Blood and Land

J. C. H. KING

Blood and Land

The Story of Native North America

ALLEN LANE
an imprint of
PENGUIN BOOKS

ALLEN LANE

UK | USA | Canada | Ireland | Australia
India | New Zealand | South Africa

Allen Lane is part of the Penguin Random House group of companies
whose addresses can be found at global.penguinrandomhouse.com.

First published 2016
001

Copyright © J. C. H. King, 2016

The moral right of the author has been asserted

Set in 10.5/14 pt Sabon LT Std
Typeset by Jouve (UK), Milton Keynes
Printed in Great Britain by Clays Ltd, St Ives plc

A CIP catalogue record for this book is available from the British Library

ISBN: 978–0–241–28235–9

Contents

A Note on the Text

Blood and Land describes Native North America today in a series of thematic but overlapping chapters. The story begins with a celebration of 'Success', the way the Native North dealt with the imposition of ideas of race across the continent. This is explained in the exceptional context of the survival of First and Native Nations through the twentieth century. The following chapter, 'Recovery', details how this happened, while 'Land', 'Others', 'Language and Literature' and 'Art and Materiality' concentrate on specific aspects of Native American culture and history. The later chapters are geographically defined, providing a fuller account of the peoples of the 'East', 'West', 'North' and 'Pacific Northwest Coast', respectively. It is often impossible to separate categories, such as ideas of land, religion and law, from each other, so many individuals and events appear in more than one chapter. What I hope this does is emphasize that history and culture are closely connected, and indeed, despite exceptional diversity, indivisible.

There are many names for the peoples described in this book. 'Native', 'indigenous', 'aboriginal', 'First Nation' and 'Indian' are all used below, and the terms mean different things to different people in different contexts. The 'Iroquois' are today usually called 'Haudenosaunee', and the numerous peoples around and north of the Great Lakes may be referred collectively as the 'Ojibwe', the 'Chippewa' or the 'Anishinaabe'. My preference is to use different terms and names at different times, better usage of differing terms in appropriate contexts perhaps being preferable to absolute distinctions of right and wrong.

Acknowledgements

There are many people to thank, all the while remembering that mistakes, and errors of emphasis and association, are mine. First, I am deeply grateful to Simon Winder at Penguin for his longstanding patience and critical advice over many years since we first spoke of the idea in 2000. Gill Coleridge, my agent, has been always been constructive. At and for Penguin David Watson, Maria Bedford, Richard Duguid and Rebecca Moldenhauer have diligently assisted with editing, map commissioning, production and picture research. Dave Cradduck compiled the index. John and Elizabeth O'Beirne Ranelagh have been the most generous of hosts, especially at Moncla with Michael Jones. Most importantly Elizabeth generously and kindly read, edited, and improved on early drafts. I am most grateful. Peter Whiteley kindly read and corrected the text: his thoughtful suggestions and useful criticisms are much appreciated. My family encouraged me: Emily, James and Henry and Neil were always there when needed.

There are also many people, many long gone and much missed, in North America who, while hardly involved in this project, have over many decades informed and helped me. These include: JoAllyn Archambault, William Fitzhugh, Travis Hudson, Ki-Ke-In, Shep Krech, Molly Lee, Henrietta Lidchi, John MacDonald, Sally McLendon, Leah Otak, George Qulaut, Morton and Estelle Sosland, Ben Stone, William Sturtevant, Don Tenoso and W. Richard West, Jr. Nicholas Thomas, at the Museum of Archaeology and Anthropology in Cambridge, appointed me Von Hügel Fellow at his museum in 2012. All these kindnesses and contributions are much appreciated.

Preface

This book outlines Native American cultural history. This is intended to try to explain why, despite facing devastation and never-ending difficulties, Native America in contemporary Canada and the United States is successful. By successful I mean also that Native America thrives as a phenomenon in both the imagination and the intellect. The success is similar in kind, if not scale, to that of much greater entities – in terms of population size and seemingly complexity – such as the Classical or Judaeo-Christian worlds, or continents such as Asia and Africa. Of course, most of us in the West come, in one sense or another, from the Classical and Judaeo-Christian traditions, while we do not come from Native North America. Instead Native America provides a touchstone of identity: about who we westerners are and particularly who we are not.

Native North America has been especially successful also in surviving, in continually changing to meet the challenges of the dominant societies, from the influence of federal state and provincial authorities to the transgressive effects of popular culture. Little more than a century ago no one expected Native North Americans to do anything other than assimilate and die away. The major practical and symbolic moments in this process in the USA were the opening up of Indian Territory to white homesteading in 1898 and the conversion of this Native homeland into the state of Oklahoma (meaning 'red people' in Choctaw) in 1907. At this point the Native population had reached a low point of around 375,000.[1] Nobody expected Native America to recover, yet recovery occurred, in a series of cycles in which new institutional frameworks were set up, then altered, abandoned and improved, sometimes all three conflicting directions occurring simultaneously. And recovery in population occurred with astonishing rapidity: today there are more than 2.5 million Native North Americans.[2]

In African America, well into the twentieth century, the racial rule ran: 'one drop and you're out': that is, one drop of African blood, a great-great-grandparent, say, and you were black. The rule now concerning Native North America is, with only slight exaggeration and mild irony, 'one drop and you're in'. This came into play in the 2012 US Senate election, when the Democrat Elizabeth Warren of Massachusetts, now a senator, was challenged on her unproven claim to Cherokee status both by her Republican opponents and by Native Americans. Yet very many people *are* now aware of having Cherokee ancestry. Only perhaps two generations ago it would have been unthinkable in most cases for individual Americans actively to embrace their Native American genes. This is a remarkable and insufficiently marked change.

When I first visited Cherokee, North Carolina, and the Smoky Mountain community of Indian people, who avoided transportation west, it was a depressed, devastated hill town. In 1991, in the only downtown mini-mall, an elder was 'chiefing', that is, dressed in Plains Indian clothing with a feather war bonnet and posing for pay with the rather few tourists. Then I visited the factories where Cherokee made genuine New England quilts for Sears and tom-toms for football fans supporting the Atlanta Braves. Fifteen years later, when I returned to contribute to an exhibition about the Cherokee in Tulsa, the Cherokee had a vast casino, as well as their own police force and all other normal municipal services owned and controlled by them, thanks to their success in the gaming industry.

Yet perhaps the most remarkable aspect of Native North America is that a tiny population has contributed so much *diversity* to the world's cultural landscape. If Native North America is considered alongside the Pacific, indigenous Middle and Andean America, South Asia, Africa or the Middle East, then perhaps something of Native North American exceptionalism becomes apparent. So what follows is, in this important sense, an account of Native American exceptionalism.

In academic studies, much is today made of the need to avoid reductionist description, in which differences are flattened out and identity stereotypes perpetuated, in order to develop more sophisticated ideas in which power and agency are returned to Native people. So emphasis is placed on concepts such as hybridity, contingency and agency, on the understanding of Native literature, film and art, on the development of cross-cultural, pan-Indian identities and the recovery of an understanding of the way both the USA and Canada grew out of reciprocal, but highly skewed, arrangements between Natives, Europeans and North Americans.

Scholarship cannot in the end entirely avoid locatedness: the specificity and the cultural geographies of the more than 1,000 Native nations in Canada and the USA. Actual origins and the development of identity are of fundamental importance, both in the distant past and in the cultural constructions from the nineteenth century onwards into the twenty-first. Frequently, however, the nuanced specifics of culture are reduced to archetypes, particularly in the media and museums. In the 1970s the museum-going public was either sceptical or uncritical and largely unaware of, and uninterested in, the cultural complexity of Native North America. Epithets such as 'red men', 'squaws', 'tomahawk chops' and the expletive 'Ho!' were still used. So the central role for the museum curator is to interpret and explain cultures through objects, and to place this understanding in a broader framework of deconstructed archetypes. That is, to reverse the process, the curator learns to take archetypes – the Arctic hunter, the Plains warrior, the Environmental, Casino and Hollywood Indian – and uses objects to explain how these simplistic formulations simultaneously communicate with yet limit and misinform the museum visitor.

The view expressed, then, is that of a museum curator. I spent thirty years at the British Museum, as curator of the North American collections. The museum had been collecting often in an incidental manner Indian and Inuit materials for 220 years without a curator. To learn about the collections and Native North America at the same time was an extraordinary privilege – and a challenge. Yet this took place at a moment of unprecedented change in the United States and Canada to do with the sovereignty-related issues that in the USA led to the development of Indian gaming and in the north were entangled with issues of energy and land and the revolution which was taking place in the curation of Native North American heritage. In the 1970s the idea that there would be a self-governing territory, Nunavut, was at most a dream; the repatriation of the Canadian constitution from Westminster in 1982 transformed aboriginal affairs. My curatorial role, for thirty years, was to explain how this happened, as it happened. I was always aware how little I actually knew about Native North America, and so, when I left the British Museum in 2012, I began again. Writing this introduction to North America has been for me a means of extending my understanding of the changes in Native North America over the last forty years.

Map 1. Cultural regions: this map derives from earlier 'cultural area' schemes developed by anthropologists in the nineteenth century and articulated most fully by Alfred L. Kroeber in 1939.

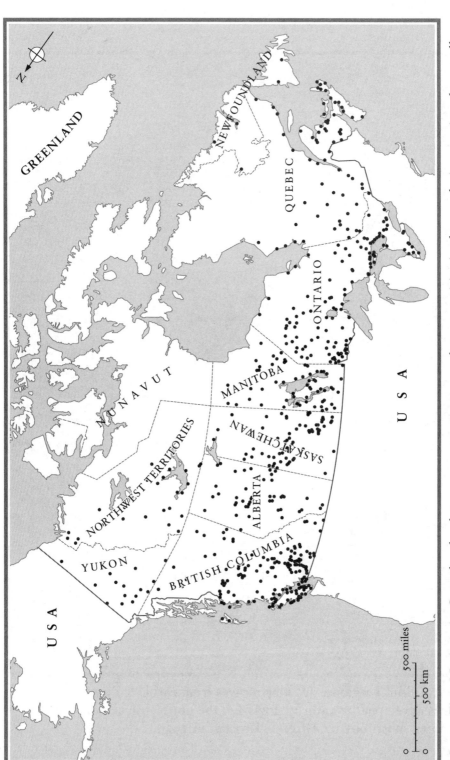

Map 2. First Nations in Canada: the dots represent reserves and communities in the north; in practice almost all are too small to be represented cartographically.

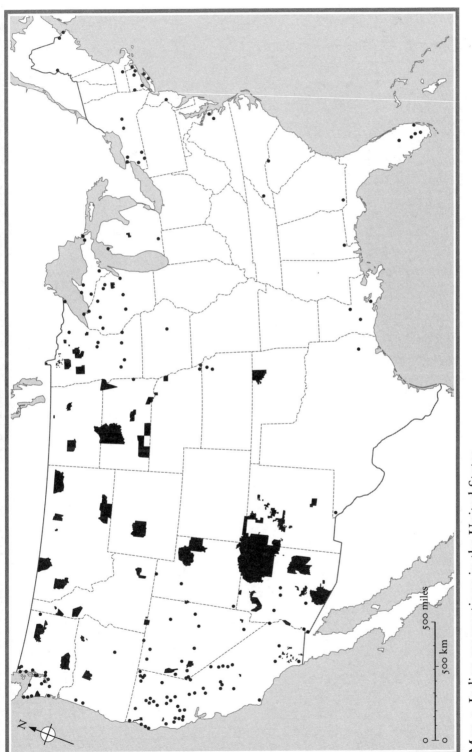

Map 3. Indian reservations in the United States.

Introduction

The history of Native North America moves in a series of cycles: periods of great change occur every twenty or thirty years, followed by calm, if not consolidation. The nineteenth century saw the defeat of the final confederations in the War of 1812; removal in the 1830s; the cataclysm of defeat during and after the Civil War of 1861–5; greatly enlarged boarding schools designed to destroy Indian culture, followed by the racially defined Dawes Act, pulverizing reservations in the name of freedom and assimilation, from the 1880s. Indian Territory, that eighteenth-century dream, was finally obliterated with the creation of Oklahoma in 1907, at the population nadir. Recovery came in the 1930s, with the New Deal instituting elected governments and rebuilding the land base, only to be followed by migration to the cities and the final assimilationist fling, of termination, in the 1950s. The recovery of the 1970s occurred across North America, with the settling of land claims in Alaska and Quebec and Greenland Home Rule. This occurred against a backdrop of renewed interested in the appropriation of the natural resources of Indian Country and an unholy activist alliance of urban radicals, chic celebrities with (but also often against) traditionalists. The corporatism of the 1970s in the north and the institution of Indian bingo and then section 3 slots ushered in the current period of unrivalled achievement, prosperity, orderliness and ordinariness. Yet in so many ways Indian Country remains in the belly of the beast, imprisoned by history in the impossible clutch of multiple deprivations.

Crucial to the future is what will happen to Indian gaming, the extraordinary phenomenon which is responsible for nearly 612,000 jobs worth $27.6 billion, $91.1 billion of output,[1] and the general empowerment of the small minority of Indian reservations with successful casinos; to Alaska Native corporations and the rather different Canadian ones; and to the mineral resources of Greenland.

But gaming is already changing with the phenomenal growth of online gambling, accessible to everyone without the need to travel. Casino visitors are ageing, and the question is: can Indian Country move gambling to the internet, preferred by the young, and even if it does what benefit could this properly bring to Indian people? The two greatest success stories of the 1990s, the Pequot Foxwoods and Mohegan Sun Casinos, are both heavily in debt, with declining revenues and new competition in the northeast of the United States. Others – the Chumash in California, Chickasaw and Choctaw in Oklahoma – flourish.

Gaming, like the extinction of land rights brought about alongside the settlement of land claims, is a highly destructive vehicle of achievement. It is suggested that between 1 and 1.5 per cent of the US population are 'disordered' or problem gamblers, and studies in the 1990s suggested that each disordered gambler costs society between $9,500 and $53,000 per year: the costs of gambling far outweighing the benefits of gaming.[2] This is even before the social costs of gambling are taken into account, alongside the high-end welfare dependency of annual per capita payments, with access often racially defined. Yet gambling will grow. John Sowinski, president of No Casinos in Florida, observed a phenomenon that governs how elected officials largely view gaming: 'The solution to having too much of it is to have more of it.'[3] If the tote or pari-mutuel gambling is doing badly, or if local gamblers are spending elsewhere, or if the state needs more money, then more casinos are required. Gambling and gaming are not going to disappear, and the growth of an empowered Native professional class (dubbed in 1970s Alaska the 'Brooks Brother Natives', a reference to the use of clothing from this WASP and Ivy League tailor), is irreversible. And of course the importance of economic class was predicted 250 years ago by David Hume, writing in 'Of Interest': 'When a people have emerged ever so little from a savage state, and their numbers have encreased beyond the original multitude, there must immediately arise an inequality of property.'[4]

Beyond Native corporations and casinos and their likely changing economic positions, and the impact of declining natural resources, and climate change and the destruction of the northern cold-based habitat, are fundamentals. These mean that Indian Country will not change, because the long centuries of churning upheaval have resulted in a resilience which ensures survival. This is in part to do with the uniqueness and hyper-diversity of Indian culture, its ability to create and rethink architecture and art; but it is also to do with the way in which Nativeness is embedded in the United States and Canada. The ragged edge of the North American accommodation with the 'Indian' is continually addressed in often startling ways. For instance, in 2014 grifter rancher in Nevada Cliven Bundy, who had failed to pay rent for grazing cattle on federal lands to the government for over twenty years, was able to challenge armed officials. He was often compared, as a victim of the Feds, on former presidential candidate Ron Paul's website, to the Lakota, whose women and children were killed at Wounded Knee in 1890.[5] It can be seen in the battle, led by the Oneida, against the racist name of the Washington Redskins, which resulted in the creation by the team owner of a foundation supplying cold-weather clothing to destitute Indians, cocking a snook at Indian deprivation. Yet these symbolic battles cloak a much greater reality, one where the meaning of 'nation' and 'Indian' is mimicked and parodied and then without a flicker of humour becomes the accepted norm.

This inversion of meaning is a regular process in historiography, particularly in the American narrative. The image of the American Indian, of the savage as American, transferred back and forth across the propaganda of the American Revolution. The image of the Native was associated with the revolutionaries of the Boston Tea Party (who wore face paint and Indian fancy dress) and the non-taxation of tea without representation. This fed into the later assumption of Mohawk or Plains fancy dress in fraternal organizations at parties, common until very recently. A recent manifestation of this was the Native head-dress worn by the daughter of the governor of Oklahoma, Christina Fallin. In a picture posted on Facebook in 2014 she captioned her image 'Appropriate Culturation', a riff on 'cultural appropriation'.

One such inverted meaning is the idea of Columbia, invented in 1738 by that critic of American patriotism Dr Johnson ('How is it that we hear the loudest *yelps* for liberty among the drivers of negroes?') as an ironic companion for Hibernia and Britannia, but taken up in all seriousness as the main symbol of the USA before being superseded by the Statue of Liberty after 1886. Johnson uses Columbia as a Lilliputian name for the country normally called America. Specifically he talks of the 'Conquests and Acquisitions in Columbia', which 'broke thro'' all the ties of human nature' in reference to the dispossession of Native America.[6] Another inversion is the song of 'Yankee Doodle' (i.e. fool), a song of the French and Indian War and then the American Revolution, in which the American *faux* dandy would stick an Indian-like feather in his hat and 'call it macaroni'. Then there is 'cowboy', the term first used by Swift in a poem to his friend and possible wife Stella and subsequently employed for loyalist irregulars in Westchester, New York, before an inversion in meaning and migration out to the freedom-loving west. Another is the whole idea of American exceptionalism, originally from de Tocqueville, but used by the communists of the 1920s and 1930s, appropriated and reworked by Republicans in the 1980s as a badge of honour and then used as an anti-federalist and anti-Washington patriotic taunt in the 2008 election.

But among cultural meanings perhaps most important is the dialectic between melting-pot America and the America of embedded but diverse ethnicity. The ideal of a melting-pot America was invented by Israel Zangwill in the aftermath of the pogroms in Kishinev and Kiev in 1903 and 1905. In his play *The Melting-Pot* (1907) he writes:

> America is God's Crucible, the great Melting-Pot where all the races of Europe are melting and re-forming! . . . the real American has not yet arrived. He is only in the Crucible, I tell you – he will be the fusion of all races, perhaps the coming superman.[7]

That is, unmentioned Indian people are not not included. Interestingly, while American Indians are not mentioned in the play, in an afterword of 1914 Zangwill says that the 'Melting-Pot of America will not fail to act [on African Americans] in a measure as it has acted on the Red Indian'. More to the point is perhaps the mid-century view of Indianness: in 1953, during the time of termination, Felix Cohen, the drafter of the 1934 Indian Reorganization Act (IRA) and of the template for tribal constitutions, wrote that:

[T]he Indian plays much the same role in our American society that the Jews played in Germany. Like the miner's canary, the Indian marks the shifts from fresh air to poison gas in our political atmosphere; and our treatment of Indians, even more than our treatment of other minorities, reflects the rise and fall in our democratic faith.[8]

The ideas, then, of nationhood and of Native American and aboriginal Canadian and First Nations are not in any sense stationary concepts, but ones in continual process, moving backwards and forwards in deeply conflicted circumstances. In the USA 'Indian' as a national symbol acts as a general formulation, whereas in Canada 'Inuit' and 'First Nations' are identity markers, each with a much more definite profile than the single, all-encompassing symbols of the USA, such as the flag and Columbia, Liberty and Indian. Land is also a symbolic marker, and loss of land is the major theme of this book. Sarah Palin neatly inverted this trope in her autobiography, *Going Rogue*, when she quoted with approval baseball coach John Wooden (1910–2010): 'Our land is everything to us . . . I will tell you one of the things we remember on our land. We remember our grandfathers paid for it – with their *lives*.' She had muddled two different individuals: the statement was actually made by Cheyenne leader John Wooden Legs (1909–81) and referred to Cheyenne participation in the Battle of the Little Bighorn.[9]

Most ironic of the transfers of moral meanings is that which relates to 'Indian Country', the expression used to refer to lands still identified and often actually occupied by aboriginal people, whether in Maine or Arizona, eastern Washington or the Everglades. Originally used in the early twentieth century, 'Indian Country' was also an expression that appeared in regular use in Vietnam, as a catch phrase describing hostile country inhabited by the enemy. The term features, for instance, in the testimony around the My Lai Massacre of 1968, when perhaps 300–500 Vietnamese villagers were killed. In the 1971 congressional hearing about the incident the following exchange occurred between Captain Robert Bowie Johnson and Congressman John F. Seiberling (1918–2008):

Johnson: Where I was operating I didn't hear anyone personally use that term ['turkey shoots' for killing civilians]. We used the term

'Indian Country'. Seiberling: What did 'Indian Country' refer to? Johnson: I guess it means different things to different people. It is like there are savages out there, there are gooks out there. In the same way we slaughtered the Indian's buffalo, we would slaughter the water buffalo in Vietnam.[10]

'Indian Country' meant, of course, sovereign country, a place in which the US military might not go. But 'tribals' still occupy the position of hostiles in the governmental mind: Akbar Ahmed, writing recently of the way in which Al-Qaeda and the War on Terror are situated in tribal areas – the Yemeni–Saudi borderlands and the Hindu Kush/Afghan periphery – used language that mimics attitudes to Native America:

> These suffering people had one thing in common: they were all part of communities living on the periphery and margins of the state. Those who represented the center of the state usually called them 'primitive' and 'savage.' Some said their time in history was up.[11]

This twenty-first-century world of extra-judicial killings, by drones and other means, is justified today, to the amazement of Indian people, by the precedent of the execution by a military tribunal in 1818 of two British traders, Robert C. Ambrister and Alexander (George) Arbuthnot, who were providing Seminole in Spanish Florida with arms to resist the encroachment of the USA. In the aftermath of the executions it was proclaimed that circumstances demanded such overriding of normal judicial procedure.[12] And in 2011 news of Osama bin Laden's successful assassination was given the code name 'Geronimo' (after the famous Apache leader also known as Goyathlay, c.1829–1909), provoking outrage; the august *Washington Post*, incomprehensibly, thought this furore was misguided – the similarity they said is in the hunt not the individual, as though the moral taint would never shift from bin Laden the terrorist abroad to Geronimo the patriot leader.[13]

It may seem outlandish to compare American attitudes to Middle Eastern tribal peoples with that to Native America. Yet there are other ways of repositioning 'Indian Country'. One, perhaps, is fiscal. In 1984 the historian Wilcomb Washburn (1925–97) noted with approval that 'The BIA's [Bureau of Indian Affairs'] budget of $1.5 billion is bigger than the budgets of the FBI, the CIA, and the Drug Enforcement Agencies combined.'[14] In the run-up to fiscal year 2014 it was anticipated that at the BIA there would be 7,900 employees and a budget of $2.6 billion; in contrast the FBI budget alone was to be $8.2 billion, with 34,000 employees, that is, more than three times that of the BIA. The intelligence agencies' budgets for 2014 are around $45 billion. But of course Washburn was writing of pre-casino time, and today for the small proportion of Indian nations with high-profit casinos much of Native American income is emancipated from government money. Further, it must be noted that some people such as the Hopi will not create casinos and may suffer from the perception that Indian nations, now rich, are less eligible for charity.

So by some markers both 'Indian Country' and Native American society are in a state of rude wellbeing, as evidenced by success in Alaska, in casino country and indeed in Nunavut, Greenland, and among the Nisga'a and Cree. But of course the Indian in Cohen's *Basic Memorandum* had to be defined, and was defined, on the basis of tribal membership, ancestral descent and blood quantum. That is a crude racial designation which still has traction in definition, in the notorious Certificate of Indian Blood, which is now perhaps in the process of withering away, a last reminder of the 1930s.[15] Overarching changes, such as the 1983 removal by President Ronald Reagan of the oversight of Indian affairs in the White House from the Office of Liaison to the Office of Intergovernmental Affairs, marked this other reality: as Washburn pointed out in 1984, the Indian people are a 'third sovereignty in the country, equal, in many critical respects, to national and state sovereignties'.[16] While Edward Said would have had us believe, in the 1980s, that the colonized always remain marginalized and dependent, on the periphery, a separate view of Native North America would suggest instead that Indianness and Indian identity are a core aspect of national identity, the subaltern survivor mutating and mimicking overarching society, subverting national characteristics, of American liberty and also of Canadian fairness.

Canada's identity is correctly considered, in contrast to the USA, as being 'soft', in the sense of flexible and supple, and 'fair'. This is because Canada incorporated from the beginning the biculturalism of French Canada, especially in religion, and features aboriginal identity internationally. Yet John Ralston Saul's nuanced and ironic treatment of these themes, A *Fair Country: Telling Truths about Canada* (2008), obscures the basic dichotomy in First Nations history. After the War of 1812, with the important exception of the Métis rebellions in 1869 and 1885, there was little or no military violence. But while the government did not preside over American-style massacres, it acted administratively more effectively and more brutally than that of the USA. Between the Indian Act of 1876 and the new constitution of 1982 Canadian First Nations lost all vestiges of sovereignty; there was no sense in this period that aboriginal people constituted 'domestic dependent nations' as in the United States. For aboriginal people Canada was neither fair or soft, until challenged by the Parti Québécois from 1968, when national identity was remade. In comparison to Congress, the much more harsh administration of the Canadian parliament created minute reserves – there are none like the Navajo reservation, at 27,000 square miles the size of the Republic of Ireland. Most significantly, there were few reserved rights in respect of the provinces in which aboriginal people found themselves. Further recovery took much longer in Canada and began in the 1970s rather the 1930s. Then Thomas Berger, symbolically equivalent to Felix Cohen, conducted the Mackenzie Pipeline Enquiry (1977) and as an activist judge and lawyer led the debate on the constitutional changes of the 1980s. Yet it was the aboriginal politician Elijah Harper (1949–2013) who led the defeat of the Meech Lake Accord in 1990, which would have enshrined the status of Quebec, but not that of aboriginal people, as a distinct society. Thus it was an Indian who refused to compromise Canada's egalitarianism and set the seal on the Canadian constitution.

I

Success

The Revd Samson Occom (1723–92) (Mohegan), who wrote *A Short Narrative of My Life*, 1768.

Colonel Ely S. Parker (1828–95), US Commissioner of Indian Affairs, Seneca soldier and ethnographer who wrote out Lee's terms of surrender at Appomatox, 1865.

Charles Eastman (1858–1939) (Santee Sioux), Ohiyesa ('the Winner'), physician, writer and activist, witness to the aftermath of Wounded Knee, 1890.

Tom Longboat (1887–1949) (Onondaga), *right*, residential-school educated winner of the 1907 Boston marathon, here at the 1908 Olympics.

JimThorpe (1888–1953) (Sac and Fox), in Carlisle football uniform, 1909; medal-winner at the 1905 Olympics, his amateur status was removed 1913, returned in 1972.

Vice-President Charles Curtis (1860–1936) (Kaw), *right*, the first
non-European to hold high office in the USA, with Hoover in 1932.
The Curtis Act (1898) destroyed Indian Territory.

Publicity image for *Silent Enemy* (1930), starring the Carlisle-educated
World War One veteran Buffalo Child Long Lance (1890–1932), whose
assumed name hid likely Cherokee-based origins.

Open coffin of Jackson Barnett (1856–1934) (monolingual Creek, OK), and the richest Indian, mourned by his fortune-hunter wife Anna Laura Lowe (1881–1952).

Ojibwe/Anishinaabe/Chippewa protest in 1937 against the removal of their Indian agency to the city of Duluth.

Myra Yvonne Chouteau (1929–2016), Shawnee prima ballerina, descendant also of French eighteenth-century fur traders.

Canadian Cree activist speaking after the ending of the Occupation of Alcatraz, 1971.

Sacheen Littlefeather (b. 1946) (Apache and Yaqui), the activist sent by Brando to decline his *Godfather* Academy Award in 1973.

Chief Dan George (1899–1981) (Tsleil-Waututh Nation, North Vancouver), playing a Cherokee confederate holding up Clint Eastwood.

Mercier Bridge, Quebec, blocked in 1990 during a protest over golf-course expansion on to Mohawk burial ground.

Governor of Taos Quirino Romero (1906–86), *centre*, with President Richard Nixon in 1970, the year of the return of Blue Lake to the Pueblo.

Karen Jim (Whitford), scholarship and Miss NCAI winner 1970, now elder at Celilo Village, which was rebuilt after the Dalles Dam destroyed Indian access to the Columbia River in the 1950s.

Foxwoods Resort Casino, founded by Pequot Richard 'Skip' Arthur Hayward, 1992.

The Battle of Hayes Pond: Lumbees breaking up a Klan meeting in North Carolina, 1958.

Suzan Shown Harjo (b. 1945) (Cheyenne).

INDIAN BURIAL PIT, SALINA, KANSAS

1950s postcard of the archaeological museum known as Whiteford's Indian Burial Pit, Salina, KS, which was closed down in 1989, the remains reinterred by the Pawnee.

I

Success

As mentioned in the Preface, Elizabeth Warren, when a Harvard law-yer, indicated her minority status – Native American and Cherokee. During her successful election campaign for the Senate in Massachu-setts in 2011–12, her claim was called into question with demands for proof of ancestry. Some Indian writers accept that she may have a smidgen of Cherokee blood,[1] others do not. But as an Oklahoman from the state with the most diverse Native history, it is a reasonable claim. What is extraordinary is that proof of race should be required in the twenty-first century – no one claiming Irish or German or Jew-ish descent would be required to furnish documentary evidence – and that a politician should associate herself with a group of people, the Cherokee, who until the second half of the twentieth century had been unfavoured as an ethnic option in the American melting pot. This account will look at how Native North Americans recovered through the twentieth century from centuries of roiling colonization, of celebratory caricature cut with actual genocide and deliberate ethnocide.

Statistics

The great success of Native North America in the twentieth century is demonstrated in bald, seemingly featureless statistics, statistics which hide highly variable situations. In the USA in 1900 there were 237,196 Indians;[2] starting in 1960, census respondents could select their race, and the number of Indians grew exponentially. In 2010, 5.2 million people recorded themselves as American Indian and Native Alaskans, 1.7 per cent of the total US population with an expectation of growth to 8.6 million by 2050, or 2 per cent of the American population. The largest Native nations were in 2010: Cherokee (819,105), Navajo (332,129), Choctaw (195,764), a compound Mexican American Indian (175,494), Chippewa (170,742), Sioux (170,110), Apache (111,810) and Blackfoot (105,304). In 2010, there were fifteen states with more than 100,000 AI/AN people: California (723,225), Oklahoma (482,760) and Arizona (353,386) leading the way, with Alaska having a 19.5 per cent Native population.[3]

The growth of Native America is symbolized by the removal of racist sporting logos in the last few decades; one major example remains: the Washington Redskins, the capital's football team. In this the underlying supposition of those refusing to support the change to something such as 'Warriors' may be that if people want to be Indian then how can 'Redskins' be derogatory – an idea that misses the historical point. Elsewhere, the Cleveland Indians logo, Chief Wahoo, cognate with Jonathan Swift's eighteenth-century primitive people the Yahoos, is only slowly being eliminated. And of course there are occasionally exceptions that prove the rule – the Broken Bow Savages being the name of the Choctaw High School team in Oklahoma – that the use of Indian names is the prerogative of Indian people.

The situation seems similar in Canada, certainly in the business of statistics, yet so much is quite different, starting with names, 'Indian' being non-preferred. In 2011, there were 1,400,685 who identified as 'aboriginal', some 4 per cent of the population, so proportionately there are over twice as many First Nations, Métis and Inuit people in Canada than in the USA. In 1900, there were around 100,000 aboriginal people in Canada, so the growth in numbers is similar. Further, while there are more than 550 nations in the USA, Canada boasts 600 bands. The comparable number of reservations and reserves masks the much smaller Canadian form of 'reserve' in number of inhabitants and also in area, so there are perhaps only 25,000 people at Six Nations, Ontario, one of the most populous reserves. In 2011, 697,505 Canadians reported themselves as being registered or Treaty Indians: a Treaty Indian is one who has 'taken Treaty', that is, someone whose band or nation has signed up to a treaty with the crown in return for payments and rights on a reserve. A registered or status Indian is one who comes under the Indian Acts from 1876, but where there may not yet have been a treaty as such, as in British Columbia. Similarly, it is estimated that in 2031 there will be between 1.7 and 2.2 million aboriginal people in Canada, some 4–5.3 per cent of the population; that is, continuing growth will occur.[4]

The first difference between Canada and the USA is that there are registered Indians whose bands have not signed treaties. Then there is another radical disjuncture between the two countries: the large number of Métis people (451,795) of mixed descent in Canada;[5] these non-status people are present in the US population, yet are not a separate feature of American statistics.[6] Undoubtedly many of those who identify as Choctaw or Cherokee are of mixed descent but aren't referred to as such, or indeed, as they might have been in the early twentieth century, as 'breeds' or 'half-breeds'.

The situation in the two countries differs much further, for instance in the definition of the north. In Alaska all Native people, Indian and Eskimoan (Aleut, Yupik and Inupiat), have been merged into the new category of 'Alaska Native', while in Canada a much more homogeneous original population of Inuit basically speaking Inuktitut has been split up, and new Inuit identities and terminology continue to appear. People are described as living in 'Inuit Nunangat', a term coined in 2010. Statistics Canada says Inuit Nunangat stretches from Labrador to the Northwest Territories and comprises four regions: Nunatsiavut, Nunavik, Nunavut and the Inuvialuit; it also includes the northernmost section of the Yukon Territory.[7] And, of course, the governmental situation in the north is radically different between Alaska, the Canadian Arctic and Greenland. Nunavut in Canada is a self-governing region, set up in 1999, largely but not completely Inuit, unlike Alaska, which became a state in 1958–9, where the Native population is under 20 per cent of the total, and where the degree of financial and other autonomy is similar to northern Quebec, where the James Bay and Northern Quebec Agreement of 1974 is, in its corporate outcome, in some ways similar to the Alaskan Native Claims Settlement Act of 1971. Yet both the Alaskan and the Canadian situations are different to that in Greenland, which is both part of Europe – the Danish queen is head of state – and yet geographically in North America. In 2013 there were 56,483 inhabitants; in contrast with the situation in the USA and Canada, this is expected by Statistics Greenland to decline by 2,500 by 2040. Greenland, like Nunavut, is self-governing; the territory was part of the EEC/EU until 1985, took Home Rule in 1999 and, after a 2008 referendum, further autonomy in matters other than defence, judiciary, police and foreign affairs.

Racial Thinking and Science

What follows describes the setting in which success came about. The definition of who is an aboriginal or Native person is a mutable concept. In a sense Native is the least imperfect of available terms, one of a series created to refer to outsiders beyond the pale of civilization, from the classical 'barbarian' to 'wildman' and 'savage', meaning woodsman, and 'Indian', which was superimposed on the Americas from the fifteenth century. The term 'red man' was popularized in the eighteenth century. John Wesley, the father of Methodism, who visited Georgia in the 1730s, may have been the first to use the term, having adapted it from southeastern peoples such as the Cherokee and Creek, who named themselves as red men in contrast with the white men, and in opposition to blacks.[8] But the idea may also have an earlier descriptive usage in reference to the use of red ochre for decoration by aboriginal people, especially the Beothuk of Newfoundland, who were in contact with Europeans from the fifteenth century and probably before and were made widely known by the trader George Cartwright in the late eighteenth century.

More significant in the eighteenth century was the development of the idea of race, in the sense of family or family line, to include a sense of ethnicity, nation and man as a biological being, and as a means of classifying varieties. Carl Linnaeus (1707–78) was responsible for systematizing ideas of variety. In the first edition of his *Systema naturae* (1735), he separated the species *Homo* into four *varietate* (Europaeus, Americanus, Asiaticus, Africanus) in the same way that other species were defined. Then in a later edition of his *Systema* (1758), Linnaeus created the new binomial term for our species, *Homo sapiens*, and by making people natural and wise he created an acceptable classification, understanding that men, like monkeys, were primates in his original category *Anthropomorpha*.

The introduction of race into natural science and the classification of man was the work of the Count de Buffon (1707–88), who believed that as species mutated through environment, they divided into races, a term to which he gave pre-eminence, although his meaning provides a sense of ethnicity, since it encompasses more than simply physical classification. Much of the formalization of the proto-social science was organized by the German scientist and anthropologist Johann Friedrich Blumenbach (1752–1840), also a monogenist, who in the 1770s and 1780s proposed four and then five division of humanity, including Americans and whites, that is, Caucasians. All shared an understanding of the origins of man based on biblical creation and subsequent degeneracy due to environmental factors. Scientific formulations in the nineteenth century combined with legal ones of blood, and of half-blood. These had originated in British law and the *Commentaries on the Law of England* of William Blackstone (1723–80), in reference to families:

> [A]s every man's own blood is compounded of the bloods of his respective ancestors, he only is properly of the whole or entire blood with another, who hath . . . all the same ingredients in the composition of his blood that the other hath.[9]

Science and the study of aboriginal America in the United States begins with Thomas Jefferson (1743–1846), who rebutted Buffon's ideas of degeneracy by sending a moose and other cervids to France to show that American species flourished to a giant size in the United States. Jefferson wrote in the 1780s of the oratory, excellence and equality of Indian people in his *Notes on the State of Virginia* (1784). He championed the friendly Mingo-Cayuga warrior Logan (c.1723–80), the murder of whose family in 1774 had precipitated Lord Dunmore's War. Further, Jefferson collected information about aboriginal people, empowering early American ethnography during and after his presidency. Yet it was Jefferson who also set up the structures for the growth of the states and advocated Indian removal. In the aftermath of the Revolution the idealism of Jefferson was, come what may, combined with the realities of a post-war world. In this, Britain still occupied American frontier forts and remained allied to Indian nations, while Americans flooded into the Ohio country and beyond and where the flourishing image of the noble savage was tempered with lurid frontier tales of Indian atrocities, captivities and of general savagery and incapacity.

US Federal Relations with Indians

Gradually legislative and diplomatic control was exerted over relations with Indian people, lands and land sale. With the constitution in 1789 the federal government inherited the British system, in which Indian affairs were organized by two superintendents and not by the royal/state governors. During the Revolution the Continental Congress had assumed control of relations with Indian peoples, and this continued afterwards. Earlier, in 1783, Congress had signalled the continuation of British policy in a proclamation of 1 September:

> The United States in Congress assembled have the sole and exclusive right and power of regulating the trade and managing all affairs of the Indians, not members of any of the states . . . and they do hereby prohibit and forbid all persons from . . . purchasing or receiving any gift or cession of such lands or claims without the express authority and directions of the United States in Congress assembled.[10]

In 1784 the Treaty of Fort Stanwix defined Iroquois boundaries, and the 1786 Hopewell Treaty allied the United States with the Choctaw and Chickasaw. But long-standing New York anti-federalist Governor George Clinton (1739–1812) strongly opposed federal leadership in Indian affairs. Eventually between 1790 and 1834 six non-intercourse or Indian non-intercourse acts (with titles such as 'an act to regulate trade and intercourse with the Indian tribes and to maintain peace on the frontiers') were passed following Congress's proclamation of 1783. All reserved the rights to appoint and regulate trade with Indians in the Indian Country and to survey, designate and acquire Indian lands.

Yet the original thirteen states retained certain rights in respect of Indians and were constant in their battles to safeguard these rights from federal authority. In a sense in some states nothing mattered more than the regulation of rights with Indian people, especially in respect to land. In the late eighteenth century this was particularly important in New York, the only original state with a large aboriginal population, which still had thousands of now patriot, pro-American Indians, Senecas and Oneidas. It was to the Senecas that George Washington turned his attention in 1790, following the passing of the first trade and intercourse act, to proclaim his good intentions. He said to the Indians in his address of 29 December:

> No State nor person can purchase your lands, unless at some public treaty held under the authority of the United States. The general government will never consent to your being defrauded. But it will protect you in all your just rights. Hear well, and let it be heard by every person in your Nation, that the President of the United States declares, that the general government considers itself bound to protect you in all the lands.[11]

Yet in the day-to-day administration and court functions, it was states that had most at stake, it was states that were determined to limit federal powers, and it was local people who were most interested in retaining lands with doubtful titles, and whose folk systems of knowledge and identity incorporated racial rather than romantic ideas about Indians. In New York in particular the state abrogated federal authority in a number of ways in legal matters. Most important was that of treating with individual Indian nations over land sales. So 'An Act authorizing the governor to appoint commissioners to treat with the Oneida Indians for the purchase of part of their lands' was passed on 26 February 1798 in New York, as the Oneida were and had been one of the principal landowners in New York. In terms of criminal law something similar happened when a Brotherton Indian in 1801 was ruled subject to state civil and criminal law even though the victim was an Indian, because the Brotherton Indians (Mohegan/Pequot Christians) were not fully acknowledged.[12] In formulating policy in the south, other states such as Tennessee and especially Georgia used New York's proactive usurpation of Federal Indian rights as precedence, arguing also that the trade and intercourse acts only applied when Indians were in a majority area and not surrounded by whites.[13] The federal acts therefore neatly illustrate the difficulties of bridging the gap between fine legislative sentiments and the impossibility of enacting those laws and in particular are associated with the almost complete absence of cases against white people charged with violence against Indians, or for taking land.

To the legal differences under state and federal law was added in nineteenth-century North America the collection of substantive information about aboriginal people. The acquisition of data to ensure equitable distribution of treaty payments was organized alongside the cross-referencing of linguistic, ethnographic and archaeological data. Racialization, in which Indian people were classified using a selection of supposedly scientific criteria, of phenotypical or genetic differences, to do with craniology and hair type and skin colour, was imposed in the early and mid-nineteenth century. And then after 1871 ideas of blood and descent became paramount, sanctified in law by the Indian Act in Canada, by treaties and by the Dawes Act in the United States in 1887 and associated with defined property rights and status. Then the original racialization of craniology and physical anthropology gradually withered away in the first half of the twentieth century. However, the embedded, ruinous idea of racial separation was left behind, a folk system expressing cultural difference maintained by legal status conferring at the same time both privilege and dependency, a hierarchy of racial difference fully expressed in economic terms. Then from the 1960s the prejudice against being Indian was reversed, in most areas except those where Native people might constitute a significant proportion of the population, where prejudice remains: Arizona, the Dakotas, New York. This meant that generally more people, at the same time as actual population increase, chose to define themselves as Indians. Finally biological anthropology, or bio-anthropology, replaced physical anthropology, beginning with the study of blood types and then moving into the study of DNA. While bio-anthropology is properly scientific, it exists alongside administrative systems and folk knowledge which maintain a de facto form of reverse racism alive, a racism focused on inclusion and the positive will to identify as Indian, rather than a racism which pathologizes and excludes.

Identity and National Boundaries

Success is hard to measure. The increase in numbers masks real differences across national borders, though the pathological underside of that success seems to be similar everywhere. Canada's aboriginal peoples, Greenlanders, American Indian and Alaskan populations have different degrees of autonomy and different ways of expressing their extremely diverse heritage. In the USA Indian people express who they are in terms of an understanding of their tribal nation, in the concept of dependent sovereign nation and in the ability to run businesses, especially gaming or gambling, because in some sense they retain a degree of independence. This arises because their identity is situated at the interface of federal and state law and authority. Most difficult are those businesses selling fuel or tobacco – 'smoke shops' that seek to avoid state taxes.

In Canada the idea of nation is left largely in the term 'First Nation', which came into use after the renaming of the National Indian Brotherhood as the Assembly of First Nations in the 1980s. Native Americans in the USA have an almost analogous organization, the National Congress of American Indians, but there is no National Chief in the USA. Yet as in Africa there are numerous instances of peoples divided across the US–Canada boundaries, which were fixed largely in the late eighteenth to mid-nineteenth centuries, separated by arbitrary decisions, arising before final migrations were made, of Canadian Inuit to north Greenland, and Inupiat from Alaska to the Canadian Arctic. Those peoples divided by the frontier include the Gwich'in and the Tlingit between Canada and Alaska; the Makah in Washington separated from the Ditidaht and Nuu-chah-nulth on Vancouver Island; the Montana Blackfoot from the Alberta Blackfoot; the Ojibwe/Anishinaabe from the American Chippewa and the New York Haudenosaunee separated from the Ontario brethren, loyalist refugees who left the USA after the American Revolution.

Functioning of the Race System

Frell M. Owl (1899–1980), a North Carolina Cherokee who worked for the BIA for thirty-three years, ending as superintendent at Fort Hall, Idaho, left an excellent account of epithets applicable in the 1960s to American Indians: breed and half-breed, competent and incompetent Indian, pagan, heathen and Christian Indian, good Indian and bad, citizen Indian and so on. He also made clear the difficulties which surround blood quantum:

A mixed-blood may possess only one-fourth Indian and three-fourths non-Indian blood and be classed as an enrolled Indian. In unusual cases, a mixed-blood with as little as one-sixteenth or even one-thirty-second Indian blood may be a tribal member. The ridiculousness of standards for classifying tribal Indians is apparent.[14]

In contrast, in Canada, while there used to be racial definitions for Indian and Eskimo, the degrees of Native blood were never articulated: you are either First Nations by descent and recognition or not. And then this absolute definition is blurred by the ill-defined notion of Métis.

US Expansion

The thirteen American colonies originated in the seventeenth and eighteenth centuries from a variety of proprietary charters and royal institutions reflecting historical moments and the individual ambitions of founders. The American Revolution and the fifteen years of constitution creation produced a muscular, supple system for the expansion of the United States, for creating territories and for spawning an ever-increasing series of new states. Contained in the south by Spanish Florida, west by French Louisiana and north by British Canada, the new country developed as a majoritarian, democratic state. This had to sanction means of extinguishing state claims to the west of the Appalachians and Indian claims to the territories designated as Native by the Royal Proclamation of 1763. Most important of the legislative acts of the continental congresses were the Land and Northwest Ordinances of 1785 and 1787, inspired by Jefferson's insufficient ordinance of 1784. These set up a new, highly enhanced system of land survey, creating townships, 6 x 6 miles, defined by lines running north and south. These began in the southeast corner of what is now Ohio, providing for the sale of lands and the provision of education and schools from land in Jefferson's imagined country of yeoman farmers, in what had been Indian Territory until 1783. In the words of historian Jonathan Hughes (1928–92):

The land ordinances became the great American colonizing machine: they left the intellectual mark of the Americans on the nation's geography as indelibly as did the Roman roads on physical England, still cutting straight across the undulating English countryside. The Northwest Ordinances were the colonial Americans' institutional thumbprint on the American continent all the way from the Ohio River to the Pacific.[15]

This simple, brilliant, highly effective Public Land Survey System was put into effect by the sometime British soldier Thomas Hutchins (1730–89), appointed the first and only Geographer of the United States in 1784, who in the 1760s and 1770s surveyed Ohio and Mississippi lands and the Florida Coast. It was the Jefferson–Hutchins system, started on the Ohio land tract known as the Seven Ranges, that effectively dispossessed Indians of land, providing later the methodology, indeed the ideology, for homesteading both in the USA and Canada.

New States

Further, the 1787 Northwest Ordinances set up the Northwest Territory, formerly Indian lands, and the system of creation of territories, pre-state formations which would be overseen by the federal government, a system adopted also by Canada. From the Northwest Territory, that is most of the lands around the Great Lakes west of New York and Pennsylvania, came the smaller territory of Indiana in 1800, and a succession of states, starting with Ohio in 1803, then Indiana itself in 1816. Occupation of these new lands was also encouraged by the continuation of the British system granting of bounty lands to veterans, this time of the American Revolution, by the US government, providing, of course, militarized frontiersmen. It was also expected that the sale of lands would assist in paying off debts run up during the Revolution. While individual land sales lagged, the development of highly speculative, if not downright fraudulent, land companies, such as the Scioto and Ohio, were part of this process of transfer of former Indian lands to white settlers.

That the USA had set up a means and a system for state territories, land survey and sales and the eventual creation of states was irrelevant to Native Americans, who had not been consulted by their British allies before the making of the Treaty of Paris. Opposition to expansion into the Northwest Territory was led by the Miami leader Little Turtle and the Shawnee Blue Jacket, who at the Battle of the Wabash, in 1791, achieved the greatest military defeat of American forces, one in which more than 600 soldiers died. The effects of this victory were reversed at the Battle of Fallen Timbers in 1794 and the secession of most of Ohio by Little Turtle (c.1747/52–1812) and Blue Jacket (c.1743–1810) at the Treaty of Greenville the following year. This ending to the Northwest War resulted in the flushing out of the British from the northwest, confirmed in the Jay Treaty of the same year.

Cherokee and Modernization

The Jay Treaty, while guaranteeing cross-border privileges to the Iroquois, also ensured that in other agreements the remaining lands of the Seneca Oneida and Cayuga would become available through the treaty process. The history of those fellow Iroquoians, the Cherokee, in the southeast was both very similar to that of the Iroquois and very separate. Like the Iroquois, the Cherokee are matrilineal, with status and inheritance traced through the female line, especially in terms of membership of the seven clans, including Paint, Wolf and Deer, with blood providing a literal rather than metaphorical link between relations. The Cherokee are, like other southeast peoples, identified as a maize-producing chiefdoms, but chiefdoms in which leadership was earned through recognition rather than simply inherited status. Inhabiting the interior upland and mountainous areas of North Carolina, Tennessee and Georgia, the Cherokee, like the Iroquois, were away from coastal areas of immediate settlement and able to trade, throughout the eighteenth century, vast numbers of deer skins: thousands at the beginning of the century, soon rising to millions. The deer trade provided resources for technology transfer and development, and the appearance of traders and the intermarriage of traders and Cherokee women gave rise to an elite of mixed descent who brought European agricultural practices, including new animal husbandry, new farming techniques and also the practice of plantation slavery. Further rapid changes to Cherokee society in the eighteenth century brought the need for long-distance diplomacy during the period of the French wars, with visits made to London in the 1730s and 1760s and the arrival of missionary education. While traditional agriculture is termed horticulture or gardening, this in part arises from a downplaying of Indian agriculture by early male European commentators part blind to the importance of female-led agriculture and to the contribution made by women to the likely large surpluses required to finance chiefly townships. However, into the nineteenth century, with the changes to Cherokee economy and society, bilateral inheritance, among people of mixed descent, came to define much economic and political leadership. That is, empowerment of the male line, as in white practice, came to be more accepted by Cherokee along with other aspects of European America.

In the aftermath of the brutal warfare of the American Revolution the Cherokee signed the first Treaty of Hopewell in 1785. This provided clear boundaries, despite American squatters being already established on Indian land, regulated trade and provided for a Cherokee delegate to be sent to Congress. Also this act promised punishment for Americans committing crimes against the Cherokee, the provision least likely to be fulfilled:

> If any citizen of the United States, or person under their protection, shall commit a robbery or murder, or other capital crime, on any Indian, such offender or offenders shall be punished in the same manner as if the murder or robbery, or other capital crime, had been committed on a citizen of the United States; and the punishment shall be in presence of some of the Cherokees.[16]

Sequoyah

The success of the Cherokee and accommodation with the United States continued through the early nineteenth century, with the further establishment of Moravian missionaries for education, and above all support for the United States in the Creek War and the War of 1812. In the 1820s the Cherokee celebrated a long series of accomplishments, to be seen perhaps as modernization and even accommodation with American ways. Among these achievements most important was the invention of a syllabary in the 1820s by George Guess or Sequoyah

(1770?–1843?), a monolingual metalworker and soldier with the USA in the Creek War. With eighty-five or eighty-six syllables written with a mixture of adapted Roman, Greek and Cyrillic characters, Cherokee were able to learn to read relatively rapidly instead of the years required with Roman-written English. Aided by missionaries, Sequoyah's system was adapted for use in printing, culminating in the appearance of the bilingual *Cherokee Phoenix* from 1828, a weekly newspaper produced in editions of 200.

During the 1820s a capital was established at New Echota, Georgia, with features including a museum, and in 1827 the first principal chief, John Ross (1790–1866), largely of Scottish descent, was elected. Ross, wealthy and educated, was a capable leader from the 1810s through to the re-establishment of a relationship with the USA after the Civil War. With the National Party he led opposition to removal from the southeast to Indian Territory. The start of the removal process began in 1802 when, in a compact with Jefferson, Georgia gave up its western territories, these becoming Alabama and Mississippi, in return for an agreement that the Congress would extinguish Indian title within the state. Gradually the Cherokee began to move west, to Indian or Unorganized Territory, originally a vast area which gradually shrank to become the state of Oklahoma, although enforced removal and the legal isolation of the Cherokee Nation was part of a prolonged process, which, as well as dividing the tribe, defined Indian Nations. In the 1820s proposals and discussions for Indian removal remained a matter of dispute. With the election of Andrew Jackson (1767–1845) removal became a tenet of federal policy. The Removal Act of 1830 provided the obligatory reasonable terms for removal, saying that Indians who 'may choose to exchange lands' would receive lands out west, be helped to travel there, be protected in those lands and provided with funding for the first year, that the new lands would be guaranteed through all time, and that compensation would be paid for all improvements made on the original lands. In the same period Georgia sought, like New York before, to extend state authority over Indian people. Much of the hostility to Cherokee was led by twice governor George Gilmer (1790–1859). It was Gilmer who initiated the prosecution of Samuel Worcester, leading to the most famous case in Indian legal history.

Worcester (1778–1859) was a missionary, the son of a printer pastor, who helped Elias Boudinot (1802–39) found the *Cherokee Phoenix*. In 1831 he was convicted of illegally living in Indian Country against state law and jailed. His case was taken to the Supreme Court. Worcester v. Georgia 1832 confirmed all that was best in the Euro-American treatment of Indian Nations, yet in effect also demonstrated the difference between the law as enacted and the actual procurement of justice. Chief Justice John Marshall made extremely explicit the rights of Indians in three cases. First, he had already affirmed in 1823 in a case about Piankeshaw/Miami/Illinois lands, Johnson v. M'Intosh, that US individuals could not purchase Indian lands. But after Georgia had imposed state laws on the Cherokee Chief John Ross took a case to the Supreme Court disputing their validity; Marshall heard the case but declined to pronounce, saying that Indian tribes were 'domestic dependent nations', that is, they were not foreign nations, and so crucially Marshall both undermined the validity of the treaties and confirmed federal privileges. In Worcester Marshall redeemed the position of the USA from a moral point of view, proclaiming:

> the acts of Georgia are repugnant to the Constitution, laws, and treaties of the United States . . . They are in direct hostility with treaties, repeated in a succession of years, which mark out the boundary that separates the Cherokee country from Georgia; guaranty to them all the land within their boundary; solemnly pledge the faith of the United States to restrain their citizens from trespassing on it, and to recognize the pre-existing power of a nation to govern itself.[17]

But in a probably apocryphal aside Jackson is supposed to have remarked, 'John Marshall has made his decision, now let him enforce it.' Further, this period of Jackson's early presidency saw also the first major gold rush, from 1828, looking for placer metal in Cherokee country and resulting in an influx of thousands of miners and speculators, many of whom were to move on twenty years later to California, taking with them Georgia practice in Indian relations. The disintegration of proper relations between state and federal authorities and the Cherokee Nation led to the Treaty of New Echota of 1835, signed by a small number of Indian people of the Treaty

Party, well-established individuals who recognized that they had no future in their traditional homelands and had the means to transfer themselves and their property out west. Among the signers, led by members of the Ridge family, was Elias Boudinot. Many of the signers moved west shortly afterwards of their own accord. The majority, however, were forcibly removed in 1838–9 by General Winfield Scott, a process taken over by John Ross, along the 800-mile 'Trail of Tears'. A large proportion of the Cherokee died: upwards of 4,000 people from the 14,000 who were moved west. And in 1839 the leaders of the Treaty Party, including Boudinot, were assassinated. Finally, in the 1860s, the Civil War divided the Cherokee Nation again, John Ross once more at the forefront of an impossible leadership, working with the Union, fighting with the Confederacy and with Confederate Indians.

The 1860s

The 1860s were more generally a catalyst for Native North America. In British North America, federation was achieved in 1867 in the aftermath of the Civil War to the south. Canada was extended westwards to the Pacific in 1871 with the inclusion of British Columbia in return for a promise of a transcontinental railway. In the USA the abolition of chattel slavery, with the Emancipation Proclamation of 1863, and the passing of the 13th Amendment in 1868 did away with the pernicious business of slavery by the account book. But what had already begun to occur, the colourization of racial difference, accelerated, during the decade in which Darwin's *On the Origin of Species* was vigorously debated in the United States.

For aboriginal Americans, the eighteenth- and early nineteenth-century dichotomy of savagery and Christian civilization was given additional strength by racial and creationist theory. Creationist theory survived in the United States longer than in Europe, supported by the tremendous authority of Louis Agassiz (1807–73), the great discoverer of the theory of ice ages in Europe, who worked at Harvard. Agassiz's thinking about race, originating after he came to the United States from Switzerland, promoted difference and polygenism during the 1850s, providing succour to the south. Agassiz went, for instance, to Brazil on a photographic expedition to prove that racial hybridity produced sterile offspring and of course failed.[18] He also in the 1860s promoted Lamarckian ideas of difference, that characteristics could be acquired and passed on with each generation, as an alternative to Darwinian theory. His work contributed to the acceptance of the earlier ideas of Samuel George Morton (1799–1851), the influential craniologist, whose work in the 1820s and 1830s sought to prove that brain size determined difference, Caucasians being the brainiest, followed by Asians.

The colour racialization of difference established itself alongside craniology in a most pernicious way in Indian Territory, during and after the Civil War, in a manner which ensured the dispossession of Native people. The 'Five Civilized Tribes', an epithet which came into use in the mid-nineteenth century to group together the peoples removed in the 1830s to Indian Territory – the Choctaw, Cherokee, Seminole, Chickasaw and Creek – numbered about 60,000 people before the Civil War. To a greater or lesser extent they themselves owned slaves and ran plantations. The Seminole, Indian people undefeated in Florida, the territory to which they fled from the United States, were mostly intermarried with freed slaves. A Works Project Administration (WPA) researcher, Jessie Ervin, recorded in 1937 the thoughts of Kiziah Love, from Colbert, Oklahoma, aged ninety-three, on emancipation from Choctaw slavery in the 1860s: 'What did I do and say? Well, I jest clapped my hands together and said, Thank God Almighty, I'se free at last!'[19] – an expressive phrase that might have been uttered by any emancipated individual in Alabama or Mississippi.

But the seeming simplicity of the words mask a complex hybrid process that was deeply destructive to Indian people and indeed today remains a toxic source of conflict in accessing tribal resources. Through the twentieth century the issue of slavery and the Civil War in Indian Territory was overshadowed by ideas of factionalism in Indian Territory, but it was a factionalism articulated in part at least by the business of slavery. And discussions of Reconstruction in the south usually referred to southern white Reconstruction, not to Indian recovery. The Cherokee, for instance, organized in 1859 a group called 'The Knights of the Golden Circle', whose constitution stated: 'No person shall be a member . . . who is not a pro-slavery man.' In terms of numbers it has been estimated that at least 7,376 slaves were held by Indian people, and perhaps as many as 10,000. Ten per cent of the Creek population were slaves, at one end, and 30 per cent of the Seminole were slaves at the other end, but the difference between bondage and freedom was least clear cut among the Seminole. Slavery was different among Indian people because of kinship, and in the nations apart from Seminole 88 per cent of Indian people did not own slaves, and those with slaves tended to be of mixed American and Native descent.

Further treatment of slaves was different: Ethan Allen Hitchcock (1799–1870), a Union general, noted: 'A slave among wild Indians is almost as free as his owner, who scarcely exercises the authority of a master, beyond requiring some thing like a tax paid in corn or other product of labor.'[20] Emancipation brought intersecting, conflicting difficulties. For the ex-slave holder the problem of labour emerged; for the non-slave-owning Indian it promised the possibility of dislodging the mixed-descent ex-slave owners from leadership roles, and above all it left a very ambiguous group of ill-defined ex-slaves, without properly understood roles or political affiliations. Treaties were imposed in 1865–6 on Indian nations designed to achieve a number of things: to end slavery and to include ex-slaves as tribal members; to end hostilities between Union and Confederate Indians; to create a territorial government, for the first time, although this did not officially happen until 1890. The Southern Treaty Commission took the view that Indian removal had not worked and a policy of assimilation would be preferable. To this end the new treaties, required because adherence to the Confederacy had invalidated previous ones, sequestered Indian lands for a variety of purposes, including ironically for settling newly incoming Indian groups, but also for the building of railways.

The actual treatment of ex-slaves varied enormously. One important Native response was the traditional one, found in all kinship-based societies, of adoption in, of making fictive kin real, by taking in African Americans and treating them as family. Lewis Johnson, Union Chickasaw, put it like this:

> I have heard much said about the black folks. They suffered as much as we did. I have always understood that the President esteemed the

colored people, and we are willing to do just as our Father may wish, and take them in and assist them, and let them help us. So I think and feel towards them.[21]

But of course, with thousands of African Americans now free, they could not all be incorporated as kin. Contrariwise, during the Civil War some people had already sought to deny rights to ex-slaves; the Cherokee freed slaves in 1863 but refused to make them members of the Cherokee Nation. Confederate Creek Daniel N. McIntosh and James M. C. Smith said it was against nature's laws to treat ex-slaves equally, and quoted Jeremiah 13:23, a favourite text of racists, to the commission:

> The antipathies of race among Indians are as strong, if not stronger than they are among the whites. The Government of the United States . . . may force us to things repugnant to our nature; but it cannot change our honest conviction and faith, any more than it can change the skin of the Ethiopian, or the spots of the Leopard.[22]

Others said that this attitude to slaves had been learned from Americans. Generally delegates understood that the idea of organizing a unified territory and vesting land in African Americans would threaten the sovereignty of the Indian Nations. Further, there was confusion as to whether emancipation and the 13th Amendment applied to Indian Territories, so that the Choctaw and the Chickasaw had the confusing opprobrium of being the last American governments to prohibit slavery. They were also mostly Confederates and most reluctant to allow freedom to bondsmen, occasionally, like Choctaw Michael Laflore, kidnapping them to bring them back to Indian Territory, and still buying slaves in late 1865. The behaviour of Confederate Indians created cross-cutting interests, associating the US drive for emancipation with imperialism and the seizure of Indian land, and the subordination of ex-slaves with the self-determination by Indian people. The Seminole, the only nation to adopt its African Americans, lost 3 million acres, and the process, with the construction of railways, prepared the way for an influx of poor whites, to be employed by Indian planters. As late as 1885 the Chickasaw governor was recorded as saying: 'the Chickasaw people cannot see any reason or just cause why they should be required to do more for their freed slaves than the white people have done in the slave-holding States for theirs'.[23]

Continued strife over the rights of ex-slaves to membership of Indian tribal nations also threatened to introduce more US interference, since ex-slaves who were denied residency or property rights might complain to the US government. One Choctaw ex-slave, J. J. Briarley, wrote to President Grover Cleveland about the killing by police of his friend Lemon Triams in 1886: 'Dont turn us loose Keep us in your Charge Mr Cleavland [sic].' Ex-Cherokee slaves were recorded as speaking Cherokee but were not acceptable as returnees from wartime exile in Texas. And finally, as among white people, what mattered most was now skin colour. In the 1880s John Mac-Donald, a black Delaware adopted by the Cherokee, was evicted from his farm by a light-skinned Cherokee, Ellen Mathes, and noted: 'Just Because I am mixed with Colored the[y] say No Negro shall have any Rite in this Nation.' Other Indians fought for the rights of ex-slaves as Indians, for instance Oktarsars Harjo, former principal chief of the Creek, who noted how the Confederate Creek wanted to deny payments to freedmen. This conflicted and difficult story has one important lesson, perhaps: that Indian people in the southeast were in this limited sense no different to southern whites, though on balance they behaved better.[24]

The Lumbee and Indian Mutiny

Among Eastern Indians the Lumbee were named after the Lumber River and largely resident in the tri-racial Robeson County. They number perhaps 60,000 people, according to a North Carolina leaflet of 2013, and while discussions about identity revolved in the 1930s about the boundary between African American and Indian, their identity is continually shifting. Today they are said to be mostly the descendants of the Cheraw and related Siouan peoples, but their background is more complex than that.

North Carolina Natives suffered egregiously from diseases and from the wars which destroyed and removed peoples such as the Tuscarora in 1711–15, when with defeat some Indians were sold into

Caribbean slavery, and many of the remaining Tuscarora were removed to New York to become the Sixth Nation of the Iroquois Confederacy. The Yamasee War of 1715–22 followed, the Yamasee being a mixed, incorporative group who evolved on the Anglo–Spanish Florida frontier and supplied the British with deer skins from the interior. After the failing of the trade, war ensued, and the Yamasee ended up in slavery or in flight to what would become Georgia and Florida.

The Lumbee avoided the fate of the Yamasee, but their current peculiar circumstance, as the largest tribe without recognition, despite a 2015 initiative in Congress, comes about for a number of reasons. One is that the March 1781 Articles of Confederation stipulated (article 9) that:

> The United States in Congress assembled shall also have the sole and exclusive right and power of . . . regulating the trade and managing all affairs with the Indians, not members of any of the States, provided that the legislative right of any State within its own limits be not infringed or violated.

That is, the original thirteen states retained some prior rights over federal authorities in dealing with Indians. The Lumbee were the most numerous of the people that fell under this heading. More importantly the Lumbee inhabit marginal land, like that of the Florida Seminole, that no one wanted and so were left to a large extent in peace, were never defeated and consequently never had their land base recognized by the federal authorities. In the 1830s, with removal of Indian nations in the south, racial lines were redrawn, and in 1835 freedmen were disenfranchised. In the 1860s the Lumbee were caught up in the Civil War, especially towards the end, when people were conscripted for war work on the coast by the rebels. At that time the Indian population was centred on Scuffletown, now Pembroke.

During the chaotic period of endemic violence, with the hardening of racial divisions imposed during Reconstruction, prominent Lumbee, targeted by the Confederacy, helped Sherman and the Union and then were duly betrayed. The prominent Lowrie/Lowry family were caught in all of this, and for an eight-year period were led by a young son, Henry Berry Lowrie (c.1845–c.1872), who killed the abusers of his family and turned Robin Hood or Zorro-type outlaw and bank robber, stealing from and killing prominent whites and escaping twice from jail. Eventually, after a particularly successful robbery, he disappeared, perhaps dying unromantically in a firearms accident. In 1885 the Indians of Robeson County were recognized as Croatan, believed to be descendants of Walter Raleigh's lost colony on the coast, by a politician philanthropist, Hamilton McMillan (1837–1916), who created a school for Indians. Through the twentieth century the ethnic and racial designation of the group kept changing, to the preferred ethnonym of Lumbee in 1953, when they become prominent again in their own right with a geographically derived name which could encompass all Indian groups.

In 1958 *Life* magazine covered the story of a Ku Klux Klan meeting, 100 strong, determined to stop integration of housing and interracial dating, that was broken up by 350 Lumbees. The armed Lumbees made off with a flag and burned a cross at what is now the annually celebrated 'Battle of Hayes Pond'.[25]

No other Indian group has been the subject of so many congressional hearings, and in the 1980s it was thought that federal approval would have cost $120 million a year. In order not to alienate other Native nations it was agreed that any eventual recognition would require a separate appropriation outside of the BIA's budget. From 1970 the Lumbee designation started, if not to fracture, then to divide under the general umbrella, so that by the 1990s there were eight participating groups: the Lumbee Tribe of Cheraw Indians, Hatteras Tuscarora Tribe, Cherokee of Robeson and those of Adjoining Counties, Tuscarora Indian Tribe of Drowning Creek Reservation, Tuscarora Tribe of North Carolina, Eastern Carolina Tuscarora Indian Organization and Tuscarora Nation of North Carolina.[26]

While the literature on the Lumbee suggests that ethnographically they are Indian, the response of white extremists to the possibility of recognition suggests that the cultural specificity of the Lumbee seems limited: without religion, language or high-profile cultural markers, it remains hard for them to be recognized as Indian. Yet this large group of people, many tens of thousands, has lived in a single area, the marginal wetlands of Robeson County, for hundreds of years, absorbing outsiders from wherever they came, in Indian fashion. In this circumstance cultural markers to do with family and lifestyle would have implicit meaning, rather than symbolic legibility, the Indian identity being a state of being and a way of life. In another country, such as Canada, where tribal specificity is less marked, the Lumbee might identify as a mixed group of varied descent: Métis (from Europeans and also Africans) and Native Americans (from Iroquoian, Algonquian and Siouan-speaking peoples). The repeated attempts both at self-designation and external designation and recognition reflect the need in American law to impose racial categories in order to obtain federal recognition. Over all of this hangs the Faustian spectre of casino economics: recognition would provide the legal framework to develop gaming industries, yet the state of North Carolina has stipulated that only two Indian nations, the Eastern Cherokee and the Catawba, might have casinos. The Lumbee have agreed to language in their recognition process that would prohibit the tribe from gaming operations. Further, the legislation which set Indian gaming revolves around land, and the Lumbee have no land and are not involved in the land claims process.[27]

The Plains and Ideas of Racial Fitness

The biological history of Native North America is correctly told as one of unmitigated disaster, where decimation of peoples occurred because of low resistance to imported diseases and European aggression. Yet in one area an exactly opposite story can be told, one where the nutritional wealth of Native North America was much higher than that of Americans. Horse-borne Indian hunters dominated the American Plains for a short period, a century or century and half, and retained the bow until the 1870s, when breech- rather than muzzle-loading carbines became available. The arrival of the horse allowed for greater mobility, and for a major reduction in the use of dogs and women for transportation, although the demands of the nineteenth-century fur and skin trade resulted in a huge increase in the labour required of Indian women in the hard, time-consuming business of scraping and softening skins. The horse allowed also for a greater ease of hunting and a reduction in the importance of the communal hunt – of hunting by driving bison into pounds and over buffalo jumps.

A comparative study has been made of the size of Plains Indian men and European and American men. Franz Boas took biometric readings of thousands of American Indians over a fifteen-year period at the end of the nineteenth century. In 1892, at the time of the Columbian Exposition in Chicago, 1,485 Indians, largely men, from eight Plains tribes were measured. These measurements have been collated, and revisited to tell a story where Plains Indians were taller and probably healthier than their Euro-American counterparts.[28] Early in the century travellers on the Plains, such as Major Long and George Catlin, had noted the great height of Indian men, and this now seems to have been confirmed. The average height of British, Dutch, French, German or Russian troops born in the mid-nineteenth century was 164–6 cm, while American and Canadian troops were 171 cm tall, and Plains Indians 172 cm.

This study of Plains Indian men also suggested that in the central Plains, where bison ecology was most favourable, height was maximized. Rainfall declines on the Plains east to west, and temperature increases north to south, so effective moisture is decreased north to south and east to west; and in the north, of course, pasture is reduced by the cold. There may have been 30 million bison at the time of optimal forage, and in the mid-latitudes of the Plains (such as the wet Black Hills) Indian men were taller than those in the north, such as the Blackfoot (172 cm) and Assiniboine (170 cm), and the Kiowa (170 cm) and Comanche (168 cm) in the south. The Cheyenne were the tallest (177 cm), followed by the Arapaho (174 cm), Crow (174 cm) and Sioux (173 cm).

A further seemingly racial inflexion to the narrative of Plains history can be given to the defeat of the US army at the Battle of the Little Bighorn. It has been argued that long-haired, blue eyed Custer was defeated not because he disobeyed orders, divided his command, was a victim of conspiracy and followed mistaken tactics, but because he was so convinced of his racial superiority that he paid little or no attention to ordinary necessary professional disciplines: the training of men and the teaching of men to form up and fire in disciplined formation. He was confident of the superiority of his forces and was sure that attack was the better form of defence.

Disease

The flu epidemic of 1918–19 began as a mutation in vast First World War camps, either at Étaples, among British soldiers, or in Kansas, among Americans, and was known as Spanish flu because neutral Spanish newspapers, without wartime censorship, reported the pandemic early. It was particularly devastating in the north. In Labrador the Inuit population dropped by 30 per cent, and two Inuit villages were particularly devastated: Okak and Hebron, the former losing 204 of 263 residents in the last two months of 1918. The dead could not be buried, so loose sled dogs ate the dead and attacked the living. In the 1980s Kitora Boas, who was twenty years old in 1918, gave understated expression to the aftermath: 'For a long time after there was this sense of decline as far as yearly activities were concerned among the Inuit and in all northern Labrador communities. A sense of let-down was in the air for a long time.' But of course this 'let-down' had been the unrecorded aftermath of epidemics in indigenous communities for hundreds of years across the Americas, as Old World pathogens took a hold.[29] On the other side of the continent Brevig Mission, an Inupiat village near Bering Strait, lost 90 per cent of its population, and in 1997 the body of a woman was exhumed from the permafrost to provide for the first enough time a large enough sample for scientific investigation.[30] Importantly the administrative response to the flu outbreak was very different in Labrador and Alaska. Labrador was a home-rule British colony, in which missionary activities dominated most aspects of life. In late 1918 the Moravian mission ship *Harmony* was late delivering supplies, and while the captain knew of the flu, no effective measures were taken to separate sailors and Inuit. During the rapid unloading of cargo transmission would have been unavoidable. In Alaska, in contrast, armed guards were used to quarantine villages; in some places – Barrow, Shishmaref, and Wainwright – this worked, whereas in others, such as Nome and Saint Michael, it was ineffective. In Labrador Inuit communities between Nain and Hopedale escaped the flu epidemic, possibly because simultaneous outbreaks of measles had an inoculating effect against the virus.[31]

Smallpox is perhaps the most notorious of Old World pathogens to devastate the New World. In the Old World smallpox was endemic, and populations were self-immunizing, which meant that nursing mothers passed on immunity to their babies. In the New World women could not pass on their own immunity and, having no immunity themselves, became ill and were unable to look after sick infants. A number of factors may have assisted in the spread of smallpox in Native communities. These include communal living, as in longhouses, flight from diseased loci and population movement by trading, hunting and warfare. Smallpox arose in the Old World after the ancient migrations to the Americas and was transmitted both from Europe and through transported African slaves, who, as often from the African interior, would also possess limited immunity to the disease. It has also been suggested that the use of sweat lodges as a means of cure may have contributed to deaths, but this seems unlikely to have been a major factor.

Most notorious is the use of smallpox as an early form of biological warfare during Pontiac's rebellion around Fort Pitt/Pittsburgh in 1763 by the British. William Trent (1715–c.1787), a fur trader and land speculator in Pennsylvania and the Ohio Valley, son of the founder of Trenton, NJ, invoiced the army in the summer of 1763 for replacements for 'two Blankets and an Handkerchief out of the Small Pox Hospital. I hope it will have the desired effect [of spreading the pox]'. These were provided to parleying Delaware leaders, Turtle's Heart and Mamaltee, the invoice actually specifying 'To Sundries got to Replace in kind those which were taken from people in the Hospital to Convey the Smallpox to the Indians Vizt: 2 Blankets 1 Silk Handkerchef & 1 linnen do'. Next month Lord Amherst, commander of the British forces, made it clear to the commander of Fort Pitt that such measures were appropriate, writing 'You will Do well to try to Innoculate the Indians by means of Blanketts, as well as to try Every other method that can serve to Extirpate this Execreble Race', inoculate meaning, whether ironically or not, to infect.[32] The history of smallpox in North America has an important place in the discussion of genocide in the United States, and effective holocaust denial is a complicated issue. But as elsewhere in Native history understanding the circumstances of this attempt to kill Indians provides important contemporary insights into the aboriginal situation.[33]

What is interesting about the historiography of the Amherst/Pontiac/Fort Pitt episode is the absence of any wider contextualization of this major event – how did Native Americans view smallpox in the eighteenth century, what measures were taken by Indian people to minimize the disease, and how did the American colonists see smallpox infection among Indian people? Of course, new epidemics were incorporated into Native belief systems. In the 1830s Cherokee beliefs were recorded by a Protestant missionary, Daniel Buttrick. When smallpox broke out, as it did every dozen or so years, a smallpox dance (called by Buttrick Itohvnv) was performed, because it was believed that evil spirits, Kosvkvskini, aroused by the absence of proper observances, were on the loose. With the performances a degree of seclusion – seven days in the Council House – was enforced, restricting movement beyond the provision of necessities.[34] Further explanation was given with animist causation, the pimple and pustules being associated with the pricks of chestnuts and the colours of choke berries. Creek towns applied quarantine, perhaps learned from the colonists, so that some towns avoided contagion. William Bartram (1739–1823), the Philadelphia naturalist, recorded in 1776 the measures taken in the Creek town of Attassee to combat an unspecified epidemic: 'At this time the town was fasting, taking medicine, and I think I may say praying to avert a grievous calamity of sickness.'[35] The British were repeatedly put out, during the colonial wars, by the reluctance of friendly allies to make themselves available during times of pestilence: Kanagatucko/Cunne Shotte/Stalking (Standing) Turkey/Old Hop (fl. 1750–62) of Chota relocated meetings out of town to Congarees in 1755 to avoid contagion, because many of his warriors had died on the way back from Charleston. The French explained to their Indian allies that the British brought disease, and Creek and the Cherokee would not commit to fight in the Ohio Valley because of the threat of disease. What this means is that in the 1760s, during Pontiac's revolt, the British were aware of the devastating consequences of smallpox and the measures taken by respected Native leaders to avoid epidemics.

Tuberculosis continued through the first half of the twentieth century as a significant disease, with a high level of mortality, gradually reduced by the 1960s as the Indian Health Service improved. In 1910 the death rate was estimated at 1,000 in every 100,000, and by 1978 was reduced to 6. As ever there is much discussion as to whether TB was present in the Americas before 1492, and in general the evidence suggests that it was not.[36] A 1933 immunization trial on First Nations children from Qu'Appelle, Saskatchewan, of a French TB vaccine received great attention in the summer of 2013. A television programme publicized a paper published much earlier which contrasted the vaccinated infants brought to medical attention with those left on the reserves, who were treated as a control group, in other words suffering a higher rate of mortality. Framing this discussion was a much earlier quote from Canada's first prime minister, Sir John A. MacDonald (1815–91), responsible for Indian policy and for keeping costs down. He boasted in 1882 that agents 'are doing all they can, by refusing food until the Indians are on the verge of starvation', the point being that malnutrition along with overcrowding are preconditions for high TB rates.[37]

Finally, and symbolically, most controversial of all is the question of the prevalence of syphilis in pre-Columbian America, and whether it was taken back to Europe by the Spanish to become the French or Neapolitan disease, in British parlance, depending on who was fighting whom. The issue is clouded, as with other pre-modern descriptions of diseases, and by the association of syphilis with leprosy and the similarity of evidence for yaws and syphilis. But the examination of skeletal materials from European leprosy suggests syphilis was not endemic in Europe, and that it probably did originate in the New World. It was prevalent in Native American skeletal materials from the USA but was a non-venereal disease that mutated to become a sexually transmitted disease at the time of European contact with the New World. Native North America is central to much history of epidemiology, and health, or rather poor health, remains a core issue in both countries.

In the USA, Native health is administered by the Indian Health Service (IHS), founded in 1955, at the time of termination. Allowed to discriminate in hiring Native people, it suffers from significant decline in funding, for instance under sequestration enacted in 2013. The service provided by the Aberdeen Area of the IHS in South Dakota was the subject of a 2010 report by Byron Dorgan for the Senate, which detailed a long list of issues cloaked as ever in inexpressive terms masking unnecessarily high death rates: chronic mismanagement, lack of employee accountability and financial integrity; recurring diversions of reduced health-care services due to lack of qualified providers or funds; five IHS hospitals in the Aberdeen area at risk of losing their accreditation or certification from the Centers for Medicare and Medicaid Services (CMS); several facilities cited as having health-care providers on staff who lacked proper licensing or credentialing; key senior staff positions remaining vacant for long periods of time, contributing to the lack of proper management; employees with a record of misconduct or poor performance being transferred to different health facilities within the Indian health system; pharmaceutical audits of narcotics and other controlled substances not regularly performed, with three service units within the region having a history of missing or stolen narcotics.

Alcohol

From colonial times traders dispensed alcohol to willing purchasers, introducing an important intoxicant. One or two intoxicants were already in use in North America, apart from Native tobacco. Indian people in a relative small area of the southern United States used the leaves of a small holly species, *Ilex vomitoria*, or *yopún* in Catawba, to create a black drink, high in caffeine, to assist in purification and celebration, rituals which included vomiting, hence the Latin name. In the southwest especially fermented drinks were made from saguaro cactus and other plants, but not, of course, distilled spirits. Alcohol, on becoming available in the seventeenth century, was also used in ceremonials and festivities for in-group rituals. In the next centuries alcohol use was widely reported in conjunction with a wide range of spiritual circumstances, including in the Ojibwe/Anishinaabe Midewiwin ceremony; by Thoreau for predicting the illness of his Penobscot guide in the 1850s; in the Ojibwe/Anishinaabe shaking tent ceremony; among the Montagnais/Naskapi/Innu in Quebec-Labrador and more

43

generally in medicine societies among the Dakota and Haudenosaunee/ Iroquois; in thanksgiving rituals and in mourning rites. Prohibition can be traced to the appearance of nativistic revivalism, of Tenkswatawa and of Handsome Lake, and to the influence of the temperance movement in Indian Country. Alcohol would inevitably be consumed with tobacco, suggesting inebriation in a social context. The author of an article that summarizes Native use in eastern North America states: 'in most societies where people drink, drinking is commonly not only a highly patterned, socially and culturally integrated activity but is usually also either a profane or a sacred act',[38] something which commentators often omit. This was also the general implication of Kathryn Abbott's study of drinking among the early twentieth-century Anishinaabe of Minnesota: that firstly studies were generally unnuanced, by age and gender and by the seasons and the association of drinking with certain activities – such as the gathering of maple sugar, rice, bringing in furs for ale, receiving treaty payments and so on, where non-Indians would be present.[39] It also suggested that drinking was used by non-Indian commentators as a rhetorical device to pathologize Indian behaviour and maintain dependency, as farmers were or were not allowed to own land in fee simple after allotment, and that in intersecting with the general prohibition movement Indian drinking lost social aspects such as the in-saloon association with saloon keeper and patrons. Further, and more recently, it has been suggested that Indian people are genetically predisposed to alcoholism, but this seems to be another myth.

Low Alcohol Use by Indians

The central perceived reality today is rather different: that alcohol use in Indian Country is seen as a non-social activity, with little benefit, so alcohol abuse and Indian Country are synonymous in the public imagination. The reality is different. An innocent-sounding, but subversive, Indian Health Service document, *Behavioral Health Briefing Book* (2011), summarizes the American Indian and Alaska Native situation in respect of alcohol and drugs. It makes one highly surprising suggestion – that in the period 2005–8 alcohol use among Native people was *below* the national average (43.9 per cent Indians against

55.2 per cent of all adults used alcohol) – but suggests that binge drinking and all other statistics for abuse, morbidity and crime is much higher. The devastation wrought by alcohol abuse remains, however, a constant factor in Indian Country, regularly sensationalized by journalists. Recently a nurse, Nora Boesem, in Newell, South Dakota, was reported as having fostered ninety-three children with Foetal Alcohol Syndrome in a fifteen-year period.[40]

Alcohol remains toxic in other ways. In recent years, from 1953, the US government has begun to delegate federal authority in certain areas, such as environmental protection, and alcohol use, to tribes. This means that regulation in these matters is localized at the tribal level, in theory, but not, as it turns out, in practice. Regulation of the liquor trade with Native people began in early colonial times, but has always been characterized by equivocation. In Massachusetts liquor sales were banned in the 1630s, but the ban was repealed in 1641 so that traders could engage with Indian people, and in 1646 the colony itself began to issue alcohol bounties for the killing of wolves. This ambivalence continued through colonial times, though it was long recognized by Indian people that alcohol use was highly destructive. By the eighteenth century alcohol sales were an accepted part of colonial trade, highly influential in enabling trade and land sales, as well as in military activities. After the American Revolution prohibition gradually became American policy. In 1802 Jefferson successfully asked Congress to legislate prohibiting alcohol sales to Indians, and this became fully codified in US law under the 1834 Trade and Intercourse Act. Less appreciated is the continued ambivalence of Native people themselves to alcohol: in the early nineteenth century the Cherokee established taverns and used alcohol as a prelude to war. In 1803 Cherokee Chief Tolluntuskee made a contract with Thomas N. Clark to establish two inns on the Cumberland Road for five years allowing him to 'keep good & reputable persons in said Houses' and to 'furnish liquors & good provisions' for travellers.[41] Later the Cherokee nation, aided by temperance societies, managed effectively to control alcohol abuse, although the right to tax alcohol became an important sovereignty issue leading up to removal in the 1830s. Indeed so important was the issue that Elias Boudinot noted non-Indian use in 1830:

Among the whites of the surrounding counties intemperance and brutal intoxication . . . may be witnessed in every neighbourhood . . . [if
you] visit the Indian elections, courts and the General Council and
make a disinterested comparison . . . we pledge ourselves that there is
less intemperance exhibited here on these occasions than among the
whites.[42]

During the period of termination, when 100 tribes were designated
for extinction, other laws relating to Indian Country were amended;
by 1949 much land on Indian reservations had been alienated, so that
large white populations now lived in Indian Country. In 1949 non-
Indian communities and rights of way were excluded from the
regulation of alcohol. In effect this means that it is often very hard to
enforce alcohol bans on Indian reservations. An important case was
heard at the beginning of the millennium around attempts by the
Yakama Nation, in Washington State, to ban alcohol. This is a large
reservation, with around 1.2 million acres, the size of Delaware, with
25,000 people, 20,000 white, mostly situated in two towns, Toppen-
ish and Wapato. In the northwest, in Indian Country, alcohol-related
deaths were seven times the national rate of 6.7 per thousand deaths.
The state appealed the tribal law as affecting trade, and the US Attor-
ney for the Eastern District of Washington issued an opinion in 2001
that Indian Country did not include communities in white areas
(where land was owned in fee simple), and so prohibition could not
apply to the two towns.[43]

The impossible situation of Indian Country in respect of alcohol is
further illustrated by the Pine Ridge Oglala Lakota Reservation.
Larger than Yakama, and the size of Delaware and Rhode Island combined, with a similar population, this reservation saw an alcohol ban
in 1889. In 2013 the ban was lifted after a vote: 1,871 for legalization
and 1,679 against. The tribal president, Bryan Brewer, who was against
legalization, pointed out: 'We know the use will go up . . . we know
there'll be more violence. There'll be more women and children who
will be abused. It will taper off. But it's something we're just going to
have to deal with . . . I hope they talk about that.'[44] Much of the alcohol
sales previously came from liquor stores in nearby Whiteclay, Nebraska,
selling millions of dollars' worth of beer, and netting hundreds of

thousands of dollars' worth of tax, which could otherwise have gone to the tribe, hence the change. In 2012 the tribe tried to have liquor sales at Whitclay outlawed, which failed, although this tiny community of a few liquor stores subsists almost entirely on Indian alcohol abuse.[45]

One way then of regarding alcohol use by Native people is that its use changed over the centuries: at first involved with religion, it then became a form of release and conviviality with war and dispossession in the eighteenth and nineteenth centuries, and then gradually one of general abuse in the twentieth century, now including crystal meth and gasoline sniffing. As ever, the writing is almost always expressionless; only occasionally do contemporary descriptions use pungent nineteenth-century language, as when recently British writer A. A. Gill describes European mining engineers waiting to pick up drunk Greenlandic 'Vegetative women to have blubbery semi-conscious sex with', a comment, in *Previous Convictions* (2007), which at least doesn't hide prejudice behind statistics.

Education and Sport

While Native education is a separate topic, during one important period, the third quarter of the nineteenth century, new schools were designed specifically to eliminate the Indian race; yet in enabling sporting success, boarding schools were later to contribute to a new Indian identity in the early twentieth century. Education of Indians, in the aftermath of the wars of the 1870s, was led by a self-appointed, fiercely dedicated group of influential, well-to-do, reform-minded Christian philanthropists from the eastern United States. They were determined to obliterate Indian culture, replace Native languages with English and turn Indians into successful Americans. In the USA two post-Civil War educational institutions were particularly important, in contributing to forced assimilation by educating Indians and creating missionary-inspired leaders for Indian Country and beyond. One, the Hampton Institute, now Hampton University, was an offshoot of the school set up in Virginia during the Civil War for the teaching of slaves fleeing the south. Between 1878 and 1923 some 1,388 Native Americans were enrolled, especially Sioux and Haudenosaunee (Seneca and

Oneida), and educated in this school, where African Americans out-numbered Indian people by a factor of four. Hampton was founded by Samuel C. Armstrong (1839–93) and the American Missionary Association, with Mary Peake as the first teacher, in the 1860s. In the 1870s Lieutenant Richard Henry Pratt (1840–1924), a Civil and Indian War veteran, organized the education of Indian hostage prison-ers at Fort Marion, Florida, some of whom he eventually sent to Hampton. Booker T. Washington, the slave-born educator (1856–1915), acted as a house father for the Indians in the 1870s. Girls lived in Winona Lodge, and boys in the wigwam; classes included a wide range of technical skills, farming and religious education. An early Kiowa student, Koba, wrote: 'I pray every day and hoe onions'.[46] Indian education ceased in the 1920s because of the hostility of employers to Native employees who had been educated with blacks, and perhaps also because of rising concern about the involvement of Indian female pupils with black students.

Pratt went on to create the much larger, from a Native point of view, Carlisle Indian Industrial School in Pennsylvania, the flagship boarding school designed to teach civilization (in Pratt's conception), an idea more recently put as 'education for extinction',[47] and espe-cially cultural extinction. An additional aspect of education at Carlisle was that of outing, of placing Indian pupils with white people to learn agriculture, especially in Quaker families. However, particu-larly because Native leaders sent their children to Carlisle, many of the most prominent Indian people of the early twentieth century were educated there. Among them was the Lakota Luther Standing Bear (1868–1939), a model student for Pratt, who led the Indian Band across the Brooklyn Bridge at its opening in 1883. American Horse (1840–1908), who favoured accommodation with the USA, sent his children there, who went on to work for Buffalo Bill.

The school emphasized sport as well as music and quickly developed good teams and an excellent reputation for Native sports. Most fam-ous was Jim Thorpe (1888–1953) (Sac and Fox), descendant of Black Hawk, from Oklahoma, who attended from 1904, won two gold medals, for pentathlon and decathlon, at the Stockholm Olympics in 1912, was subsequently disqualified on the grounds of competing for money but had the medals restored posthumously to him in the

1980s. Tom Longboat (Onondaga) occupies a similar place in Canadian athletics and took part in the marathon in the 1908 Olympics, where the sensational finish, and the removal of the Italian winner Dorando Pietri for being helped to his feet, brought athletics and the Games to mass attention for the first time.[48]

Carlisle had an outstanding football team, to which Thorpe contributed, and which for twenty-five years from the 1890s regularly competed with Ivy League teams. In 1907 the Carlisle team, including Thorpe, beat the University of Pennsylvania in front of 20,000 people. In the extraordinary season of 1911 Carlisle won ten of eleven games, including beating Brown, Johns Hopkins, Pennsylvania and Harvard, when Harvard was favourite, Thorpe scoring all the points.

Carlisle was the model for the boarding school system across the USA but eventually failed. The accommodation, originally a barracks, was returned to the army in 1918 as a hospital. The founding of schools nearer reservations, a reluctance of people to travel far away from Indian Country and war recruitment were all contributory factors in its demise.

2

Recovery

Henry Roe Cloud (1884–1950) (Ho-Chunk), *right*, major Indian leader of the 1930s.

Representatives of various tribes attending an organizational meeting of the National Congress of American Indians, founded 1944.

Russell Means (1939–2012), Lakota activist and actor, wearing dream-catcher earrings and raising a Black Power salute.

Different stories during the Civil Rights era. Louis Tewanima (1888–1969), Hopi runner, silver medallist at the 1912 Olympics, and Jesse Owens (1913–80), four-time Olympic gold medallist 1936, fundraising in 1954.

The Seminole Tribe of Florida received federal recognition 1957. Here, in the 1940s, Harry S. Truman is receiving a Seminole shirt in an act of Indian diplomacy.

John Echohawk, executive director of the Native American Rights Fund.

Helen W. Peterson (1915–2000), Oglala leader, in the 1950s.

Morongo Casino. In California v. Cabazon Band of Mission Indians, 480 US 202 (1987), his Indian nation enabled gambling to begin.

Ben Nighthorse Campbell (b. 1933) (Cheyenne), US senator and judo competitor at the 1964 Olympics.

William Wayne Keeler (1908–89), Principal Chief of the Cherokee Nation and head of Phillips Petroleum.

lly Mills (b. 1938) (Oglala), in 1964 after winning the marathon at the Tokyo lympics.

Wilma Mankiller (1945–2010), first female principal chief of the Cherokee Nation, who took part in the Alcatraz Occupation in 1969.

Edison Chiloquin (1923–2003) (Klamath), refused payment for his land when the tribe was terminated, the land being restored by President Jimmy Carter in 1980.

LaDonna Harris (b. 1931), Comanche politician who fought termination, 1971.

ndian Pavilion at Expo '67, the centenary year, when Quebec and aboriginal Canadians irst fully assumed national roles.

Elijah Harper (1949–2013), Ojibwe Cree leader who upset the 1990 Meech Lake Accord, which privileged Quebec without First Nations Recognition.

Vine Deloria Jnr (1933–2005), Lakota politician and writer, 1981.

Julian Pierce (1946–88) (Lumbee), politician and nuclear chemist, murdered during a judicial election.

President Barack Obama meets Elouise Cobell (1945–2011), banker activist who obtained $3.4 billion redress from the federal government for incompetence.

2

Recovery

Citizenship and the First World War

In one of those counter-intuitive episodes, the bitter campaign against the Pueblos in the early 1920s occurred at the same time as Indians, for the most part, in fits and starts, finally became citizens.[1] Many people, particularly those who had taken allotted land, were already citizens. Further, after the ending of the First World War, a 1919 act enabled Indian people to apply for citizenship in recompense for their wartime participation. Perhaps the most telling comment from the Native community came from the early physician Carlos Montezuma or Wassaja (c.1866–1923) (Yavapai-Apache), who after leaving the BIA became very critical of the agency's work and ridiculed the spectacle of Indian people fighting in a European war, in a sense foreshadowing the post-9/11 Indian bumper sticker: 'fighting terrorism since 1492':

> We Indians are ready to defend the country of our forefathers as we have been doing these five hundred years against all odds, but what are we now? We are nothing but wards; we are not citizens and we are without a country in this wide world.[2]

Opinion, however, both within and outside the Native community was divided as to whether citizenship was a good idea. Charles Eastman, Ohiyesa (1858–1939) (Santee Sioux), was one who advocated a mixed approach that would bring the benefits of Indian culture together with eventual citizenship; his father had taken part in the Santee Sioux revolt of 1862, and he was one of the first Indian physicians, tending the injured after the massacre at Wounded Knee in 1890. He put it like this in 1919:

we think each race should be allowed to retain its own religion and racial codes as far as is compatible with the public good, and should enter the body politic of its own free will, and not under compulsion . . . he was forced to accept modern civilization in toto against his original views and wishes.[3]

Some white people felt that allotment had allowed too many Indians to become citizens too quickly, but nevertheless the Indian Citizenship Act (ICA), a Republican proposal, went through in 1924 and protected Indian rights while providing citizenship. Some 125,000 people out of 300,000 became citizens, without having to apply. Some remained to be convinced.

Afterwards Clinton Rickard, who campaigned to maintain cross-border access in Iroquois country, put it like this in his autobiography, *Fighting Tuscarora*:

United States citizenship was just another way of absorbing us and destroying our customs and government . . . We feared citizenship would also put our treaty status in jeopardy and bring taxes upon our land. How can a citizen have a treaty with his own government?[4]

In Canada citizenship came much later: Canadian nationality law was established only in 1946–7, and citizenship for indigenous people in 1960; before then this right came with abandonment of First Nations status. However, rights to vote in Canada are straightforward in comparison to those of the USA.

Although the US ICA of 1924 may be seen as an aid towards assimilation, it did not necessarily confer rights to vote, even though the 15th Amendment (1870) had made this guarantee. States with large populations therefore took measures to eliminate African and Native Americans by insisting on residency and then disqualifying Indians who lived on reservation because reservations were separate from electoral districts! Or because they were wards, or could not speak English. It was only really after 1945 that the issues around voting were cleared up, and even since then they have generated substantial case law. In 1965 Congress passed the Voting Rights Act to enfranchise racial minorities; but this has been challenged most recently in 2013, when the Supreme Court ruled, because of the equal sovereignty of the states, that states no longer need to obtain pre-clearance from the federal government for any changes in voting rules. This means that various voter ID laws remain in place and in effect if not by prescription discriminate against minorities. So, for instance, a 2004 Arizona act requires photo ID. While regulations are in a constant state of flux, a 2011 review of the report, *Citizens Without Proof*, suggested that many people were thus disenfranchised: 'Most prominently, the study found that 11% of voting-age American citizens – and an even greater percentage of African American, low-income, and older citizens – do not have current and valid government-issued photo IDs.'[5] And this is likely to include a high proportion of Native Americans.

Indian Affairs during the 1920s

In other ways improvement in administration of Indian affairs came in a roundabout fashion. Following the Teapot Dome scandal of 1923, Hubert Work (1860–1942), an activist and efficient interior secretary, was appointed to end corruption and deal with the agricultural crisis of the 1920s. Work served 1923–8 and introduced effective reforms to improve management of public lands and water. He created new National Parks, especially in the east. One aspect of the criticism of the Department of the Interior was the questions raised over the bungling incompetence of its Bureau of Indian Affairs and the mishandling of the Pueblo issues of land and dance in the early 1920s as addressed by John Collier and the Indian Defense Association. Work enabled, by commissioning the Institute of Government Research, the statistician and progressive administrator Lewis Meriam (1883–1972) to prepare with private funding the report *The Problem of Indian Administration* (1928). Gathering information over three years, the often-designated 'Meriam Report' provided a devastating critique of conditions on reservations and in schools high rates of TB, of corruption in the Indian services in places like the Yakima valley, where Indian irrigated land was still being illegally appropriated. Immediately the report had the effect of reducing the allotment of lands to Indians (that is, stopping the alienation of reservation-held communal lands) and laid the way for the Indian New Deal of the 1930s. Health, education, statistics and finance were at the heart of the account, but no anthropologists were appointed to the commission. However, the only Native American on the Meriam Commission, Henry Roe Cloud (1884–1950) (Ho-Chunk/Winnebago), who was brought up in a hunting and logging community in Nebraska, was perhaps the most prominent leader of the 1920s and 1930s. Sometimes regarded as the first Indian graduate of Yale, he actually held an MA in anthropology and was both a supremely effective orator and an innovative educator. He had campaigned as a student for the release of Geronimo and the Citizenship Act of 1924 and generally was interested in modernization. He did not see that hunting, and the traditional life that went with it, were sustainable in the twentieth century.

The Indian Reorganization Act 1934

Henry Roe Cloud was also to act as chief advocate for the legislation, touring the country to persuade tribal people to vote in favour of tribal governments. The Indian Reorganization Act (IRA or Wheeler-Howard Act) is titled very explicitly to do with the modernization of Indian Country, for instance mentioning 'Home Rule', the concept used in Ireland in the nineteenth and early twentieth centuries. This referred to self-government and does not of course mention cultural survival:

> An Act to conserve and develop Indian lands and resources; to extend to Indians the right to form business and other organizations; to establish a credit system for Indians; to grant certain rights of home rule to Indians; to provide for vocational education for Indians; and for other purposes.

John Collier (1884–1968), commissioner of Indian affairs 1933–45, was responsible for the Indian Reorganization Act. He was born into a family prominent in the resurgence of the south and incidentally in promoting the integration of African America. His father, Charles A. Collier (1848–1900), sometime mayor of Atlanta, was president of the Cotton States and International Exposition Company, which organized the fair in 1895. He arranged the appointment of Booker T. Washington (1858–1915), the last African American leader born into slavery, as commissioner for Alabama. At the fair Washington made a conciliatory and accommodationist speech to the senior Collier, his 'Atlanta Address', which could in a Native American context be read as an assimilationist text:

> I but convey to you, Mr. President and Directors, the sentiment of the masses of my race when I say that in no way have the value and manhood of the American Negro been more fittingly and generously recognized than by the managers of this magnificent Exposition at every stage of its progress.[6]

Just as Washington's position was criticized for being too accommodationist, so too was John Collier's Indian New Deal, with the Indian law which arose with the IRA criticized for being assimilationist.

Felix Cohen and Indian Law

Much of the law itself, and subsequently in the late 1930s and 1940s of its implementation and codification, was the responsibility of Felix Cohen (1907–53) of the Department of the Interior and the Department of Justice. He organized the Indian Law Survey, which oversaw the compilation of forty-six volumes of Indian Law. He went on to create the *Handbook of Federal Indian Law* (1941), not before being sacked in 1939, for reasons at least connected to his perceived radicalism, and possibly also because of anti-Semitism. Cohen had a wonderfully refreshing view of the world, for instance talking of first-use property rights in reference to agricultural land, by providing the absurd instance that the first person to breathe a certain volume of air would own the rights to use that air, in a magically titled 1935 article for the *Columbia Law Review*: 'Transcendental Nonsense and the Functionalist Approach'. As well as drafting the IRA, Cohen also provided the template for the creation of the Indian constitutions that were required for tribal governments. Cohen as a progressive and legal pluralist favoured full and appropriate consultation with Indians, at a time when consultation was severely limited and when Indian Service administration of reservations was authoritarian. Intellectually supple and administratively savvy, he brought to the process of creating Indian governments an understanding of the need for expediency to ensure administrative success; and this expediency led to the creation of around 100 governments with constitutions that are often strikingly similar, following his 1934 *[Basic Memorandum] On the Drafting of Tribal Constitutions*. This of necessity needed to override the earlier concerns of different governance, of cultural norms that might vary from people to people. One further aspect of this was the need to show that the IRA was successful, and so, while tribes were encouraged to write their own constitutions, anyway a controversial activity, the constitutions were rushed, in order to demonstrate success. The constitutions also had to be approved by government. Therefore tribes late in writing their constitutions in order to ensure success were tempted to follow previously drafted, rushed and formulaic constitutions that had been approved by the secretary of the interior. As Kevin Washburn put it: 'While the IRA thus helped to preserve the platonic notion of tribal governance, it necessarily substantively changed tribal governments and helped displace and smother traditional tribal governance.'[7]

Implementation of the Indian Reorganization Act

While the IRA has been criticized for forcing Indian nations to produce non-Native-type constitutions, much of the criticism may be seen as irrelevant: the important point is allotment ceased, and assimilation stopped being the goal of the BIA. But the tribal constitutions, enabling a degree of self-government, were only partially successful and not always very to the point. So, for instance, the already self-governing Pueblos, both western and Rio Grande, generally only adopted constitutions to formalize already existing governmental organization. The new Hopi councils, started and restarted, were not initially successful in dealing with Navajo encroachment on Hopi land and with the US government and then had difficulties dealing with demands for access to energy resources. Similarly, the Navajo through the 1930s, with a variety of constitutional measures, with factions for and against, regularly refused to adopt the IRA. That the IRA did not promulgate a form of government unwanted on the reservations is indicated by the successful rejection of the act by the Navajo in 1935 and by the election in 1938 of Jacob Morgan as chairman. Morgan (1879–1950), son of a Navajo scout for the US army in the 1886 Apache campaign and missionary, was strongly opposed to Collier and to the livestock reduction programme that was an essential part of the act in enabling recovery for overgrazed land. From Morgan's perspective the owner of a 500-sheep herd could afford a 10 per cent reduction in sheep, whereas a 10 per cent loss of a fifty-sheep flock might mean starvation.

What the act achieved, however, was exceptional. Importantly, it recognized that the improvements that needed to take place, including in education, had to be effected in circumstances that were radically different to those of 100 years earlier: a revolving loan fund was provided for economic development, funds were provided to buy back lands, and allotment stopped. The end of allotment effectively meant that, while reservations were left with checkerboard patterns of land ownership, the situation did not progress to a stage where Indian land simply disappeared. Most interestingly from a contemporary perspective the buy-provisions have been used, although much challenged in the courts, in the self-government era from the 1970s for tribes, with casino and other funding, actually to increase reservations.

Termination

The situation of the Indian, more so in the United States than Canada, is essentially unstable. In a sense there is more variation within the concept of 'Indian' than between the ideas of non-Indian and Indian. Within the political process, campaigners and advocates are always looking for new ideas to change and improve the situation of Native North Americans. This has been attempted by removing assets, that is, opening treaty land to homesteaders in 1887 to provide good examples of farmers for Natives to copy, or indeed by legislating Indian people into existence, by recognizing them as nations, or out of existence, as with termination in the 1950s. These policies oscillate in an unstable system between assimilation and separation, and it could be said that termination policies were a reflection of a new sense of US self-purpose that arose in the 1940s, in part through a feeling that the New Deal had achieved its goals. In this way, then, the Indian New Deal in the USA ran out of steam and became unimportant with the arrival of the Second World War, the growth of war industries and the move of Indian people into cities for work. Importantly, while the IRA of 1934 had brought to an end the loss of land and introduced tribal charters and government, it had not really expunged the deeply situated goal of assimilation, which was reinvigorated by the success of migrants moving to cities for war work. In 1943 the Senate reported on the cost and inefficiencies of the BIA and IRA, the Indian Claims Commission from 1946 may have been designed to settle outstanding issues, and in 1949 the Hoover Commission reported again on Indian Affairs at a time when government was seen more as a menacing octopus than a servant of the people.[8] Hoover called for the 'complete integration' of Indians 'into the mass of the population as full, tax-paying citizens'.[9] There was not, as with the Dawes Act or the IRA, a single act which introduced the new policy, but instead the Hoover report acted like the Meriam Report, the precursor of a House Concurrent Resolution 108, in 1953. This laid out policy without any legal force. It was declared:

> to be the sense of Congress that, at the earliest possible time, all of the Indian tribes and the individual members thereof located within the States of California, Florida, New York, and Texas, and all of the following named Indian tribes and individual members thereof, should be freed from Federal supervision and control and from all disabilities and limitations specially applicable to Indians.[10]

Termination in the 1950s

The new policies were put in place by a former New Deal Democrat, Dillon Myer (1891–1982), who was commissioner of Indian affairs from 1950 to 1953. Myer had been put in charge of the War Relocation Authority (1942–6), which oversaw the removal of Japanese Americans from the West Coast (though not, of course, from Hawaii, since, given their preponderance in numbers, that would have shut the territory down). Myer thought that most Japanese Americans were loyal, but that loyalty tests were required, denied that camps were concentration camps and would not, later on, countenance an apology, displaying exactly the same confused self-reinforcing teleology which dominated Indian policies. Myer was thought to have been effective, at least in avoiding harsher measures, and since he had known nothing about Japanese America before starting war work thought himself that it would not matter that he knew nothing, as commissioner, of Indians and Indian policy and could appoint similar know-nothings in the BIA. He aimed to remove the federal government from Indian affairs as soon as possible, with honour. The former secretary of the interior, Harold Ickes, who had appointed Collier, called Myer a Hitler and Mussolini rolled into one.[11]

Terminated Tribes

The Indian tribes to be terminated included especially the Menominee in Wisconsin and the Klamath in Oregon. What is interesting is that among the tribes to be terminated were several in California, as well as the Oneida in New York and Seminole in Florida, who were to be conspicuously successful in the late twentieth century. And again the amounts of land involved were enormous – more than 3,000 square miles. Legislation was required for the termination of each tribe, and again, as so often before, the munificent language used acted to beguile and confuse the opponents of assimilation. It was designed more especially to bring on board Indian people whose aspirations sought to overcome the restrictions of federal regulations. One of the leaders seeking change was Napoleon Bonaparte Johnson (1891–1974), first president of the National Congress of American Indians (NCIA) in 1944, a Cherokee lawyer who sought to end the BIA, but whose organization was later to lead in the fight against termination. From 1954 to 1961 Helen W. Peterson (1915–2000) (Oglala), from Pine Ridge, was executive director of the NCAI and responsible for leading lobbying against Termination Acts with all their pernicious effects. Beyond the freeing-up of land ownership, the special relationship of trust with the federal government was finished, state laws and state taxes were imposed, federal programmes to tribes and individuals were stopped, but above all sovereignty was ended.

Public Law 280

Public Law 280, of 1953, was enacted alongside 108 to allow certain states to assume jurisdiction on Indian reservations: in California,

Nebraska, Wisconsin, Minnesota, Oregon and later, after statehood, Alaska. The thrust of the law was an illogical paradox: Indians were said to have reached a stage of acculturation and development in which they were as socially advanced as other state citizens; yet it was also said that they lacked law and order and therefore required law enforcement.[12] As Felix Cohen pointed out, at the time Indians were in fact subject to numerous bodies of law, many of them specifically Indian-related federally empowered measures. The absurdity of this, on usually law-abiding reservations, was further recognized in a BIA report on Wisconsin which indicated that: 'the fact that there is relatively little serious lawlessness in most Indian communities where there are limited or no facilities for protecting persons or property is a tribute to the stability of the members of these communities'.[13] Finally in the 1960s, when the extra costs of law enforcement became apparent, several states retroceded the right to criminal jurisdiction to Indian tribes. The effect of PL 280 was to remove important areas of jurisdiction from tribal governments, that is reduce sovereignty, and then fail to replace effective policing with state law enforcement in what were often remote communities. Termination and PL 280 were accompanied by other measures designed to reduce costs and, in the name of freedom and equality, accelerate assimilation. These included measures to close schools and conversely ensure that Indian children were educated at schools far from their own reservation, reduce Indian health care and hospital funding and accelerate relocation of Indian workers to cities. Relocation to cities was an extreme form of assimilation favoured during the 1950s and, unlike the casual move to urban war work in the 1940s, failed miserably. In some areas returnees to reservations were 90 per cent or more, and even the BIA's own statistics in the 1950s indicated that 24–30 per cent of migrants returned to reservations. Much of this was because Indian people, despite the BIA and boarding schools, did not have the education to find permanent work. In fact most jobs they found were seasonal railroad and agricultural work, the least secure positions at the time.

Termination in Oregon

The disaster of terminations can be traced through the story of the destruction of one of the largest of tribes. Termination proceeded with individual acts against the Klamath in 1954. Orme Lewis, Assistant Secretary of the Interior, wrote in 1954:

> It is our belief that the Klamath Tribe and the individual members thereof have in general attained sufficient skill and ability to manage their own affairs without special federal assistance . . . Their dress is modern, and there remains little vestige of religious or their traditional Indian customs. Most of them live in modern homes, many of which are equipped with electricity, water and sewage disposal . . . The Klamath Tribe has been considered one of the most advanced Indian groups in the United States.[14]

Three years later it was said that most adult Klamath men did not work, that the majority had criminal records beyond driving offences and that there were few educated people among them. Nevertheless the act imposed on the tribe a disposal of forested tribal lands; individuals were given the option of receiving land or money if they withdrew from the tribe. The vote was held in 1958, and of the 2,133 eligible 400 didn't vote and 1,649 elected to withdraw from the tribe and receive money. The BIA had run the forestry business on a sustainable basis, and the tribe was the only one which repaid administrative costs to the BIA. The sudden demand for withdrawal from the tribe and for money precipitated factionalism within the tribe, and the sale of the vast majority of tribal lands. The reservation forest had a sustainable yield of $2 million a year, from 750,000 acres. Because of the collapse of the price of timber, as precipitated by such a sale, most of the forest failed to find a buyer, and so in 1959 the federal government acquired 525,680 acres of forest for $68,716,691; 135,000 acres was retained by Indian people, and this was acquired by the federal government in 1972. The Klamath lands are now part of the Winema National Forest, named for the Modoc leader of the 1870s who assisted in the defeat of her cousin Captain Jack or Pinktuash (c.1837–73) in the last war on California soil.

Fighting Termination

From the tribal perspective at the time and now there was no need for termination: as Laurence Lee Witte put it to Congress in 1954:

We are citizens of the United States or citizens of the State of Oregon; above and beyond that we enjoy the privilege of hunting and fishing . . . our property is tax exempt as far as the proceeds from the timber is concerned. I do not think we are under bondage . . . We have a home; we have income from our per capita sources . . . this is our permanent home; any form of liquidation or termination should come from the Klamath people themselves.[15]

Further acquiescence in the bill was obtained by duress, by withholding treaty moneys, according to the 2014 Klamath tribal chairman, Allen Foreman, and the federal management of the lands has been disastrous, with a collapse in deer and fish populations, even though the tribe retains hunting rights. The best of the stories from this episode is that of Edison Chiloquin (1923–2003), who refused to take money for this land; eventually President Carter in 1980 signed a specific bill, the Chiloquin Act, enabling him to retain 580 acres. While the tribe was restored in 1986, it received no land basis, and the catastrophic management of the Klamath basin continued into the new millennium.

Continued Race View

Throughout the twentieth century, the lines of racial discourse remained most controversial in relationship to African Americans. It might be assumed that political engagements on the ragged edge between Indian and African American would soften and blur and disappear. Yet in many ways the classification of people of mixed descent around the categories of Indian, African American and freedmen remains a live issue, with vigorously articulated historical and scientific analysis pursued to determine the 'truth' of these relationships. In the early twentieth century tribal rolls, derived from the time of the 1887 Dawes Act, included freemen, descendants of the slaves brought west with the removals of the 1830s. Recently the issue of who is and who is not an Indian, especially in Oklahoma and because of annual per capita income derived from casinos, has become live again, particularly among the Cherokee and Seminole. Further threat of disenrolment has become an aspect of everyday life, apparently marginal, but central to the question of how racial issues may or may not be deactivated. In the soap opera *House of Cards* (2014), the casino boss, Daniel Lanagin, played by sometime performer for Diana Ross Comanche Gil Birmingham, threatens an employee with disenrolment for indiscretion.

Yet the African American aspect of this issue is much broader than a question of loss of benefits, whether nation- or tribe-wide. This goes back to the racial policies for African America in the late nineteenth and early twentieth centuries, where the hypodescent rule ensured that one drop of African American blood meant you were classified as 'negro', enabling regulation of mixed marriages, which only ended with the Civil Rights era. In the south the extra categorization of African Americans resulted in the scooping up of Indians as people of colour and, after the passing of the IRA in 1934, an even greater determination to reclassify Indian people as blacks. And today there is also the evidence provided by gene testing; that is, scientific tests are available to show how much, if at all, African Americans are descended from Indian people.

The absurdities of racial categories reached their nadir in Virginia and North Carolina in the 1920s and 1930s, following the passage of Virginia's Racial Integrity Law, 1924, and its associated Sterilization Act. This simplified racial laws, defining two categories, 'white' and 'colored', 'colored' including Indians. Everyone's race was recorded, and mixed marriages were criminalized. However, because many of Virginia's oldest families claimed descent from Pocahontas, an exception was allowed for Native Americans with one-sixteenth Indian blood or less to be classified as 'white'. Together these laws enabled the sterilization of what were regarded as imbeciles and the feeble-minded to take place, and after court cases Virginia laws and practices were copied in other states. The tenor of 1920s field research into questions of descent is provided by Arthur Eastabrook and Ivan McDougle's *Mongrel Virginians: The WIN* [White Indian Negro] *Tribe* (1926) about the Monacan Indians in the Blue Mountains, defined variously as 'low down' yellow Negroes, Indians and 'mixed'. Now the Monacans are a non-profit and state-recognized tribal organization with a museum and an annual powwow. Even at the time (1927) *Nature* dismissed the scientific value of the study because, it was said, of the high rate of participation of women active in prostitution.

Racializing Indians in the South

With the passing of the IRA, however, a problem appeared for the administrators: non-federally recognized tribes could apply for federally recognized status and institute themselves as sovereign tribes. Virginia racial laws were promoted by Walter Plecker (1861–1947), state medical and statistical administrator, who advocated the reclassification of Indian people as of colour if necessary simply by issuing papers which denied Indian identity. In 1943 he wrote of Indians:

> now for some time they have been refusing to register . . . as negroes, as required . . . Some of these mongrels, finding that they have been able to sneak in their birth certificates unchallenged as Indians are now making a rush to register as white. Upon investigation we find that a few local registrars have been permitting such certificates to pass through their hands unquestioned and without warning our office of the fraud.[16]

If coloured people insisted on perpetuating racial fraud then they would face a year in jail. Virginia's race act was repealed in 1967, leaving the matter of the non-federally recognized tribes still under discussion.

In North Carolina, where there were also numerous race acts, Harvard anthropologist Carl Seltzer examined the people of mixed descent then known as the 'Cherokee Indians of Robeson County' in 1936. A total of 209 people, now Lumbees, were measured using anthropometric techniques to determine whether they met the blood quantum levels, and he discovered, for instance, that full siblings in the Brooks/Locklear family were of different race! Notoriously he used the pencil test to determine whether or not a person was a Native or African American: a pencil was slipped into the hair of the individual, and the person shaken to see if the pencil would fall out of the hair. If the pencil fell out of straight hair, then that person was Indian; if it remained in crinkly hair, why then of course that person was coloured.

Yet Native and African American ancestry is real and important. Many African Americans are recorded as of Indian descent: Jimi Hendrix (1942–70), Eartha Kitt (1927–2008) and Rosa Parks (1913–2005), for instance. In a recent study it was suggested that one in five

African Americans have Native American ancestry, and that in Oklahoma there is a higher proportion of African genes, as one would expect: only 14 per cent of African Americans have Native ancestry, but these people have 2 per cent or more of Indian genes.[17] Much was made of Native American ancestry in the PBS series *Finding Your Roots*, hosted by Henry Louis Gates Jnr in 2012 and 2014. Many people want to have Native American ancestry, and in this African Americans are no different from other people. Winston Churchill's son Randolph claimed that his grandmother's family had Iroquois ancestry, a highly unlikely possibility, since the alliance was supposed to have taken placed in Sackville in what is now the Canadian province of Nova Scotia, home of Mi'kmaq not Haudenosaunee.[18]

Eugenics and Sterilization

The eugenics movement was founded by the British scientist, anthropologist and statistician Francis Galton (1822–1911). This non-science promoted hereditary hygiene, incorporating eventually the sterilization of supposed degenerates. In the UK well into the twentieth century this was aimed at protecting class privilege, and in the USA to protecting race. In both countries eugenics was considered, for most of its history until the 1930s, a progressive science, and in the USA Virginia and North Carolina promoted sterilization but largely did not sterilize Indians. Plecker in Virginia was a promoter and wrote to Germany in the 1930s in approval of the Nazi programme to sterilize German Africans. Even though eugenics fell swiftly out of fashion in the 1940s the idea of sterilization as an instrument of social policy to reduce birth rates continued to take hold in Indian Country. This reached a climax between 1970 and 1976, when some 25–50 per cent of Indian women were sterilized, a total of 25,000 by the end of 1976. This was, ironically, during the period when ideas of self-determination were taking hold. Sterilization did reduce the number of Indian children. Between 1970 and 1980 the number of children born to each Apache woman was reduced from 4.01 to 1.78.[19] Generally abuse was widespread and included the sterilization of minors without consent, coercion into consent, signing post-operation and so on. Among one Northern Cheyenne group, Mary Ann Bear Comes Out found that the IHS had sterilized 56 out of 165 women aged thirty to forty-four. Abuse of sterilization in turn inevitably caused marital problems, divorce, alcoholism and guilt. At the end of this same period, in 1976 the Indian Health Care Improvement Act was passed, mandating the passing of control of Indian health to tribal governments, thus ending sterilization programmes.[20]

In Canada similar programmes existed, on a smaller scale. In a four-year period, 1971–4, of 580 women sterilized at federal hospitals, 551 were aboriginal.[21] More pernicious, perhaps, were the earlier medical experiments conducted on indigenous people without consent in the 1940s and 1950s, particularly in Manitoba and in residential schools. During the 1940s various medical and anthropological surveys were conducted among starving Cree communities in the Subarctic, their deprivation worsened by the reduction in welfare transfers, a decrease in the price of furs and an increase in reliance on store-bought white foods. In consequence it was recognized that northern and western communities might provide laboratory-type conditions for establishing a better understanding of vitamin and mineral deficiency. What they found instead, however, was that malnutrition might be at the root of the so-called Indian problem: in the preliminary report of 1942 the following was noted: 'It is not unlikely that many characteristics, such as shiftlessness, indolence, improvidence and inertia, so long regarded as inherent or hereditary traits in the Indian race, may, at the root, be really the manifestations of malnutrition.'[22] Experiments were then conducted on malnourished children. At Alberni Residential School on Vancouver Island, home to Nuu-chah-nulth people, it was discovered that riboflavin deficiency was highest. The medical officer then conducted an experiment, published in 1953, to establish the improvements that might occur if milk consumption was increased. Intake of a daily 8oz (half the Canadian recommended amount) was maintained for two years before being tripled; and of course the malnutrition in Alberni was occuring at a time when there was still access to unlimited quantities of Pacific salmon species, the traditional food staple of coastal British Columbia and an excellent source of riboflavin. Residential schools were also used in testing supplements to improve dentition, an initiative which brought forward a prohibition on the introduction of new types of oral hygiene until the experiment was completed. Inevitably the prolonged experimentation was conducted without the consent of parents or children, against emerging post-war rules about medical experimentation, in circumstances in which medical experimentation was increasing rather decreasing and where in the USA results from German wartime experiments on the effects of cold on camp inmates assisted in preparation for space travel. A series of thank you letters from children in the Alberni school from 1952 indicates the degree of compulsion: one child said: 'Tell the nurse I said thank you for the pokes she gave me'; another complained that she 'didn't understand the words that Doctor Brown was saying. I was listening very carefully too'; other letters reassured staff that nothing had hurt.[23]

Native Activism

The long shadows of termination and eugenics, born of progressive ideas of the 1870s and 1880s designed to assimilate the remnants of the 'disappearing' Indian population, took some thirty years, from the 1950s to the 1980s, to be dispelled, along with the threat and realities of the IHS sterilization programme. Both were defeated by the moves to self-determination. What is remarkable about these termination and sterilization programmes is that they were instituted a little before but principally during the era of the Civil Rights movement: that is, as African America successfully fought ancient measures, new federal measures of dispossession, of land and body, were still being imposed on Indian people. One of the most useful ways of looking at the third quarter of the twentieth century lies in the comparison of the gradualism of Indian politics, promoted especially by the National Congress of American Indians, founded in 1944 to counter assimilation and then termination, with the activism of the 1960s and 1970s. For Native Americans, unlike for African Americans, the ancient federal relationship, and the BIA, with all its faults, provided avenues through which politicians and lawyers could mount an effective campaign both to bring the new programmes to an end and to introduce an era of self-government. Of course, activism was important, especially in relation to fishing in Washington State and the Pacific Northwest, and occupation played a role, for example in the two occupations of

Alcatraz, and those of the Bureau of Indian Affairs and Wounded Knee. But in a way gradualism was a more important aspect of the revolution of the 1970s than the dramatic efforts and rhetoric of the American Indian Movement, which might be better seen as the penumbra, as the controversial finale of mid-century movements, or as curtain raiser or catalyst to the successes of the 1970s and 1980s.

In this view the quieter stories from the 1940s and 1950s onwards belong to a generation of Indian leaders such as Earl Boyd Pierce (1904–83), lawyer for the Cherokee nation and historian. Rose Crow Flies High (1918–94) (Mandan Hidatsa) was successful both as a politician in the 1970s, when she was tribal chair, and as an advocate and quilt maker; but she also helped plan the 1968 Poor Peoples' March on Washington, DC, organized to demonstrate against the failure of Johnson's War on Poverty. Helen Petersen (1915–2000) (Cheyenne/Sioux) was the first woman president of the National Congress of American Indians in the 1950s. Slightly later the American Indian Chicago Conference (1961), advocating self-determination, inspired leaders such as Clyde Warrior (1939–68) (Ponca) to found the National Indian Youth Council in 1961 with Mel Thom (1938–84) (Paiute), its first president. NIYC was active in fishing politics and in turn inspired the American Indian Movement (AIM).

Hank Adams

Most interesting of the people around NIYC is Hank Adams (b. 1943) (Assiniboine-Sioux), who in the 1960s and 1970s transcended many categories of leadership, being a social worker, administrator, activist and negotiator. He was active in anti-suicide programmes and in the fishing controversies of the 1970s in Washington State. Perhaps most importantly he organized the research that enabled the Boldt decision, in which the US government took Washington State to court in 1974 and won, confirming that Indians had the right to fish and to a share of the catch, to go through. The fishing issue was part of the nineteenth-century treaty process in which hunting and fishing rights were guaranteed, and with the disappearance of the bison nationwide fish became the subsistence resource and country food. Fishing rights were guaranteed to the Nisqually by the 1854 Treaty of Medicine

Creek. Billy Frank Jnr (1931–2014) was first arrested for fishing at home in 1945, when he was fourteen, and was later arrested fifty times. Adams helped with the research which enabled the Boldt Decision, 1974, protecting fishing rights. Adams as an activist was also involved in the early 1970s occupations by AIM and negotiated the ending of the Bureau of American Indian and Wounded Knee affrays. In this sense, and in his achievements, he is much more significant than the roster of activists, much better known, associated with AIM, such as Russell Means (1939–2012) (Lakota), Dennis Banks (b. 1937) (Anishinaabe) and Leonard Peltier (b. 1944) (Anishinaabe and Lakota).

American Indian Movement

AIM, though very different to what would now be considered terrorist groups, such as the Weathermen, is the movement that everyone remembers: AIM communicated the distress and the experience of Native America; it was the catalyst without itself being the agent of change. Instead it was the expression of new underlying aspirations. But its three moments of high drama are very different to each other. The second occupation of Alcatraz,[24] beginning at the end of 1969, was organized by Native students in California, especially Richard Oakes (1942–72) (Mohawk) and others originally from out of state, and involved the Lumbee writer Dean Chavers. The occupation received support from well-heeled Bay area residents and stars and attracted international attention. Dennis Banks visited the occupation and took home with him activist ideas to put into effect elsewhere.

Alcatraz, the former site of a prison of ill repute, was due to be returned to Indian ownership as stipulated by a treaty under which surplus federal land no longer required should go back to Native ownership. The occupation in November 1969 began casually, with false starts and, as with AIM, had an urban origin: in this case in Bay area alterity rather than in the Twin City deprivation that had underpinned the earlier founding of AIM.

Oakes, a sometime steel worker from St Regis, New York, who came west, went to college and married a Pomo. In 1969 speculation about a revisit of the Lakota 1964 occupation of Alcatraz triggered the new occupation after the San Francisco Indian Center burned down in

October. This precipitated the early need for a forum bringing together Native voices in the Bay area. Oakes recruited supporters at California colleges, including Edward Castillo (b. 1948) (Luiseño-Cahuilla), a historian, while Ojibwe Adam Nordwall/Fortunate Eagle (b. 1929), head of the United Bay Indian Council, was the principal organizer, and John Trudell (b. 1946) (Santee Dakota) acted as radio spokesman.

Initially the occupation was well organized, with a council and democratic decision making, but after one of Oakes's children was accidentally killed, precipitating his departure after a few months, divisions between the occupiers increased, the banning of alcohol lapsed, and newcomers from the street community arrived on the island. The government in Washington took a conciliatory view, mostly refused to countenance a violent end to the protest and allowed it to wither, if not away, then through the removal of water and power and the fire that occurred shortly afterwards, which destroyed three buildings including the lighthouse, to a state more than a year later where the few remaining occupants could be safely removed. AIM, like the Indian Council, was involved with urban issues but took note of the way the federal government's hands were tied and embarked on a prolonged activist campaign, starting with the occupation of a replica of the *Mayflower* in Philadelphia, Thanksgiving 1970.

The Nixon Era

Together, Alcatraz and the two AIM occupations of Wounded Knee and the BIA were examples of urban activism, as opposed to the rural activism of the fish-ins and the Canadian radicalism from the 1980s onwards. Richard Nixon, the wayward libertarian, Quaker racist but an advocate for equal opportunity, was explicitly responsible for adopting self-determination, in the heady atmosphere created by Alcatraz and three publications: *House Made of Dawn* (1968) and, rather differently, *Custer Died for Your Sins* (1969) and *Bury My Heart at Wounded Knee* (1970). Nixon was perhaps most significantly influenced by his Cherokee football coach, Wallace Newman, who impressed upon him that he didn't believe in the nonsense of being a good loser: the point was to win.

Nixon's Indian policy came out of his ideas for New Federalism, for a reduction in administration, and was created in part by Vice President Spiro T. Agnew, who chaired the National Council on Indian Opportunity (NCIO), and Donald Rumsfeld, then director of the Office of Economic Opportunity, and especially by Democrat lawyer Leonard Garment (1924–2013), who with his assistant Bradley H. Patterson Jnr originated the statement and briefed the press after Nixon's 'Special Message to the Congress on Indian Affairs' of 8 July 1970. The statement is admirable in its intentions and in its eloquent sentiments acted as a moral template for all of the momentous changes, including especially financial success, which occurred in the next fifteen or twenty years. Nixon said, for instance:

> Federal termination errs in one direction, Federal paternalism errs in the other. Only by clearly rejecting both of these extremes can we achieve a policy which truly serves the best interests of the Indian people. Self-determination among the Indian people can and must be encouraged without the threat of eventual termination.[25]

This was followed up by a whole series of measures which turned the federal relationship with Indians around. Most important of the acts, with huge symbolic performance, was the return of the sacred land around Blue Lake to the Taos Pueblo at the end of 1970, but in 1973 the Menominee were restored. In the same year the BIA budget was doubled. In 1974 the Indian Financing Act stated, rather in the manner of the 1953 statement, which conversely had brought in termination:

> It is hereby declared to be the policy of Congress to provide capital on a reimbursable basis to help develop and utilize Indian resources, both physical and human, to a point where the Indians will fully exercise responsibility for the utilization and management of their own resources and where they will enjoy a standard of living from their own productive efforts comparable to that enjoyed by non-Indians in neighbouring communities.

Nothing could be more explicit in indicating a determination to foster tribes in the neo-liberal sense of being equal and separate. Nixon's policies had an afterlife with the 1975 Indian Self-Determination and Education Assistance Act, which again is determinedly liberal in outlook, enabling tribes to take control of services from the BIA:

> To provide maximum Indian participation in the government and education of the Indian people; to provide for the full participation of Indian tribes in programs and services conducted by the federal government for Indians and to encourage the development of human resources of the Indian people; to establish a program of assistance to upgrade Indian education; to support the right of Indian citizens to control their own educational activities.

Alaska Native Claims Settlement Act

Yet the defining and most radical moment of this period lies not in the generalized statements and acts, and the beginning of the roll-back of termination, but in the passing of the Alaska Native Claims Settlement Act (ANCSA) in 1971. Like the return of Blue Lake to Taos, the Alaskan settlement was deeply embedded in Washington politics and was an issue to be turned to political advantage in a state with a Republican governor. In early 1971 the main issues for the administration were the need to build a pipeline south from the oil field, the desire not to go back on Nixon's positive stance towards Indians and to benefit Alaska. John Ehrlichman (1925–99), domestic affairs adviser in the White House, laid out these points, and the secretary of the interior, Rogers Morton (1914–79), offered to give Native Alaska 40 million acres and $1 billion, which is what was written into the bill passed in December. Yet of course Native rights in Alaska were terminated, although ownership in the corporations that were created to hold these rights could not, eventually, unlike allotted lands following the Dawes Act, be alienated to non-Natives.

Child Welfare

In all countries with significant minorities the issue of child welfare is central to discussions of cultural self-determination. Of particular importance is the role of multigenerational care in the transmission of language and culture. In this much-conflicted area, ideas of cultural norms are central. Particularly contentious is the dominant society's mid-twentieth-century practice of the adopting-out of aboriginal children from multigenerational families with shared ethnic values of child care. Children were placed in adoption, or with foster parents, supported by payments for care. In both the USA and Canada the modification or ending of out-of-community adoption in the late twentieth century became a fundamental part of the movement towards self-determination. In the USA the 1978 Indian Child Welfare Act (ICWA) was passed to remedy the situation in which in 1969 and 1974 some 25–35 per cent of Native children were in institutions or were adopted or fostered. The act was sponsored by William Byler, director of the Association on American Indian Affairs (AAIA) 1962–80. In his published evidence, 'The Destruction of the American Indian Family', he noted that in 1971 34,538 children, or 17 per cent of the total, were in BIA boarding schools. He emphasized the irony that, whereas Indian people had been forced on to reservations at gunpoint, they were now being told that reservations were unfit for children and forced to send their children off to schools.

In 1974 Byler had pointed out that adoption was not about physical abuse:

> a survey of North Dakota tribe indicated that of all the children that were removed from that tribe, only one percent were [removed] for physical abuse. About 99% were taken on the basis of such vague standards as deprivation, neglect, taken because their homes were thought to be too poverty- stricken to support their children.[26]

As it was put in 1995 by a lawyer working in the Dakotas with the ICWA: 'Non-Indian judges and social workers – failing to appreciate traditional Indian child-rearing practices – perceived day-to-day life in the children's Indian homes as contrary to the children's best interests.'[27] At the time of the act, in 1977, Chief Calvin Isaac of the Mississippi Band of Choctaw noted that 'culturally the chances of Indian survival are significantly reduced if our children, the only means for the transmission of the tribal heritage, are to be raised in non-Indian homes and denied exposure to the ways of their people'.[28] One of the other contributory factors leading to the ICWA was the Indian Adoption Project of 1958–67, sponsored by the Child Welfare

League of America. With this project some 395 children were adopted by white families; in the 1970s a study was undertaken suggesting that the project was proceeding successfully; yet in 2001 Shay Bilchik, the director of the Child Welfare League, apologized for the scheme, saying: 'No matter how well intentioned and how squarely in the mainstream this was at the time, it was wrong; it was hurtful; and it reflected a kind of bias that surfaces feelings of shame.'[29]

Yet it was not clear that the act was working, and it was said only: 'At the very minimum, the existence of the act has brought attention to the unique needs of Indian children and provided state agencies and judges with a valuable, cross-cultural educational tool.'[30] Since 1978 hundreds of cases have occurred, helping define Indian adoption. These can be highly contentious and deeply destructive, with an element of racially construed justice remaining all too possible. Most recently a prolonged case concerning a girl with an absent Cherokee father and Latino mother working with Latino adoptive parents was taken to the Supreme Court (Adoptive Family v. Baby Girl 2013), where the non-Indians won, and the Cherokee Nation and Cherokee father backed down, only to be sued by the adoptive family for court costs of $1 million. This suggests that something more than welfare underlies public–private behaviour and the performance of adoption law.

Adoption in Canada

In Canada many of the same practices and concerns operated, and the ICWA of 1978 became a catalyst for change north of the border. In the 1980s, with the repatriation of the constitution, reviews and reports such as the Federation of Saskatchewan Indians' *Indian Control of Indian Child Welfare* (1983), this changed. This phenomenon, when First Nations children were collected up and removed from their natal homes, is referred to in Canada as the '60s Scoop': 11,132 status Indian children were adopted between the years of 1960 and 1990, 70 per cent into non-Native homes.[31] However, this may, according to Allyson Stevenson, exaggerate the number of children apprehended and not give due recognition to the effects of colonization and endemic problems existing on reserves, and so to the real benefits of adoption into a non-First Nations family.[32]

Violence

In this perspective, of a groundswell in non-violent movements, the two main activist moments of the 1970s tell a lesser story, acting as metonyms or symbols of the gradual improvement in Indian Affairs. But they also kept the longstanding agenda of gradual improvement of the Native situation in the public eye. Nixon's Indian policies did not benefit the urban half of the Indian population, out of which the American Indian Movement was born in 1968 to deal with issues of housing and poverty and prejudice.

The Trail of Broken Treaties march of 1972 occurred at the time of Nixon's successful re-election. When the marchers reached Washington government spokesmen refused to meet with them. The Bureau of Indian Affairs was then occupied, and much damage was done. Nixon, who had no relationship with the Civil Rights Movement, was contemptuous of radicalism, and his administration sought to split the movement through the creation of the National Tribal Chairmen's Association (NTCA) instead of engaging directly with it. Indian advocacy had an establishment of traditional leaders used to working with the Bureau of Indian Affairs, but the federal administrators adopted a divisive strategy. Further, of course, in believing in self-determination for Native Americans, Nixon was echoing his prejudice against integration of African Americans, assimilation and integration being in an opposed relationship in this period.

While Alcatraz stimulated positive thinking about Indian affairs, the occupation of the BIA can be seen as sending a mixed message, even though consequently Marlon Brando sent Sacheen Littlefeather to refuse his 1973 Academy Best Actor Award for *The Godfather*, to great publicity.

The week-long BIA occupation was ended by Leonard Garment and others appeasing the occupiers and sending them home with a grant of $66,000.[33] This polarized the difference between reservation and urban Indians. They each caricatured the other: 'red apples' for the reservation people (red on the outside white inside), and 'Assholes in Moccasins' for the members of AIM.

The occupation of Wounded Knee in 1974 arose around similar

issues. It was organized by AIM but concerned primarily with the lack of justice in racially motivated killings in the Dakotas. There were important differences from the earlier occupations: while both Alcatraz and the BIA occurred in arenas without traditional leadership, the occupation of Wounded Knee took place with a similar newsworthy interest in Indian Country itself, but also with settled Native leadership and sharply drawn white–Native racial lines.

Wounded Knee further bitterly divided Indian people, perhaps in a way which had been taking place since the appearance of Praying Towns, seventeenth-century missionary settlements involved in King Philip's War of 1675, between modernizers and pan-Indianists. In the 1970s AIM, like earlier pan-Indianists, sought to create a national narrative. Here the urbanized leaders of AIM were working against the local Native establishment, and so against those with sustainable political and economic networks.

AIM Leadership

What occurred at Wounded Knee in 1974 is that AIM became something akin to a paramilitary organization rooting for revolution. Richard Oakes had been inspired by revivalist ideas, such as the White Roots of Peace, which emphasized the Tree of Peace, the foundation of Haudenosaunee/Iroquois ideas of the universe, situated as the tree was on the back of the turtle. Others were not inspired by ideas of peace, and Russell Means, for instance, viewed self-determination as a plot to bolster the colonialism of the BIA. AIM in the Twin Cities area was originally involved in monitoring violence against Native Americans, listening in to police radios and arriving at incidents involving Indians before the police to try to prevent violence. Similarly in South Dakota, murders, for instance that of Wesley Bad Heart in 1973, were the reason for AIM's arrival outside of traditional Chippewa and Dakota territory.

Some hundreds of Oglalas and others led by Russell Means occupied the small town of Wounded Knee for seventy-one days. Although much visited by the media, ease of access, unlike island Alcatraz, meant that violence was always much closer to the surface, and with violence against Indians came the need for self-defence. Further, President Richard Wilson (1934–90), of the Rosebud Lakota, who had supported AIM in their investigation of the death of Raymond Yellow Thunder in 1972, had later that year already distanced himself from AIM's destructive actions. He was therefore seen by AIM as a non-traditional representative arising from the 1936 Indian Reorganization Act election constitution for the tribal nation. Wounded Knee took place following a failed attempt to impeach Wilson, and more generally was about revising the Rosebud/Oglala Treaty and replacing the Wilson government with something traditional and hierarchical. The confrontation was armed and violent, but Nixon insisted on quiet negotiation, and the siege was ended with an agreement to investigate Wilson's government.

Other Oglala, and especially the transformational Lakota journalist Tim Giago (b. 1934), continue to defend Wilson and excoriate AIM for the polarization of the community. The violence during the occupation, with two Indian people killed, resulted afterwards in both Means and Dennis Banks being put on trial for violent offences; the charges were dismissed because of irregularities. But the violence continued, with multiple deaths and confrontations between the tribal police, labelled 'Goons', the FBI and the traditionalist supporters of AIM. This climaxed in 1975 with a stand-off at the Jumping Bull place. Two FBI agents, searching for Jimmy Eagle, who had stolen a pair of boots, were killed. Leonard Peltier (Chippewa-Lakota) was successfully prosecuted and found guilty in 1977 of the two execution-style murders, despite multiple irregularities in the proceedings. Whether Peltier was responsibile for the murders is another matter, obscured and made more difficult by the murder of another AIM activist, Mi'kmaq Anna/Annie Mae Pictou Aquash (1945–75). For this murder fellow First Nations activist John Graham was convicted in 2010. Aquash, it was said in court, had heard Peltier describe the murders of the FBI agents.

Benefiting from AIM

One question arising from AIM, Wounded Knee and the mid-1970s violence in South Dakota is who, if anyone, benefited. And one answer is the lawyer and later long-serving governor of South Dakota William Janklow (1939–2012). In 1974, when he was running for state legal office, Janklow was accused of raping his fifteen-year-old babysitter, Lakota Jancita Eagle Deer (1952–75), while he was director of the Rosebud Sioux Legal Services in 1967, an accusation he shrugged off. Janklow benefited from the polarization of politics brought about the violence of 1974–6, becoming governor in 1978. The deaths of Eagle Deer, from a hit-and-run accident, and her stepmother, Delphine Eagle Deer, killed by an unknown assailant in 1976, are two of the many deaths of the period where coincidences merge with conspiracy theories. Many of these theories swirl round the activities of Richard Wilson and the tribal police force, and the FBI's involvement with agents provocateurs and informants. What is important about the violence and the prolonged confrontation at Wounded Knee is that both acted as a catalyst for the continued reformist behaviour of the Ford and Carter administrations, which resulted in the acquisition of land for the Kootenai and Havasupai, for instance, while actually ensuring that the moderate centre, rather than traditionalist and urban Indians, would lead later developments in Indian Country.

Canada

The Canadian situation is very different. As mentioned previously one of the main issues in the USA is how the privileges available to Native North Americans are ringfenced by the long history of pre-1871 treaties and the tension between state and federal law. In contrast, the post-confederation, post-1867 Indian Acts imposed on Canada's First Nations elected chiefs and councils to run reserves; that is, chiefs would be elected under western democracy-style conventions. Often opposed, by the second half of the twentieth century this came to be seen as an aspect of cultural genocide, an imposition designed to ensure that aboriginal people became good white Canadians, contrary to an informed understanding of the heterogeneous cultural values of diverse aboriginal peoples – and of ancient of consensual aboriginal democratic traditions. Over time, however, diverse systems of voting arose in Canadian First Nations. In the 2010 parliamentary report 'First Nations Elections' these were said to be of four forms:

> 252 Indian bands (or 41%) hold elections in accordance with the election provisions of the Indian Act. 334 bands (or 54%) conduct 'custom elections' under custom codes developed by the band. 29 First Nations (or 5%) select leaders pursuant to the provisions of their self-government agreements . . . approximately 10–15 bands follow other leadership selection mechanisms, such as the hereditary or clan system.[34]

One central issue, where more than 50 per cent of aboriginal people don't live on reserves or traditional territory, is who should be eligible to vote, normally defined under: 'Subsection 77(1) of the Indian Act' which 'provides for the eligibility of voters, stipulating that an elector must be 18 years of age and be "ordinarily resident on reserve"'. A membership or 'custom' code for a single First Nation allows a band to set out its own procedures for electing government. It may simply mean a difference in the length of time between elections or relate to culture or residence.

Canadian Factionalism

The on-reserve residence stipulation for voting was overturned in 1999 by the Supreme Court (as contrary to the equality rights of off-reserve members). But the tension between aboriginal organizations representing all Indian people and those representing on-reserve residents, the Assembly of First Nations, remains important. Pierre Brazeau was involved in the Congress of Aboriginal People (CAP), founded in 1971 to represent off-reserve aboriginals. A 2008 report suggested that band elections were undemocratic. CAP and Brazeau were denounced as a stooges for the federal government by Cree Chief Lawrence Joseph, head of Saskatchewan First Nations.[35] The personalities of the antagonists illustrate two contrasting leadership styles: Lawrence Joseph is a long-standing leader, who worked for thirty years in federal jobs, early on as a pilot and prison officer, and is a semi-professional musician with his own band and an Anglican lay reader as well as head of Saskatchewan First Nations. Brazeau, on the other hand, is a young (b. 1974), charismatic politician, the youngest senator in Canadian history (Conservative Party), from the important Algonquin/Anishinaabe reserve 130 miles north of Ottawa, Kitigan Zibi/Maniwaki. He was national chief of the CAP and more controversially recently was involved in a celebrity boxing match for charity with Prime Minister Justin Trudeau, arrested for sexual assault and investigated for abuse of parliamentary expenses and in the summer of 2015 was working as a bouncer. The expenses problem mirrors exactly that in other democracies: claiming to live far from parliament, but actually living nearby.

Power and Money on Reserves

But the difference in leadership styles reflects extremely well the problems of small-community democracy, where elections, under the Indian Act, are disturbingly frequent – every two years – and where the power and resources available to band council leaders are significant, and where, apart from government patronage employment, access to benefits and income is often limited. Chief Terrance Nelson (of the Roseau River First Nation, Manitoba) put it like this:

> To understand why elections are so divisive in many First Nation communities, you have to look at the economy of First Nations people and communities. First Nations in Canada are at the 63rd level of the United Nations living index. Many First Nation communities are extremely impoverished, with some having up to 95 per cent unemployment . . . So becoming a member of chief and council not only means a guaranteed income, but if you want it, it also means the control of most of the wealth in the community. It is, therefore, easy to understand why elections in our community are so intense.[36]

However, Chief Nelson was himself removed from office by court order shortly afterwards. Rights to self-government and self-determination were reaffirmed in the 1996 Aboriginal commission. Yet the conclusion of the 2010 report indicated the extent to which aboriginal people need a new, non-Indian form of band and reserve governance that is not based on a colonial situation.

First Nations Democracy

In general the issues of democracy are not so simple: in British Columbia, Northwest Coast peoples lived in a flexible, class-based society in which ownership (of wealth, beaches, fish weirs) and rights were hereditary and articulated through highly elaborate belief systems and an impressive body of oral literature. The Haudenosaunee in Canada have a poorly functioning electoral system in, say, the Mohawk community of Kahnawake, Quebec. Yet since before European contact there existed well-functioning councils with their own form of democracy, involving the raising up or election of fifty chiefs or *sachems* to the Council of the Iroquois, supported by clan mothers, in a matrilineal society. In the 1920s the government replaced the chiefs and council with an elected chief; the 2010 report on elections quotes Ellen Gabriel, president of Quebec Native Women Inc., who said that in the 2006 Mohawk Council election only 28 per cent of people voted and that:

> I am a Longhouse person. As I said, I do not vote in my band council elections because we had a government and still have a government that existed before Europeans arrived here. It was made illegal in the 1920s and it is still illegal. The government refuses to deal with traditional people's governments.[37]

Further, in the 1980s the elected Mohawk Council instituted a moratorium on becoming Mohawk: any Mohawk who married, lived with or was in a common-law relationship with a non-Mohawk was denied rights and privileges; and this was further changed in 1984, when a 50 per cent blood quantum rule was adopted.[38] Understanding all the meanings of these rules, and how the electoral systems impact on membership, is complex and difficult, but clearly they are divisive and non-productive.

Membership Rules in the USA

One aspect, then, of bloodlines is the business of recognition, of whether a First Nation or Native people has sufficient attributes to be a tribe. In Canada this issue is rolled into the catch-all identity of Métis and mixed descent on the national level. In the USA it is always open for a cohesive people like the Mashpee Wampanoag of Cape Cod to undergo a federal recognition process, now organized under the Commission on Indian Recognition. The Mashpee, like the Lumbee, failed initially to be recognized at the federal level, although eventually they prevailed, and as of January 2014 have a compact with the state of Massachusetts and plans to create a casino resort, Project First Light. Another aspect of recognition and of Indian status is disenrolment, whereby people formally enrolled are taken off the register because of some technicality in the registration of their bloodlines. Of course it is perfectly reasonable and correct for tribal nations, who since 1905 and the Waldron decision, in which Jane Waldron (of mixed descent) won the right to claim an allotment, have had the right to define tribal membership, to exclude people with improper or incomplete claims to tribal membership, since these provide health and educational benefits, and in the case of the prosperous tribes many additional benefits, including per capita payments. What is much more surprising is the existence of limited overviews of the importance of blood. In the 1990s Meyer and Thornton looked at tribal membership rules for more than 300 nations and categorized them: 20 tribes required 50 per cent or more Indian blood; 148 required between 25 and 50 per cent of Indian blood; 98 had no blood requirement. Those with most resources have the most sharply defined blood quantum requirements.[39] Tribal nations no longer have to use blood for tribal definition, and yet most do. And, of course, as people continue to marry out the amounts of Indian blood decrease, and definition of Indians might then need to change. One example of a relatively recently constituted tribal nation with a high income is that of Shakopee Mdewakanton Sioux in Minnesota. The community was organized in 1969 with thirty-three people defined as members in the following three ways:

> The membership of the Shakopee Mdewakanton Sioux Community shall consist of: (a) All persons of Mdewakanton Sioux Indian blood, not members of any other Indian tribe, band or group, whose names appear on the 1969 census roll of Mdewakanton Sioux residents of the

Prior Lake Reservation, Minnesota, prepared specifically for the purpose of organizing the Shakopee Mdewakanton Sioux Community and approved by the Secretary of the Interior. (b) All children of at least one-fourth (¼) degree Mdewakanton Sioux Indian blood born to an enrolled member of the Shakopee Mdewakanton Sioux Community. (c) All descendants of at least one-fourth (¼) degree Mdewakanton Sioux Indian blood who can trace their Indian blood to the Mdewakanton Sioux Indians who resided in Minnesota on May 20, 1886.[40]

A bingo operation was set up in 1980, and casinos followed, with an exponential increase in new members. In 2012 the *New York Times*, reporting on a 2004 divorce case, noted that tribal membership had grown to 480, with individual incomes at $1.08 million, and according to the president Stanley R. Crooks they have 99.2 per cent voluntary unemployment. The tribe has given away hundreds of millions of dollars since gaming began, which is, of course, a much higher percentage of donations than made by any public corporation, generosity being a continued aspect of Indian culture.[41]

Disenrolment

On the other hand there is the much more difficult spectacle of tribal nations tightening rules, which has the effect of excluding Indian people who failed to enrol when it was a relatively simple matter. Then what happens is an extremely disagreeable process in which the tribal court looks into the documentation. So, for instance, there are 306 Nooksack in 2014 threatened with disenrolment because the BIA does not have the papers proving membership to the 1940 roll. And tribes, being sovereign nations, have the final say. Another aspect of all this is the business of peoples with African American heritage disenrolling freedmen. For the Cherokee and the Seminole in Oklahoma this is very different: for the Cherokee it is to do with former slaves who should not be excluded, having been adopted into the tribe after the Civil War; for the Seminole it is because of the inclusion of Maroons from free African communities who moved west with the removals after the Seminole Wars.

Indian Nations are able to define their own legal identity. As indicated, this can be directly couched in racial terms, and this can be altered in very explicit ways to benefit Indian people. A 2000 Senate report, 106-464, proposed a bill to alter the blood quantum requirements for two Native nations in Texas, the Tigua/Tiwa, seventeenth-century refugees from New Mexico, and the Alabama-Coushatta refugees from the state of Alabama. Both nations were terminated in the 1950s and then restored. For both, unrelated, peoples the proposal was to decrease the blood quantum requirement from an eight to a sixteenth, to stop descendants of Indians being classified as non-Indians. The cost of health and other benefits was estimated at $1,500 a year, and so for the 550 Alabama-Coushatta people who would become Indians the total cost annual cost in 2001 was estimated at $1 million per annum.

Membership in Canada

Whereas in the USA with the Indian Reorganization Act of 1934 Indian tribes could define membership through the female line, Canadian law was, from the first nineteenth-century Indian Acts, much more restrictive. The term used is 'status': people on the Indian Register, created in 1951, have Indian status as defined by the federal department of Aboriginal and Northern Affairs. Membership ran through the male line only, until 1985, when law C-31 changed the Indian Act to enable descent to be reckoned through the female line. Brazeau was an off-reserve beneficiary of the bill. Yet without proper resourcing such a huge influx of new members of First Nations bands was difficult and deeply divisive. 56,800 new status Indians were expected, whereas 114,512 were added during the first fifteen years of the Act. In 2012 the Federation of Saskatchewan Indian Nations put it like this:

> In 1985, Bill C-31 reinstated the status of thousands of First Nation people who were unfairly disenfranchised. The federal government made the changes without proper consultation, accommodation and the resources needed to properly study the bill. The bill continues to cause problems for First Nations with respect to a lack of resources, assimilation and divisiveness in the communities.[42]

Whenever improvements are made to the situation of First or Indian Nations, resourcing is an issue, causing factionalism and dissension and slowing down and subverting the delivery of justice. Yet the federal authorities recently repeated the incompetent handling of Bill C-31 with a drive to recruit more First Nations people to aboriginal status in Newfoundland. The Qalipu Mi'kmaq, recognized in 2007, were in 2014 expected to recruit 10,000 members but had 100,000 applicants and with 23,000 acceptances in 2014 had become the second-largest First Nations band.[43]

3
Land

Codex-style Spanish painting, perhaps by a missionary-trained Indian artist, 1720s, showing a 1720 battle between Europeans on the Platte River, Nebraska.

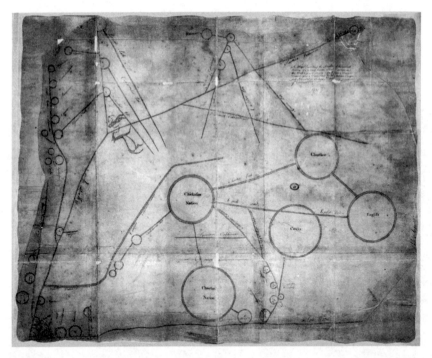

Chickasaw (?) map of what is now northern Mississippi and Alabama showing settlements and trade routes, socially and spacially considered, the Mississippi River on the left.

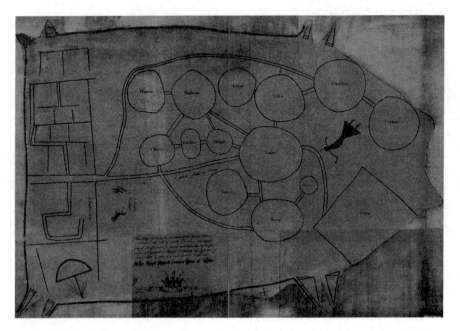

Catawba map of *c.*1721 showing Native Nations as circles and Charleston, SC, as a grid system on the left, with a ship to indicate trade.

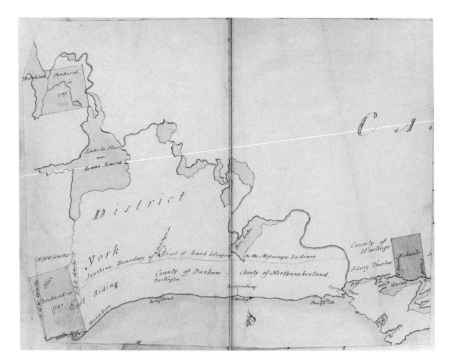

The Haudenosaunee were forced to relocate on to purchased Mississauga land in what is now Ontario after the American Revolution.

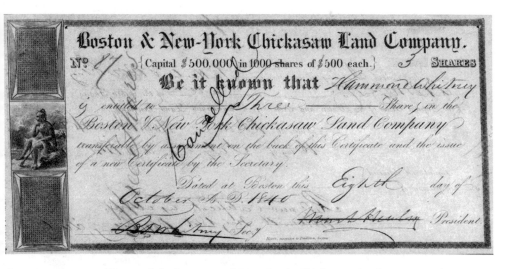

An 1836 share certificate of the Boston and New York Chickasaw land company. In 1835–7 virtually all of the northern half of Mississippi was sold at auction.

Native view of treaty-making: Little Skunk (Cheyenne), drawing, before 1879.

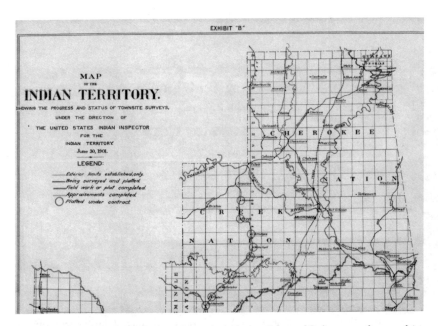

A 1901 Cherokee Nation map, showing the rapid establishment of townships three years after the 1898 act of Charles Curtis (Kaw) forced the dissolution of the governments of the Five Civilized Tribes.

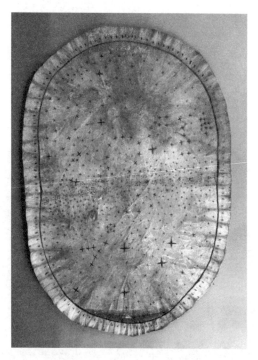

Pawnee star chart kept with the Big Black Meteoric Star bundle. At two o'clock on the upper right side at edge moving towards the middle are Seven Stars or Pleiades, during winter, and the Big Stretcher or Big Dipper.

Ikmalick, Inuk from Nunavut, drawing a map of the Arctic coastline, Boothia, for John Ross, 1830s.

Governor General Vanier paying treaty money at Cold Lake First Nation, perhaps the first time that a governor general of Canada actually presented the treaty money. Alberta, June 1961.

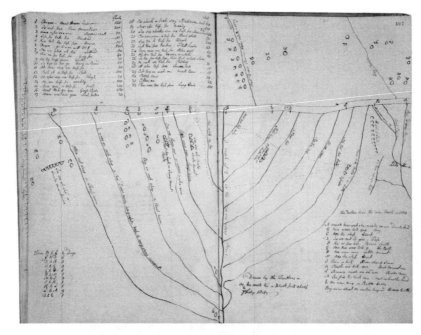

'Map Drawn by Feathers or Ac ko mok ki a Black foot chief 7 Feby 1801'.
Used by Lewis and Clarke to cross the USA in 1804 via Arrowsmith's
1802 map.

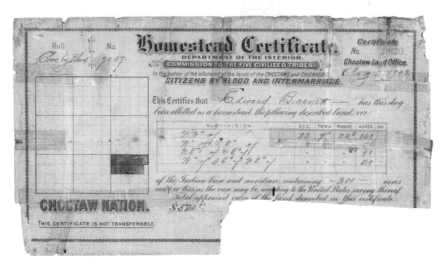

'Choc by Blood' map section of a Homestead Certificate issued to Edward
Barnett, Choctaw Roll No. 7037, 11 August 1903.

Louis Riel (1844–85), Métis politician, 1870, executed after the North West Rebellion.

Ada Deer, Menominee politician (b. 1935) and the first Indian to head the Bureau of Indian Affairs, had Menominee land restored in 1973.

James Billie (b. 1944), the Seminole leader who introduced bingo and gambling and is also a folk and country singer.

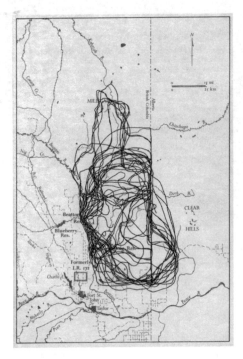

Resource use map, Beaver Dunne-za, BC, from the 1970s, a map laying the foundations of many land claims.

3
Land

First thoughts

Colonization required rationale. European ideas of rights to land in North America derive from seventeenth-century political thinking, especially that of Hobbes and Locke. John Locke (1632–1704) believed that every man had a natural right to property; Thomas Hobbes (1588–1679) maintained that rights came from the sovereign.[1] These basic, conflicting ideas were combined with the proposition that land unused or underused by its inhabitants could be appropriated. This had perhaps been most elegantly put by John Donne (1573–1631): 'In the Law of Nature and Nations, a Land never inhabited, by any, or utterly derelicted and immemorially abandoned by the former Inhabitants, becomes theirs that will possesse it.' However, appropriation had to be sanctified by the extinction of natural rights; that is, unused or abandoned land could be purchased. This was neatly summarized by Samuel Purchas (1577?–1626) in talking of America which:

> hath yeelded many benefits, both opportunitie for lawfull purchase of a great part of the countrey from the Natiues, freely and willingly relinquishing and selling the same for Copper, or other commodities (a thing of no small consequence to the conscience, where the milde Law of Nature, not that violent Law of Armes, layes the foundation of their possession).[2]

And the overarching assumption encapsulating these propositions is that Christianity provides the justification for the actions of the colonizers.

Purchase

These ideas underlay all that happened from the late seventeenth century onwards: aboriginal people had rights in the land, but because they did not use the land in an agricultural (with plough), as opposed to horticultural (no plough), sense, these rights could be acquired by the sovereign and successor states, for transfer to those who might also have natural rights in property, life and liberty. Europeans therefore through the seventeenth century sought to buy, with trade goods and by divine right, territory that was 'under-used'. The need to protect Indians, from their own worst selves as non-Christians and from settlers, flowed from these attitudes, and with it the idea of reserving territory for Indian people. Of the early colonists Roger Williams (c.1603–83), founder of Rhode Island, was the principal innovator. Only occasionally were Indian leaders recorded as acting strategically, as when the Matinecock leader Suscaneman on Long Island sold small lots to appease, and ambiguous lots to forestall, the loss of larger lots, and so delay the ensuing litigation.[3] In New England and other colonies land was purchased from Indian people, although very often their leaders in reality had little idea of the transactions they were entering into. In the aftermath of the French and Indian/Seven Years War and Pontiac's Rebellion, which nearly succeeded in driving off the Europeans, an edict was issued in 1763 by George III, reserving land across the Appalachians to Indian people, an idea as irksome to Americans as taxation without representation. Ironically it was this seemingly liberal idea of entrenching Indian rights that led to dispossession, a pattern repeated through the nineteenth and twentieth centuries. Reserving lands for aboriginal people, which began as a beneficial policy, became in the young United States an idea on its own capable of reorganizing Indian policy in line with the requirements of settlement and the moving frontier. Spain from the sixteenth century had assumed the rights of the crown in land and the right to make land grants. These policies were first codified in 1681 in *Recopilación de las Leyes de los Reynos de las Indias*. After the American Revolution both in Florida and Louisiana, as the balance of power shifted, treaty making and accomodation with Indians became ever more important.[4]

Jefferson

It was Thomas Jefferson (1743–1826), third president (1801–9), intellectual, slave-owning liberal and writer of the Constitution, who developed the idea of Indian Territory into a working concept that enabled dispossession and removal. He initially advocated proper, fair treatment of Indians, but after the Louisiana Purchase of 1803, that is, the acquisition of France's territory west of the Mississippi, he came to favour removal. In his early life, in recording what he thought of Outacity the Cherokee on his way to London in 1762 and in his 1784 account of Virginia, he demonstrated in detail his admiration and respect for Native Americans and his conviction that they could and would, in the best belief in noble savagery, contribute to America with all-important virtues, for instance: 'he is brave, when an enterprize depends on bravery; education with him making the point of honor consist[ing] in the destruction of an enemy by stratagem, and in the preservation of his own person free of injury'.[5] Jefferson took a contradictory position on Indians, similar to that held as a slave-owning democrat. He believed in Indians as hunters but encouraged their development into farmers, with the assistance of missionaries and others, and the possibility of intermarriage with white people. He hoped that with education by missionaries and agents, Native people would willingly sell surplus land. The funds so released could then pay for the costs of their education.

Jefferson was usually incorrect in both assumptions – that Indians would happily become farmers and sell lands – but he recognized that the USA would create policy by force. Indian nations were, in general, already in equilibrium with their lands: the farmed produce, largely of women, was complemented by access to vast territories for hunting by men; and this Indians would not readily give up. Yet, when faced during his presidency with regular correspondence indicating this, Jefferson responded by lecturing Indian people on the need to farm, and for women to become spinners and weavers. His policy was taken up and continued by Madison and Monroe and further extended by Jackson.

In a sense the ideal individual in the Jeffersonian dispensation was

Benjamin Hawkins (1754–1816), the North Carolina planter who had been appointed superintendent of Indian affairs south of the Ohio by Washington, set up the Creek agency, learned Muskogee, wedded a Creek woman, Lavinia Downs, and built a large landholding with African American slaves. Yet such leadership was insufficient, and the tension between the traditionalists and the non-traditionalists was such that a civil war – the Red Stick War (the traditionalists used red clubs and sticks) – broke out between the Creek factions in 1813. The defeat of the Red Sticks, led by Upper Creek men, who believed that a return could be made to traditional ways, terminated the last pan-Indian movement against the United States. This was inspired by the Shawnee/Creek leader Tecumseh (1758–1813) with his brother Tenk-swatawa, the Prophet. Defeats at the Battle of the Thames in the north and Horseshoe Bend in the south ensured that no quasi-independent Indian state would appear in the midwest, and that the United States would be free to deal with the Five Civilized Tribes.

Jackson and Removal

Andrew Jackson, commander of the American forces which defeated the Red Sticks, and the British at New Orleans in 1815, campaigned in 1829 for the presidency and for removal of Indians, following fifteen years of further treaties with southern Indians. The Supreme Court case of 1823 Johnson v. McIntosh was a landmark. In this Chief Justice Marshall formalized a new idea, arguing that the 'Right of Discovery' took precedence over the right of occupation, and that only the federal government could dispose of Indian lands.[6] Here, he muddled the right of discovery with the underlying right to treat with Indians. Congress passed the Indian Removal Act in 1830, which was followed by eight years of negotiations, land purchases under duress, forced removals and war, collectively known as Nunna daul Tsuny, literally the 'Trail where they cried', now the 'Trail of Tears', for the removal of the Cherokees, of whom alone between 4,000 and 8,000 people died.[7] Indian Territory had been formally created in 1834 in what is now Oklahoma and Kansas by the Indian Intercourse Act, replacing the 1763 idea of Indian Territory east of the Mississippi.

Cherokee Removal

The process of negotiation and removal was different for each nation: The Chickasaw, comparatively rich and compact, were removed in relatively good stead. In contrast, the Cherokee, who had successfully adopted much of the American way of life, with a written syllabary and constitution, had a far more difficult time: in the 1820s the state of Georgia passed laws removing Cherokee rights, fought by principal (from 1827) chief John Ross (1790–1866). He was a sometime Indian agent, adjutant under Jackson in the Red Stick War, founder of Chattanooga in 1816 and, following the Removal Act, focus of the process of removal. The Treaty of New Echota of 1835–6 provided for the complete removal of remaining Cherokee to Indian Territory, with a promise of $5 million (interestingly to be compared to the $23 million paid for all of Louisiana in 1804), a difference which highlights the separation of owning land with title, in fee simple, and possessing land as federal government or crown, a distinction which would have confused Indian negotiators. That Ross supported the treaty but later fought against it was, as ever, to do with factionalism. 16,500 Cherokee and 1,500 Cherokee slaves were obliged to go west, to join the 5,000 already there, though the majority of Cherokee were opposed to the treaty and its consequences. Most of the removal took place in 1838–9, but it had begun in the 1820s. Much of the process was recorded and published, including the expenses incurred by removal and the value of relinquished property. So Mary Doherty's plantation in Georgia was listed on 26 October 1832: 'One double house, entry between, two good chimneys. Good under floors, upper in one room $110. Four corn-cribs, worth $24. Barn and smoke-house, worth $40. Good land, good fences, a draw-well in the best order. Fruit trees, very likely and thriving.'[8] No wonder, then, that incomers wished to acquire Cherokee property.

Undefeated Seminole

In contrast to the Cherokee and Chickasaw, the Seminole fought a second prolonged war in 1835–42, the most expensive war in Indian history, following the 1821 secession of Spanish Florida to the USA.

The Treaty of Payne's Landing of 1833 prescribed movement west and was signed by Seminole representatives under duress and renounced on their return to Florida. The war which followed was partially conclusive, with more than 1,000 deaths in the American forces and removal of more than 2,000 Indian and African Seminole. It was followed eventually by the Third Seminole War in the 1850s and further paid removals. More than 20,000 Creek were removed largely under provisions of the 1832 Treaty of Cusseta, the climax being reached in 1838 in Alabama in a conflict called the Creek War, fought between squatter settlers and Creek, who, after refusing to leave, were forced away by the army. By the Treaty of Dancing Rabbit Creek, of 1830–31, the Choctaw ceded a great central northwest-to-southeast swathe of what is now the state of Mississippi. Those who somehow remained behind were unusually and for the first time allowed to become US citizens.

Defeat in the Civil War

The Civil War brought about the emancipation of African Americans and a new interest in the settlement of Native American land issues, but above all a new determination to assimilate Indian people into America. The Five Civilized Tribes, largely with the Confederates, again fought on the losing side and were expected in defeat to bring in African Americans as tribal members. Surprisingly in the US during the Civil War, such was the power of the government, violence against Native Americans was maintained, as was also the rapid growth of railroads. The first transcontinental track opened in 1869. Continued warfare in the American west, and especially the culmination of the Modoc War in the lava beds of northern California in 1873 and the destruction of George Armstrong Custer at the Battle of the Little Bighorn in 1876, resulted in renewed demands for final settlement of Indian issues. These were led by new organizations, and by writers determined to assist Indian people. Ironically the culmination of their efforts was the General Allotment or Dawes Act of 1887, which more than anything led to the impoverishment of Indian reservations. One of these advocates was Alfred B. Meacham (1826–82), former abolitionist and Methodist minister. As Indian commissioner negotiating with the Modocs, he was wounded in 1873, saved by the interpreter Winema

(1848–1920) and then wrote two books describing the Modoc War. *Wigwam and Warpath; or, The Royal Chief in Chains* (1875) was the first, and he campaigned with his saviour Winema for redress.

Post-Civil War Activism

A similar process attempted to redress the wrongs done to the Ponca by the Second Treaty of Fort Laramie (1868. This gave Ponca land to the Sioux and resulted in their removal in 1877 to dry land in Indian Country. Standing Bear (*c.*1829–1908) sought to return the remains of his deceased son home and was arrested and in turn sued for habeas corpus in 1879, for the first time successfully by a Native American.[9] Famously he challenged the court to classify him as non-human. To the judge he said, like Shylock, of his hand:

> That hand is not the color of yours. But if I pierce it, I shall feel pain. If you pierce your hand you also feel pain. The blood that will flow from mine will be the same color as yours. I am a man. The same God made us both.

In 1879–83 Standing Bear, with the help of Suzette LaFlesche (1854–1903), toured the USA and Britain and gained the support of prominent Americans including the poet Henry Wadsworth Longfellow (1807–82). Another legendary advocate for Indian improvement, who had heard Standing Bear, was the writer Helen Hunt Jackson (1830–85), who saw herself as a post-Civil War Harriet Beecher Stowe, publishing *A Century of Dishonour* (1881) about Indian policy and *Ramona* (1884), the tragic California Indian romance set in Mexican California, which in the 1916 movie version included an entirely different Luther Standing Bear (1868–1939), a Yankton boarding school-educated storekeeper, actor and writer in the 1920s and 1930s.

Campaigns

But perhaps the most influential advocates of change were religious groups. The Board of Indian Commissioners, set up in 1869 as part of Grant's Peace Policy, oversaw the supply of proper provisions under treaties and the development of missionary education to reservations. The liberal determination to assist Indian people was, through both individuals such as Meacham and government policy, closely associated with churches. The Quakers were especially active both in Indian advocacy and in education, gathering, for instance, at the Lake Mohonk resort, New York, to discuss the way forward. Advocacy and the need to educate, improve and, as people saw it, assimilate Native Americans worked in a counterintuitive manner to develop the imposition of severalty, that is the imposition of private 'several' ownership on Indian reservations. The Women's National Indian Association was set up in 1879 and campaigned for severalty, and the Indian Rights Association, from 1882, campaigned for citizenship and the incorporation of Indian people into the United States. Others campaigned against the provision of private title in Indian lands, mostly notably the Indian Nations themselves. Importantly, the Five Civilized Tribes of Indian Territory were able for more than a decade to avoid allotment of land, that is severalty, to Indian individuals. Otherwise a fairly disparate group argued against allotment of Indian lands. These included Lewis Henry Morgan (1818–81), the railroad lawyer and anthropologist. Perhaps more surprising was the opposition of the Colorado politician Henry M. Teller (1830–1914), Secretary of the Interior 1882–5. He was the instigator of a Code of Indian Offences (1883), which prohibited Native religion. Interestingly he understood that the morally offensive part of the Dawes Act was that it was undertaken in the spirit of helping Indian people. The real aim [of allotment] was:

> to get at the Indian lands and open them up to settlement. The provisions for the apparent benefit of the Indians are but the pretext to get at his lands and occupy them . . . If this were done in the name of Greed, it would be bad enough; but to do it in the name of Humanity . . . is infinitely worse.[10]

The Dawes Severalty or Allotment Act 1887

The Allotment Act was created by Henry Dawes (1816–1903), a Massachusetts senator and congressman, a liberal who abolished the treaty-making process in 1871, bringing in the era of Indian governance by statute, and helped set up the first National Park, Yellowstone, at that time. Dawes in the 1880s was gradually won over to the idea of allotment. In less than fifty years, between 1887 and 1934, the Indian land base decreased from 138 million acres (560,000 km²) in 1887 to 48 million acres (194,000 km²). This much was something more than simply breaking treaties; it was a process with an articulated and spurious ideology of betterment and advancement and in this sense more heinous that simply a matter of seizing land. Under this act 160 acre lots were allocated to Indian families, or 80 acres to individuals, the actual amounts varying whether pasturage or arable lands were involved. After a period of twenty-five years, fee simple ownership was provided, so that individual Indian families came to own their own land. The land that was not so allocated could then be distributed by sale to non-Indians, resulting in land rushes to the west.

The Curtis Act 1898

The Allotment Act was amended and changed to 'improve' and speed up the process, but the most important change was that also instigated by Henry Dawes. In 1893 he became chairman to the Commission of the Five Civilized Tribes, the Dawes Commission, which advocated the extension of allotment to Indian Territory and removal of self-government by Indian nations. In this he was successful, with the passing of the Curtis Act of 1898, named after the Native American Charles Curtis (1860–1936), of Kaw ancestry, one of the first Native Americans to reach high office, becoming vice-president in 1929. The essential problem of the act is that Native Americans were unfamiliar with American law, with the payment of taxes and with making a will. Much land was alienated, through sale and by leasing.

Fractionated Land

Indian people were already farmers before the Dawes Act: with the passing of the Dawes Act they were enabled to lease land to non-Indian people. That is, there was a choice – to farm or not to farm – whereas before there had been no choice. Even where land remained in Indian hands it became hopelessly divided, through generational division under intestate law. This is the issue of fractionated land. Fractionation is a scientific term used to discuss the break-up of a chemical compound into components, by distillation or freezing. The use of the term therefore neatly expresses the intentionality of the Dawes Act. A US government report of 2011 puts the effects of the process like this: 'The General Allotment Act of 1887 divided tribal land into parcels and allotted them to individual Indians. At that time, each Indian owned 100 percent interest in their allotment. Because wills were not widely used, smaller and smaller undivided interests descended to successive generations. Today, some of the original allotments are owned by as many as 1,000 individual heirs'.[11]

Indian people in the USA, and indeed the Department of the Interior and Indian Affairs, do want to rectify the situation. Fifty years earlier, in 1960, the consequences of the division of land issue was put as follows:

For many years we have recognized that one of the most serious problems facing our American Indian population is that of [inherited] land. With each passing generation the difficulties of solving this problem multiply and if some solution is not forthcoming it will be so acute by the turn of the century [i.e. 2000] that the Federal Government will be unable to bear the burden of handling the administration of the land and the Indians will find their estate so fractionated that their utilization will be nearly impossible.[12]

Fractionation limits the tribes' productive use of the land: it is costly to the federal government to administer the approximately 4.1 million fractionated interests on 99,000 fractionated tracts, and the 267,000 individual account holders. Minute parcels of land in multiple ownership are useless either for joint or individual use. The mismanagement of land trusteeship, and of accrued funds, was addressed in the long-running case Cobell v. Salazar (1996–2009). Eventually a payment of $3.4 billion was agreed, both providing settlement of individual suits over mismanagement and enabling the buying back of fractionated land into tribal ownership. Yet long delays have undermined the settlement: cheques were due to go out in 2014, but some 30,000 plaintiffs had no known addresses or their whereabouts were unknown.[13]

The manner in which allotment occurred also affected its out-come. So while the intentions of the Dawes Act were to liberate and to individualize the economic opportunities of Indian people, the outcomes were shaped externally. So, for instance, the reservations and sections of those reservations selected early on for allotment were the most fertile, best-watered areas, resulting in the early alien-ation of much of the best land. The Dawes Act was intended to stimulate Indian farming and certainly increased agriculture in Indian Country; Indian people already had the rights to farm on reservation, and many Indians were already farmers before 1887. The additional right acquired after 1887 was that of leasing or alien-ating the land. So if you were an Indian farmer with an allotment and had the choice of leasing out your land or actually working the land, and had been born into a buffalo-hunting family, the tempta-tion was there to lease the land and not to farm. The Dawes Act therefore had a negative effect on Indian people who were already farmers and on those who might have become farmers, the opposite of what was intended by Congress.[14]

Oil Lands

The main provision of the Dawes Act was to allow reservations to be divided into 160 acre allotments, one for each Indian family, in trust for twenty-five years. Soon after, the law was changed to enable Indian people to sell or lease their land. So instead of thrift, industry and indi-vidualism being encouraged by the act, the opposite occurred. Indians became small-scale landowners, rentiers. Occasionally impoverish-ment by alienation was replaced by sudden wealth, with highly disruptive effects. While most land, in the east and south of Indian Ter-ritory/Oklahoma, was held by the Five Civilized Tribes, in the northwest the Osage were removed from Arkansas and Missouri ultimately fol-lowing three treaties of 1808, 1818 and 1825. Their apparently useless new land was discovered early in the twentieth century to be oil rich. So in 1957 the Osage celebrated fifty years of the closing of the tribal list of members, with statehood in 1907, with a festival accom-panied by oil maps showing where their wealth came from. Before 1924, Indian people were not US citizens, but wards, in effect minors who could not own oil leases. Therefore white people moved in on Indian people to become guardians, by marriage or fraud, of Native oil fortunes; and if that failed murder was a possibility: sixty Osage were killed during the early 1920s. So turbulent had oil-rich Oklahoma become by the early 1920s that one of the first main activities of J. Edgar Hoover's FBI was fighting crime among whites and Indians there.

Among the families set up by the Oklahoma oil boom on Indian land was that of the Gettys at Bartlesville. Another was that of sometime Oklahoma governor E. W. Marland (1874–1941), of Ponca City, who was involved with Miller's 101 Ranch, the successful Wild West show operation. What is interesting about Marland is that his biography, *Life and Death of an Oilman*, was written by the historian John Joseph Mathews (c.1894–1979), of Osage, trader and tracker descent. This reversed the trope of Indians being celebrated by white authors. Mathews's account of Marland, the creator of a vast company, eventually to become Conoco, is a respectful biography, omitting details of the marriage to Marland's de-adopted stepdaughter.

Canada

Canada originally shared with the American colonies a joint view of aboriginal affairs and land title. This changed rapidly after the American Revolution, when the United States set up a comprehensive if only partially functional reservation system, under the control of the federal government and Congress. Only those signed treaties that were ratified by Congress went into effect; that is, half of the treaties signed by Indians were given force of law. In Canada the nationwide business of treaty-making began only in 1871, four years after confederation, and the same year that the treaty system in the USA ended. The new Canadian confederation created the rather modest number of eleven treaties across large swathes of Canada between 1871 and 1921. In each area representatives were brought together and allocated reserves, rather than reservations, with rights in land, hunting and fishing, and annual payments. The premature ending of the process in the 1920s meant that in the middle of the twentieth century much of Canada was unceded territory, still with aboriginal title. This territory included much of the land around Hudson Bay, except to the south, and most of Canada west of the continental divide. Treaties had been enacted in what is now Canada, before 1871, and these small-scale ownership were designed to regularize land ownership locally. The Royal Proclamation of 1763 was superseded in the USA by American law after 1783, but in Canada retains importance until today. The 1982 constitution, in the Canadian Charter of Rights and Freedoms, mentions specifically the rights retained by aboriginal people from 1763 in these terms:

> The guarantee in this Charter of certain rights and freedoms shall not be construed as to abrogate or derogate from any aboriginal, treaty or other rights or freedoms that pertain to the aboriginal peoples of Canada including (a) any rights or freedoms that have been recognized by the Royal Proclamation of October 7, 1763; and (b) any rights or freedoms that now exist by way of land claims agreements or may be so acquired.

However, the proclamation is ambiguous, both providing for land and hunting rights for aboriginal people and insisting that these rights were derived from the crown.[15] The new importance of First Nations at this time was symbolized by the effective leadership of the Cree/Ojibwe politician Elijah Harper (1949–2013) in defeating the Meech Lake Accord, which in the 1980s would have given Quebec special constitutional status, an absurdity when First Nations were not consulted.

Haudenosaunee Land

A number of different types of colonial settlements can be mentioned. Most interesting, because in Canada it is unique, is the purchase of lands from the Algonquian Mississauga in order to provide territory for the Mohawk, Six Nations and other aboriginal allies of the British, who in being loyal to the crown suffered removal after the American Revolution. This grant of 1784, of what is known as the Haldimand Tract, originally consisted of six miles either side of the important Grand River, which flows more than 150 miles through Ontario to Lake Erie, some 2 million acres. As with many other 'grants' to aboriginal people, however, much of this territory was rapidly alienated to settlers, ironically in part because Joseph Brant or Thayendanegea (*c.*1742/3–1807), the Mohawk leader during the American Revolution, advocated land sales and intermarriage with First Nations. Brant had been celebrated by Boswell in an interview in 1776 on one of his visits to London. In a sense the creation of Six Nations was a culmination of the policies of the superintendent of Indian affairs, Sir William Johnson (*c.*1715–74), who was responsible for treaty-making and keeping Indians on the colonial side up to the eve of the American Revolution.

There had been earlier treaties following the lease-making and patent assignments of the seventeenth-century colonies. In Nova Scotia a series of treaties was signed between 1725 and 1761 which both maintained aboriginal rights and ensured British control. That of 1725, which pertained to New England as well as Nova Scotia, made clear the rule of law:

> If any Controversy of difference at any time hereafter happen to arise between any of the English & Indians for any real or supposed wrong or injury done on either side, no private Revenge shall be taken for the same, but proper Application shall be made to His Majesty's Government upon the place for remedy or Redress there in a due Course of Justice we submit Our selves to be Ruled and Governed by His Majesties Laws and desiring to have the Benefit of the same.[16]

Between the Treaty of Paris of 1783 and the joining of British Columbia to Canada in 1870 occasional agreements, especially around the Great Lakes and at Niagara, were made to regulate aboriginal affairs and land transfers. But before and beyond the creation of Six Nations Reserve, the other treaties which alienated land from First Nations, in the east and in what is now British Columbia, were relatively unimportant in comparison to the major post-confederation secessions of land.

French Canada had had a slightly different view on aboriginal land rights, first viewing land as entirely at the disposal of the crown, ownership seeming irrelevant in the vast tracts of hunting Canada involved in the fur trade. Also, aboriginal peoples including the Iroquois and those of the Maritimes were regarded as allies and so would have no need to surrender land. In addition, the French crown, unlike the British one, regarded conversion an elemental part of the process of colonization, perhaps because the Pope, in dividing the

Americas between Spain and Portugal in 1494, might otherwise regard French colonization as illegitimate.

Treaties as Deals

At the centre of the confusion about treaties and treaty rights, in both countries, is a basic divergence in the understanding of the purpose of a treaty. The aboriginal view is of treaties as charters, semi-sacred documents vital in the protection of sacred land. This is set against the practical administering of rights in which competing claims and interpretations determine actual behaviour. And in Native North America this meant initially the behaviour of colonists and citizens, of traders, and in the nineteenth and twentieth centuries mineral claims and the exploitation of natural resources in business. In western diplomacy, the definition is rather different. If 'an Ambassador is an honest man sent abroad to lie for the good of his country',[17] then American, British and Canadian military and other leaders were simply lying for the good of their nations. Another reference, from the nineteenth century but relating to the seventeenth, is even more explicit in accurately caricaturing the behaviour of diplomats: 'Cardinal Richelieu seems to be considered the founder of the present system of diplomacy properly so called. I can find no better signification for the word which typifies the pursuit than double-dealing . . . it is expressive of concealment, if not of duplicity.'[18] These are the words of Thomas Colley Grattan (1792–1864), an Anglo-Irish journalist and diplomat who helped negotiate the Webster-Ashburton Treaty of 1842, settling boundary problems between the USA and Canada, so he certainly knew about treaty-making, this one, for instance, causing a world of difficulties among Great Lakes peoples. Double dealing, then, may be considered an integral feature of the treaty-making process, whose effects may require later resolution, likely to be dependent on the degree of support and authority from federal authorities.

Canadian Treaties

The eleven Canadian treaties signed by the crown in the late nineteenth and early twentieth centuries are both similar to American treaties and also very different. Treaty 7, dating from 1877, set up reserves for the largely Blackfoot peoples of southern Alberta. While hunting rights in non-reserve lands were preserved, the actual size of reserves was extremely small. The reserve for the Kainai or Blood people, of the Blackfoot, is 1,400 square kilometres (550 square miles), which is modest, indeed positively parsimonious, in comparison with the vast tracts allocated by western treaties in the USA. In the USA the Navajo reservation is 27,000 square miles. Across the border from the Kainai Reserve is the reservation of the Blackfeet (sic) in Montana, with nearly 6,200 square miles of territory.

Western Land Rights

Discussions with Indian people about land rights varied. In Canada from the eighteenth century the form of rights held by aboriginal people in land was a matter of debate. Joseph Brant, the Mohawk leader allied to the British in the American Revolution, argued that the lands obtained with the Haldimand Grant should be available freehold to his people. This attitude soon disappeared. First Nations reserves in non-treaty Canada were determined in size by administrative order under the Indian acts and are often extremely small. British Columbia, for instance, joined the Canadian confederation in 1870–71 and was until recently largely without treaties, a situation which pertained also to American Alaska, purchased from Russia in 1867 and having only one main reservation created for the British missionary William Duncan's ideal community of Tsimshian at Metlakatla. Reservations in British Columbia are minute, often barely more than village sites. In Canada between 1874 and 1951 the Indian Act, with regular amendments, defined relationships between the federal, provincial and territorial governments, between aboriginal people and non-aboriginal people, through what is now called the Department of Aboriginal Affairs and Northern Development, neatly encapsulating the importance of aboriginal people for Canada – a department designed to administer aboriginal people, by implication within the broader remit of Canada's northern frontier. After 1951, without consensus as to how to manage the Indian Act, this legislation was left alone, while other measures relating to aboriginal people were enacted separately.

Recovery of Rights

In a sense governance of Native North Americans by statute, outside of any sense of basic rights and equality in treaty relations, lasted in both Canada and the USA until the 1970s, when resource extraction required the settling of issues in the north. In Canada, with the Calder case of 1973, it was acknowledged that First Nations had rights in the land, and then in 1997 the Delgamuukw case confirmed, with oral testimony, that question of sovereignty, outside of any treaty, had not been tested in court. In 2014 aboriginal rights to original territories were confirmed in a case brought by the Chilcotin/Tsilhqot'in in relation to commercial logging. The Supreme Court ruled inter alia that:

> Aboriginal title flows from occupation in the sense of regular and exclusive use of land. In this case, Aboriginal title is established over the area designated by the trial judge. Aboriginal title confers the right to use and control the land and to reap the benefits flowing from it.[19]

American Indian Congress 1944

In the USA after 1945 pressure to solve the Indian problem, no doubt with a sincere wish to better the lot of Indian people, brought about the idea of termination, that is, the aspiration to finish the government-to-government relationship between Native American Nations and the federal government. Native anticipation of this process resulted in the founding of the American Indian Congress (1944). There was no successful counterpart to this movement in Canada, which came about because of the huge transfer in the USA of Indian populations to cities for war work. While Indian people have generally sought a measured separation from the USA, American policy-makers have sought and to some extent still do seek policies which, in empowering Indian people, also assimilate them. Tribes had in the nineteenth and early twentieth centuries regularly been eliminated. Much criticism was voiced in the 1940s of the Bureau of Indian Affairs, and later in that decade the commission, chaired by ex-President Hoover, included Indian policy in the proposals designed to reduce executive government. The commission's 1949 *Report on Indian Affairs* called for integration of Indians as tax-paying citizens. In Canada the National Indian Brotherhood, now the Assembly of First Nations, was founded in 1967 and came to the fore with the 1969 proposal to repeal the Indian Act and pass responsibility for aboriginal affairs to the provinces. The campaign against this idea was led by the Cree author of *The Unjust Society* (1969), Harold Cardinal (1945–2005), and others.

Termination

Fourteen acts were passed by Congress between 1955 and 1961, covering individual tribes or groups of tribes. Three very large terminations were enacted of the Menominee in Wisconsin, and of the Mixed Blood Utes and Klamath out west. There were 109 tribes involved, with 11,000 people and 1,362,000 acres. For most of the smaller tribes the land was simply sold, and proceeds given to the tribes, whose relationship was now with the federal government rather than the states. For larger tribes the choice was between immediate sale and receipt or participation in a public trust: some 600,000 of the more than 800,000 acres of the Klamath reservation in Oregon were sold in 1961. For the Menominee a state corporation was established, but they fought for the restoration of status, achieved in 1973. The Menominee reservation included in the nineteenth century 350,000 acres of white pine. A successful sawmill was set up, and by the 1950s the BIA held $10 million for the tribe. With termination the reservation became a county in Wisconsin, but it did not have a sufficient tax base to run a county, and so the tribe went from being one of the most self-sufficient to being among the most impoverished. In short, termination was catastrophically misconceived; it took a decade to stop, longer to reverse.

Activism and Assimilation

Certain developments from the 1950s and 1960s counteracted assimilation by termination. First, there was the civil rights movement, which acted as a catalyst and provided a background to the Chicago conference of 1961. At this the Montana Native administrator and activist D'Arcy McNickle (1904–77) drafted the Declaration of Indian

Purpose, an essential text for increasing the activism and self-projection of Indian people. Part of the text reads as a conventional account of wrongs suffered; part dismisses ideas of paternalism and charity:

> the Indian has been subjected to duress, undue influence, unwarranted pressures, and policies which have produced uncertainty, frustration, and despair . . . What we ask of America is not charity, not paternalism . . . We ask only that the nature of our situation be recognized and made the basis of policy and action.[20]

This non-paternalistic setting-free, first of northern peoples and then of the federally recognized tribes, occurred in the 1970s. Actual administrative change was moved forward by an entirely different sort of development: the discovery of oil in Alaska in 1968–9 and the simultaneous need in Canada to organize First Nations rights to deal with hydroelectric development, at a time of the celebration of Canada's centenary in 1967. From these developments flowed an extraordinary series of administrative changes, including the recognition of definite but limited land rights and in some areas a small but real degree of autonomy.

Corporations

The absence of treaties in Alaska and much of Canada meant that resource development from the 1960s onwards required the settlement of land claims; but of course the loaded term 'treaty' was, and is, never used. This is important from the US point of view, because a treaty implies possession of sovereign rights, which were withheld from Alaskan Natives. Land claims required research showing land use to be undertaken on a massive scale; for instance, for the Alaska Native Claims Settlement Act (ANCSA) and for the Mackenzie Valley pipeline enquiry maps had to be prepared showing Native land use. Of these ANCSA is most interesting because it put in place a neo-liberal view of Native America, in which rights were granted to American-style corporations, both empowering Native Alaskan individuals and giving them a degree of freedom which may ultimately mitigate against the survival of Native corporations in general Native ownership.

ANCSA was enacted into law on 18 December 1971. It was

intended to settle outstanding land claims and establish clear title to Alaska's land and resources. To do this, the act established twelve regional corporations and a method of conveying surface estate (land) and subsurface estate (mineral and other resources) to each regional corporation. ANCSA also established 'village corporations', which were given, subject to valid existing rights, the right to the surface estate (land) in and around the village, as identified in section 11 of the act, as amended. The amount of land to be conveyed was identified in section 14(a) and allotted according to the Native population of the village as follows: for between 25 and 99 people, 69,120 acres; for between 100 and 199 people, 92,160 acres; for between 200 and 399 people, 115,200 acres; for between 400 and 599 people, 138,240 acres; and for 600 or more people, 161,280 acres.[21]

Alaskan Termination

But the other aspect of the 1971 act, the termination of other rights, is also very clear:

> Beyond that in Section 4 (b) All aboriginal titles, if any, and claims of aboriginal title in Alaska based on use and occupancy, including submerged land underneath all water areas, both inland and offshore, and including any aboriginal hunting and fishing rights that may exist, are hereby extinguished.[22]

This extinguishment of title in exchange for settlement was already government policy, through the Indian Claims Commission (1946–78), a prelude to termination, something neither the Hopi nor Lakota will tolerate. With ANCSA about 150 million of 345 million acres in Alaska were withdrawn, roughly half for Native settlement and half for public purposes. So as part of the seemingly generous proposals in ANCSA, the Bureau of Land Management (BLM) administers 75 million acres of land in Alaska. Their remit is as follows:

> The BLM manages more than 245 million acres of public land, the most of any Federal agency. This land, known as the National System of Public Lands, is primarily located in 12 Western states, including Alaska. The BLM also administers 700 million acres of sub-surface

mineral estate throughout the nation. In Fiscal Year (FY) 2011, recreational and other activities on BLM-managed land contributed more than $130 billion to the U.S. economy and supported more than 600,000 American jobs. The Bureau is also one of a handful of agencies that collects more revenue than it spends. In FY 2012, nearly $5.7 billion will be generated on lands managed by the BLM, which operates on a $1.1 billion budget. The BLM's multiple-use mission is to sustain the health and productivity of the public lands for the use and enjoyment of present and future generations. The Bureau accomplishes this by managing such activities as outdoor recreation, livestock grazing, mineral development, and energy production, and by conserving natural, historical, cultural, and other resources on public lands.

In November 2012 they sold hydrocarbon rights to a small section of Alaska for $898,900 on 14 tracts on approximately 160,088 acres of the 22.8-million-acre reserve. The U.S. Geological Survey has estimated that there are 896 million barrels (mmbbls) of mean technically recoverable oil and 53 trillion cubic feet (tcf) of mean technically recoverable natural gas within the NPR-A.[23]

While Indian affairs and the management of federal lands are separate operations in the USA, they seem to act in analogous manner to the Canadian federal department. So perhaps with a conflict of interest the BLM and the Bureau of Indian Affairs are both divisions of the Department of the Interior. Continued refusal to accept the way in which Indian-derived national lands are not for privatization can be seen in the way BLM lands may be used for hunting and grazing. In Nevada the case of Cliven Bundy, who refuses to pay BLM fees for cattle grazing, following the Sagebrush Rebellion, is in a direct parallel with land seizures from Indians in earlier times. Further, the American Land League provides support for those states campaigning to turn over BLM lands to local control. In Canada 90 per cent of land belongs to the crown in many provinces.[24]

Maps

One way of considering the treaty process and land is to look at maps. It is a commonplace in postmodern cultural studies that knowledge is power. Flowing from this were the rhetorical flourishes with which colonial maps were deployed. So, for instance, Captain George Vancouver (1757–98), a much-disliked martinet of an explorer, gathered information from the Spanish and his own extraordinary four seasons of surveying to create the first coastal charts of North America from Baja California to southern Alaska.

While treaties might be enacted with definitions based on the distance that could be walked, or covered by a deerskin, or within sound of a gunshot, it was the gradually regularized measurement systems which ensured proper disposal of land alienated from aboriginal peoples. The systems in use in the USA and Canada are largely British, but with area-appropriate alternatives in French and Spanish North America. The basic surveying device is that of the metal chain, a series of 100 links measuring 66 feet, invented in the early seventeenth century by mathematician and theologian Edmund Gunter (1581–1626) in London. In young America, in 1785 and 1787, the Public Land Survey enabled territories from the Ohio onwards to be surveyed and often sold site unseen. An analogous system for the Canadian west was adopted in the late nineteenth century. Allotments in the west were initiated with the US Homestead Act of 1862 and imposed on Indian reservations from 1887 were 160 acres, or a quarter of a square mile.

Acquisition of Indian lands is the other side of the frontier dream: first the purchase of title from Indians, in a treaty, which might or might not be ratified by Congress, then perhaps the reduction of reservation size in subsequent treaties and finally the disposal of 'surplus' reservation lands to homesteaders. In 1908 parts of the Rosebud reservation in South Dakota were opened up to allotment: prospective farmers could purchase lots from the US federal government at $10 an acre. Decisions were made by staking and by lottery, a process common in the west. There was a dream of riches, analogous to the gold rush. The breaking-up of the Sioux/Lakota reservation resulted in joyous land rushes, in which thousands of people descended by wagon and train on different towns in the prairies, checked out soil quality and were lucky, or not, in the allocation of farms. A mere forty years earlier, in 1868, the Lakota chief Red Cloud, Mahpiya Luta (c.1822–1909) had defeated the US army, recently victorious in the Civil War, and secured for himself and his people at the Treaty of Fort Laramie the vast Great Sioux reservation, half of what was to become the state of South Dakota, all of the lands being west of the Missouri. The most intensive period of mapping of the United States occurred at the time of the Homestead Act of 1862, and more importantly for our story of the General Allotment Act of 1887, which forcibly opened Indian reservations to settlement by European Americans as a means of ameliorating the conditions of Native America and solving the Indian problem. Indian lands are usually associated with the trope of broken treaties, but the destruction of the land base actually arose through the selling-off of Indian lands to homesteaders and not simply through the breaking, or non-ratification by Congress, of treaties. In the next fifty years two-thirds of Indian lands were lost: 60 million acres was disposed of by the government as surplus under the initial act. Under the Burke Act, 1906, a further 27 million acres was alienated. This measure replaced a system of grants of land in trust for twenty-five years, with one of grants in fee simple or outright ownership, if the Indian was deemed 'competent and capable'; Indians were deemed competent generally if of mixed descent, and in becoming liable for the payment of taxes, an unfamiliar process, of course, were likely to forfeit their land.[25]

The Cost of Fractionation

The intention of the 1887 Dawes Act, as of subsequent acts, was to allocate lands to individual Indian people, assisting in their assimilation; but it was also seen as enabling cultural genocide. Presented as a liberal, forward-looking gesture, it enabled Indian people to be free eventually to dispose of the land and also to lease it to non-Indians. Then, as mentioned, with inheritance down the generations – in large families – farms came to be divided into unusable small tracts, a process called fractionation. Original nineteenth-century grants to Indian individuals of 160 acres might today, because of the absence of will-making, have dozens or even a hundred or more owners, making use of that land almost impossible. The effects of fractionation can be seen in the situation of one parcel of land detailed in the 1980s (Hodel v. Irving, 481 U.S. 704, 713 (1987)). Tract 1305 of the Sisseton-Wahpeton Oyate of the Lake Traverse reservation in the Dakotas is 40 acres and at the time of the case had 439 owners and produced $1,080 in annual income; one-third of the owners received .05c per annum, two-thirds less than $1. The cost of administering this income in the 1980s was $17.5 million, increasing along with a burgeoning number of owners to $42.5 million per annum in 2003. Theodore Roosevelt called the 1887 Dawes Act on 3 December 1901 'a mighty pulverizing engine to break up the tribal mass', and indeed it was just that. And it was mightily assisted by foreigners and by criminal organizations, such as the Benson Syndicate in California and the West, which was contracted for land surveys. One foreigner involved in lands was an acquaintance of Red Cloud, an Englishman called William Blackmore (1827–78), a lawyer and speculator in land grants, who bought up Hispanic claims in the American west and brokered them to European clients.

Maps and Treaties

Wayfinding and map-making are ancient aspects of Native culture. There is a famous map of the great Sioux reservation of 1868, including the gold-rich Black Hills, then sprawling from South Dakota into other states. Such maps can be compared to a ledger book drawing of a Plains scene in which space, the arrangement of tipis and water and the movement of people conform to the tradition of Plains pictography, without horizon and scale, people rather than places. Plains captives began to use paper instead of skin to describe their histories and in the absence of accessible drawing materials used blank ledger books and even printed trade catalogues for their art.

The discussions of treaties are usually accompanied by large-scale maps, showing reserves, reservations, successions of land and current settlements. A fuller perspective is provided by looking at the way aboriginal people visualized the land and understanding something of the technical context in which land was taken and divided. Maps, in the Native way, can be seen as a state of mind, intellectual knowledge with a spiritual and not just technical dimension, enabling, for instance, wayfinding in travelling and hunting. Maps also extended beyond the earthly world and included sky maps. The indigenous view of landscape, as something holistically part of a single whole, can be contrasted with the way in which lands were surveyed and broken up for farming.[26] But that is not the end of the story. The third era of cartography is that which began in the 1960s. Map-making became the central process in the recovering of differing degrees of autonomy, in Alaska and in Canada, and in what Alaskans call rather dismissively the Lower 48, that is, mainland US.

Native Maps

Explorers, traders, missionaries and administrators from the sixteenth century collected and used Native map-making skills. Native North American maps were created long before European contact and were produced for a wide variety of reasons:

> as messages or instructions to others; as interactive planning; in order to reconstruct past events and record them for posterity; to make sense of the world beyond that of direct experience and relate it to the known world; and to divine. The list is not exhaustive.[27]

Maps were constructed of all sorts of material. One example given is of a Mi'kmaq chief in 1761 who used his first finger and thumb to form a circle and to show how his people was about to be crushed by the force of colonial settlers between New York, Montreal, Boston and Halifax. Another example given is of sand, where among the Nuu-chah-nulth of Vancouver Island a raid on another village was preceded in the 1860s by a sand map created on the beach three-dimensionally to show the layout of the village to be attacked. A similar example was recorded by Colonel Dodge, a friend of the speculator Blackmore, who described a Comanche raid into Mexico in the 1820s. Each day as the Indians were travelling south those who knew the route would sketch out the day's journey in dust before setting off. What is remarkable, then, about Native American maps is threefold: the extent of the knowledge; the ephemerality of the maps actually created – only a small number of maps survive; and the alternative ways of seeing in which environment, time, social space in the form of settlements, perspective and horizon may be different, and the way in which water is more important than dry land.

Maps of the Southern US

A handful of maps – less than half a dozen – of the southern United States survive in manuscript on paper copies from originals which may have been on skin. These are social maps, in which villages and alliances are depicted across hundreds of thousands of square miles, with tracks between them where the walking time is depicted as the main coordinate, time as we know it today trumping distance. They were retained by early eighteenth-century colonial governors such as Francis Nicholson (1655–1728) and show Chickasaw, Creek and Cherokee communities, and how they relate to the arch-rivals, Britain and France.

Mound Surveys

What is exceptionally interesting about these maps is that they have a superficial similarity to the layouts of large ancient ceremonial trading and burial settlements. These were created along the rivers of the Ohio and Mississippi Valleys by the indigenous Hopewell culture at the beginning of the first millennium AD and by the peoples of the Mississippian period at the beginning of the last millennium with influence from Mexico or Middle America. A site such as Mound City in Ohio, 2,000 or so years old, covering approximately 13 acres, has a well-laid-out square earthwork enclosing burial mounds. That at Newark, not far away and approximately of the same date, is on a much grander scale, with geometric earthworks many hundreds of metres across, and with avenues and linking features inside the main enclosure. These foretell the aesthetics of the village and day-walks depicted in maps created by Indian allies in the eighteenth century. Larger still is the Mississippian settlement at Cahokia, Illinois, where a vast disciplined geometric arrangement of pyramids and other earthworks may have supported a town larger than London in 1066.

Two further features are noteworthy: first, the skill set required to survey and create such an immense geometric complex – without paper, clay tables or other permanent materials for chart creation; and second, the cartographic knowledge available 2,000 years ago, which must have been a day-to-day reality in trading societies in touch with

Lake Superior for copper, North Carolina for fossilized shark teeth for ornamentation and the Gulf of Mexico for marine shells – which probably had currency functions as well as aesthetic, symbolic and status ones.

Water Maps

One main alternative to the walking map is the water map, and indeed many more water – coast, river and lake – maps survive than walking and settlement maps. Many of these come from northern North America, and approximately thirty are found in the Hudson's Bay Company Archives in Winnipeg. One of the most famous is that by a Blackfoot called Feathers, drawn for fur trader Peter Fiddler at the beginning of the nineteenth century. Covering between half a million and a million square miles, this shows the drainage of rivers, along with settlements, into the Missouri-Mississippi, going down in a 'V' to the Gulf of Mexico. Further, very neatly, towards the top of the page is a thin horizontal line indicating the barrier of the Rocky Mountains, in effect a non-place. And running off the page towards the top edge of the sheet on the left are two further rivers, probably the Columbia and the Snake, draining into the Pacific. What is remarkable here is the way that knowledge, the presentation of information in a way that can be of practical use, is more important than scale accuracy. The significance of such a map is demonstrated by the incorporation of Feather and Fiddler's information about the northern Plains and Rockies in Arrowsmith's 1802 engraved map of North America. Published in London, this was used by Lewis and Clark, following Jefferson's Louisiana Purchase of 1803, to travel to the West Coast up the Missouri and over to the Columbia in 1804–6. The expedition depended on Native and fur trader knowledge for travel and interpretation, the Canadian Charbonneau (1767–1843) and the Shoshone Sacagawea (1788–1812) assisting the Americans.

Private Speculators' Maps

William Clark would have been very familiar with Native wayfinding. Later in St Louis when administering Indian affairs, he assembled a cabinet or museum full of items no doubt representing transactions between himself and Native America. A unique item on deer skin is a map of the Mississippi, Wabash and Ohio drainages, with the largely French-founded settlements marked. This turned up forty years ago at Stonyhurst College in Lancashire, UK, having probably been brought from Clark's museum in 1825. Without documentation, the map is again of very uncertain origin, but it may have been a river map designed to show Indian nations and land cessions made to the Wabash Land Company, a speculative venture with an illegal assignment of land from one or more Indian leaders rather than from the crown or federal government. These doubtful corporations issued stock and sold land to urban speculators and to settlers.

Native American land maps are more often water maps, because these were valuable not just for travelling, but also for marking marine, riverine and lacustrine shellfish. There is a modern archaeologist's map of the Bay Area in California, which is dotted with numbers each representing a shell midden (mound of empty shells). For Native America what matters are the coasts and even more the interior waterways, and this is reflected in the prominent borrowing of Native names for rivers and lakes as names for states and provinces – for instance Ontario and Saskatchewan, Connecticut, Michigan, Mississippi, Tennessee and Wyoming. Algonquian- and Iroquoian-speaking peoples in eastern North America created river and coast maps used by cartographers.

Other Maps

Two other map types should, however, be mentioned. One is the war record, on the Plains, showing with pictographs actions in which the artist-warrior depicts his exploits on a wearing robe. And the other is the star map, a Pawnee depiction of the heavens, where an accurate representation of constellations by the Pawnee is associated with a broader cosmology, rather than being purely about wayfinding. Little is known about how maps were created by Native Americans, how they were imagined and dreamed. For the Yup'ik, the Eskimoan-speaking people of southwest Alaska, stories are traditionally accompanied by the use of drawings in dirt or snow, drawn with a story knife of walrus ivory. Maps are likely also to have been visualized in this way. The most exotic and material of all maps are the Greenland coast maps, carved in wood and, as tactile objects, capable of being used in the darkness of kayaks, say under the deck of a kayaker paddling home.

Of course what cartographers (and cartography is a term which apparently only dates to the nineteenth century) mean by a map is a drawn or engraved chart; and Inuit and Arctic peoples assisted from the first exploration of North America with charts, which were drawn en route. Encounters between Europeans and Native North America were initially often to do with exchange of information, transactions to avoid violence and obtain food, but above all, the need, across language barriers, to receive directions. Most surviving physical maps are from the north, and especially from the Arctic. In the nineteenth century William Parry, in searching for the Northwest Passage, obtained a map of the Foxe Basin by Iligluik which he later had engraved. In the 1830s John Ross, in recording his location of the magnetic north pole, drew two map-makers, Ikmalick and Apelagliu, at work. But for Inuit the understanding and appreciation of landscape, for making it comprehensible and usable, is a multisensory, multigenerational project in a state of constant updating and improvement. It is a process that is both fixed in a moment of time and yet constantly changing. Of most importance are the categories by which this landscape is named, and so controlled and used – for of course without physical, immutable maps names provide the entry point to understanding. A way of memorizing and memorializing the landscape is fundamental to making it usable. Henshaw lists Inuit features used for naming:

> Climate sensitive features: Sea ice conditions, ocean currents, seasonal camping locations, snow conditions, nesting areas, temperature conditions, animal migrations, wind directions. Ecological features: Presence of specific plants and animals, animal products, signs of animal presence, animal behaviour. Topographic features: Terrestrial (mountains, cliffs, hills, peninsula), hydrographic (shorelines, passages), aquatic (lakes and rivers). Metaphorical features: Mythic associations, zoomorphic, and anthropomorphic. Harvesting activities: Hunting, processing, caching areas. Routes: Travel, resting spots, safe anchorages. Camps: Camp sites. Other: Archaeological sites, historic events, Inuksuit.[28]

And the essential point here is that in the Arctic land formation includes seasonal changes to the landscape in the form of ice developing and then melting, and the necessary naming of different forms of ice – linguistic exuberance is the end feature. If much of the territory that needs to be traversed is sea ice, ice that is constantly changing, then the idea of fixed maps is useless, as may also be fixed terms. What is needed for travel is an understanding of seasons and weather that can be constantly updated.

Inuit Travelling

We see living in a single place as a fixed condition, while Claudio Aporta, in his recent study of routes, trails and tracks in the Igloolik area, says that travelling 'was not a transitional activity between one place and another, but a way of being'.[29] In this sense, Inuit mobility is more than just part of a 'seasonal round' related to subsistence; rather, movement itself constituted a core element of Inuit culture, and especially of memory. Native North Americans are sometimes called nomads or nomadic, Latin terms for wandering herd pastoralists, also suggesting a degree of aimlessness, when movement was deliberate and well considered and when aboriginal people were only marginally involved with domestic animals, particularly the dog.

Naming the Landscape

Cartographic knowledge is all-important while maps themselves may, perhaps, be irrelevant: Ashevak Ezekiel of Cape Dorset/Kinngait in the late twentieth century described through an interpreter how Inuit acquired this knowledge:

> in the past when Inuit camped at certain spots . . . they were familiar with the area only so each camp had its own knowledgeable information and names and they exchanged [information about routes and place-names] if you passed through [they would say] 'this is the route' and 'it's safer' [to go this way], etc.[30]

That is if you do not have maps, names become all-important. If you are walking in mountains, the names of features on a map are useful;

if you are hunting in a movable landscape of ice the names of features are the only points of reference: toponymy in the mind in effect becomes the map.

But there is another important reality here: that cartographic knowledge in Native North America was a social function, maintained by oral tradition in the abstract and useful only in so far as it existed in the minds of users. The decline and disappearance of this knowledge in the north is highly dangerous, as well as detrimental to identity. John MacDonald in his account of Igloolik Inuit and the heavens gives good examples of how names matter and how the loss of knowledge of toponymy is crucial: some young people who were lost out on the sea ice stopped and radioed for help, asking that someone come out on a snowmobile to rescue them. They knew the landscape and could use it, but because they could not name the landscape they could not describe where they were; in a sense the landscape was only half mapped. In another instance, when young people had set off from Igloolik and arrived in the wrong community, the elder Noah Piugattuk spoke to the two young men: 'I lectured them saying that they were ignorant because they could see the sun and the ground . . . They were old enough but they were not trying to learn.'[31]

Dreams

For cartographers, understanding the landscape is a literal scientific project. For Inuit it can be a matter of dreams. One theory of dreams is that they provide a way of ordering disordered experience and information, a reflective space in which to make sense of nonsense. Aipilik Innuksuk, a late twentieth-century elder from Igloolik, talked in an interview of being lost on sea ice in an unexpected storm and without any notion of the landscape from which he could return to his camp. He built a temporary shelter of snow and slept spasmodically, waking himself frequently to warm up and to check that his dogs were still in harness. In one of these moments he dreamed exactly of where the camp was: 'I heard somebody say to me "The direction of your camp is right on your lee side; if you go downwind you can get home!"' He didn't act immediately because he was unsure about the information but waited until morning and realized that his dream had been correct. Aipilik finished the interview by saying: 'This was not the only time I was given directions in my sleep. Should other people have similar experiences I would advise them to do as they are told.'[32] Wayfinding then may also be dependent on maps lodged in the unconscious; and dreams, as we now know, are vitally important in the processing of experience and knowledge.

Symbolic Maps

Finally, dreams of routes and maps can become entirely symbolic, and while seemingly non-functional act to give symbolic weight to embedded ancient knowledge. Hunting caribou is the all-important activity in the north, required to obtain fat meat for winter sustenance and thick winter coats ready for turning into clothing. For the Innu, or Montagnais Naskapi, the head of small family hunting bands in the eastern Subarctic would have a dream predicting where the annual migration of caribou would occur towards the end of the summer. He would relay the dream to his wife, who would paint the dream on a coat, which he would wear at the mokashan ceremony before the end of summer hunt. These coats are entirely abstract in design, but they act to situate the understanding of the hunt in a social context. Of course, the migrating routes of caribou would tend to be the same each year, that is, the technical ecological knowledge about caribou movements would be fairly fixed but no doubt sorted out in dreaming mode to take account of recent events such as weather. And for Subarctic people hunting and trapping territories might specifically be owned and possessed by individuals and family. Anishinaabe George Copway (1818–69) put it like this in the 1840s, before describing an incident when he came across a group of trappers whose furs he himself seized without protest:

> The hunting grounds of the Indians were secured by right, a law and custom among themselves. No one was allowed to hunt on another's land, without invitation or permission. If any person was found trespassing on the ground of another, all his things were taken from him, except a hand full of shot, powder sufficient to serve him in going straight home, a gun.[33]

New Maps

What happened in the late twentieth century was the development of new maps relating to new forms of the recording of traditional information. These were necessary for evaluating aboriginal land claims. The end result was the development of Native toponymy and Native land-use maps, especially in the 1960s, and in the crucial sense that knowledge is power, power flowed back to aboriginal people. However, these maps, as expressive measures of communication and authority, only occasionally involve the Native renaming of features, such as Denali for Mount McKinley in Alaska, the highest peak in the US. There in general traditional names of European and American origin have been maintained.

More dramatic maps and mapping changes have occurred in Canada. Canada was created round the nationalization of Rupert's Land from the Hudson's Bay Company and the land grants made for the creation of the Canadian Pacific Railway. This was completed in the 1880s, using an American-style land survey. Further large chunks of Rupert's Land and the Northwest Territories were taken for the creation of the prairie provinces in 1912 and for the extension of Manitoba, Ontario and Quebec. Settlement, much later, of northern land claims proceeded from the 1970s in a variety of ways which further divided up the Northwest Territories and provided a degree of self-government. The main agreements are as follows, and new arrangements are currently coming into effect in Labrador:

The James Bay and Northern Quebec Agreement (1975). Under this three categories of land were created for the Cree and Inuit in New Quebec. 3,250 square kilometres (1,250 square miles) were reserved for Inuit villages/settlements and 2,158 square kilometres (830 square miles) for Cree villages/settlements, and 14,000 square kilometres (5,400 square miles) of land with exclusive harvesting rights were confirmed for Cree and Inuit. These are self-administering, that is, a degree of self-government is provided for. The vast majority of land is Category 3, reserved for the province but where aboriginal people have rights to hunt, more than 900,000 square kilometres over which title was otherwise surrendered.[34] The Cree lost more land to flooding than they gained as Category 1 for exclusive harvesting. One of the major initiatives arising from this was the creation of Avataq, which means float, as in the kind of sealskin float used for walrus hunting and whaling. Avataq is an organization that maintains archives and collections for Nunavik, the Inuit area of northern Quebec. Much is highly innovative, for instance mapping sounds and maintaining oral history.

The Inuvialuit Final Agreement (1984). The Inuvialuit were accorded legal control over their land with ownership of 91,000 square kilometres (35,000 square miles) of land including 13,000 square kilometres (5,000 square miles) with sub-surface rights to oil, gas and minerals. Furthermore, the Inuvialuit established the right to hunt and harvest anywhere in the claim area, particularly as primary harvesters on certain lands known to be rich in wildlife.[35]

The creation of Nunavut (1993, 1999). The most significant of the Canadian land claims settlements is that of the Inuit self-governing territory. The agreement was signed in 1993, organized by a commission of nine people, and went into effect in 1999. Nunavut has a 1,877,787 square kilometre (725,018 square mile) land area and a population of 31,000. The 2012–13 budget was $1.45 billion, of which 92 per cent comes from the federal government.

Greenland is very separate. It became a self-governing overseas administrative division of Denmark in 1979, and under Home Rule discussions continue about the possibility of full independence perhaps in 2021, 300 years after colonization. The essential difference is that the political map of Greenland has not changed in the way that the maps of Alaska or Canada have changed since 1971. However, the same kind of mapping of traditional land use, territories, and today especially the ice cap and ice patterns, continues.

Land-use Maps in Canada

In the rest of Canada, that is to say Canada which includes the provinces, territories and especially the areas of settlement established by the original federal treaty process of 1871–1921, land-use maps have become increasingly important. That in British Columbia is based on the Aboriginal Mapping Network, an organization that provides links to historical materials on aboriginal mapping, which hosts maps in areas of British Columbia and Ontario where claims are underway. In British Columbia the first agreement to be reached was that of the Nisga'a along the Nass River in the northern part of the province. Their agreement was signed in 1999, the first for a century, and went into effect a year later. It was prompted by the 1973 Calder case before the Supreme Court in Ottawa. This reversed an earlier decision and ruled that aboriginal title existed before the creation of the province of British Columbia. In the 1980s and 1990s the extinction of rights became a defining issue for aboriginal people, and while the language of the Nisga'a agreement is less inflammatory the effects are the same: 'All rights and title to non-Nisga'a lands are effectively surrendered in exchange for the rights and for the rights and benefits defined in the agreement.'[36] Some of the provisions are as follows: $196.1 million dollars (in 1999 dollars); 2,019 square kilometres (780 square miles) of land; an average yearly allocation of 44,588 sockeye salmon, 11,797 coho salmon, 6,330 chum salmon, 6,524 chinook salmon and 4,430 pink salmon, protected by the treaty; a water reservation for domestic, agricultural and industrial purposes.

Land Studies

For the necessary land claims agreements to take place in Alaska and Canada, a large number of groundbreaking studies were funded and published in the 1970s and 1980s, in which aboriginal land use and toponymy became entrenched in legal and administrative thinking.[37] Probably the most interesting of the mapping projects from this period is Hugh Brody's *Maps and Dreams*, published in 1981. This created detailed maps, both conceptual and physical, to show how hunting and trapping were sustained by the Beaver or Dunne-za Indians of the 1980s, with their traplines, their areas for hunting big game and their berry-picking and fishing areas. What Brody does is accentuate the business of dreaming and the importance of conceptual maps, but his maps, like all Native maps, are centred on water. Fewer mapping projects about Alaska Native land use were organized in this period, though there had been a couple of earlier ones about Inupiat land use in northwest Alaska. If one thinks, however, of cultural domains in the Arctic, then other matters, like the whale for the Inupiat, become the central focus, as explored by Tom Lowenstein in *Ancient Land Sacred Whale* (1994) at Point Hope. One actual land study had been undertaken in response to Edward Teller's Project Chariot in the 1950s to excavate a new port at Point Thompson, Alaska. This was to use nuclear devices near a number of Native villages including Point Hope. Opposition to this idea contributed to the development of the environmental movement in the 1960s. Project Chariot was a characteristic northern absurdity of the Cold War.

Water Rights

As mentioned, underlying the conceptual difference between Native and non-Native map-making is an attitude to water. While oil and gas rights on land are the most valuable form of mineral rights, water rights are perhaps the most contentious, requiring negotiation and legislation. Water rights were often included in treaties, and water no less than land was alienated frequently by squatting on Indian lands. There is therefore now in the waterless west a long series of water disputes, which are in a way more important than land disputes and give rise to endless legal cases. Darcy S. Bushnell, ombudsman for water rights in New Mexico, summarized the issues in 2013: one nation, the Navajo, claims nearly a billion acre-feet on one river, the San Juan, in one state, New Mexico, per year. Many tribes do not have access to drinking water, but all require water for farming, hunting and gathering, fishing, and spiritual activities. Access to water was guaranteed by treaty, and since Native people were there first their water claims are the senior ones. Of course, non-Native neighbours also require water for many of the same reasons.[38] Bushnell also summarized the situation in respect of the settlement of Native American claims:

> To date, twenty-eight settlements have achieved a federal settlement act and are involved in implementation. Sixteen settlements are in progress with two, the Blackfeet Water Rights Settlement of 2011 (Montana), S.399/H.R 3301, and the Navajo-Hopi Little Colorado River Water Settlement (Arizona), S.2109/H.R. 4067, having been

introduced in the 112th Congress. Many more tribes' water rights remain to be addressed, including tribes with claims on the Colorado River, the more than 100 California tribes with federal recognition, the Oklahoma tribes which share [the basins of] two rivers [Arkansas and Red] and many more in the mid-west, the east, Alaska and Hawaii.[39]

But of course the shortage of water is a general affliction in the Americas. This may be addressed by the selling of Canadian water, even enforced by the terms of the North American Free Trade Agreement (1994).[40] Reliance on case law may not necessarily protect Indian water rights. In general in the US it was argued in a 1996 article 'Conquering the Cultural Frontier: The New Subjectivism of the Supreme Court in Indian Land', by David Getches (1942–2011), that the Supreme Court, so often assumed to be textualist in its literal readings of the constitution, was in Native affairs increasingly political in its interpretation of Indian law.[41]

The Conceptual Globe

The central issue of cartography is conceptual: how to conceive of the earth, and how to project knowledge on that conception. In a recent review article David Wootton introduced to his discussion of the fraught nature of maps the magic realist criticism of normative reality, citing a Jorge Luis Borges short story of a map of an empire the size of the empire itself:

> In that Empire, the Art of Cartography attained such Perfection that the map of a single Province occupied the entirety of a City, and the map of the Empire, the entirety of a Province. In time, those Unconscionable Maps no longer satisfied, and the Cartographers Guilds struck a Map of the Empire whose size was that of the Empire, and which coincided point for point with it. The following Generations, who were not so fond of the Study of Cartography as their Forebears had been, saw that that vast Map was Useless, and not without some Pitilessness was it, that they delivered it up to the Inclemencies of Sun and Winters. In the Deserts of the West, still today, there are Tattered Ruins of that Map, inhabited by Animals and Beggars; in all the Land there is no other Relic of the Disciplines of Geography.[42]

But of course the map as big as the empire it represents, which perhaps the English-educated Borges took from Lewis Carroll, is exactly what Native Americans have in their mind when they are wayfinding. In the Arctic the ability to travel is connected to an understanding of the stars, of wind and tide, of ice, of snow and of animals. In Africa it may rely on driven sand, or animal spoor or similar, and in tropical forests on the breaking of twigs, leaves and footprints and light through a dense forest canopy. This understanding of the landscape can only exist in the mind: no map of that moment in time showing driven snow, animal tracks, pressure ridges and fractured ice has any need to be recorded because it is changing all the time. So the Borges story of an empire whose map was as big as the empire and found to be useless and left to decay neatly reverses the trope of the Native whose knowledge really does enable him to see the whole world, in a form of magic realism, as a map, a map of his or her empire.

4

Others: Beings, Believing and the Practice of Religion

'Two-Spirit' man We'wha (1849–96).

Windigo, 1977, by Norval Morrisseau (1931–2007).

Indians Hunting the Bison, 1843, by Karl Bodmer (1809–93).

George Copway (1818–69 (Ojibwe or Chippewa)), known as
Kahgegagahbowh, Methodist preacher and First Nations leader.

California prayer board, Salinan.

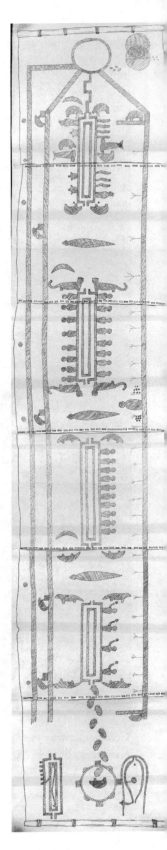

Ojibwe/Anishinaabe birchbark scroll,
early twentieth century, used in Midewiwin
ceremonies to resolve conflict and
ensure good health.

Pablita Velarde (1918–2006),
Santa Clara, Tse Tsan (Tewa for
'Golden Dawn'), from *Green
Corn Dance*, 1956.

Inuit shaman in a trance, Hudson Bay, *c.*1900–1905.

The annual Sun Dance ceremony at the Kainai (Blood First Nation) Reserve, near Cardsto
Alberta, 1953.

Qingailisaq, a shaman, with parka created for him after meeting a group
of *ijiqqat* humanlike supernatural beings, while hunting caribou, 1902.

Navajo sand painting, Wind Doctors Ceremony, for healing.

Dancer with deer effigy, in an annual renewal ceremony for community good health and hunting, Northern California.

Sxwayswey mask dance, used in naming and cleansing ceremonies among Coast Salish people, Cowichan, BC, early twentieth century.

Wovoka (1854–1923), 'Cutter', or Jack Wilson, Paiute leader who founded the Ghost Dance Religion.

Quanah Parker (c.1853–1911), Comanche rancher who lost most of his 44,000 acres with allotment, and the leader who established the Native American Church.

Pueblo Buffalo Dance.

Hopi Katsina dance.

Tablita dancers and singers, San Ildefonso, symbolizing maize/corn praying for rain.

Prince Charles, or Mekaisto (Red Crow), a great Kainai name given to him in 1980 at a smudging ceremony, Mi'kmaq, May 2014.

Cheyenne sweat lodge frame, early twentieth century.

4
Others

Windigo

The landscape of Native North America is inhabited by non-human persons, animals, plants – others, religious beings. Some beings are, or seem to be, evil. Windigo, for example, is a cannibal being among the historic Anishinaabe and other Algonquian-speaking peoples, nations of the boreal region west and north of the Great Lakes. Windigo would possess people through their dreams: just as animal spirits would appear in dreams to aid with hunting and locate prey, Windigo would instil a craving for human flesh and predestine the dreamer – in a time of famine and starvation – to kill and eat people. While rarely occurring, once Windigo was identified in the community every effort would be made by appropriate practitioners to cure the victim, with drumming and sweat lodges and shaking lodge ceremonies. If healing failed then the victim was executed, as happened to three possessed people – Makanin, Wiskahoo and Moostoos – during the fur trade period. Fear of Windigo among Anishinaabe and Cree, placing very rare cannibalism as an aspect of hunting, might have meant people were actually less likely to eat human flesh, say in the spring, the regular time of game scarcity.[1] So cannibalism was given a proper cultural context and a way of rescuing the victim, with a degree of understanding which Europeans and Americans could not muster in the Arctic or Pacific, when white people succumbed to the ultimate hunger – choosing, as was their wont in the nineteenth century, the young and people of colour. First Nations knew that cannibalism was something to be resisted, but that resistance was not always possible. 'As Sidney Castel, a [twentieth-century] Cree of Northwestern Manitoba succinctly phrased this,

"Never mind if you put good food out for it. It [Windigo] won't touch it. That's not what it's hungry for." You, the hungry one, will become Windigo and eat human flesh.'[2]

In Native belief systems non-human spirits exist everywhere: in material form, such as plants, animals and landscape, and in immaterial forms such as Windigo. These beings provide a way in which hunters can engage with and to the necessary extent control the world around them; they include beings to be hunted – caribou and moose – and beings to be grown – such as maize – and beings which may ensure sufficient water. They are also about practice, about the way in which rituals, part of rather than separate from everyday life, were and are enacted to rescue people in danger of becoming possessed by evil spirits. Generally rituals of belief reinforce and reassure; they ensure that animals allow themselves to be hunted, or that clouds and rain appear at the right time to ensure the growth of maize. Windigo has also been used as an apt metaphor for the rapacious consumption of western culture by Jack D. Forbes (1934–2011).[3] More generally Native religion is about the practice of beliefs, about the existence and prevalence of beings – some human and some non-human – and the use of materials and made objects as symbolic repositories of these beliefs, the latter regularly categorized as art. To label these phenomena simply as religious would be to distort and inhibit understanding of the underlying ideas of hunting and farming, and of kin and relationships, even as they involve ritual and belief.

The account here concerns overarching themes, with additional accounts included in the second half of the book in the area chapters. Much is omitted. So not mentioned are the winter Zuni Shalako ceremonies, which occur after the harvest scheduled by the Bow Priests, or the Sun Dance on the Plains, offered individually traditionally for renewal in advance of the buffalo hunt. Both these are now usually closed to outsiders. Unique but also with some similarities are the World Renewal Ceremonies, including the Jump Dance, White Deerskin and Acorn Feast, in northwest California. There, the world having been created by pre-human immortals, the ceremonies are performed on hallowed ground of the ancients.

Religion

Of all the imposed portmanteau categories which situate Native North America in a European-American world, 'religion' is perhaps that most open to abuse. It can, of course, be descriptive and analytic as a term, but is more problematical when appropriated by new age believers and misunderstood, maligned and romanticized. Native religion is also highly politicized, popularized imagery serving ambiguously within Native communities as a means of identity and ensuring that, to a certain degree, academic authority lies in an objectified, detached reality outside the community. Consequently in the middle ground, sitting between popular culture and its situation-specific, irony-inflected usage by Indian people, lies a long string of ideas, both overworked and often under-considered. These include: Trickster, Coyote, Great Spirit, ideas of the Turtle World, Mother Earth,[4] Happy Hunting Grounds and so on. Instead, Native religion is best understood as concerning belief systems and world views that surround and derive from other beings – non-human beings – which determine what happens, not in defiance of practice, but alongside and interacting with everyday life. Fundamental to this view of religion is that it is social and communitarian, specific to all that happens and to the ceremonies which Indian people may view as an aspect of the everyday instead of something distinct. Underlying this, and all of the numerous differing belief systems in Native North America, is also the idea of the sanctity of kinship: relatedness between people, and between people and non-human beings, is fundamental to existence. So seemingly individualistic occasions, such as the vision question to obtain a helper spirit, or the sweat lodge, or the memorial speeches made at potlatches or powwows, are all socially embedded. They occur alongside rituals of purification with corn pollen, tobacco, bird down, sweet grass and cedar bark.

This means that all activities have a fundamentally religious aspect, whether it is to do with hunting seals, buffalo or whales, collecting eagle feathers, stripping cedar bark for clothing or digging spruce roots for basketry. Belief systems explain why things go wrong when taboos are broken, as in the Arctic when mixing land and sea activities, or for the Cherokee in the nineteenth century, when youth guarding maize fields might engage in sexual experimentation and so, in polluting the corn, cause smallpox epidemics. For Plains people, ideas of buffalo as a sacral presence in all aspects of life were and are embedded in the association of women and buffalo with fertility, the magical qualities of white buffalo, the sacrifice of the body and the self, at the Sun Dance in rituals of self-mortification with buffalo crania, and literature, prayer and worship. Misuse of religion and misunderstanding, especially around conservation, today is especially associated with animal beings. Yet whether animals are killed for health reasons, to stop the spread of disease, or protected for the conservation of the species is irrelevant to original Native beliefs, which stress the interdependence of buffalos and humans, not domination of buffalos by humans. Controversy especially surrounds the culling of the Yellowstone buffalo herd, the last free-roaming herd in the USA, which may be seen as causing ecological devastation, because buffalo being at one with the land protect the environment. Instead, with the now disproved idea of preventing the spread of brucellosis beyond the park, buffalo are killed annually to protect ranch cattle.[5] In contrast the many thousands of wood bison in Alberta and northern Canada do not generate controversy, though the municipality of Wood Buffalo, it should be noted, is where the polluting tar sands are situated.[6] And while whaling is an accepted part of Inupiat life in northwest Alaska, it is prohibited for the Makah in Washington State, where the right to hunt whales is recognized, but permission to hunt is withheld, even though there is a population of at least 15,000 whales in the eastern Pacific.[7]

Shamans

Against the preponderance of Native North American ideas taken up by the dominant societies to help the understanding of others sits the Siberian concept of shaman. Entering North America through Alaska, shamanism is the major conceptual contribution of Russian America, and of Siberia, to contemporary culture. The term 'shaman' comes from the Evenki (formerly Tungus) term. It originated in the Siberian/Chinese borderlands, a land of reindeer herders, as the term for a religious practitioner or priest and entered English via Russian travel literature in the seventeenth and eighteenth centuries, and then from the Russian after the purchase of Russian America in 1867, where it was applied to Tlingit beliefs.[8] Thereafter, within twenty years, it was in use in the literature for the Cherokee and the Navajo, and for Inuit. In describing Native American religion 'shaman' sits with 'medicine man' over the older biblical term 'sorcerer' (with today a retained sense of witchery and evil), a process of changing terminology which both authenticates ideas of aboriginal beliefs and exoticizes them. 'Medicine man' seems to come from the seventeenth-century French Jesuit descriptions of New France,[9] and thence into English by the end of the eighteenth century, and provides a more colloquial idea of the religious leader, still preferred in much of North America. 'Doctor' is also used. Neo-shamanism, that is, the use of individual spirituality to achieve self-realization, sits uneasily both with Native American religion and new age movements. As an authentic religious idea, contemporary shamanism requires the rapid simplification of recorded received practice into rituals, without language and culture, a symptom of ennui or anomie for the disassociated. These might, for instance, derive from the Sun Dance, but their main feature is the almost complete cultural decontextualization, that is, the practitioner and the claimed messages sit outside any lived context – a matter of preaching holistic behaviour by people who have never hunted or listened to reindeer herders. For the purposes of the discussion here, 'shaman' is used in reference to the northern and northwestern part of the continent, and 'medicine man' elsewhere.

New Age Movements

'Modern man' has for a long time, to paraphrase Jung, been 'in search of a soul'.[10] Jung visited Taos in the 1920s. But in the 1990s activists and academics began to write about and campaign against new age spiritualists who had been adopting Native North American practices since the 1970s, designating this as a form of cultural imperialism. 'Plastic shaman' is the pejorative colloquialism that arose at that time for what are often commercialized activities.[11] The new age movement draws on a creative, derivative soup, a mishmash of ill-digested ideas, many taken from eastern mysticism, combined with ideas about crystals, the self, dream catchers and sweat lodges. Websites such as New Age Frauds[12] and Plastic Shamans out fraudsters, and Philip J. Deloria wrote about these people in his book *Playing Indian* (1998).

One of the most established new age teachers is Lynn Andrews, who has written numerous books and has an elaborate website offering courses to PhD level, using a smoothed narrative incorporating multiple Native American ideas in a four-year course. Each year is a 'Lodge', and the first year is 'Lodge of the Winds', with references to mother earth, heartline spiral, beauty kachina and so on. Her course is based in Sedona, Arizona, an important centre of new age spirituality. Sedona is also where a major tragedy took place in 2009, when three participants died during a retreat at Angel Valley. Angel Valley's website is explicit:

> Angel Valley is . . . a bridge to a new reality to a 5th Dimensional Consciousness, to a state of remembering and knowingness, to a world of love and synchronicity, where our inner child can experience the magic of our imagination.[13]

The deadly occasion at Angel Valley was a Spiritual Warrior weekend, attended by fifty-six people at $10,000 a head, organized by James Arthur Ray, author of *Harmonic Wealth* (2008). It included a sweat lodge, designated a 'hellacious' event, where participants were ordered to ignore distress signs. The three who died were not elderly males with heart conditions, but in their thirties and forties. Ray was sentenced to twenty months in prison for negligent homicide in 2011,[14] lost his millions and was interviewed by Piers Morgan on CNN on release in 2013 as a celebrity with something to explain.[15]

Twentieth-century Shamanism

The development of Inuit syllabics in the 1890s for the production of bibles and hymnals permitted the wide distribution of Anglican missionary materials through the early twentieth century, through the new fur trade posts, annual trading voyages and visits by the Canadian North West Mounted Police. In Nunavut, however, the recording of shamanic activity and the appearance of Inuit prophets continued well into the twentieth century. In the eastern Arctic in the early part of the century some twenty such movements have been identified. These were led by a male camp leader, an *isumataq* or 'one who thinks'. The leader might also be a shaman, someone who, for instance, by identifying how a food taboo might have been broken, would be able to deal with problems as they occurred and with spirits. One of the most important and well-documented movements arose in the Igloolik area between Baffin Island and Melville Peninsula during the early 1920s. Anglican bibles and hymn books were in circulation, but there were no missionaries present. In 1920 a shaman, Umik, and his son Nuqallaq killed a trader, Robert Janes (called Sakirmia), north of Mittimatalik (Pond Inlet).[16] Father and son moved south and in the winter of 1921–2 rapidly converted thirty-five families around Igloo-lik. Thirkel Mathiassen (1892–1967), a member of the Danish Fifth Thule expedition, described Umik's status as a prophet in some detail just a few years later. People travelled with a white flag on their sled or *komatik* and lined up to sing a hymn to greet anyone coming into the camp; everyone would shake the visitors' hands three times. Inside the snow house was a crucifix which Mathiassen tried to buy, but was told he could not because it was a powerful amulet. Other features of the cult included the appearance of new spirits, for instance at the seal breathing hole, *aglu*, a portal to the world of animal spirits. The Bible had arrived only a few years earlier.

Christianity in Greenland

This pattern in the Arctic, of leaders and shamans turning into proph-ets and then converting to Christianity, is an old one, extending back to the middle of the eighteenth century in Greenland. Greenland had been Christian, under the Norse medieval settlement, before the arrival of the modern Thule Inuit in the fifteenth century and the dis-appearance of the Scandinavian settlements. Indeed at one time the late medieval archdiocese of Nidaros/Trondheim included the Isle of Man, the Orkneys, the Shetlands, Iceland, Norway and Greenland. In the early eighteenth century, Danish/Norwegian and German mis-sionaries combined trading and proselytizing in what is now west Greenland. Mass conversion occurred, along with revival movements led by shamans, as Inuit moved towards the trading settlements around what is now the Greenland capital Nuuk. The appearance of prophets occurred after the arrival of Christianity and before conversions. One of the best-documented leaders of the period is that of an Inuk called Imaneq (c.1710–70), who came from south Greenland and lived north at Pisugfik ('the place where you pass' – from island to island), a settlement 50 miles from Nuuk, in the period 1768–70. He had a dream, saw Jesus and was told to give up his old ways. In the 1770 account of David Crantz:

> An old angàkoq, familiar to us, by name Immenek, who for many years had heard the gospel here and by our Greenlandic helpers, has changed his mind . . . he sent to us his stepson and three men of his housemates to ask for some Brethren to come to Pisugfik to read the Gospel.[17]

When a close female relative became ill, maybe his wife, and he was unable to heal her, he acquired a simple and childish temper, so that account goes, and converted to Christianity, taking the name Melchior. Following his failure as a shaman, he took the opportunity of leading in the conversion of his community, thirty-eight strong. In the nineteenth century stories of Imaneq were recorded, and watercolours of him created by Aron of Kangeq.[18] Today Greenland has an integrated Lutheran church, and the bishop of Greenland is Sofie Petersen, from Sisimuit, a large industrial community known for fishing and aluminium, appointed in 1995. But this Christianity lives with and by a non-Christian understanding of an animate world.

Tlingit shamans

The Russian use of 'shaman' transferred into English in the first two-thirds of the nineteenth century in reference to Tlingit practices in southeast Alaska. At this time Tlingit shamans were powerful individuals, often leaders in their own community, one in each village and clan. The shaman's powers were wide-ranging: ensuring a supply of animals to hunt, the occurrence of salmon runs and good weather, finding missing persons; they would also have medical knowledge. The shaman would provide amulets to help and protect people and deal with the consequences of spirit possession by land otters (river otters rather the larger sea otters, ambiguous, hugely powerful creature of land and water). Alongside these would be other animal helpers, such as crane and octopus. While these were not related to the moiety and family crests carved on regalia and totem poles, understood within clans, they would sit alongside other abstract and mythic creatures. Shamanic authority was passed on after death from one individual to another. At the burial of the deceased with his regalia irresistible spirit possession would occur and once suggested would require the novitiate to prepare himself by fasting, living in the forest and seeking spirit helpers. An animal, falling dead at his feet, would furnish the shaman with a slice from the tongue, and other parts to provide amulets, held together in a bag.

Medicine

Tlingit shamanism also involved medical knowledge of protection and curing. A large spiny plant, Devil's Club (*Oplopanax horridus*), related to gingseng, was hung in houses to ward off evil.[19] The three main smallpox epidemics between 1775 and 1862 were explained as 'disease spirits' riding in canoes and taking the spirits of the dead with them from village to village; again Devil's Club would be placed round doors and windows to keep away the disease. Devil's Club provides a good example of the apparently efficacious use of an important botanical resource in shamanic practice and elsewhere: it helped to deal with TB, diabetes and rheumatism and aided shamans to achieve a trance-like state, as a result of the plant's hypoglycemic properties. In use as an analagesic through to the end of the twentieth century, and no doubt beyond, Devil's Club was employed by dozens of different peoples in the Pacific northwest. In 1981 Annie York, from Spuzzum in the interior of British Columbia, kept short lengths of dried stick to use as an infusion to prevent weight loss and relieve flu.[20] More recently, after full scientific analysis it was reported that: 'traditional uses of O. *horridus* have been supported by the identification of compounds in the plant that have biological activities that are consistent with ethnobotanical uses of this species. This is another confirmation of the value of ethnobotanical knowledge.'[21] Or, to put it another way, the 'being' in Devil's Club, no less than the being in that all-important yellow cedar bark used on the Pacific Northwest Coast for clothing, has a sacred reality which transcends the simple label of religion.

Inuit Shamans

In contrast, in the eastern Arctic the Inuit shaman, *angakoq*, used little or no paraphernalia or medicine. Drumming and singing enabled the usually male shaman to enter a trance and to sort out problems relating to the lack of animals for hunting – by determining, for instance, which taboo had been broken, such as preparing land animals on sea ice, and how this might be rectified to have the animals return. Nineteenth- and twentieth-century records of eastern Arctic shamanism were obtained by a wide range of people in limited circumstances; the New England whaler George Comer (1858–1937) famously obtained photographs of a shaman going about his business in a snow house. Knud Rasmussen (1879–1933), the part-Greenlandic Danish eskimologist, described Inuit belief systems and practices with the formulations of intellectual and spiritual cultures. These elegant ideas can be applied to Inuit belief systems in the contemporary world from which practising shamans have disappeared. What thrives today in Nunavut and Nunavik are the fundamental elements of shamanic traditions embedded in a broad cosmological framework, crossed with Christian beliefs that both are antithetical to shamans and to an extent (for instance prayer for the appearance of animals) replace them. Twenty-first-century Inuit practice includes:

> belief in *tarniit* (shades, souls), *tuurngait*, nonhuman beings (such as *ijirait* [caribou-people] and *tuniit* [people who inhabited the land before the Inuit]), the Inuit naming system, the sharing of country food, the need to communicate or confess transgressions or exceptional experiences.[22]

Religious Rights

Native American religion does, of course, exist as an objective fact, ensuring the survival of aboriginal peoples. In particular, it is legally sanctified through the US constitution (1789), and through the Canadian Charter of Rights and Freedoms (1982). These two codes allow and protect the expression and performance of religion in many important respects. The 1st amendment to the US constitution begins: 'Congress shall make no law respecting an establishment of religion or prohibiting the free exercise thereof . . .', and the 14th amendment (1868) ensured that civil rights could not be curtailed or changed by state law. Fundamental to the treatment of Native religion in the USA, however, is the following paradox: for aboriginal people religion is part of the whole of everyday life, and the US constitution insists on a separation of powers, and of religion from the state. Thus fundamentally, whatever the laws say, the US constitution undermines Native American belief and practice, while protecting it objectively, so setting up a process which fragments belief systems while seeming to guard them. In the nineteenth century, with the assumption of assimilation and of racial inferiority, Native religions were subject to specific measures to ensure their disappearance, particularly through missionary activities and the boarding and BIA school systems. Recovery began only in the last third of the twentieth century with the 1968 Indian Civil Rights Act (ICRA), which explicitly wrote into law the constitutional protections for American Indian religion. Further, this ensured, with some restraints, that no tribal government could interfere with religion. This re-establishment was taken further in the 1978 American Indian Religious Freedom Act (AIRFA), which states unequivocally:

> that henceforth it shall be the policy of the United States to protect and preserve for American Indians their inherent right of freedom to believe, express, and exercise [their] traditional religions . . . including but not limited to access to sites, use and possession of sacred objects, and the freedom to worship through ceremonials and traditional rites.[23]

Yet in 1988 in the Supreme Court case Lyng, worshipped lands in northern California were not protected from road building and tree cutting, because those activities did not compel anyone to do anything contrary to their beliefs.[24] In Native America, wilderness is an inhabited land, replete with beliefs and ideas, while for non-Natives wilderness is the objectified part of the landscape, untouched and unaltered and idolized platonically for its essential rather than lived qualities. However, further protection was given in 1993 by the Religious Freedom Restoration Act, which helps protect religion, say on sacred land burdened with laws imposed from outside.

The situation in Canada was, and is, different, but had similar results: the federal constitution of the new state (the British North America Act) gave the new government control over Indian affairs from the start in 1867, and First Nations were governed under the Indian Acts from 1876 onwards. These included the prohibition of ceremonies until the 1951 Indian Act dropped these requirements. It was, however, the new 1982 constitution which, in section 2(a), guaranteed 'freedom of conscience and religion'. The basic difference between Canada and the USA is that in the USA the disestablishment of religion provided a context for the vigorous growth and development of sects, from the *Mayflower* onwards to the religious awakenings in the eighteenth and nineteenth centuries, as recognized by de Tocqueville in the early nineteenth century. The second awakening, for instance, in the early nineteenth century gave rise to extraordinary new sects and religious phenomena alongside traditional churches. These included Native American prophets before and alongside Nat Turner (1810–31), the visionary rebel against slavery in the African-American revolt of 1831, and the eruption of Mormonism in the same decade. In Native terms this occurred in the burned-over districts of western New York, especially with Handsome Lake (c.1735–1815) as a prophetic leader, where there were no unconverted people to be brought into the new forms of ecstatic religion.[25] In contrast, Canada was largely settled by members of churches, and religious effervescence calmed by numerous established Christianities working, often closely, with the state and with provinces and colonial powers. The head of state is the defender of the Church of England. Whereas in the USA diverse and diffuse access to law allows for challenges to the status quo by individuals, Canadian traditions did not allow this freedom.[26] Instead, in the USA disestablishment of religion and the fragmentation of jurisdictions allow for more vigorous legal support for Native advocacy in religious disputes. Whether this means that Canadian First Nations have a different religious life to that of related peoples in the USA, as a consequence, is a moot point.

Religion in Prisons

Late twentieth-century developments in the USA allowed for the reintegration of Native ceremonies into Native American life. Thus the use of eagle feathers or of other protected species by Native Americans is now permitted. Native Americans are allowed to practise religion in prisons and penitentiaries – the word penitentiary in the USA indicating penitence, repentance of sins, thus placing prisons, in a secular society that guarantees freedom of religion, in a religious framework. Prisons and penitentiaries are important loci in which free exercise of constitutional freedoms have been considered in the courts. In 1973–5 Jerry Teterud, of Cree descent, brought actions against the Iowa State Penitentiary claiming that American Indian religious rights were violated by the prohibition of long hair. The Eight Circuit upheld Teterud's appeal because the judge recognized that, while American Indian beliefs were not easily labelled as religious in a normative western sense, they might nevertheless be religious. The court also recognized that Native religion was not exclusive and could be combined with, for instance, Christianity. But another aspect of Native religion in penitentiaries is that Native religion provides a robust set of beliefs and practices of benefit to non-Natives, prison inmates often with divided selves and identities. Anthropologist Hugh Brody made a film in 2005–8, *The Meaning of Life*, in a prison with many Canadian First Nations inmates. This documents the way in which generalized inclusive prayers may help non-Native individuals recover their lives when more conventional activities do not. Inmates thus become real penitents in the medieval sense – but for the modern world, and in Canada as well as in the USA.

Religion and the Law

The legal framework protecting and fostering religion comes out of centuries of persecution of Native American belief systems: prolonged attempts by missionaries, the Department of War, the Department of the Interior, the Department of Indian Affairs, the Bureau of Indian Affairs and other agencies to eradicate religious practice. Many of these arose in response to catastrophic change. The European American and Canadian colonization of the continent produced frequent religious responses to the destruction wrought by war and disease and rapid technological and social change.

As already mentioned, religion, like many other terms such as nature and wilderness, does not exist except as an all-important construct, as a means of protecting and objectifying beliefs and practices that maintain Native life. Part of this involves a view of animals as being non-human persons who must be propitiated and understood, prayed with as much as prayed to in order to ensure that they make themselves available to be hunted. Connected to these beliefs are rituals which uphold these relationships socially: these include the first occasions on which young people take their first animal, or the first salmon of a spring run of fish, or the providing of water to the freshly killed seal. All these rituals speak of the respect required in the animal–human relationship. Among horticulturalists green corn celebrations have similar weight.

This idea of beings extends beyond living creatures to the landscape itself. Mountains, lakes and waters have their own being and spirits, and this is something with which everyone engages intimately. In contrast, behaviour towards animals is that towards non-human persons, rather than the distinct category of 'animals'. In Canada protection of hunting rights are more closely associated with subsistence; but in the USA the use of country food has also been associated with the exercise of religious rights. In an Alaskan case of the 1970s, a Dene/Athapaskan man, Carlos Frank, was prosecuted for taking a female moose for a memorial potlatch, but his right to do this, as a matter of practice, was upheld. The court noted that the 'freedom to believe is protected absolutely' under the First Amendment.[27] Like the belief systems associated with the buffalo, those attached to whaling among the Makah in Washington and the Nuu-chah-nulth in British Columbia are especially strong and in both cases associated with women. Traditional prayers and songs would address the hunted whale off Vancouver Island, while the chief's wife would stay still at home, personifying the hunted creature.

Totemism

Relationships with kin also extend to the immaterial. A vital concept is that of totemism, from the Anishinaabe *ododem*, meaning family or relation, which enables people to create relationships with non-human people. This might be for the purpose of symbolic distinctions between clans and families, in order, for instance, to identify whom one might or might not marry. First described by fur traders and explorers around the Great Lakes, and fully formulated by the Native preacher Peter Jones in the middle of the nineteenth century in relation to clans, the concept was given a wider definition in the late nineteenth and early twentieth centuries by the anthropologists Alexander Golden-weiser and Franz Boas. Boas noted that the 'clan totem has developed from the individual manitou (spirit) by extension over a kinship group'.[28] For instance, he described the way in which personal spirits encountered by individuals would become the family clan or lineage symbol. Claude Lévi-Strauss used totemism to argue that there are fundamental structural ideas underlying the social world, which oper-ate to separate and articulate culture and nature. Earlier, Emile Durkheim had used ideas of totemism, transferred to Australia, to explain the origins of religious life in group identity. Few Native American ideas have been as influential in helping us to understand belief systems and deep structures of thought and practice.[29] These ideas of totemism then seeped into understandings of other cultures, just as the Polynesian idea of 'taboo' became both an analytic and a generic folk term in Native North America as elsewhere.

Education, Christianity and Indian People

Religion and education were central features of New France and New England from the earliest colonization. In Quebec the early seminar-ies were not successful. These were the responsibility of Father Charles Lalement (1587–1674). Unlike the schools set up in Japan during in the previous century, they did not replace existing educational institu-tions, did not seek to convert the parents of converts, did not teach practical skills, were expensive and found difficulties in recruiting pupils.[30] In seventeenth-century New England, where the goal of missionaries was to 'reduce' Indians to 'civility',[31] similar difficulties arose. Indian education in Christian ways was marked by pious hopes and in the long term almost always moral failure; yet modernizing Indian leaders were most often evangelical Christians who employed in hybrid ways their new religion to further Indian rights. Perhaps most importantly in the seventeenth and eighteenth centuries much of the flow of learning, and its complex of behavioural ethics, went in the opposite direction, from Indian people to New Englanders or, as the historian James Axtell calls them, the New English. While European technology and the horse enabled the conquest not just of Mexico and Peru, but also the Spanish frontiers in the USA, something rather different happened in North America. The establishment and survival of the English colonists and French *voyageurs* depended on the more general flow of educational knowledge from Algonquian- and Iroquoian-speakers to the newcomers. In New England the early tales are of the Abenaki Samoset (c.1590–1653), the Wampanoag Massasoit (c.1581–1661) and the Patuxet Squanto (1585–1622) helping the incomers with information about maize and about hunting. An early description of Native help and education indicates the extent and sophistication of the horticultural tuition – although, alas, it leaves off any account of the spirituality that was a necessary component to the life of the successful Native farmer. The Indians were, wrote William Wood in 1634,

> our first instructers for the planting of their Indian Corne, by teaching us to cull out the finest seede, to observe the fittest season, to keepe distance for holes, and fit measure for hills, to worme it, and weede it; to prune it, and dresse it as occasion shall require.[32]

Further, it was only by adopting Indian technology – the snow shoe and the moccasin – and Indian techniques in warfare, especially skulking rather than marching through the wilderness, that the English survived through the seventeenth century. The fur trade and much of the exploration of the North American continent were predicated on Native North American knowledge and practice shorn of beliefs.

Captives

The predilection of Europeans for Indian ideas went beyond the co-opting of knowledge. Most remarkable of all is that, when captured on the northern frontier of what was to become Maine, for instance, the English preferred the Indian way of living, something recognized long before Linda Colley's book *Captives* (2002) highlighted it. Benjamin Franklin, for one, was quite clear about this, writing in 1753:

> when white persons of either sex have been taken prisoners young by the Indians, and lived a while among them, tho' ransomed by their Friends, and treated with all imaginable tenderness to prevail with them to stay among the English, yet in a Short time they become disgusted with our manner of life, and the care and pains that are necessary to support it, and take the first good Opportunity of escaping again into the Woods, from whence there is no reclaiming them.[33]

Slightly later, the French aristocrat turned frontiersman J. Hector St John de Crèvecoeur (1735–1813), author of the first American bestseller, *Letters from an American Farmer* (1782), and the writer who asked first 'What is an American?', spoke of thousands of white people who had become Indians, when no Indians had become Europeans. [34]

Missionaries

Morally speaking, then, Europeans tended to prefer to become Indians, rather than vice versa. Yet the important educational efforts to Christianize Indians in the seventeenth and eighteenth centuries cannot be dismissed simply as failures; more realistically, they were partially successful, in providing limited circumstances for the exercise of Native leadership and for the intermingling of traditions in the 'Praying Towns' of New England, Kahnawake in New France/Quebec and other communities.

Fourteen 'Praying Towns', autonomous villages for Algonquian-speaking Christians, were created by John Eliot (1604–90).[35] Eliot had translated the Bible into Massachusett (1661, 1663) and created a grammar. He preached in the home of Waban, an early convert who later warned of the difficulties with the Wampanoag but was nevertheless accused of being a traitor and locked up in the 1670s. The Praying Towns were not as successful as hoped. Praying Indians were distrusted and treated as second-class citizens. John Sassamon (c.1600–1674), who had attended Harvard briefly in the 1650s, symbolized the fraught relationship between colonist and Christian Native, caught between the two worlds; his death, by murder or accident, precipitated events leading to King Philip's War in 1675–8.[36] In this the Praying Towns were destroyed. The people of the most important town, Natick, fled to Boston, where they were imprisoned; many died, and the community did not recover.

Eliot was Overseer at Harvard (1642–85), where a building for an Indian College was created in the 1650s. While rather few Indians were educated at Harvard, the Indian College was used for the printing of the Massachusett materials. Harvard's failure to educate more than a few Indians, due in part to early deaths from disease of students, was replicated a century later at Dartmouth, founded in the 1760s with funds raised in part by Samson Occom in Britain. Yet in important ways Christian Indians both preserved a degree of Native beliefs to serve alongside imported English superstitions and were able to act as literate advocates in Indian affairs. Other eighteenth-century missionary communities, at Stockbridge, for the Mahican and Mohawk, and Occom's own Brotherton, for Pequot and Mohegan, were relocated west to Wisconsin during the time of removal. Significantly, then, on important occasions Native Americans sought later and worked with missionaries – other examples include the visit to Queen Anne in 1710 of four Native New Yorkers applying for assistance and, later the services of Samuel Kirkland (1741–1808), Presbyterian, among the Senecas and Oneidas, Asher Wright (1803–75) among the Senecas, and Cyrus Byington (1793–1868) among the Choctaws.

Algonquian Missionaries

Immediately after Independence and the separation of church and state in the USA, while Indian people recognized the importance of speaking English, few innovations or initiatives were made either by missionaries, other than Quakers, or by the federal government until the War of 1812. The Quaker Thomas McKenney (1785–1859), early in his life as a controversial Indian reformer and scholar, was superintendent of Indian trade from 1816 and an advocate for the Indian Civilization Act (1819), which provided $10,000 for education. McKenney then became the first superintendent of Indian affairs in 1824 and an initial promoter of the Indian Removal Act (1830).[37] A small number of highly influential Methodist Native ministers in the USA and Canada were writers and advocates during the first half of the nineteenth century. William Apess (1798–1839) published the first Native autobiography, *Son of the Forest* (1829), and like Occom before him campaigned for Indian lands rights, falling foul of Anglo-America. Apess organized the Mashpee revolt of 1833, which resulted in the return of rights to the Indians, such as that of electing their own selectmen and state recognition of Mashpee as a district.[38] Kahkewaquonaby or Peter Jones (1802–56) was a translator, his *Life* (1860) and *History of the Ojebway Indians* (1861) being published posthumously.[39] Kahgegagahbowh or George Copway (1818–69) (Ontario Anishinaabe/Ojibwe/Mississauga), a Methodist missionary, the first Canadian First Nations writer to publish his autobiography (*The Life, History, and Travels of Kah-ge-ga-gah-bowh, (George Copway) a Young Indian Chief of the Ojebwa Nation* (1847) and *Sketches of the Ojibway Nation* (1850)), used Christianity to condemn injustice against Native North Americans and advocate the importance of a homeland for Indians. He was later to become a recruiter for Union forces in the Civil War and eventually a Catholic missionary to the Mohawk.[40] While meagre government subsidies for Indian education were provided federally for and by missionary societies before the Civil War, occasional missionaries such as Bishop Henry Whipple (1822–1901) acted as effective advocates. The Episcopalian Whipple campaigned for better reservations and for leniency after the Dakota uprising of 1862, which he fully blamed on the USA, and in other causes.[41]

Boarding and Residential Schools

In the aftermath of the Civil War, and in the context of the final two decades of Indian wars, separate systems of Christian education were instituted by educators of military background. Most influential was Richard Henry Pratt (1840–1924),[42] who took part in Indian wars in the

1860s and identified a need to educate and assimilate Indians rather than simply destroy them. In the 1870s he began a programme at Fort Marion/St Augustine, Florida, to convert and educate male prisoners under military discipline and organized the transfer of pupils to the Hampton Normal and Agricultural Institute, Virginia. This had been founded in 1868 by General Samuel Armstrong (1839–93)[43] for the moral and practical education of former slaves and from 1878 took Indians too. Pratt founded the Carlisle Indian Industrial School the following year on the principles of equality and assimilation; he cut students' hair and soon prohibited the speaking of Native languages. Progressive leaders, such as American Horse, advocated the sending of children to Carlisle, and the school developed a high reputation, with significant achievements, especially in sports, at the beginning of the twentieth century: notably at baseball and with the success of the athlete Jim Thorpe. By that time seemingly localized rather than national boarding schools had been established, such as Chemawa Indian School (from 1880) in Oregon, Sherman Indian High School (from 1892) in Riverside, and Carlisle, further reduced by Indian recruitment in the army, closed in 1918.

Indian boarding schools in the USA continued to grow in importance until the 1970s – for instance, Mount Edgecumbe High School opened in Alaska in 1947. These schools were both highly effective at creating a bicultural elite and deeply destructive of the basic tenets of Indian culture. Further, boarding schools contributed, through close living conditions, to the spread of disease, for example TB. In Canada, as in the USA, education and assimilation were enforced from 1884 with compulsory schooling, following the advocacy of lawyer and journalist Nicholas Flood Davin (1840–1901). Residential schools represented a highly destructive means both of assimilation, with a strong Christian component, and of eradicating Indian culture. In many ways these schools were catastrophic. Some thousands of pupils died while being educated; many more were abused; this is now the subject of the Indian Residential Schools Truth and Reconciliation Commission, set up in 2008, under which compensation is payable to former pupils.[44] In Canada recent First Nations leaders such as National Chief Phil Fontaine (1997–2009) survived residential schools and achieved important redress, in Fontaine's case including an audience with Pope Benedict XVI in 2009. While the residential school system has disappeared in Canada, the boarding school system survives on a small but significant scale in the USA. Sexual abuse occurred in all denominations, even the Eastern church, which was and is well accepted in Alaska. Among the Tlingit, converted in the nineteenth century to Russian orthodoxy, ritual to do with memorial and mourning gradually gained ground across cultures towards Tlingit practice. This was described in the late twentieth century in this way: 'We added the Orthodox ceremony to our old ways of comforting each other. We made the two cultures work for us.'[45]

Black Elk and Seattle

Other hybridizations of belief systems occurred elsewhere. Two exceptional texts provide insights not only into the beliefs and practices of the leaders whose speeches and words were written down, edited and published, but also into the process of mythopoeic, cross-cultural elaboration and hybridization which has sometimes taken place. One is *Black Elk Speaks* (1932), the words of a Lakota medicine man caught in the processes which ended buffalo hunting in the period of missionaries and war. He finished up, and is remembered in the community, as a zealous Catholic catechist. Black Elk's speeches were taken down, very indirectly, by John G. Neihardt (1881–1973), a Nebraskan mystical poet, who as a teenager had published *The Divine Enchantment* (1900), a narrative poem about Vishnu, Krishna and Nirvana. In the words of W. K. Power, Black Elk's teachings, refined by the removal of excess and a simplified context, 'created the perfect noble Indian of the past, a full-blown psychic and seer, one who lived up to the image and romantic expectations of most white people and a few non-whites', no less real for having been adapted in this way.[46]

The other is text is the speech of Chief Seattle, Sealth (1786?–1866) (Duwamish), spoken to Governor Stevens in the 1850s, which includes a prayer-like admonition seemingly celebrating the integration of religion, of Natives and non-Natives, but actually profoundly pessimistic.[47] This runs:

> Tribe follows tribe, and nation follows nation, like the waves of the sea.
> It is the order of nature and regret is useless. Your time of decay may

be distant, but it will surely come, for even the white man whose god walked and talked with him as friend with friend cannot be exempt from a common destiny. We may be brothers after all. We will see.

Yet the whole construct relies on late recording, translation and heavy intervention, over more than a century, with speculative bumper sticker additions made, for instance by scriptwriter Ted Parry in 1972: 'How can we buy or sell the sky?'[48]

Animism and Landscape

Seattle's speech was made in awe of the natural world, particularly the waters, the mountains and the trees, and of the beings which inhabit those inanimate features in the animate world. This now problematic idea of personhood in objects and animals was recognized long ago by early travellers and by proto-anthropologists in the nineteenth century. E. B. Tylor, the Oxford anthropologist, boldly imported it into his *Primitive Culture*: 'I propose here, under the name of Animism, to investigate the deep-lying doctrine of Spiritual Beings, which embodies the very essence of Spiritualistic as opposed to Materialistic philosophy.'[49]

The idea of animism is found in the vitalist theories of the Enlightenment scientist Georg Ernst Stahl (1659–1734), but it is now predominantly associated with the idea that only some beings are human. But in a real sense in Native North America being, knowledge and the material merge. While the more abstract idea of 'being' works much better than 'animism' in understanding the crossover between humans and other persons, 'animism' provides a more rounded term. In this sense there is today both an old animism and a revitalized one, which perhaps took hold with Irving Hallowell's work with Anishinaabe in the mid-twentieth century.[50]

Animate Landscape

The Black Hills of South Dakota and Wyoming are a mythical landscape for the immediate Native inhabitants, the Lakota and the Cheyenne. This mythical quality would likely have been articulated in analogous if not similar belief systems from the very first occupation thousands of years ago. The Lakota artist Amos Bad Heart Bull (c.1868–1913) drew a map of the Black Hills at the turn of the twentieth century. Clearly shown are Bear Lodge Butte/Devils Tower and a large geographical feature called the Race Track.[51] More generally Black Elk and others left a copious oral history associating the Black Hills with stories of Fallen Star, the culture hero whose villages are both in the heavens and in the hills. That the Lakota may not have occupied the Back Hills for more than a century or two, from the late eighteenth century, is irrelevant to the belief-rich landscape as understood by the Lakota up to the end of their occupation in the late nineteenth century. Most importantly, the Black Hills were firmly included in the Great Sioux reservation of 1868, illegally terminated, and still in dispute because of the non-acceptance of the monetary compensation offered in recompense for so much sacred territory.

Devils Tower

Devils Tower in the Black Hills neatly illuminates the conflict of Lakota beliefs and the non-Native construction of the landscape. This natural monument is associated with the Summer Equinox, Sun Dance and Monster Bear in Lakota belief. First ascended by non-Natives in 1893, it became the first US National Monument in 1906 and today is climbed by 4,000 visitors a year. Agreement was reached in 1995 that climbers would be asked not to climb the Tower during June, at the time of the Sun Dance, and the National Park Service says that 85 per cent of climbers respect this self-imposed regulation, which is voluntary, due to the separation of state and religion. In earlier mythology, that of the Kiowa, Devils Tower is called Tree Rock and is associated with the story of children pursued by a bear who find shelter on a tree which raises them up to safety.

Two other monuments also illustrate the divided use of sacred sites. Mount Rushmore, with carvings of four presidential heads, implicitly celebrating the idea of Manifest Destiny, was conceived by the Ku Klux Klan member and Mormon artist Gutzon Borglum (1867–1941) and created between 1928 and 1941 on a sacred trail. Also in the Black Hills, and in a sense more egregious and seemingly offensive in its import, is the carving of Crazy Horse (d. 1877) by one of the Mount Rushmore carvers, Korczak Ziolkowski (1908–82), made to celebrate the Lakota spiritual leader who refused to be depicted in photography in his lifetime. While the monument has generated funding for Native American projects, it remains unaccepted by at least some of Crazy Horse's descendants. In 2003 one of these, Elaine Quiver, said that in Lakota culture consensus is required for an undertaking of this kind and that the sculptor did not ask permission before starting carving on the mountain with dynamite in 1948. Of the project team she said:

> They don't respect our culture because we didn't give permission for someone to carve the sacred Black Hills where our burial grounds are . . . They were there for us to enjoy and they were there for us to pray. But it wasn't meant to be carved into images, which is very wrong for all of us.[52]

Others are reconciled to the sculpture as akin to the Easter Island figures (*moaia*), but of course the point about those deities is that many were overturned when they failed the Polynesian inhabitants of Rapanui, while others were incorporated in the succeeding Bird Man religion, a celebration of the first spring harvester of bird's eggs.

Apache Mountain Spirits

While among the Lakota and Kiowa and others the spiritual life of the landscape, and the sacred nature of sites, can be understood most simply in reference to oral history, among one group of peoples – the Apache – mountain spirits (*gaan*) are danced in masked performances. They are maintained as sacred beings and yet at the same time employed in projecting Apache identity and nationhood. Accepted by the Apache, the anthropologist Greenville Goodwin (1908–40) had this to say of *gaan*: 'They are a people who resided on earth long ago, but departed hence in search of eternal life and now live in certain mountains, places below the ground, as well as living and traveling in clouds and water.'[53] These beings, and many others, control everyone's life, and to them is due appropriate respect and observance, which, if rendered appropriately, will result in wellbeing. In 2007 the National

Museum of the American Indian returned thirty-eight sacred objects to the Apache to be restored to the mountains, including masks, which travelled in cases with holes in so they could breathe.[54] That a complex of beliefs should have become essentialized and objectified as an identity marker is to render it neither inauthentic nor insincere.

Apache Mountains

Apache dancers who summon the spirits have other roles. On their current reservation the Mescalero Apache have their own casino, Inn of the Mountain Gods, which features *gaan* dancers as the central emblem on their logo, and *gaan* dancer sculptures. This is hundreds of miles east of their nineteenth-century territory in southeast Arizona, alongside the Pinaleño Mountains and adjacent to the White Mountain Apache. The Trinity Test site, where the first nuclear test bomb was detonated in 1945, is near to the sacred Oscura Mountain Peak.

The Pinaleño Mountains, in Western Apache territory, were the subject of a prolonged battle in the 1980s and 1990s about the use of sacred peaks for the placement of telescopes by the Smithsonian Institution, the University of Arizona and European partners. All were attracted by the height of the peaks and the clear sky. The Indian Claims Commission recognized Mount Graham, originally part of the White Mountain reserve, as part of the original homeland, although removed from the reservation in 1873. The arguments as to whether the telescopes should be built rested on a number of issues: the extent to which the Western Apache, including the White Mountain Apache, were agriculturalists, and so not involved with mountain spirits; the length of time they had lived in southeast Arizona; and the seeming absence of archaeological remains – entirely normal for a semi-nomadic people without major settlements. In order to obtain permission to build the telescopes environmental impact laws were amended, and advocates provided selective views of the importance of the mountains to the Western Apache. One of these advocates, the late Charles Polzer, a Jesuit ethno-historian and curator, was reduced to describing in the *Frankfurter Rundschau* the opposition to the telescopes as being part of a 'Jewish conspiracy', unfortunate in that German institutions are involved in constructing and using the facility.[55] As so often Native advocacy is associated with environmental concerns of the wider community. In the case of Mount Graham, these issues are a threatened squirrel subspecies, and the removal of first-growth trees. While the struggle relating to Mount Graham was about religion, other analogous instances of struggles which could be couched in spiritual terms instead rely on the broader compass of cultural survival. In the 1980s, during the last phase of the Cold War, the Labrador air base at Goose Bay, a suitable sparsely inhabited region where few people would be affected, was made available to NATO for training,. However, the Innu and their primary subsistence and cultural mainstay the caribou were threatened, particularly by the many thousands of often low-level sorties each year, which adversely affected caribou reproduction.[56] The abuse of the sacral quality of landscape is the most important issue in Native North American religion.

Haudenosaunee

Much of what is known about Native American religion should be questioned, yet at the same time protected from obtrusive inquiry. In 1990 the Native American Graves Protection and Repatriation Act (NAGPRA), administered by the National Park Service, was passed: this enabled funerary remains, sacred objects, articles of patrimony, to be returned to the originating community from museums – a major improvement to religious freedom. But it also resulted in the imposition of rigid definitions on supple categories of belief. In some cases a ritual complex, such as that of the False Face Masks – medicine masks – of the Iroquois, was researched and worked on before the sacralization, in the western sense, brought the ceremony new secrecy and retirement from public view, at least in the USA. William Fenton (1908–2005) published his account of these beings in 1987 as one of his last achievements, and perhaps his greatest monograph.[57] False Faces protect against disease and may have assumed their distorted forms in the early contact period as a result of exposure to imported epidemics. In 1937 Fenton summarized the Seneca ritual complex:

> The Faces claimed to possess the power to control sickness. They instructed the dreamers to carve likenesses in the form of masks, saying

that whenever anyone makes ready the feast, invokes their help while burning Indian tobacco and sings the curing songs supernatural power to cure disease will be conferred on humans who wear the masks.[58]

Under NAGPRA many False Faces have been returned to the appropriate longhouses, as required for religious purposes, and yet in Canada False Faces may still be carved and sold to non-First Nations people. Separate from the False Face Society is that of the Bushy Heads, the plaited or braided Corn Husk Masks, which are not considered religious in the same way; they appear in the Midwinter Ceremonies, represent the three sisters as maize, beans and squash and have the ability to make prophesies. While not religious, Corn Husk Masks are expressive of a belief system and practice, as are other important aspects of Iroquois/Haudenosaunee ritualism – especially those to do with the Condolence Ceremony. These involve the use of strings of wampum, shell beads, and wampum woven into belts, creating mnemonic devices; while not sacred as such, they provide the foundation records of the Iroquois Confederacy. It is appropriate, then, to regard both these ceremonies as religious and also everyday, with responsibility for the use and appearance of masks and belts determined by community; and it is correct that this should stand, even if the several peoples are divided and disagree, and even if there is a considered academic view as to their secular nature. Conversely, the Hamatsa Dance, a central ceremony of the Kwakwaka'wakw in British Columbia, was once seen as a secret event, and while performances may be observed by all at potlatches, retains a sacred aspect, spiritual without being religious. The Canadian Museums Association and Assembly of First Nations, without legislation, produced the 1992 *Task Force Report*. With equality, partnership and provision for repatriation, it is non-confrontational and collaborative in providing for a similar process.

Native American Church

Another vexed and important aspect of religious freedom arises in the case of the Oklahoma-founded Native American Church of 1918, [59] originally promoted before his death in 1911 by Comanche chief and modernizing rancher Quanah Parker (c.1845/52–1911). In this syncretic religion drumming, praying and the use of beaded whisk fans of protected macaw feathers are associated with the consumption of peyote button cactus, found in Texas and northern Mexico. This visionary sacrament helps to concentrate the mind, and enables ceremonies to continue for long periods. Persecution of peyote use began in the early twentieth century, as the abuse of other narcotics also came under legislative scrutiny, and prohibition came under federal or state statute. Controversy within the Native community around peyotism led to the disintegration of the Society of American Indians in the early 1920s.[60] Nevertheless the Church survived and prospered, despite regular challenges to the use of this cactus. In one particular case brought against Mary Attakai (Navajo) in Arizona in 1960 a guilty plea was mitigated by lawyers claiming her rights to full protection of religion and the equal right to exercise her religion. Most interestingly, Judge McFate explained with pointed phrases why peyote use was not prohibited, because it was only used for religion or medicine, was not habit forming or a narcotic and was used for worship: 'Its use, in the manner disclosed by the evidence in this case, is in fact entirely consistent with the good morals, health, and spiritual elevation of some 25,000 Indians.' In another case, Woody, 1964, the California Supreme Court pointed out: peyote 'serves as a sacramental symbol similar to bread and wine in certain Christian churches'.[61] Eventually in one of the federal regulations designed to implement the Comprehensive Drug Abuse Prevention and Control Act of 1970 (21 C.ER. 1307.31), the Native American Church was made exempt from prohibition.[62]

Syncretic Religions

Two concepts are employed to describe syncretic religions, such as the Native American Church, which have to some extent been applied elsewhere. What is interesting is that it is Native North American societies which provided the real people or the actual data to encourage anthropologists to formulate theories – theories which found their own limits but which importantly took forward discussions. One concept, now obsolete, is that of nativism, to describe a movement which disdains and rejects the values and behaviour of incoming groups and believes that language and beliefs are innate rather than learned. Originally this might be applied to Native North America, and to movements labelled as involving magic rather than religion; today nativism may be applied, in a twisted sense, to settler societies seeking to limit new entrants into that society. That idea was systematized in the 1940s[63] and replaced in the 1950s by a more influential one. This is the idea of the revitalization movement of Anthony Wallace. He not only brought together worldwide movements with a definitely cross-cultural approach, but placed them in a system of religious innovation, moving from equilibrium to change, and back to equilibrium, that anticipated Stephen Jay Gould's formulation a decade or two later of punctuated equilibrium. Both paradigms involve a model with a stable situation followed by one of turbulence and then perhaps return to equilibrium.

Native Prophets

Wallace's formulation is very ambitious: he enumerates prophets or near prophets across cultures, from his own scholarly interest in the Iroquois:

> the Haudenosaunee: Handsome Lake case (Seneca, 1799–1815), the Delaware Prophet (associated with Pontiac, 1762–65), the Shawnee Prophet (associated with Tecumseh, 1805–13), the Ghost Dance (1888–96), and Peyote; in Europe, John Wesley and early Methodism (1738-1800); in Africa, Akhenaten/Ikhnaton's new religion (in ancient Egypt), the Sudanese Mahdi (the Sudan, 1880–98), and the Xhosa Revival (South Africa, 1856–7), or Simon Kimbangu (c.1890–1950), the Congo prophet who spent the last thirty years of his life in prison; in Asia, the origin of Christianity, the origin of Mohammedanism (c.610–50), the early development of Sikkhism (India, c.1500–c.1700), and the Taiping Rebellion (China, 1843–64); in Melanesia, the Vailala Madness (New Guinea, c.1919–c.1930); in South America, a series of *terre sans mal* movements among the forest peoples, among the Tupi-Guarani, from early contact to recent times.[64]

Today, while Handsome Lake's Longhouse religion survives, the most famous religion of them all, the Ghost Dance, is gone. This was the accomplishment of Wovoka (c.1856–1932) (Northern Paiute), both a well-educated Christian and one capable of controlling the weather, who predicted a solar eclipse in 1889. He also proclaimed that white people would disappear, the Ghost Dance's central tenet that was so alarming to Americans. While of course Wallace's ideas have been subject both to extension and to revision, that of revitalization provides a basic concept. It can be used as a stalking horse, to stimulate and take forward proper discussion of similar but actually highly varied religious movements, and their role as the driving force behind social change, protecting elements of traditionalism at times of maximum stress. In this the idea of a revitalization movement also represents a major contribution of Native North America to intellectual history.

Creek, Seminole, Religion and War

One of the most interesting revitalization movements in Native North America is that of the Creek in the southeast of the USA. It is significant, because they were part of a process that led directly into nineteenth-century wars in the present state of Florida, wars which ultimately failed to subdue the Seminole – descendants of Creek fleeing from Spanish west Florida to the east and south to avoid US incursions. The movement and the prophets are important because the languages, symbols and communications used fit Wallace's paradigms so neatly and they involved magic. To add another dimension, they were entirely integrated with the issue of slavery.

The Creek or Red Stick War (1813–14) and the Seminole Wars (1816–58), seldom bracketed together, combine belief and colonization from the American Revolution onwards. The southern frontier, like the northeast frontier around the Great Lakes, remained a contested area after the American Revolution and the Treaty of Paris of 1783. For much of this time the Creek and the British were allies with the Spanish in Florida; Creek leaders were often descended from Creek women and Scottish trader fathers, behaving as Creek and receiving the benefits due to them in a matrilineal society. In the south, the Creek divided between the Upper Creek in the northern parts of what would become Alabama and the southern Lower Creek, who lived more closely and intermarried with non-Natives. British interference, largely around trade, based in the Bahamas, combined with the

Creek interest in resuming an independent existence, which meant an ambiguous relationship with Spanish west Florida – allied to Britain in the Napoleonic War. Tecumseh (1768–1813), of part Shawnee origin, with his brother Tenkswatawa (1775–1836), organized resistance to America in the Great Lakes region, Indiana and Ohio, fighting eventually for British North America in the War of 1812. Tecumseh encouraged the Upper Creek on the Alabama River system to resist American encroachment, as particularly represented by the more accomodationist Lower Creek, on the Flint-Chattahoochee river system in Georgia. During his visit to the south in 1811, with the prophet Seekaboo, Tecumseh spoke to 5,000 people at Tookaubatchee, urging them to abandon the white man's ways. A new federal wagon road was built about that time from Georgia to the Alabama settlements, encouraging American migration. The Upper Creek, inspired by a series of prophets and known as Red Sticks from their use of red-painted clubs, attacked the Lower Creek- and American-held Fort Mims in the summer of 1813 and massacred most of the several hundred people inside. The attack on Fort Mims was led by another of the prophets, Paddy Welch, and William Weatherford (Red Eagle).

But the most influential prophet of this period was Hidlis Hadjo (in English Crazy Medicine) (c.1770–1818), also known as Josiah Francis, who was much influenced by Seekaboo. Francis claimed magical powers: he could, he said, remain underwater for a prolonged period and fly through the air, skills taught to him by a familiar spirit; in addition people opposed to him died in mysterious circumstances. He created a settlement, Ecunchattee, or Holy Ground, which was protected, he claimed, by an invisible barrier against attack. Like other revitalization movements, the Red Sticks rejected Euro-American ways and the rapid encroachment on Creek land used for cotton plantations. Hidlis Hadjo also claimed to have been able to write; a message opened by the Spanish governor and ally of the Creek contained just scratches, however, and the governor was first angry and then laughed. Following the massacre at Fort Mims, Holy Ground was attacked and destroyed, there being no invisible barrier to protect the Indians against the militia forces sent against them. Consequent on this unsuccessful revitalization movement, Andrew Jackson forced a treaty taking more than 20 million acres from the

Creek. He went on the offensive against the Creek, regarding them all as Seminole, that is rebellious mixed-blood African and Native Americans.[65] Removed alongside the Creeks were both the Cherokee and Choctaw with Pushmataha (c.1760–1824), who had remained loyal to the United States.

Revivalist Movements among Algonquian-speaking Peoples

Of the revivalist movements, the one with the most substantial body of material was the Ojibwe or Anishinaabe Grand Medicine Society, or Midewiwin. This was performed in a Mide lodge, using birch-bark scrolls with engraved pictographic stories. Mide practitioners sought to ensure the wellbeing of the wider Ojibwe, who traditionally occupied much of the country north and west of the Great Lakes into Manitoba and Saskatchewan. Through the society, the intellectual life of the Anishinaabe was passed on down the generations, young men rising by degrees. Analyses of the Midewiwin are, it is suggested, focused on the historic moment when authority of dreams came to be replaced by secular authority, as the fur trade developed and declined, and control of the environment disappeared. Much has been revived in the USA by Edward Benton-Banai (b. 1934), who recorded the story of the earth diver's origin of the world: when a succession of animals sought to recover earth from the floods, the muskrat successfully brought up mud but died in the process, the mud being transferred to a turtle's back to create the world. Nanabozho/Nanabush/Wenabozho, the trickster hero, made and makes the stories available and ensures the passing on of secret knowledge. As the myths of the Anishinaabe remain available, so recovery of the Midewiwin and Anishinaabe identity continues and is maintained.[66] While the Mide society is not, unlike many other movements, associated with specific leaders, other Algonquian movements are. One such is that of the Kickapoo prophet Kenekuk (c.1790–1852), an originally dissolute young man who, on revelation, used prayer sticks with pictographs that recalled both black-letter bibles and rosaries and offered public confession of sins followed by punishment to ensure discipline at a time when the Kickapoo were threatened with dissolution and removal.[67]

Indian Shaker Church

Other prophet movements became official churches, such as the Indian Shaker Church of the Pacific Northwest. Unrelated to the Quaker-derived Shaker movement, this church arose in the 1880s and was incorporated in Olympia, Washington, in 1910. The founder, John Slocum (Squaxin, of the wider Coast Salish people, speaking Lushootseed), died and was reborn in 1882, and when near death again afterwards was revived by his wife, who was shaking and praying. Together they combined elements of Native religion with Catholic and Protestant features. Today the church continues in its mission to heal, in both Canada and the USA. An important element is the individually owned song, important property in tradition ritual. God's presence is contained in the songs that heal. In the words of Patricia Sanchez (Quinault) in the 1980s: 'When you join the Shake, you get your gifts, and . . . you get a song. It don't come to you all at once, but you get your song. And you're known by that song . . . It's yours.'[68]

The Calumet Ritual

The calumet or pipe ritual in eastern North America and the Plains is perhaps the oldest ceremonial complex in North America in continual, albeit much changed, use. The highly decorated ash pipe stems, employed in supplication through bird intermediaries with the world above, may have existed as ritual instruments as far back as the Archaic, when they were also used as throwing sticks (atlatls) and were adorned with bird stones.[69] In the nineteenth and early twentieth centuries, the Hako ceremony of the Pawnee, with highly decorated ash stems, became the type ritual, involving as it did the blessing and ritual incorporation of children into society using calumets and bird symbolism, with highly poetic songs and celebratory music and meaning. In an explanation of a song recorded by Alice Fletcher at the turn of the twentieth century the owl came to one holy man and said, 'Put me upon the feathered stem for I have the power to help the Children. The night season is mine. I wake when others sleep. I can see in the darkness and discern coming danger.'[70] The calumet ceremony, while ancient, also spread rapidly after the dislocation and destruction brought about by European contact and is, for instance, associated with the Eagle Dance among the Haudenosaunee.[71]

Pueblos and Christianity

Pueblo religion and the interaction between Christianity and Native religion among Puebloan (town) peoples of New Mexico, Arizona and the greater southwest followed a different course. This is because, despite an initial relationship between the Spanish and the Pueblos which was as destructive and transformative as elsewhere, what occurred was a degree of resistant integration, compartmentalized amalgamation, with the incorporation of substantive and symbolic elements of Christianity into traditional belief systems, while leaving Indian cultures intact. In other words, syncretization associated with Indian prophets occurred differently in Pueblo society. Each of the several dozen Pueblos in the seventeenth century was – indeed is – a tightly knit society with cross-cutting priestly associations and clan systems, matrilineal and patrilineal. These organizations, highly educated in mythology and religious practice, were – and are – able to ensure the cooperation vital to continuing success in the fertilization and watering of meagre arable lands. Religion is closely associated with agriculture, especially in the western Pueblos, with the sacred nature of enabling rituals, seasonal and calendric, upheld by priesthoods who organize education and initiation. Priests maintain symbolic and practical association with sources of spiritual power, especially the land, water and crops, both in public performances and in secluded ceremonies conducted in the *kiva* (the Hopi chamber) to ensure survival. In the east, Rio Grande Pueblos, with greater access to water, curing societies, for instance involving bear shamanism, are more prominent. The fragility of Puebloan culture is underlined by the collapse of major Puebloan settlements in medieval times and the abandonment of large villages, for example Pueblo Bonito in the twelfth century and Cliff Palace, Mesa Verde, Colorado in the thirteenth. Yet perhaps because of the strength required to maintain communities in arid lands, many Puebloan people incorporated incoming European material culture from the sixteenth century and adopted and adapted Spanish Christianity and so endured more successfully than, for instance, Native hunting communities on the Plains. The significant exception to this is the Hopi, often hostile to modernization in the nineteenth century, like the Seminole. They had, much earlier, been accepting of refugees from the Rio Grande Pueblos after the Pueblo Revolt, whose descendants remain at Hano.

European Colonization of the Pueblos

Missionary activities among the Pueblos were, for the most part, closely associated with military force. The initial European military exploration in 1540–42 was led by Francisco Vázquez de Coronado (1510–54) from New Spain in search of the mythic and near-mythic sites the Seven Cities of Gold (Cibola) and Quivira. Visiting western Pueblos and the Colorado River, as well as the villages along the Rio Grande, and penetrating northeast to Kansas, Coronado's expedition brought with it missionaries but found no gold. Returning after injury, Coronado was accused of crimes against Indians, attacking Pueblos and torturing headmen. The written records of the expedition stimulated further exploration, and the next settlement project, that of Juan de Oñate (c.1551–c.1626), followed in 1598–1607. Oñate was accompanied by soldiers, colonizers and priests, who laid the initial foundations for a permanent presence in several Pueblos. The Indians at Acoma initially accepted the Europeans, but later revolted in response to rape. After reconquest and enslavement men over the age of twenty-five were sentenced to lose a foot. Three priests remained after Oñate's departure, but that number rapidly increased, while the number of Pueblos decreased through the seventeenth century. Missionary efforts were much less successful in the western Pueblos of Acoma, Hopi and Zuni; with perhaps 20,000 converts and thirty priests, there was little chance of enforcing Christian orthodoxy, except, partly, with the whip, but nevertheless parallel compartmentalized worlds arose, with the *kiva* and plaza for Indian ceremonialism, and the church for the Franciscans.

The Pueblo Revolt

Revolts, especially revolts in response to the determined destruction of Indian paraphernalia, masks and prayer sticks, were a cyclical feature of religious and colonial life. The most successful revolt was that of Popé (c.1630–88), from San Juan, in 1680, a revitalization movement in which the Europeans were swept out down to El Paso and a return was made to traditional beliefs and culture. An Indian explained in the 1680s:

> In order to take away their baptismal names, the water, and the holy oils, they were to plunge into the rivers and wash themselves with . . . a root Native to the country, washing even their clothing, with the understanding that there would thus be taken from them the character of the holy sacraments.[72]

The return of the Spanish, relatively peacefully under Diego de Vargas (1643–1704), in 1692 was accompanied by only moderate emphasis on Spanish systems of governance and economic exploitation, appropriate for a distant frontier colony. Later revolts, in 1696, were not treated leniently.[73] The recreated Hopi Christian community at Awatovi, was destroyed in 1700. Consequently while superficially enforced, separate systems of ritualized belief co-existed: prayer sticks amulets, masks, tobacco and corn pollen on the Native side, and crucifixes, statues, holy water and incense on the Christian side. In the nineteenth century, with the crumbling of Spanish structures, Indian people in the Pueblo were left much more to their own devices, reinforcing parallel but syncretic practices maintained for their own purposes, rather than for those of the wider church.

Recent Catholicism in the Pueblos

In the nineteenth and twentieth centuries the American Catholic episcopate resumed duties in the Pueblos, emphasizing the importance of combating heathenism. This continued into the second half of the twentieth century, when many communities were without priests. The Indian communities were both romanticized and, if unaccepting of new appointees, pressurized by the withholding of ministrations and visits.[74] Most important at this time were two developments at Isleta, south of Albuquerque. There a German-born priest, Fred A. Stadtmueller, took a very literal view of his duties from the 1950s to the 1970s, fighting against Indian dancing in the church, eventually remodelling the church and concreting over the dance ground to the fury of the Indian people – who dubbed swastikas on the parsonage – for whom touching the sacred ground was an essential part of the dance. Indian people, factionalized, also accused him of immorality with his housekeeper. He was after a long campaign forced out of Isleta by the governor Andy Abeita, in handcuffs, though allowed to return for his belongings and to close the church. He had begun his duties in the 1940s flying himself from parish to parish and ended his days regularly visiting Isleta Casino for a meal, a Monsignor respected and acknowledged by other guests.[75]

The Franciscans, unlike the Jesuits from the seventeenth century and low church New Englanders and high Anglicans from the nineteenth century, did not generally engage in work with local languages, did not publish bibles and other materials in Indian tongues, though they had Indian acolytes and Indian representatives in the Pueblos. Gerónimo Boscana (1776–1831) wrote the only detailed account of Native Californians in the missionary period, first published by Alfred Robinson in his *Life in California* (1846). Generally, however, Native people served in the church until the late twentieth century. When Edward Savilla from Isleta was ordained, in 1976, he maintained that it was possible to be both Catholic and a tribal loyalist, his point being that he still needed to assuage the fear that Native priests would divulge aspects of traditional religion.[76] Perhaps, ironically, the absence of linguistic analysis by the Franciscans and the reluctance to publish materials in Tewa or Tiwa, for example, helped protect Pueblo society. In many, if not most, missionary histories, missionaries have borrowed ideas and figures from the indigenous cultures and elided them with their own Christianity, in order to ensure successful evangelization. Although dangerous, with the possibility that Christianity would be reformed around Native beliefs, this has been a conscious and unconscious strategy, sometimes connected to the idea in the Americas that God implanted in heathen societies ideas which would enable their eventual conversion.[77] To emphasize this, churches were built on top of kivas.

Hopi Success

Literature and legend, belief systems and their borrowings can also be protected, retired from regular public scrutiny by non-Natives. The success of the Hopi in secluding intangible culture is symbolized by the rise and fall of the imitative Smoki ceremony of Prescott, sometime capital of Arizona. The Smoki were in some ways a fraternal organization. Between 1921 and 1990, white men red-faced up and danced to the *tsu'tsikive* (snake ceremony) – to help preserve the performance, they said, to the horror and amusement of the Hopi.[78] The snake ceremony was meant to ensure rain; but in the 1930s it was determined that some of the snakes used in the ceremony had been defanged, said by some to be contrary to Hopi beliefs and epistemology. President Calvin Coolidge was made an honorary Smoki in the 1920s; Theodore Roosevelt had viewed the actual ceremony in 1913 at Walpi. In 1990, when Vernon Masayesva was Hopi tribal chairman, after picketing, the Smoki ceremony was abandoned. This success contributed to the formal founding of the Hopi Cultural Preservation Office (HCPO) in 1996.[79]

Rattlesnakes and Believing

In popular culture the snake ceremony is reduced to a rain dance, situating explanations for the lack of rain. More recently, with mock hilarity, the seemingly endless drought in the American southwest has been associated with the rattlesnake round-up at Sweetwater. This communal event, beloved of Texans and others, may be seen not only as the reckless endangerment of a species, but, from a Native point of view, as courting an ecological disaster by acting disrespectfully towards harbingers of rain.[80] This can be seen as an inversion of an opposite trope: that of the disrespectful conservationist. Conservation, by limiting hunting, alters the relationship between people and animals. For instance, in the Arctic, the conservationist may be seen to bring about the decline in numbers which the conservators are intent on avoiding: among the Yupik failure to hunt geese is an act of disrespect which may reduce geese populations. The retirement of the Snake Dance from public view and the determination of some to exterminate rattlesnakes sit alongside other campaigns. The seemingly extreme demands of the HCPO, for instance, to control access to photographs in fact sits quite reasonably with the attempt to control the presentation of Hopi belief systems in a way which is both accurate and respectful and so which does not offend. The film *Hopi: Songs of the Fourth World* (Pat Ferrero, 1983), for example, explains the layered belief systems, religion and life of the Hopi in a measured, intelligible way: it relates maize symbolism to the four-colour and to the four-cardinal-point symbolism; to the calendar; to farming practice; to the weather; to the ancestors spirits, *katsinam*; to the creation of food, such as flat bread and cornmeal; and to clothing and the basketry symbolism used in marriage. And while all of these points are made visually and through sound, they are also very much metaphysical, of the mind, and in that sense speak to Hopi belief systems and religion, *navoti*.

California

Native Californian religion reflects the great ethnic and linguistic diversity of the coastal region, yet many of its features – shamanism, the use of the drug Datura to assist in dreams, revivalist movements such as the Bole-Maru – are found elsewhere. Perhaps exceptional is the Franciscan missionary endeavour, from 1769, symbolized by the canonization of the Catalan Junípero Serra (1713–84) in 2015. Serra's ascent to sainthood was assisted by the 1986 *Serra Report*, which did not include contributions from California Natives and omitted accounts of brutality, which the governor Pedro Fages (1734–94) recorded in the 1780s as excessively severe, that is harsh beyond the norms of the time.[81] Against this are the lyrical accounts of visitors evoking the magical quality of the missions. These include Robert Louis Stevenson, who visited Carmel in 1879, when he commented on the beauty of the service, the wonderful singing and the quality of the Latin.[82]

Mississippian Beliefs

A separate network of peoples and belief systems also using snake symbolism existed to the far east of the Pueblos. The southern and central valleys of the United States, and surrounding areas west into Oklahoma, east to the Mid-Atlantic Coast and north to the Great Lakes, were home to the societies of the Mississippian culture from AD 800 to European occupation in the eighteenth century. In that period Mississippian culture adapted to accommodate the central role of maize, beans and squash horticulture,[83] largely derived from Mexico. Vast ceremonial complexes, such as Cahokia, Illinois, home to ten or twenty thousand people, were constructed at the turn of the first millennium. These were run by stratified chiefly societies in which priests mediated between cults concerning lineage and ancestor worship, sanctified chiefly families and emphasized earth and fertility, renewal and wellbeing through rituals such as the green corn ceremony, which flourishes to this day, as among the Creek and the Seminole. Held in summer, when corn ripens, this festival brings people together to remind them of mutual obligations, moral behaviour and the importance of gratitude for the blessing of food.

At its height in the centuries before contact, Mississippian society likely consisted of related, but probably antagonistic, chiefdoms, alternating war and trade, and ritual interaction in games such as chunkey, 'running hard labour'.[84] Cults to do with the upper and the lower worlds represented by falcons, underwater snakes and feline beings were accommodated on flat-topped temple mounds, sometimes of huge size, such as Cahokia, Etowah, Georgia and Moundville, Alabama. Of overriding importance was the business of trading, especially in regalia and ritual objects, including seated stone figures, sometimes relating to chunkey, trophy head pots, often superbly decorated with tattooed designs, elaborate forms of ceremonial weapons, including stone sceptres, and copper repoussé and marine shell ornaments carved with motifs relating to war and redemptive cults, including especially the sun/directional cross, tear- or falcon-eyed warriors and serpent figures. In the 1930s and 1940s, these burial and temple mound finds were seen as relating to what was termed the Southern

Cult, later modified as the Southeastern Ceremonial Complex. During the eighteenth and early nineteenth centuries most traditional belief systems among historic peoples were highly modified if not destroyed; the Caddo of the river systems west of the Mississippi retained much of their culture in Oklahoma until the late nineteenth century, when the Dawes and Curtis Acts forced allotment in the 1890s. In the end what is significant about Mississippian ceremonial and belief is that, associated with new ideas from Mexico, a syncretic North American religion, no doubt with regional inflections, arose. Elsewhere among ancient aboriginal peoples, it is usually suggested that belief systems antecedent to those of the present dominated: so that the world views of ancient northern whale hunters, Plains buffalo hunters, salmon fishermen and acorn gatherers in California are assumed to have been similar to those of their distant descendants.

The Hohokam, flourishing c. AD 1050–1450 in the Phoenix Basin in Arizona, a culture with canal-irrigation agriculture, may have had similar belief systems. These are poorly understood but are likely also to have related to farming and were expressed in worship on large temple mounds.

5
Language and Literature

Black Elk (1863–1950) (Oglala Lakota); *left*, religious leader, 1887.

Mohawks in school in 1786, from a primer. Christian education was both ethnocidal and enabling – for leaders to protect and modernize Native society.

Battiste Good, Wapostangi, or Brown Hat, Brule (c.1821–?), winter count 1880, showing single years marked by battles, wounds, single-event pictographs, going back to 900.

quoyah (1770?–1843?), from Tuskegee, TN, the Cherokee silversmith who invented one the rare writing systems produced by a previously non-literate people, 1821.

Navajo 'code-talkers': Corporal Henry Bahe Jnr and Private First Class
George H. Kirk operate a radio set, December 1943.

Maria Tallchief (1925–2013) (Osage), first US prima ballerina, with her
Chicagoan husband and their daughter, the Oxford-educated poet Elise
Maria Paschen, 1959.

Zitkala-Ša, Gertrude Simmons Bonin (1876–1938), Yankton writer and activist.

Thomas St Germain Whitecloud II (1914–72), Ojibwe/Anishinaabe/Chippewa physician and author of hobo tale 'Blue Winds Dancing' (1938), with his wife, 1939.

Arthur Wellington Clah (1831–1916), (Hlax) Tsimshian trader, leader and diarist for over fifty years.

Will Rogers (1879–1935), Cherokee performer and orator, with his wife on the French liner *Île de France*, 1934.

Freshmen's page from the Phoenix Indian School Yearbook *The New Trail*, 1933, indicating how new pupils from Arizona and New Mexico presented themselves in a self-produced publication.

Alfonso Ortiz (1939–97), San Juan Pueblo, pre-eminent Native anthropologist.

Luther Standing Bear (1868–1939) (Ota Kte/Plenty Kill), Brule, or Mochunozhin, writer, activist and actor, 1935.

Buffy Sainte-Marie (b. 1941), Cree singer, writer of the Vietnam protest song 'Universal Soldier' (1964), here with Johnny Cash.

Oren Lyons (1930–), *right*, Haudenosaunee activist on the world stage and competitive Lacrosse player, talking to a journalist.

Bea Medicine (1923–2005), Lakota anthropologist.

Nora Dauenhauer (1927–), Tlingit elder and writer.

Louise Erdrich (b. 1954), Ojibwe/Anishinaabe/Chippewa novelist.

5

Language and Literature

The languages of Native North America are exceptional for their extreme diversity. This developed over a relatively short period of time. The records of languages, the literatures and oral history and the influence those languages have had in linguistics are also unique: as in other ways, Native North America altered the way the world is seen. The first major question is: how did American languages develop such diversity so quickly? Alternatively, is deep time required to explain this? Did people arrive in the Americas much longer ago, earlier than the 12,500 years BP, which was the general consensus for migration to the Americas until recently? Language families or phyla (from the Greek for race or tribe) and language isolates, apparently unrelated to any others, seem to have developed between around 12,500 and 40,000 years ago, a much shorter time span than in, say, Melanesia and Australia, first inhabited around 60,000 years ago. Historically there are both language isolates and more usually language families spread over a wide area, such as the Algonquian, though many of these languages now also face extinction.

It is very hard to categorize North American languages, which are lexically diverse, in that they have a large number of words; they also create complex words with long streams of phonemes (indivisible sound elements), which makes comparison and the creation of dictionaries difficult. One important point is that they are agglutinative: suffixes and prefixes enable instant terms to be created to describe, explain and fix, momentarily or permanently. For instance, the agglutinative process can create an ever-larger number of words for snow or indeed any other phenomenon.[1] Conversely, simple words may have complex meanings, or broad meanings. In Yup'ik the verb *qamigartuq* means 'he goes seal-hunting with a small sled and kayak during the spring'. Yup'ik also includes words with far more general meanings than comparable English or French words. For instance, *qelta* is translated as 'fish scale', 'tree bark', 'eggshell', 'peel', though one could argue that *qelta* would be best translated by 'outer layer' or 'skin'.[2]

North American languages have been at the centre of the discussions in linguistics since the nineteenth century and are the subject of a number of different mapping schemes. Their contribution to linguistics is disproportionately large, given the small number of speakers. That almost all Native North American languages are likely to disappear from everyday use is an exceptional loss, not simply to Native nations, who are losing much of their linguistic and cultural identity, but in general. Further, the recent recording of languages has been dilatory. Edward Vajda asks, for instance, whether all the huge recent effort devoted to discussions about Universal Grammar – originally a Baconian and then an Enlightenment construct reframed by Noam Chomsky, that grammar formation is hardwired to the brain – in the second half of the twentieth century would not have been better applied to describing languages now irretrievably lost.[3] One of the other paradoxes of Native North American languages is that their exceptional stability was suddenly replaced 300–400 years ago by rapid change. In particular, Spanish, French and English quickly spread across North America.[4] Languages were lost through language shift in three ways: when Native North Americans adopted a European language; through migration, as Europeans invaded Native lands; and through expansion, when European languages spread on to adjacent lands.

North America is thus a continent of great language diversity, with major differences that require particular explanation. If it is accepted that people arrived 12,500 years ago, one explanation is that languages mutated and changed very quickly, but of this there is no evidence. Language diversity is often found in mountainous parts of the world, where population movement between different ecological zones, especially between mountain valleys, is difficult, ensuring that languages remain discrete. Two such areas of language diversity are the Caucasus and Melanesia. But this is not often the situation in North America. Language diversity in North America is general, and in the case of often mountainous California very substantial, with more than sixty different languages in diverse ecological zones: desert, montane coastal and riparian. The question, then, is: how did such diversity arise, and how was it maintained? The answer to this question is related to the way in which the continent may have been inhabited: complex patterns of migration, the problematic interpretation of technology and hunting and the domestication of plants.

Linguists use the comparative method to determine how languages are related and whether they are descended from a common ancestral tongue. In a way, the idea of language difference, for instance between that of the Inuit and neighbouring Algonquian-speaking Cree and Innu, is simple to understand, in that they are mutually unintelligible. But other concepts are used, all of which on examination are more problematic. One such is the idea of dialect, where one person's different dialect becomes another person's different language. Differences in language, as opposed to differences in dialect, foster an appeal to uniqueness, separateness and nationalism, all of which are substantial. Ideas of language and dialect shift are therefore highly politicized. The easiest way of understanding dialect is to look at English dialects in North America: not simply those of Native and African America, but also those of New England, the US Midland dialect relating to the Canadian dialects, and so on.[5] The two largest Native languages, Navajo and Inuktitut, have different dialects: two for Navajo and six for Inuktitut in Nunavut alone. Navajo is perhaps a different language to those of the related neighbouring Apache, and Inuktitut is a different language to that of the Alaskan Inupiat, called Inupiaq. Movement and separation create new dialects: it is difficult to pinpoint when dialects became languages as people moved east in the Arctic, and south from the Subarctic. The Thule Inuit spread eastwards from the Bering Strait to Greenland in the first millennium and the Athapaskan moved south to California, Arizona and New Mexico in the second millennium AD, the latter migration perhaps occurring after the two White River volcano eruptions in Alaska in the same period.[6]

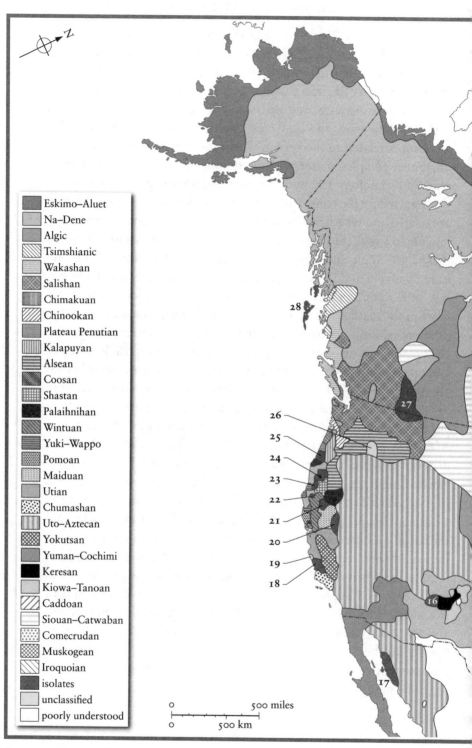

Legend:
- Eskimo–Aluet
- Na–Dene
- Algic
- Tsimshianic
- Wakashan
- Salishan
- Chimakuan
- Chinookan
- Plateau Penutian
- Kalapuyan
- Alsean
- Coosan
- Shastan
- Palaihnihan
- Wintuan
- Yuki–Wappo
- Pomoan
- Maiduan
- Utian
- Chumashan
- Uto–Aztecan
- Yokutsan
- Yuman–Cochimi
- Keresan
- Kiowa–Tanoan
- Caddoan
- Siouan–Catwaban
- Comecrudan
- Muskogean
- Iroquoian
- isolates
- unclassified
- poorly understood

0   500 miles
0   500 km

Map 4. Native North American languages.

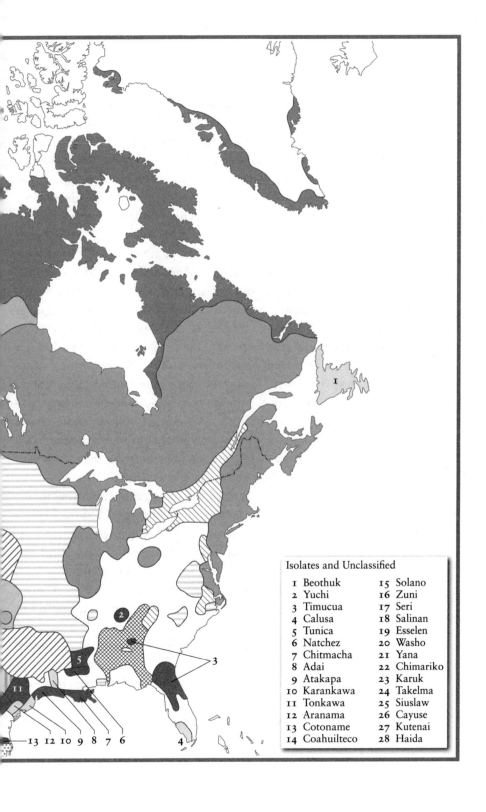

Isolates and Unclassified

1	Beothuk	15	Solano
2	Yuchi	16	Zuni
3	Timucua	17	Seri
4	Calusa	18	Salinan
5	Tunica	19	Esselen
6	Natchez	20	Washo
7	Chitmacha	21	Yana
8	Adai	22	Chimariko
9	Atakapa	23	Karuk
10	Karankawa	24	Takelma
11	Tonkawa	25	Siuslaw
12	Aranama	26	Cayuse
13	Cotoname	27	Kutenai
14	Coahuilteco	28	Haida

First Records of Native Languages

From first European contact words were collected. The early collectors of words, of vocabularies, were largely explorers and more importantly missionaries, working to introduce Christianity to Native North America. From the beginning of European intrusion vocabularies were recorded and reprinted, to ease communication of conquest, commerce and conversion. These seemingly straightforward documents freeze in time momentary meetings, opening understandings on these often misrecorded occasions with sometimes no doubt apocryphal words. Thousands of vocabularies, later dictionaries, acting as windows into the microcosm of contact, survive and are highly expressive evocations of language practice, ones which situate a number of different aspects of history. Truncated conversations in Pidgin or lingua franca – reduced, formulaic languages developed on the frontier to facilitate cross-ethnic transactions – for instance, are expressions of mutual understanding and misunderstanding, demonstrating especially the way in which European Americans found difficulty in rendering the non-concrete. This was based no doubt on a prejudice that Indian people did not have the intellectual ability to comprehend ideas beyond the mundane – but it is likely that prejudice worked also in the other direction: Native Americans believing that their European counterparts could not understand the non-concrete.

War, trading, religion and the business of deception and lying that is diplomacy are also important aspects of vocabularies. But the interest goes much further, of course: the vocabularies were used by early writers and travellers as symbolic markers of the exotic, the beautiful and the remarkable, as for instance in the business of understanding John Smith's exchange with Pocahontas published in 1612 in his *Map of Virginia*: 'Bid Pokahontas bring hither two little Baskets, and I will give her white beads to make her a chaine / Kekaten pokahontas patiaquagh ningh tanks manotyens neer mowchick rawrenock audowgh', leaving hanging the nature of the relationship between Smith and Pocahontas. Or the use of Narragansett by Roger Williams (1603–83) in his *A Key into the Language of America* (1643), long before *Gulliver's Travels* (1726) or *Rasselas* (1759), to pour scorn on the unchristian behaviour of professed English Christians. In poetry following the book's lists, Williams compares the English with Native Americans: 'If Natures Sons both wild and tame, / Humane and Courteous be: / How ill becomes it Sonnes of God / To Want Humanity?'[7]

First Systematic Collections

Thomas Jefferson, with the American Philosophical Society, and Wilhelm von Humboldt, at the turn of the nineteenth century, became involved in different ways in the comparative collection and theoretical study of American languages. The first full scheme was created by Peter Stephen Du Ponceau (1760–1844), soldier and linguist, who suggested four language families, the first three of which survive: Greenlandic (Eskimoan), Iroquois (Iroquoian), Lenni-Lenape (Algonquian) and Floridian.[8] John Pickering (1777–1846), classicist and lawyer, followed him by providing an orthography in 1820. Of the Americans involved in recording Native literature in the early nineteenth century, the most important, and most controversial, was Thomas McKenney (1785–1859),[9] who was responsible for regulating trade with Indians from 1816, as a government activity in opposition to John Jacob Astor (1763–1848) and then the American Fur Company. Most significantly of all McKenney was in charge of the Office of Indian Affairs (later Bureau of Indian Affairs). While McKenney is most noted for assisting in the passing of the first Indian Education Act in 1819, providing federal funds for missionaries, and of the Removal Act of 1830, he also acquired and accumulated in his office copious texts, vocabularies and portraits of Indian leaders. Of especial importance were the Great Lakes Algonquian/Ojibwe/Anishinaabe texts used in the multi-volume *History of the Indian Tribes of North America*, which was published from the 1830s.

A first attempt at a comprehensive understanding was that of the Swiss American Albert Gallatin (1761–1849), politician and financier, in the first half of the nineteenth century. In his first scheme in 1836 he identified many of the language groups correctly, successfully mapping the Iroquois, Sioux, Esquimaux and Creek in the southeast and the Algonkin-Lenape, and Athapascas (sic) in the Subarctic northwest.[10]

But his reach extended only up to the eastern edge of the continental divide, and he had no materials for the complex regions of the west beyond the Rockies. John Wesley Powell (1834–1902), the innovative, authoritarian anthropologist and geologist, created the first comprehensive scheme, which was published in 1891. This described fifty-eight language families. He improved Algonquian by adding Plains languages such as Cheyenne, Arapaho and Siksiska and in the Athapaskan group added the languages of the Californian peoples to those of the north and the southwest. However, he did not accept the existence of the Uto-Aztec language family, containing the Ute, Shoshone, Comanche and the Nahuatl-speaking Mexica/Aztecs. In 1911 Boas published his *Handbook of American Indian Languages*, and two of his principal students, Alfred Kroeber (1876–1960) and Edward Sapir (1884–1939), situated language as the basis for cultural anthropology. Powell and Boas' achievement is much more than that of simply classifying languages: they also, by organizing North America on a language basis, dealt a substantial blow to the evolutionary organization of knowledge and to social evolution, especially in the way Native American might be presented in museums, which had been espoused by an earlier generation of proto-anthropologists such as the American Lewis Henry Morgan and the Briton E. B. Tylor (1832–1917). However, Morgan, in initiating rigorous kinship studies, may be considered the founder of comparative anthropology, with his *Systems of Consanguinity and the Affinity of the Human Family* (1871). In comparison with Boas' geography-based ideas, or with Tyler's comparative ethnography in *Primitive Culture*, also published in 1871, Morgan's theories of kin were derived from, and analysed, Native American categories.

This seemingly simple question is much broader. Kinship and the role of women underwrite much behaviour and most cultural norms in Native society, both confirming gender as an important marker and conversely assuming equality. A similar process, articulated and expressed entirely differently, applies to homosexuality, and to the occasional cross-gendered upbringing of children. From the early colonial period, early commentators noted and were puzzled by this phenomenon, termed *berdache,* originally from the Arabic for slave, but later with additional pejorative connotations. The *berdache,* usually a man living as a woman, was often possessed of significant spiritual powers. More recently 'Two-Spirit' became the accepted term for the expression of gender variance, a single phrase neatly avoiding the rigid categories of gay and lesbian.[11] It is reasonable to suggest that, unusually in pre-modern societies, in Native North America gay, or ambiguously gendered, people, lived functional lives which acknowledged identity.

Twentieth-century Language Organization

North American language families, or stocks or phyla, were determined with some ease and had become well established by the end of the nineteenth century. Each of the classificatory systems contributed to the formulation of the next one, of course, but the schemes generally came to be of two types: those that emphasize the differences and uniqueness of some languages, and those that seek, by using broad classificatory terms, to create general schemes. Colloquially these two groups are termed the *splitters* and the *lumpers*. Sapir created in 1929 a new survey of American languages, which reduced the number of language families to six. Two more recent theories have both emphasized the simplified structure of Sapir's scheme and extended greatly the possible time depth for arrival from Asia. Sapir also published on a number of hugely important topics, including phonemes (the smallest units of sounds that can be distinguished from each other and cannot be subdivided) and Athapaskan languages. He also worked with Ishi (*c.*1860–1916), the last Yana speaker in California. Sapir proposed the idea of the Na-Dene or Athapaskan language group in 1915, and it is the situation of Na-Dene, and the place of Haida inside or outside of the group, that acts as a defining issue for North American languages today. Lumpers do not accept the Haida language as an isolate but include it in Na-Dene. The Na-Dene group of languages, the northern Athapaskans of the Subarctic and the southern Athapaskans or Apacheans, the Apache and Navajo, were joined in the early twentieth century by Tlingit, and then much later Eyak on the Northwest Coast. Later, this larger group of Na-Dene languages, without Haida, was associated with a Siberian language, Ket, by Edward Vajda, who has proposed a near-acceptable Dene-Yeniseian language family, spanning Siberia and North America.[12]

Language and Native Arrival in North America.

The fundamental question underlying the classification of American languages is that of how the Siberians populated the Americas. The most widely accepted theory is that people came across the Bering Land Bridge, a vast band of land measuring hundreds of miles north to south that connected Siberia to North America during the ice age. Crossings continued after the submersion of the land bridge under the waters of the Bering Strait: the last crossing involving the development of a language community was that of the Eskimo-Aleut language group around 1,000–2,000 years ago, and was accomplished by boat. Bering Strait remained an active crossing point until the 1940s, when the Cold War prohibited the toing and froing of Siberian Yup'ik to Alaska for trade and marriage.

The Na-Dene were the second major group of people to migrate into the Americas across the land bridge. Where the consensus breaks down is in the understanding of when the earliest Americans moved to the Americas, that is the people who preceded the Na-Dene, and whether they constituted one group. The presumption is that either, during the last glaciation, people moved from Asia, then south down along the coast, on land submerged 10,000 years ago, or that they moved inland and south through the Northwest Territories and Alberta east of the Rockies between ice fields. The more likely trail south along the Northwest Coast allows for the much later important role of the Tlingit and the Haida, and the now extinct Eyak, in the discussion of the Na-Dene.

Conventional discussion of North American language classification suggests, then, three populating movements of people into the Americas, followed by great stability through time, a large number of small families and isolates, and the large families such as Eskimo-Aleut and Na-Dene/Athapaskan. The two late twentieth-century discussions which challenged this approach were those by the lumpers Joseph Greenberg (1915–2001) and Johanna Nichols (b. 1945). Greenberg worked with African languages and those of the Pacific and the Americas. In 1987 he proposed in *Language in the Americas* that all the isolated American families and individual languages should be subsumed into a single early family of migrants, the Amerind, to sit alongside Na-Dene and Eskimo-Aleut. While this is not generally accepted, for the time being, because of what is seen as Greenberg's cavalier treatment of data, the idea can be modified in a way to suggest that a single umbrella group of earlier non-Na-Dene immigrants to the Americas might include all the languages derived from early migrants, extending back tens of thousands of years. This broad grouping would include language isolates and unrelated families or phyla.[13]

Glottochronology

The idea with which this intersects is that of Johanna Nichols, a Berkeley linguist working with Slavic languages who has studied grammar and, like Joseph Greenberg, is interested in classification. The kind of data she uses includes features such as numerical classifiers. These are seldom used in European languages such as English, with exceptions such as *pair* of shoes or *head* of cattle, but are common in Asian, Pacific and American languages. Nichols has used this interest in broad language structures to try to establish the depth of time between languages and language groups, that is, the glottochronology.[14] Glottochronology was a new technique developed by Morris Swadesh (1909–67)[15] and others in the 1950s to look statistically at language constants through time. This can determine how languages shifted and became separate and may provide figures for time depth. Crucially glottochronology depends on the idea that language change takes place at a constant rate. This is not always the case, as was demonstrated by Knut Bergsland and Hans Vogt in 1962, when they compared the retention rates for modern and early Norse/Scandinavian and Caucasian languages and found that they differed.[16] However, it is agreed that while the statistics and the methodology of glottochronology are not perfect, they provide a controversial model whose deconstruction furthers the history of language. The end result is that the discussions about lumping or splitting major language groups and about the time depth for the separation of languages provide parameters for the study of language. This means that it is now accepted by Roger Blench (b. 1953), a Cambridge linguist specializing in African languages, and others that language separation in North

America may have occurred over a very long time during a peopling process that in terms of antiquity is similar to, though not as ancient as, those of Melanesia and Australia.[17] Further, recent archaeological investigations at the Friedkin site in Texas confirms the existence of a pre-Clovis people dating to 13,200–15,500 BP who used a variety of blade, bladelets and bifacial chert tools.[18] Previously excavated sites and dates, Meadowcroft Rockshelter (19,000 BP), Cactus Hill (18–20,000 BP) and Bluefish Caves (14,000 BP), did not always receive similar acceptance.

Language Loss

The best and most authoritative source for the state of languages worldwide is the Summer Institute of Linguistics (SIL), a Presbyterian missionary organization founded in the 1930s, designed to translate the Bible into Latin American languages. SIL publish an online account of the status of languages in the world, *Ethnologue*, so providing regular updates of those languages which are threatened, shifting, extinct or indeed reviving.[19] The work of SIL may be controversial, and certainly was during the 1980s, when they were, like the Jesuits in the eighteenth century, expelled from some Latin American countries. Their work is, however, especially useful in contextualizing the status of North American languages and in summarizing the status of individual aboriginal languages.[20] The terminology used by SIL is very simple and effective. At the top level a language is institutional, and at the bottom level a language is either dormant, with no speakers, or actually extinct. So for North America only Greenland has one Native language, Greenlandic Inuktitut, which is used at an institutional level. Below the institutional level is a provincial designation; in Canada where there are no aboriginal languages embedded at an institutional level nationally, as English and French are, Inuinnaqtun, or Western, and Eastern Inuktitut are designated provincial languages or statutory working languages. Five Algonquian languages, varieties of Cree and Naskapi/Innu and Attikamekw, are developing, that is, are growing with language initiatives, as is Dogrib/Tlicho. The rest are threatened, moribund or dormant: none is labelled vigorous.

Triumph of Hybrid Nativism

Non-Native language use suggests in another sense the destructiveness of colonialism, usefully seen perhaps as the success of a hybrid nativism. Competence in English leads to education, achievement and leadership roles which cross ethnic boundaries. This was true of people of mixed descent in the Subarctic north or on the Florida frontier in the eighteenth century and remains true today: U. P. Gad explains it well for Greenland: competent, high-achieving Greenlanders constantly need to express their identity, not merely through Native language, but through gait – walking with a roll rather than straight upright – and eating country food. The use of English as a third language to replace Danish might be a dangerous way of avoiding this conundrum. He points out that: 'the elite is more Danish than the subaltern which is more Greenlandic than the elite'.[21] Language shift and language competence are important aspects of this identity, which means that people in leadership roles rely on the regular performative use of language, and on material symbols including jewellery and feathers and pan-Indian ceremonialism, ensuring that these elements of aboriginal culture will survive. One way of seeing aboriginal languages in North America is to compare them to Irish in Ireland (the only minority language that is a national language in the EU), where more than half the population have a degree of competence, but only a small number (138,000) are native speakers, and only a million are fully competent, out of an island population of 6.5 million.[22] And as in Ireland there are important dialect differences, the idea of 'Red English' being created for the use of expressive Indian English by Anthony Mattina in the 1985 translation of a Salishan text.[23]

In the United States, with far greater language diversity, the situation is much more difficult. While there is only one institutional language, English, there are no aboriginal languages in general use at a provincial/regional level. Ironically the only state with a second official language is Hawaii since 1978, but the Hawaii state website of 2014 did not display any Hawaiian bilingualism, apart from 'welcome' in Hawaiian, 'E Komo mai!', and the tag of 'Aloha State!', a generic greeting. In 2015 the different website features only the Office of Language Access and the acronym LEP, limited English proficiency, overriding the important bilingualism and Hawaiian immersion schools with the importance of teaching English to immigrants.[24] The only Native American language that is developing is Central Siberian Yup'ik, spoken on the islands between Alaska and Siberia, and on both mainlands. For *Ethnologue* the baseline date year for extinction is 1950, when the survey began, and since then one language, Wyandot/Wendat, has disappeared in Canada, and twelve have disappeared in the USA. Six languages are reawakening, that is, are successfully undergoing revitalization: two in California, four in the eastern US, but the numbers are small. More than fifty are nearly extinct, thirty moribund. The statistics for some of the major languages are interesting and tragic: of the 100,000 Sioux people, 25,000 speak some elements of a Siouan language to an elementary level. For the Cherokee 10,000 of 140,000 people are speakers, mostly in the conservative United Keetoowah Band of Oklahoma and Arkansas. The threatened languages include the Inupiaq dialects in north and northwest Alaska, and the Central Yup'ik, where 10,000 people of 21,000 are speakers. 171,000 Navajo of 266,000 are speakers. The reasons for Navajo being described as a threatened language are not straightforward, but to do with the dispersal of the population, the perceived status of English and the reluctance of monolinguals and bilinguals to speak Navajo, and not, as among Siouan or Eskimoan speakers, for reasons to do with dialect and orthographical difference. Importantly *Ethnologue* emphasizes when and how language shift takes places, focusing particularly on the moment when there cease to be any speakers of child-bearing age, because it is at that moment that infants cease to be immersed in an aboriginal natal language. A language is likely to die the moment the last female speaker passes child-bearing age.

Navajo

Of all aboriginal languages, Diné, or Navajo, is the most spoken and most likely to survive in continental North America. Half of the Navajo speak Diné, and as in the Arctic there is a flourishing radio station, KDND, founded in 1978, which uses Navajo and works as a

community network available to all for broadcasting and communication, alongside the Navajo Nation Television Network (NNTV).
KDND has 100,000 listeners in any week. The collapse in the numbers of young people speaking Navajo occurred in the late twentieth
century. In the 1970s 95 per cent of the school intake at Rough Rock
and Rock Point spoke Navajo; and most of them didn't speak English. In the mid-1990s James Crawford commented on the lack of
prestige of the language when he visited a school in Chinle with the
Navajo code-talker Carl Gorman and the students were reluctant to
admit to speaking Navajo.[25] Since then bilingualism in schools and
elsewhere has increased enormously in importance, with, for instance,
the development of a computer programme to aid learning of Navajo
by the software company Rosetta Stone. Diné is, however, classified as
endangered, and in a sense the increased symbolic use of Navajo by
the Navajo Nation marks the threats to the language and the efforts
undertaken to increase use. The place of Navajo in the USA can be
gauged by statistics from the survey of 2011.[26] Some 170,000 spoke
Navajo in that year, with a mere 195,000 speaking other Native languages; some 37 million people speak Spanish, and 884,000 African
languages. Most interesting is that there were 211,000 speakers of
Hmong, members of an Asian clan-based minority who, like the Pawnee in the nineteenth century and the Navajo in the twentieth century,
fought alongside the USA – in their case, in the Second Indo-Chinese/
Vietnam War, before they moved to the USA.

The major Navajo contribution to the Second World War was in the
form of several hundred Navajo speakers, whose translations of messages made them impenetrable to the Japanese – there were no Navajo
dictionaries and vocabularies generally available until the 1940s,
when, as it happens, they were distrusted by the Navajo, since they
were used to help implement the controversial forced livestock reduction programme. One Navajo, Joe Kieyoomia, was captured by the
Japanese and tortured but didn't know about the code talking, and
went on to survive the Nagasaki bomb in his concrete prison cell.[27]
The story of the code-talkers is perhaps the major manner in which
the national story of the USA is articulated with Navajo history.[28] Yet
it is significant that popular knowledge of Native North American
languages should be reduced to this one momentary point when they

contributed to the US war effort, instead of being celebrated for their own importance. In Canada at the same time recent statistics recorded highly optimistic numbers for aboriginal language use. It was said that the 'majority of people who reported an Aboriginal mother tongue [213,000] speak it at home', and that sixty languages were reported to be in use, especially Cree (83,000) and Inuktitut (35,000).[29]

Eskimo-Aleut

The other great language block in North American is that of the Eskimo-Aleut, especially Inuktitut and Greenlandic in Canada and Greenland. The situation in Greenland is straightforward; there the language is systematized and standardized and used as the first language in schools, and even in some tertiary education. While western education in West Greenland began in the eighteenth century, in most parts of Nunavut and Nunavik it only began around 1960. In that sense, with a relatively homogeneous series of dialects, and self-government since 1999, it should be simple for Inuktitut to be the dominant language. Yet instead of instituting monolingual education, with English taught as a second language once literacy in Inuktitut was established, Nunavut schools espoused bilingualism, with apparently disastrous results. Further preservation of English-language education became a priority after 1999. Bilingualism programmes are acting as a bridge to the learning gained by education, and once the bridge is crossed, the bridge is burned, and Inukitut atrophies.[30] The long series of problems identified by M. L. Aylward include the following: the difference between Inuit parents who want their children to be fluent in Inuktitut, before learning English and those who want to their children to be fluent first in English for their own advancement; the problem of educating Inuit to be teachers, when the Inuit in the teaching programmes cannot read or write; and the use of the Inuit and English streams as a means of seperating good students from bad ones. In one community the Inuktitut stream, termed 'General', is for poor students, while the academic stream in high school is the English stream, so kids would implicitly understand that the General Inuktitut stream would label them as inferior. This was put by a teacher so: 'if you are Inuit . . . you will be put in the not-so-smart stream or the non-academic stream . . . So I think they are already facing a brutal, brutal world. Anything we have done to try to make them feel powerful is gone.'[31]

Inuktitut in Nunavut

The Canadian Inuit Language Protection Act of 2008–9 provides for full implementation of the use of Inuktitut. So for instance, from 2011 Inuit have had the right to work for the government of Nunavut in their own language. From 2012 municipalities have had to offer services in the Inuit language. And by 2019 all school grades will have the right to an Inuit language education.[32] Yet there is little evidence that the actual issues of language in Nunavut, as outlined in 2010, have been addressed. In 2010 Nunavut Tunngavik Inc., the organization responsible for monitoring Inuit self-government, produced a report, *Our Primary Concern: Inuit Language in Nunavut*, outlining the dilemmas faced in Nunavut and in eloquent language set out the decisions that needed to be taken, without explaining that, without an illiberal paternalistic authority, in a society where consensus is required for decision-making, there is no simple way forward. So in Nunavut for Inuktitut to survive a decision has to be taken as to whether to use Roman orthography or syllabics, a decision has to be taken as to which of the six dialects is to be used, and then the difficult process has to be undertaken by Inuit of in effect eliminating the other five dialects of Inuktitut. Only by doing these things can standardized texts be prepared and published, whether it is for Inuktitut or bilingual education. One of the dialects, Inuinnaqtun, is about to disappear. Perhaps the most important point about Inuktitut is that in communities where it is the dominant language it is often not the preferred language in the home. In 2006 for 54 per cent of Nunavut Inuktitut was the mother tongue, but for only 44 per cent is it the preferred language at home, suggesting a decline in prestige.[33]

Language in Alaska

The challenges in Alaska are different, but the outcomes likely to be similar: a shift away from the main Eskimo-Aleut languages, Inupiaq and Yup'ik. Yup'ik, spoken in dialects through most of southwest

Alaska and into Siberia, is, like Inuktitut, a language that should, it might seem, be easy to maintain. A recent study, however, documents the way in which a number of factors threaten Yup'ik. This study looked at the twenty-two schools and 3,800 pupils in the Lower Kuskokwim School District.[34] It describes the measures taken from the 1970s to ensure the teaching and incorporation of the various Yup'ik dialects in education. So, for instance, the capital Bethel provided in 1995 the first Yup'ik immersion courses. By 2001, 82 per cent of all village schools in this school district, eighteen of them, used Yup'ik as a primary language of instruction from kindergarten (age 5–6) to grades 2 to 3 (age 7–9); that same year federal legislation was passed to ensure that standardized tests in English and maths would ensure 'No Child Left Behind'. The tests are termed, without irony, 'high stakes testing', referring to the need to pass the test if the student is to proceed further. Schools that failed the test became eligible for further funding, but of course no school would want to fail. This means that: 'US policies designed to ostensibly promote mainstream academic achievement are becoming de facto language policies, intensifying pressures on educators, and schools providing heritage language instruction in endangered language contexts.' Or, to put it another way: the drive for basic skills in maths and reading acts against Native language survival. Other initiatives seek to expand immersion, but the scale of these is limited. A two-week summer school was developed from 2003 by the Yup'ik Language Institute, organized from the University of Alaska, with two elders teaching. While this format, of immersion learning in a third space away from family and schools, is important, it is not clear that it can regain the initiative in protecting Yup'ik.[35]

Language in Piniq

The very difficult situation of Native languages can be looked at through an account of Central Yup'ik proficiency in southwest Alaska. Leisy T. Wyman, an Arctic linguist, also published a study which sympathetically and in great detail shows how and why young people shifted from being bilingual Yup'ik speakers, in the mid-1990s, to monolingual English speakers in 2000–2001, already a long time ago.[36] In the fictionally named community Piniq of 500 people she compared her experience as a participant observer and as a teacher in a school of seventy pupils at two periods five years apart. She labelled two cohorts of students as the RS, or Real Speakers, and the GB, or Get By students. The Real Speakers were those born in the late 1970s. What is special about the Central Yup'ik and the Lower Yukon School District is that traditional knowledge was and is available for everyone, as is the ability to hunt from the land. Yet for a group whom Wyman calls *nukalpiat*, or great hunters, as indeed for northern hunters elsewhere, English education and the values of hunters did not mix easily. This was, as everywhere, because young hunters were expected to stay in school and learn, even when the weather might be perfect for subsistence activities on the land or in the bush. Male pupils fell behind female ones early on at school. *Nukalpiat* were seen as disruptive, as youth at risk, by outsider teachers, and as future leaders by local teachers. In their final years of high school they expressed their dissatisfaction with English education and sorrow at recognizing that the teachers had such low expectations of them that they would not be taught calculus. On the other hand, after leaving school, some of these Real Speakers and great hunters dropped using English, expressing what Wyman calls linguistic survivance, that is, using language to express choice, power and cultural survival, as when using bilingual jokes to mock the president. Part of the issue is to do with the failure of English teaching, yet the paradoxical triumph of limited bilingualism lay in the difficulty of attracting outside teachers, who often left after one year, did not socialize and in some cases did not even get off the plane on first arrival; the gradual increase in distance between elders and youth; and the perception that English might provide employment, in a community in which only 40 per cent of people had jobs.

Educational Policy

Documents designed to improve Native education and literacy in aboriginal languages are produced regularly. They usually contain lofty sentiments hiding low priorities. This is well indicated by the flat, non-rhetorical and generally unpersuasive language used. So a 2007 document indicates that the Ontario Ministry of Education will: 'encourage faculties of education and community colleges to attract, retain, and train more First Nation, Métis, and Inuit students to become teachers and education assistants who are knowledgeable about their own cultures and traditions'.[37] Instead what is required is an explanation of how aboriginal teachers in isolated communities or depressed cities are to be properly valued and paid. Further, there is every reason for national state and provincial educational systems to include elements of aboriginal language and culture, if only to anchor identity with symbolic use. In other regions cultural myopia extends beyond language. So the 1998 California document for history education, revalidated in 2009, for kindergarten to grade 12, is particularly disingenuous if not dishonest. It deals appropriately with the Armenian genocide, with the Holocaust, but not with treatment of Indian people, state-sponsored militia bounty hunting or the loss occasioned by the post-1849 Gold Rush. As for the missions, ethnocide is covered with the question: 'Discuss the role of the Franciscans in changing the economy of California from a hunter-gatherer economy to an agricultural economy', that is, the destruction of Native California is glossed, nineteenth-century style, as social evolutionary progress. Indian wars and removals happened outside the Golden State, named Indians are not from California.[38] On the other hand, the Native Group Advocates for Indigenous California Language Survival has since 1992 organized education in the extinct and moribund languages of California, with the Breath of Life Workshop for California languages without speakers and the Master-Apprentice Language Learning Program.[39]

Suicide, Loss and Revitalization

One important aspect of language extinction is the likely correlation between loss and youth suicide, a pre-eminent marker of cultural distress. Taking data from bands in British Columbia from the period 1987–1992, it has been shown that in those bands with at least 50 per cent of the population conversationally competent in the aboriginal language, suicide was much lower not simply than in other bands, but also than among the non-aboriginal young.[40] In the period studied one youth committed suicide in the sixteen bands with high rates of language ability, while eighty-four people killed themselves in the 136 bands with low language competence. In Alaska the Tlingit began a high school programme in the Juneau School District, the Tlingit Culture, Language and Literacy Program, at the beginning of the millennium and published a study after ten years.[41] The difficulties and benefits seem clear cut, even when the initial intake was at a disadvantage in the English language: that is, students lacked both the book and the school speech of their non-Native peers. The initial aim was for first-year students to learn 100 words; by year ten of the programme this had risen to 171 words and phrases. The benefits include a high visibility for Tlingit culture, both locally and nationally; the teaching of respect for elders and parents; the development of a sense of a community, as in the traditional longhouse; the integration of elders into the programme; the inclusion of student teachers in the programme, both to help and to learn; and the involvement of family members in family evenings. Persistent programming difficulties were to do with competition for time and resources, the image of the programme as remedial and perhaps not being challenging enough for the brightest Native students, the shortage of programme leaders, the difficulty of moving on to the next school and the general issue of ensuring enough family support.

American Legislation

In the USA as in Canada language loss is addressed by important initiatives, designed to increase Native language use. The most significant of these was the Native American Languages Act of 1990, which came out of Polynesian language experience and success with Hawaiian. Like so much else, it was sponsored by Senator Daniel Inouye (1924–2012).[42] With little funding, this was followed by the Esther Martinez Native American Languages Preservation Act of 2006, which does provide funding for the creation of immersion nests, for instance, for teaching under-sevens. State initiatives assist. In 2003 New Mexico passed an Indian Education Act, with $2.5 million in funding, while in 2009, Minnesota provided $1.9 million for Ojibwe/Anishinaabe and Dakota language preservation, with immersion schools, and in 2010 Michigan passed a bill which permits non-qualified Native speakers to teach, and for students to receive foreign language credits for Native language classes. Some 500 programmes have been funded by NALA 8.[43] The issue remains, as for Navajo and Yup'ik, how Native people, whether reservation- or corporation-based, can find the fortitude to insist on Native language first.

Oratory

Native North American linguistics and the survival of Native languages are the central contested issues of aboriginal survival. What is not contested is the importance of the historical records, the oratory and literature, however they may be interpreted. The core feature of Native oratory is rhetoric, that is, the art of public speaking with the intention of influencing listeners. Much of recorded early oratory relates to speeches made at times of treaty-making and war, a severely limiting genre, although highly important in indicating the quality and richness of Native rhetoric. It must be remembered that 'oratory among Native American tribes at this time both grew out of and facilitated public affairs and was integral to a tribe's social and political life. Oratory was the tool by which individual members participated in and shaped a tribe's collective decision-making',[44] whether about war or peace or hunting. Speaking, of course, in all its formal and informal aspects, would of necessity include prayers and healing, storytelling of family and fable, educating in the most general sense, whether about hunting and the practical but animistic arts of the chase or about the equally practical but highly spiritual understanding of landscape and the environment. Until long after contact and the heyday of Boasian anthropology in the decades of Native nadir, relatively little oral literature was well and accurately recorded.

Many of the earliest recorded speeches were those of great leaders during conflicts, for instance, from Pontiac (d. 1769), the Ottawa/Oddawa leader, who extracted the Royal Proclamation of Indian Territory beyond the Appalachians in the 1760s from the crown. In 1763 he reminded the French in Detroit:

> It is now seventeen years since . . . all the nations of the north came with the Sac and Fox Indians to destroy you. Who defended you? Did I not? Did not my people? . . . I am the same French Pontiac who seventeen years ago gave you his hand.[45]

If rhetoric, for Samuel Johnson was the art and elegance of speaking with propriety, it is also designed to move and persuade and inspire, and was also considered the 'mother of lies' in seventeenth-century Europe.[46] The difference is that in aboriginal society an orator would know, and probably be related to, the people to whom he was talking, while in the United States rhetoric, spoken in Boston, New York or Washington, in the speeches of Jefferson or Jackson, would be distanced and separated from continued relationships with the listeners, say on the frontier and in the middle ground between Indians and Americans.[47]

Rhetorical Missionaries

Missionaries, no less than Indian leaders, used rhetoric to inspire their listeners, and in the American colonies, missionaries inspired both Indians and non-Indians. The spectacular rhetorician of the Great Awakening, the first American religious revival and precursor to revolution, Jonathan Edwards (1703–58), preacher in the 1750s to the Stockbridge Indians, was associated with Hendrick Apaumut (1757–1830), the Mahican loyalist prophet. Apaumut took up the Salvationist way forward for Native America, speaking of 'the great men of the United States' with their 'Liberty' and how 'they begin with new things, and now they endeavour to lift us up the Indians from the ground, that we may stand up and walk ourselves; because we the Indians, hitherto have lay flat as it were on the ground'.[48] The great orators of the early republic, Red Jacket, Cornplanter, Little Turtle and Black Hawk, were aware that the defeat of the French, the snuffing out of French influence and the generally mistaken alliance with the perfidious British, and all the attendant switching and changing of sides, required a diplomacy of allusion and illusion in order to maintain moral authority and hope as power slipped away, especially with the defeat of the Indian confederacy at Fallen Timbers (1794), the Treaty of Greenville (1795) and others and the forced international boundary through Indian Country. The eclipse of Indian leaders at the turn of the eighteenth century occurred, of course, during the period of the French Revolution and the Napoleonic Wars, which caused such heart-searching in the new republic. Napoleon himself spoke in a terse, vigorous, but burning style to inspire his troops, yet after 1815 was both commemorated after his defeat by the British and, like Native Americans, made the subject of humiliating displays – of his coach, for instance, in 1816 in London. All of this relates directly to the eruption of romanticism, especially in the depiction of the also defeated tribal Scots by Walter Scott, whose writings were mimicked and then superseded by James Fenimore Cooper, the son of a successful speculator in Indian land in upstate New York.

In Cooper's work there are many examples of Indian oratory, for instance that of Natty Bumpo, an Indian adopted frontiersman of mixed descent. Eloquence became an ambiguous feature of public life in the young republic.[49] Near-apocryphal patriot New Englander Brother Jonathan was a long-winded talker[50] whose literary development reached its apogee in the second quarter of the nineteenth century in an eponymous New York newspaper (starting in 1839 and again in 1842). The ambiguous attitude towards oratory sat alongside Samuel Drake's *The Book of Indians of North America* (1834), which included speeches. In this way, in a sense, Native treaty talk provided a patchwork narrative, an equivalent of Boswell's record of Johnson, or Napoleon's St Helena table talk, creating a multi-vocal rendering of Indian history. The power engendered by Native eloquence did not result in any overarching triumph, but instead is symbolic of a formidable resilience, of an ability to think quickly and express things vividly in terms which could be understood by both whites and Indians. This exuberance of Native oratory did not, of course, necessarily provide any political gains for Indian people, but in a sense confirmed the triumph of the textual record over the oral, never more so than in the fine print of the treaties themselves, especially when ratification and implementation by Congress and the federal government was required.

Indian oratory has an exceptional ability to inspire and to incorporate the listeners in the projects of the speaker; the inspiration comes from the importance of speech in all societies with shifting and unstable hierarchy, in which authority is often largely non-inherited, and in which personal qualities are paramount in leadership. Native leaders, in encounters from the seventeenth century, but especially in the eighteenth and nineteenth centuries, were both heroic figures and cast by Euro-Americans in Homeric roles as often tragic figures, cloaked in the exoticism of difference and revered as noble savages. In this they were, of course, enemies worthy of defeat and doomed to be destroyed.

The first self-projected noble savage is the Muslim hero lover Almanzor, from Dryden's *Conquest of Granada* 1672, who declaims rhetorically:

> But know, that I alone am king of me.
> I am as free as nature first made man,
> Ere the base laws of servitude began,
> When wild in woods the noble savage ran.

Indian speeches often have this kind of apocryphal – in the biblical sense of being of doubtful authenticity – literary quality, about being free and about being the king of me, and were recorded by travellers, missionaries and soldiers, often facilitated by interpreters, and rendered into acceptable English. The extent to which the transcribed speeches and recorded autobiographies are accurate remains a moot point. But the eloquence was and remains real, as does the humour and the rhetoric, and all had been learned and developed in purely aboriginal circumstances. If the archetype of the Indian speech is the male leader lecturing a silent white audience about his own integrity and the way in which the land is not for sale, and that European Americans are hypocritical in their love of liberty and ability to deceive and so on, then of course the speech formation must come from diplomacy between Native peoples. When Indian peoples did move, notably on to the Plains with the coming of the horse, then the need for long discussions to obtain consensus before travel and warfare grew; similarly with the accelerated violence of the seventeenth century in the northeast, the fur wars, the divisions and alliances brought about by European intrusion, then need for oratory may have become paramount. Whatever the realities of these speeches, they remain the preferred entry into Native literature for most people.

One of the early writers to stress Indian eloquence was the scientist and colonial official Cadwallader Colden (1689–1776), whose 1727 *History of the Five Indian Nations* repeatedly speaks of the Indian genius for oratory, comparing it to that of classical politicians, and includes numerous Seneca and other speeches, in a tract designed to promote closer cooperation between the Haudenosaunee and the British. He incorporates a standardized Iroquoian phraseology and usefully integrates a wampum belt-giving and other transactions, in a sense implicitly emphasizing that the mnemonic devices woven into the belts were an aspect of literary transaction. He described negotiations of the 1690s, thirty years earlier, to stop wars in which the Iroquois were caught between the British and the French. The talks were between the first mayor of Albany, Peter Schuyler, and the great Onondaga leader Teganissorens or Decanesora (fl. c.1690–1725), whom Colden compares to Cicero. The Indian uses metaphorical language and admonishes Schuyler for his deceitfulness:

> Children of the Five Nations, I have Compassion for your little Children, therefore come speedily, and speak of Peace to me, otherwise I'll stop my Ears for the future . . . Now Tariha [messenger] return home, and tell the Five Nations, that I will wait for their coming till the Trees bud, and the Bark can be parted from the Trees [i.e. springtime] . . . I am truly grieved to see the Five Nations so debauched and deceived . . . by Quider [i.e. Schuyler].[51]

Thomas Jefferson similarly compared the Mingo/Cayuga/Oneida chief Logan, allied to the crown, to Cicero and Demosthenes in his Notes on the History of Virginia (1788). He republished, fourteen years after the event, the speech made by Logan in 1774 for the Virginia governor Dunmore, complaining about the retaliatory murder of his family, the act which gave rise to Lord Dunmore's War and the seizure of what were to become Kentucky and West Virginia:

> I appeal to any white man to say if ever he entered Logan's cabin hungry, and he gave him not meat; if ever he came cold and asked, and he clothed him not . . . Such was my love for the whites, that my countrymen pointed as they passed, and said, 'Logan is the friend of white men.'[52]

Whatever the authenticity of 'Logan's Lament', art of the elegy, of the lament for the dead, remains a central feature of historic and contemporary Native literature.[53]

How! and the Hollywood Injun

Contrasting with this excellent early oratory was the twentieth-century racist stereotype of the stoic, silent Indian. This final bad joke, often retold, is in the same tradition as the fictional pidgin English, babyish and exoticizing, distancing and demeaning, with both real and invented vocabularies attributed to Indians from the early nineteenth century. In this pidgin the words are often spoken slowly, suggesting a lack of fluency, in complete contrast with the lucidity and eloquence of the recorded oratory. The end product, a style of speech, not a dialect, is what Barbara Meek ironically calls HIE, *Hollywood Injun English*, in an article about *How!*, the possibly Lakota greeting first recorded in the 1810s by the traveller John Bradbury (1768–1823) when out west with Mandans (a village-dwelling Plains people) and others.[54] The characteristics of this language include the absence of differential tenses, as in the speech of children – everything is said in the present – the use of *um*, the absence of articles *a* and *the*, and the use of *me* for *I*. But this goes beyond a mere simplification of language: the use of this reduced version was seen to represent a real essence, rather than an accident of speech and circumstance, enabling the practice of linguistic segregation. In consequence English, as the dominant matrix language, absorbs elements from embedded Native American languages, English being the normative language and HIE being the foreign, not original, indeed non-American language. HIE is a relatively homogeneous style of speaking into which *tomahawk*, *tipi*, *squaw* and other Native words are combined with non-standard English, with stereotypical terms such as *paleface* and *heap big*. These epithets come from a variety of sources. *Paleface* is said to have been popularized by a veteran of the Second Seminole War, G. A. McCall (1802–68) in a story about a masquerade ball in Florida in *Tales from the Frontier* (1868), but this and many of the other terms can be found in the works of Washington Irving, James Fenimore Cooper, Henry Rowe Schoolcraft and Mark Twain, writers who helped create America and Americans and in a doing so gave the Indian a cardboard identity to represent subservience to a dominant United States.

First Writers

With the first records of oratory came the first writers. They emerged out of the missionary experience, from the schools, which were seldom as successful as expected and which, if they did establish good Christian Native communities, were then dispossessed by disbandment westwards, like the Stockbridge, or over time like the Mashpee Wampanoag. Samson Occom (1723–92), the Mohegan autobiographer, preacher and likely descendant of Uncas, the seventeenth-century ally of the English, was taught and befriended by Eleazar Wheelock Lebanon, Connecticut (1711–79), subsequently the founder of Dartmouth College in New Hampshire. As a teenager Occom developed a yearning to teach and better fellow Indians. In his autobiography he records that he recognized that Indian people were well able to distinguish alphabetical letters by ear, but not by sight. So he glued letters to cedar chips, put them on a bench and had his pupils fetch and carry the correct letters; he also jumbled them up and then reordered them into the alphabet. He was a man of many parts, growing his own corn, raising pigs, carving his own spoons and ladles and an expert shot who paid for his powder and shot by selling feathers, no doubt used for bolsters. He also wrote of the differential treatment he received compared to that accorded to white missionaries, of the wretchedness of slaves and the hypocrisy of the so-called civilized in the treatment of others. Sent on a speaking tour of Britain (1766–7) to raise money for Indian education, he was extremely successful, securing a pledge from the Earl of Dartmouth (1731–1801). This arrangement was subverted by Wheelock, and Dartmouth College was set up as a fundamentally non-Indian institution, following on from his earlier Latin and Indian schools.[55]

In the nineteenth century Occom was followed by others, combining fiery Christianity and a passionate, well-expressed sense of Indianness, people who wrote for their own kind. William Apess (1798–1839), the Methodist Pequot, who published the first Indian book, *A Son of the Forest: The Experience of William Apes, a Native of the Forest* (1829), fought for the rights of the Maspee on Cape Cod in the 1830s and turned King Philip into a national hero.[56] Very different was the autobiography and lament of the war leader Black Hawk, the *Life of Ma-Ka-Tai-Me-She-Kia-Kiak or Black Hawk, embracing the Tradition of his Nation-Indian Wars in which he has been engage . . .* (1834). Unlike most of the other early Native writing this was written by a major political leader who fought the US during the War of 1812, outside of any Christian framework of modernity. In Canada slightly later two Mississauga Methodists, from the north shore of Lake Ontario, converted, spoke, translated, wrote and assimilated in the USA and Britain, as well as Canada. Peter Jones or Kahkewaquonaby (1802–56)[57] published posthumously the *History of the Ojebway Indians* (1861), while George Copway or Kahkakakah-bowh (1818–69) published earlier a similar but differently structured text, the first Canadian First Nations publication *The Life, History, and Travels of Kah-ge-ga-gah-bowh, (George Copway) a Young Indian Chief of the Ojebwa Nation* (1847).[58] This was also the period when James Evans (1801–46), another Methodist missionary, with Ojibwe/Anishinaabe assistants, developed a syllabic system for Algonquian languages.

Cherokee Initiatives

In the southern United States also, missionaries converted and inspired Indians to adopt Christianity, religion providing a pathway, through education and writing, to modernization. While many of the earlier missionaries were Moravians, the Second Great Awakening inspired the foundation of new, and now fully American, missionary societies: the American Board of Commissioners for Foreign Missions (ABCFM), in 1810, and the American Bible Society, in 1816. Both were particularly active among the Cherokee, that Indian nation most successful in taking up the economic and social opportunities of peace and plantation society. The successful syllabary of silversmith George Guess or Sequoyah (1770–1840) was inspired by observing the use of a newspaper by white people. He tried this out on his young daughter, and quickly, by manuscripts only, reading and writing spread through the Cherokee nation. In turn this was taken up by Elias Boudinot (c.1804–39) and Samuel Worcester (1798–1859), the missionary who in 1832 established at the Supreme Court the idea if not the reality of Cherokee sovereignty. He obtained metal type in Boston and used it to make the bilingual newspaper *Cherokee Phoenix*, the first Native North American newspaper, established at New Echota in 1828. Boudinot, educated by the Moravians and the ABCFM, believed that, following the Removal Act of 1830, Cherokee should move west, and he signed the removal treaty of 1835 but was assassinated by anti-removal traditionalists in 1839. In a sense Boudinot, like other, earlier leaders such as Joseph Brant, and his contemporaries Jones and Copway, was caught at the point where modernization and traditionalism together fail, because of circumstances, to produce a stable way forward.

Early writing in the USA

Algonquian/Anishinaabe/Ojibwe equivalent texts were created or recorded in a similar manner to that of Copway, Evans and Jones by Indian agent Henry Rowe Schoolcraft (1793–1864), whose magnum opus was the six-volume *Historical and Statistical Information Respecting the . . . Indian Tribes of the United States* (1851–7). But more influential were the texts obtained with his part-Ojibwe wife Jane Johnston for his *Algic Researches* (1839). Johnston was the first Native woman writer, and together they produced and published fourteen issues of *The Literary Voyager* or *Muzzenyegun* between 1826 and 1827.[59] This brought early attention to the trickster hero Manabozho, who in Schoolcraft's words 'wielded the arts of a demon, and had the ubiquity of a god'. These stories of Manabozho were taken up by Longfellow and conflated with the Iroquoian/Haudenosaunee founder hero Hiawatha to create what he saw as a national romantic narrative, after the Finnish epic *Kalevala*, with a romantic shamanistic subtext, *The Song of Hiawatha* (1855). Subsequently Henry Rowe Schoolcraft, following the popularity of the poem, compounded the incoherence by republishing legends with the entirely ridiculous equation of the two heroes. Horatio Hale eloquently compared the confusion as similar that which might have been made by an inquiring Chinese traveller in medieval Europe mixing up King Arthur with King Alfred, and both with Odin.[60] Schoolcraft, involved in negotiating the dispossession of Michigan Indians, incidentally provided the texts to create this American hybrid tale.

In the same period another Iroquoian, Cherokee rather than Haudenosaunee, wrote the first Native American, and indeed first Californian, novel. John Rollin Ridge or Yellow Bird (1827–67), of the Cherokee plantocracy in Georgia, whose modernizing father and grandfather signed the removal Treaty of Echota in 1835 and were subsequently assassinated, moved west. He became a journalist, poet and early Native novelist with the story, with a strong racial cast, of a Robin Hood-like bandit, *The Life and Adventures of Joaquin Murieta* (1854), much later believed to be part inspiration for the Zorro stories.

White Education

Many of the first Native leaders in the Euro-American world, including Occom, Apess, the Delorias, were Christian-educated, as were many subsequent generations of American and Canadian Native leaders. But the institutions of education, such as Armstrong's Hampton Normal and Agricultural Institute and Pratt's Carlisle Indian Industrial School, were renowned for their brutality, their sexual and emotional abuse and, of course, their prohibition of Indian language and culture. But a recognizably Indian literature emerged out of this obnoxious, continuing process. Sherman Alexie, in his comic teen novel *The Absolutely True Diary of a Part-time Indian* (2007), skewers the type of hopeless down-at-heel reservation teacher in his portrayal of Mr P. This skanky old white man, who is always sleepy, comes to class in his pyjamas and feels guilty about how much he beat Indian kids when he was younger to get rid of their culture. He mentors the hero Arnold after Arnold has broken his teacher's nose.[61]

In Canada Indian schools have an unambiguous reputation. So if Richard Henry Pratt, the founder of the boarding school system in the USA, is known for his catchphrase, 'kill the Indian and save the child', then the corresponding system in Canada, termed the 'residential' school system, is remembered for enacting this with terrible literalness. Some 3,200 of the 150,000 pupils in these schools, open for more than a century until 1996, are recorded in the 2015

Honouring the Truth Reconciling the Future as dying – from abuse and, mostly, disease.[62]

After the Civil War

Indian writers and activists who came of age after the Civil War and before the domination of the boarding schools were from very diverse and complicated backgrounds. In this period, for the first time, Indian women were published. Sarah Winnemucca (1844?–91) (Northern Paiute) from Nevada, self-educated as a child living as a companion in a white family, fought and wrote eloquently for Indian rights and was the first woman to achieve national prominence. She advocated military rather than corrupt BIA management of Native affairs. She was also one of those rare people who set up a school herself. In her autobiography, the first by an Indian woman, she records bloodying a male assailant while travelling in a company of men: 'Some one laid a hand on me and said, "Sarah!" I jumped up with fright and gave him such a blow right in the face. I said, "Go away, or I will cut you to pieces, you mean man!"'[63] As with her later contemporaries she was obliged to work with non-Indian groups. Caught cross-culturally, she demanded respect from speakers and advancement, while styling herself photographically and in print as an Indian princess. The Canadian Mohawk Pauline Johnson (1861–1913), with the aboriginal name Tekahionwake ('double-life'), played the same dual role, subverting white ideas of Indianness, with a reliance on romantic imagery, to educate and inform North American and Indian audiences.[64] Similarly Sophia Alice Callahan (1868–94), the first American Indian Creek woman novelist, in *Wynema: A Child of the Forest* (1891) created a romantic tale which both educates about Creek life and explains the difficulties of Native existence.

The First Leaders

Professional leaders, with tertiary education, emerged after the Civil War. Of Natives in the nadir years of the early twentieth century, perhaps most famous was Charles Eastman or Ohiyesa (1858–1939)

(Dakota), born in Minnesota. Of mixed descent, he was an early practising physician, responsible alongside the missionary poet Elaine Goodale, supervisor of education in the Dakotas, who would become his wife and collaborator, for ministering to the dying after Wounded Knee. Together, with Eastman as author and Goodale as editor, they published numerous volumes of memoirs (*Indian Boyhood* (1902)), stories and how-to books and worked vigorously for the proper treatment of Native people, helping to establish the Boy Scouts of America, including Boy Scout troupes for Indians. Eastman and Goodale were in one sense Christian assimilationists, realistic modernizers who believed in on-reservation day-schools, where education would have a wider feedback into the community. Eastman travelled to Europe in the 1910s and 1920s, speaking for his people at the London Universal Race Conference of 1911, and helped to set up the short-lived but highly influential Society of American Indians. His partnership with Goodale is well documented by a niece and others. As part of his work habits, he would make notes, and these would be organized at the end of the day, following domestic duties with their six children. The partnership came to end, however, perhaps because of Eastman's involvement with other women, and he wrote nothing on his own, though he worked on accounts of Pontiac and Sacajawea. In the 1920s Eastman was professionally involved with an unusual philanthropic widow, Florence Brooks-Aten (1875–1960), with whose foundation he served, and on whose behalf he visited Europe to lecture. At the time Eastman had retreated from the world, back, it is reasonably suggested, to an Indian identity in Canada.[65]

A similar partnership, only this time son and mother, was that between between Omaha Francis LaFlesche (1857–1932) and the first Harvard woman ethnologist, Alice Fletcher (1838–1923), interpreter in the 1879 Standing Bear case, in which Standing Bear was declared a person for the purposes of habeas corpus, a judgement that eventually ensured citizenship for Indian people.[66]

While Eastman was brought up a refugee in Canada from the 1862 war, a contemporaneous Indian physician, Carlos Montezuma or Wassaja (c.1866–1923) (Yavapai-Apache), had been captured as a baby in Arizona and sold to, befriended and brought up by the Neapolitan photographer Carlo or Carlos Gentile. Performing in Wild West shows, and then educated at the University of Illinois while working in a pharmacy, he went as a physician to Pratt at the Carlisle Indian School, being both a modernist, in advocating education and advancement, but also a radical in his early and continuing denouncements of the Bureau of Indian Affairs.[67] As a physician at Carlisle he was involved in looking after the famous football team, highly important in giving Indian people a national presence in an all-American activity, and something on which he commended his good friend the arch-assimilationist Pratt. He assisted Eastman in the setting up of the Society of American Indians, the first national organization run by as well as for Indians. But in this he was also passionately opposed to the Bureau of Indian affairs and eventually set up his own journal, *Wassija*. While originally an assimilationist, he became increasingly involved back home in the Fort McDowell Yavapai Nation, as an advocate and resident.

Montezuma wanted to marry perhaps the greatest woman activist writer at the turn of the twentieth century, the multitalented Zitkala-Ša, Red Bird, or Gertrude Simmons Bonnin (1876–1938), an Indiana-educated Yankton writer and composer, who not only spoke of her own experience growing up and co-authored the first Indian opera, *Sun Dance* (1913), but was also a journalist and editor. Later she campaigned against the oil extraction abuses of 1920s Oklahoma. Both Montezuma and Zitkala-Ša were involved with Carlisle School and the assimilation project of Pratt; Zitkala-Ša subsequently turned against Pratt and broke off her engagement with Montezuma over her insistence on remaining independent and furthering her writing. She wrote forcibly about the retention of Yankton values, for instance in an *Atlantic Monthly* article, 'Why I Am a Pagan', in 1902.[68]

Two First Nations physicians preceded the Americans Montezuma and Zitkala-Ša but were editors as well as writers. One was the Ojibwe Peter Edmund Jones (1843–1909), who edited his own newspaper, *The Indian*, which ran for twenty-four issues in 1885–6.[69] The other was the part-Oxford-educated Mohawk Oronhyatekha (1863–1907), who took over the US-based Order of Foresters and over a twenty-year period turned it a successful fraternal (that is mutual self-help and insurance) organization, which had on his death in 1907 distributed $20 million in funds to 100,000 people. He edited the order's journal and published *History of the Independent Order of Foresters* (Toronto, 1894).[70]

Writer Families

The mid-nineteenth-century penetration of missionaries westwards provided education for a limited number of converts. The Episcopalians set up their mission among the Yankton in South Dakota in 1859. One of the early converts was Philip Deloria, Tipi Sapa or Black Lodge (1854–1931), ordained a priest in 1892, and a freemason, who worked through his 'Planting Society' for the conversion of Sioux to farming while maintaining his traditional position. He was followed by his daughter and other members of his family.[71] Ella Deloria (1889–1971) (Dakota), with a degree in education from Columbia (1914), worked with Boas and his school to record primary Sioux literature and write both literature and polemics. The strength of her work can be seen from extensive details used in the texts: for instance, a Dakota seasonal greeting equivalent to Happy Christmas or Thanksgiving is: 'Now the tracks are visible', that is, as the first snow deer slots become visible, and so hunger recedes, a time of winter celebration (1954). She wrote of how a suitable punishment for murder, beyond immediate retaliation or death by ordeal, might be adoption into the family of the deceased (1944). Her polemical account of Dakota and Indian life, *Speaking of Indians* (1944), addresses a series of interconnected issues: the problem of race, which, then as now, is essentially about hierarchy, and in that sense remains alive and toxic; and issues to do with Christianity and the churches, writing as a Christian, yet emphasizing the need to acknowledge the damage caused by Christianity alongside its function as a vehicle for modernization. But throughout the work, and in her biography and then in her two-generation novel from the 1940s, *Waterlily*, what matters most is kin and kinship, and relatedness. Two of her own kin, her nephews Vine Deloria Jnr and Philip Deloria, followed her in her profession.

Vine Deloria Jnr (1933–2005) was both very similar to, and entirely different from, his aunt. A Christian-educated ex-marine, he wrote brilliantly and amusingly, for instance, in *Custer Died for Your Sins* (1969), about what he considered to be unprovable anthropological theories designed by academics to further their careers, such as the Bering Strait theory of arrival in the Americas from Asia. So he was no ethnographer, but instead an embedded Standing Rock communitarian, writing across cultures about both the generalities and the specifics of Sioux and Native America culture and about why these things are important for the United States. More than that, Vine Deloria Jnr was also a politician, an activist who worked from the inside and a director of the Congress of American Indians, the campaigning organization born in the hopeful, but especially for Indians difficult, war year of 1944. But by the mid-1960s he was caught between direct action and the need for book-keeping. He was a distinctly contrarian figure with a millenarian aspect, a coyote trickster person, who teased and infuriated and got things right, enabling change. In one of his later articles he decried the way that, with the New Deal arrangements for tribal governments, American Indian leaders had become involved in clientelism, that is, dependency on the US government, moving from being landlords to welfare recipients. Of course, he would have had a half-outraged, half-outrageous view of the conflicted absurdities of the impending changes to casino culture. At the extreme edge of his interests were Pre-Columbian contacts: he was certain that Columbus was not the first, that Barry Fell and the *oghum*/Irish/Gaelic inscriptions prove that other Europeans were in America first – not just the Vikings, but the Basques and the Bristolian fishermen. Deloria was involved in the foundation in 2004 of the National Museum of the American Indian, a national institution that could run an authoritative agenda, backed with artefacts that speak not simply to individual experience but to cultural complexity.

The multifaceted work of Vine Deloria Jnr was not atypical. Just as Charles Dickens and Mark Twain were novelists and journalists, and politicians such as Teddy Roosevelt, Benjamin Disraeli and Winston Churchill were writers and politicians, so many, if not most, twentieth-century Native writers were rather more than simply poets and novelists.

Indians Reinventing the West

Central to the whole business of Indian literature and performance is the imaginative writer who passes, who makes ethnic origins irrelevant and takes a proper place in the general scheme of things. One such was the one-sixteenth Cherokee poet and playwright and Hollywood scriptwriter Rollie Lynn Riggs (1899–1954) from Claremore, the site of the 1818 season of strawberries Battle of Claremore Mound. In this fight the newly arrived Cherokee who, long before the Trail of Tears, were already modernizers, dispossessed the more traditional Osage. In *The Lonesome West* (1927) Riggs, who had had a bitter childhood dominated by his stepmother, turned the site into Blackmore. With an ear for Oklahoma dialect, for the guitar and super-hybrid folk songs, Riggs, whose gay identity was not revealed until the twenty-first century, reworked the sometime Scottish, Irish, or even royal Henry VIII song 'Green Grow the (Holly) Lilacs' into a Broadway play of 1931, which ran for sixty-four performances and in which Lee Strasberg played a Syrian peddler. The musical, with its Surrey with a fringe on top and Indian turnips, was taken up by Rodgers and Hammerstein and turned into *Oklahoma!* in 1943, with a new score and minor changes, a reprise if you like of John Rollin Ridge and Zorro, and an affirmation of American identity in wartime. In Hammerstein's words for the *New York Times* after the opening, 'Mr. Riggs' play is the wellspring of almost all that is good in *Oklahoma!* I kept most of the lines of the original play without making any changes.'[72] Towards the end Curly's Aunt Eller pronounces quite specifically that Americans are foreigners in pre-1907 Indian Territory: 'Why, we're territory folks? We ort to hang together. I don't mean hang. I mean stick. Whut's the United States? It's jist a furrin country to me. And you supportin' it! Jist dirty ole furriners, ever last one of you!'[73] Perhaps more to the point is *Cherokee Night* (1930), which explores the business of being Cherokee, from grave-robbing on the Claremore Mound (predicting the 1930s robbing of Spiro Mound) to blood identity and the Cherokee clan system. Exceptionally Riggs wrote two plays with gay aspects, one based on prostitution in the US navy, *The Cream in the Well* (1947), and the other, *The Year of Pilar* (1938), set in the Yucatan, in which a Mexican aristocrat is involved with a Mayan.

Humour

In contrast the larger-than-life Will Rogers (1879–1935), a public figure in a way that Riggs never was, became perhaps the most famous Cherokee celebrity, but one whose ethnicity is muted. Of established Confederate stock, Rogers was a cowboy cattle man, the 1920s epitome of Curley from 1940s *Oklahoma!*, a graceful performer who both eschewed the Wild West format and transcended that of vaudeville and for whom, as a speaker and humourist, silent movies weren't good enough. He was to serve, incidentally, as mayor of Beverly Hills. Unlike characters in Riggs' plays, he was a non-tragic figure, until actual tragedy struck, in his airplane death in Inupiat territory in northernmost Alaska in 1935. His sense of humour was ironic and laid back – slow-burn jokes rather than wise cracks – and in that sense very Indian indeed. And of course the point about cowboys is not that they were free, but that they appeared to be free; they are a rural proletariat, usually landless and without a future, and distinctly descended from the medieval Piers Plowman. In Rogers' life and Horatio Alger's, the well-heeled writer identifying with the dispossessed, the cowboy appeared in the very American context of the ancient 'Dowel, Dobet and Dobest': do well, do better and do best. For the fourteenth-century Piers, 'Dowel' meant 'No creature to bygyle, Nother to lye nor to lacke . . . Ne to spille speche'. Rogers was the American who refused to beguile, lie or lack. Instead he roamed about the USA, his columns syndicated to 600 newspapers, without spilling speech. His style was copied by Bob Hope. He said that the point of treaties was to allow enough time to reach for a rock (to brain Indians), that his ancestors would have met the *Mayflower*, that 'It was as hard to find an American in New York as it was to get a passport', and of Trotsky that he had never met a man he didn't like. And when Kaw Charles Curtis was nominated for election as Republican vice-president in 1928, Rogers said they'd together run the white people out of America.[74]

Other Native writers contributed to the story of the west, such as

John Milton Oskison (1874–7), who wrote a fictionalized biography of Sam Houston, *Texan Titan* (1935), long before the renaissance. John Joseph Mathews (*c.*1894–1979) (Osage) wrote biography and tribal history as well as a novel, *Sundown* (1934), around the time of Osage wealth- and oil-based prominence. His biography of E. W. Marland (1874–1941), oilman and sometime governor of Oklahoma, includes an account of working with the 101 Ranch, a Wild West show and operation, and an oil company on Ponca land, finding oil in a location used by Indian people for platform burials and paying for the right to drill.[75]

Newspapermen

The first national periodicals by and for Indian people were the creation of the first-generation leaders. Of the early periodicals most important and influential was the *Quarterly Journal of the Society of American Indians*.[76] The Society of American Indians (SAI) (1911–23) was the first national American Indian rights group founded for and by American Indians themselves, rather than by white liberals intent on helping and saving Native people. It was organized and run by highly educated modernizers, who wrote as part of their professional and Indian lives. The editor and contributors to the *Quarterly Journal of the Society of American Indians*, later the *American Indian Journal*, included Charles Eastman (Santee-Sioux), Carlos Montezuma (Mohave-Apache) and Sherman Coolidge (Arapaho). That journal emphasized modernization and education, was against Wild Westing, i.e. Wild West shows, and advocated race pride. Arthur Parker,[77] the editor, emphasized the difference of his journals from those produced by under BIA aegis such as the Carlisle Institute's *Red Man* or the *Indian School Journal*, published in the Chilocco Indian School in Oklahoma (Smithers). They fought against the image of the Dying Indian. This is epitomized by the sculpture of the *End of the Trail* (1915), by James Earle Fraser (1876–1953), portraying a slumped warrior on horseback. The classical sculpture *The Dying Gaul* in Rome occupies a similar position of inauthentic romanticization. The editors also maintained a slightly contradictory relationship with Indian boarding schools, recognizing the need to fuse the best of the old ways with the best of the new ones. The SAI also advocated the granting of citizenship to American Indians, which was obtained. It was replaced in 1924 after the 1928 Meriam Report and the New Deal by Collier's BIA, and then by the founding of the Congress of American Indians (1944). This struggled at a time of indifference to Indian problems through the war years and the active intransigence of the termination period of the 1950s, regrouping after the Chicago Conference of 1961. Ernie Benedict Kaientaronkwen (1918–2011) (Mohawk) was highly influential at this time, having edited, between 1939 and 1941, the *War Whoop*, said to be the first newspaper in Akwesasne, and in 1968 founding *Akwesasne Notes*, which was to become the most important Indian newspaper.

Two more recent, and rather different, scholar-journalists and writer-thinkers are important. They were both Sioux and both founders of periodicals. Tim Giago (b. 1934) (Lakota), from Pine Ridge, is a writer, editor and publisher who has created a number of newspapers, the most central of which, originally the *Lakota Times* (founded in 1981), is now known as *Indian Country Today Media Network*, owned by the New York casino Oneidas since 1998. Giago's strong, trenchant reviews reflect the need to ensure an Indian historiography written by Native Americans rather than white activists and scholars. He also founded the Native American Journalists Association in 1984. Crucially, like many Indians, he had a successful career in the 1950s as a very young sailor in the US Navy, serving in Korea. He has a specific viewpoint on AIM and the occupation of Wounded Knee in 1973. The village was burned to the ground rather than simply occupied, leaving the thirty-five residents homeless. Giago's father had worked in the 1930s for the store owners, one of whom, Agnes Gildersleeves, was Ojibwe/Anishinaabe. Further, he takes Russell Means and the urban-based near-terrorists to task for inspiring violence and for vilifying the then tribal chairman Dick Wilson and he squarely blames AIM for responsibility in the killing of Anna Mae Aquash,[78] the Mi'kmaq, and for the destruction of vital Indian records during the occupation of the BIA in Washington. His real point is that ordinary, quotidian Indianness is different from radicalism, that it requires grounded persistence in cultural values rather than imposed, destructive standpoints taken from outsiders. One of his sharpest pieces relates to the Republican Tea Party, named after the Boston Tea Party, when people dressed up as Mohawks, not known to be residents of the city, so that blame for the tea dumping would fall on Indians, a signature dishonesty defining the USA and yet to be comprehended.[79]

Wičazo Ša Review (*Red Pencil Review*) was founded in 1985 by Elizabeth Cook-Lynn (b. 1930) (Lakota) and others as the first Native academic journal, with a more radical outlook than the mainstream or tribal press. The first tribal newspaper was the Navajo one, today the *Navajo Times*, founded in 1960. The *Lakota Times* and many others founded in the 1980s can be considered part of the Native renaissance of the period. In Canada *Nunatsiaq News*, founded in 1973 around the time of the northern Quebec settlement, acts as a source of both news and scholarly articles about the history and culture of Arctic Canada.

In the 1960s

The term 'Native American renaissance', coined by Kenneth Lincoln, both celebrates the very real growth in American Indian writing since the 1960s and obscures the writing, associated with leadership, that was anyway taking place in the mid-twentieth century, for instance the work of Muriel Wright (1889–1975), the Choctaw historian of Oklahoma,[80] or (William) D'Arcy McNickle (1904–77), Kutenai and Salish anthropologist and administrator, Oxford- and Grenoble-educated thanks to the proceeds of the sale of his allotment, who wrote through the middle of the twentieth century and worked with the New Deal BIA and then various private initiatives, especially those of the Congress of American Indians, publishing all the while.[81] Indian writing, certainly with Vine Deloria Jr and N. Scott Momaday (b. 1934), changed and moved away from the margins. Momaday's *House Made of Dawn* (1969), about a Pueblo man coming home, murdering and recovering through his grandfather, won the Pulitzer Prize for Literature, bringing Native literature to wider public and inspiring others. With the political successes of the 1970s, this ensured a renewed interest in early texts written by Native people, or collected from them, and these developments were associated with the launching by William C. Sturtevant of the Smithsonian's *Handbook of North*

American Indians in 1978 and the mixed blessing of art revival and consumption, appropriation and appreciation.

Native Anthropology

Sitting alongside the publications and archives assembled by anthropologists and then linguists, after about 1910, are the oral history and language resources gathered from the late twentieth century as part of language regeneration and survival by people who may be termed scholar elders. Most prolific of these was the late Alfonso Ortiz (1939–97) (San Juan Tewa), who was pre-eminent in his field. Albert White Hat (1938–2013) created the first orthography, textbook and glossary for the Lakota languages and translated dialogue into Lakota for the film *Dances with Wolves* (1990) at a time when the average age of Lakota speakers was sixty.[82] Emory Sekaquaptewa (1928–2007) was the senior contributor to the *Hopi Dictionary* (1998). Vi Hilbert (1918–2008) created collaboratively *Lushootseed Dictionary* (1994) for the Upper Skagit people in Washington State. Freda Ahenakew (1932–2011) trained as a Cree linguist in Canada and produced *Cree Language Structures* (1987), children's books and other literature. Many of the most important scholar linguists were and are women: home-based, longer-lived and more traditional than men, they are more likely culture carriers. The anthropologist Bea Medicine (1923–2005) eloquently described the Lakota world.

Vizenor

One of those influenced by Momaday is Gerald Vizenor (b. 1934). Like Momaday and other writers, he is a military man, educated in the services during the 1950s, before becoming perhaps the most questioning and most prolific Native writer. He can in the manner in which he emerged and took on the various establishments also be read against an earlier generation of writers about war, James Jones and Norman Mailer, but moving on from their traditional narrative to his own magic-realism, beyond that of the sometime anthropologist Kurt Vonnegut, Native rather than Latin American in origin. In style, however, he is very different, using language in a distinct and stimulating manner to explore history, ideas and himself. His best-known phrase is 'survivance', that is survival and resistance, which, in lesser hands, can become an in-group marker rather than a term of analysis or, as Vizenor may half intend, ironic. What Vizenor's poetics achieves is a reworking of non-linear styles of oral and original literature in mock-serious attacks on received wisdoms. He returns again and again to the centrality of the ethnic specific Indian, the Anishnaabe/Chippewa/Ojibwe, of White Earth, Minnesota. He derides the dead-letter anthropologist, Hiroshima peaceniks, university bigwigs and a caricatured flotsam of personality types who live off the body Indian, some Native and many not. Yet these seemingly hurtful satires continually invert themselves, in a humorous manner which vaporizes any cruelty, to reveal the seriousness of Vizenor's purpose: a bone court to hear the natural rights of (Indian) bones in museums, critiques of Banks and Means and invented San Francisco solar dancers, 'a ruck of urban warriors'. This style is often referred to as that of a trickster, by Vizenor himself and others, but it can also be taken at a more fundamental level: literal, rather than literary, history taken down by linguists during the nadir years. Others then and afterwards create from their own stories and extended cultural context fiction and lightly fictionalized narratives which often transcend genre. These include Leslie Marmon Silko (b. 1948), with *Ceremony* (1977), about a veteran returning to his Pueblo community, and the bleak vision of James Welch's (1940–2002) *Winter in the Blood* (1974). The Navajo poets Luci Tapahonso (b. 1953) and Rex Lee Jim (b. 1962) speak of racist hairdressers, sheep and the stars.

Folk Star

Most interesting of the writer-performers of the second half of the twentieth century, and dating to before Momaday and the Native American renaissance is the Cree Canadian-American singer Buffy Sainte-Marie (b. 1941). She achieved early success and was involved with a long series of folk and rock musicians in the early and mid-1960s. She participated in the anti-Vietnam War movement, AIM activism in the 1970s and the residential school controversy of the 1980s, which were also subjects of her music. 'Universal Soldier'

(1964) was recorded by Donovan and Neil Diamond; 'Until It's Time for You to Go' (1965) was successful for a range of singers, including the Four Pennies, Neil Diamond and Elvis Presley. Other compositions achieved permanent recognition in movies: 'Up Where We Belong', to which she was a co-contributor, won an Academy Award in *An Officer and a Gentleman* (1982). Most startling was her involvement with *Sesame Street*, for many years through the late 1970s, where she might for instance wash or bathe with her infant son, Dakota 'Cody' Starblanket Wolfchild. While there is a recent biography of Sainte-Marie,[83] and she is much celebrated, especially in Canada, she is not written about in the academic context of indigenous literature, her success and hybridity begging the same questions about identity that, for instance, bother the reputations of the Ridges and Will Rogers.

Outside Folklore

If Buffy Sainte-Marie is a folk singer, then it is worth considering whether transcribed oral texts are folklore. While all texts must be both authored and authentic, that is, be real and accurate, ideas of authorship and authenticity may confuse and distort the literatures and languages seen from within. Alan Dundes described folklore as 'autobiographical ethnography – that is, it is a people's own description of themselves', though the term 'folklore' is not always popular in Native North America, as it implies a Eurocentric knowledge base. In the nineteenth century 'folklore' was applied to the oral culture of civilized societies, but in a hierarchical context. Since Indian societies were deemed savage they were not considered to have folklore.[84] Associated with this characterization of the 1880s was the ethnocentric notion that Native American folk tales had no form or morphology, that they could not be characterized and analysed structurally. Yet folklore in and from Native North America is an important idea, one which enabled the collection and study of oral history. In the first half of the twentieth century American anthropologists edited the *Journal of American Folklore*, which had been founded in 1888 by the American Folklore Society. Further structuralists, such as Claude Lévi-Strauss, for instance in his analysis of the Tsimshian folk hero Asdiwal, developed a specific understanding of the way myths and history work.[85] So Dundes in the 1960s looked at Native American stories for structures. One common structure has four parts: Interdiction (i.e. prohibition from action), Violation, Consequence and an Attempted Escape from the Consequence. One Cree example given is that a boy is told not to shoot a squirrel by his sister, he shoots the squirrel, is swallowed by a fish and is saved by the sister when she cuts open the fish.[86] Folklore, then, is a category which could be, but is generally not, used in Native North America, except for the Smithsonian's annual Folklife Festival, founded in 1967, which celebrates diversity, for instance at the presidential inaugurations of the Bicentennial in 1976 and for the opening of the National Museum of the American Indian 2004.

Dance

Celebration of the mid-twentieth-century Indian ballerinas is placed in the same limbo: acknowledged at the National Museum of the American Indian and commemorated with a group biography[87] and other writings, but not featured in the public or academic perceptions of American Indianness. Scholars seldom have the intellectual apparatus to engage with indigeneity where it flows with the mainstream. Yet, like Buffy Sainte Marie, the Oklahoma ballerinas are in this peculiar way marginalized by the lack of informed discussion. This group of dancers is centred on Maria Tallchief (1925–2013), Marjorie Tallchief (b. 1926), Rosella Hightower (1920–2008), Moscelyne Larkin (1925–2012) and Yvonne Chouteau (1929–2016). Maria Tallchief, an oil-rich Osage Oklahoman, worked with the Ballet Russe de Monte Carlo, then George Balanchine, whom she married, and the New York Ballet during the 1940s and was much honoured in France. The success of the assimilated, the mainstreaming of Indian peoples, signifies perhaps the eclipse of ethnicity.

New Partnerships

Many elder scholars worked collaboratively. One such lifetime collaboration, but much more than that, was between Nora Marks (b. 1927) and the late Richard Dauenhauer (1942–2014), poet and translator from New York, who have together published half a dozen or so texts, anthologies and writings from the Tlingit of southeast Alaska. These are very varied. The stories include extensive biographies and a full explanation of mourning ceremonies. The important role played by drumming music is emphasized. Elders also explain the development of politics around the founding of the Alaskan Native Brotherhood by William Paul (1885–1977) and others from 1912. They wrote about the fights against canneries, which occupied prime sites along waterways and destroyed much of Alaskan fisheries, and about discrimination. The narratives created by the Dauenhauers defy easy categorization, since they depend on a wide variety of sources – personal inspiration and experience, family clan and village traditions, community if not ethnographic research as well as archival research.

Less conventional is the story of Michael Dorris (1945–97) and Louise Erdrich (b. 1954). *Love Medicine* (1984), Erdrich's account in a conversational, oral narrative style of different generations of Anishinaabe, alienated yet belonging, is a Joycean riff on Native America. The tale of their own family could be written as a Greek tragedy, or like a story from the Book of Job. Yet it is too plainly a Native American morality play about two writers who dared too much and fought too hard to transcend the limits set by the Indian story. Dorris was a war orphan from Kentucky, an undefined Indian, the brilliant first chair of the Dartmouth Indian programme and an anthropological fieldworker in Subarctic Alaska. He adopted, as a single male, a boy with foetal alcohol syndrome, for whom he strove to create a normal life. He wrote about – exploited some were to say – his son Abel in his 1989 account *Broken Cord*. At the time and later he was criticized by Elizabeth Cook-Lynn[88] for blaming the victim, Abel's mother, when he advocated the incarceration of pregnant alcoholics to save children. For Cook-Lynn, and many others, culture-based therapy models are necessary to ensure that Indian women are not to be blamed and can recover as Indians, and especially that their children are raised by men as well as women. When Dorris and Erdrich's marriage broke up, they accused one another of trying to kill their children. When their biological daughters accused Dorris of sexual and physical abuse, he took his own life.[89] In a published tale from Alaska Dorris talked of 'the capriciousness of codified law: what shouldn't be, nevertheless was'. What shouldn't have been was in Dorris' tragic life.[90]

Erdrich, the survivor, continues to write fiction in neo-realist Chippewa/Ojibwe/Anishinaabe country, comparable to Faulkner's Yoknapatawpha, and has had success with *Shadow Tag* (2010) and *Round House* (2012), continuing to explore romance and reality, violence and family.

Joking and Survival

Diné and Inuktitut are not going to disappear but they are changing, and their use is likely to shift continually semantically and structurally, and by incorporating outside terms, in the process perhaps becoming stronger. In a way, the future of Navajo may be similar to that of Welsh, which has more speakers. Between 2001 and 2011 the proportion of Welsh speakers (in a population of 3 million) decreased from 21 to 19 per cent. Surprisingly Welsh is only increasing in urban areas, where it is changing, not simply with new words, but with simplification and slang. As one commentator puts it, 'better a slack Welsh, than a slick English'.[91] There is a Welsh joke that could become a generic Native North American joke: 'I can speak English and Welsh, but neither of them properly.' Indian humour is particularly acerbic in laughing at and with non-Indians: so a definition of 'Being Indian' is for instance 'Having your non-Indian spouse dancing in full regalia at your tribal Pow-Wow' or 'Meeting at least two dozen anthropologists before you're 21' or 'Having White do-gooders continue to do for you instead of with you'.[92] Whitemen jokes are all-important, emphasizing their lack of reserve and effusiveness: 'Whitemen make lots of noise . . . it sounds too much like they mad at you. With some you can't be sure about it; so you just got to be careful all the time,' said one Apache in the 1970s.[93] One direction in which Navajo and other languages are going is the development of reservation-specific slangs. In Navajo as in English, many terms are acidly self-ironic, ethnically ego-directed: so 'jigháán' (*tchaan*) means 'rezzed out', or 'hill billy', which also has the sense of self-reliant; 'buckle bunny' describes a groupie who hangs around bulldogging rodeo stars (the buckles are awarded to winners), but the expression has rather more meanings than 'groupie'; 'snag' means a boy or girl friend, hence 'snagging' describes making out; 'Arthur Yazzie' means arthritis, as in 'Arthur

Yazzie stole my wife'; the Zuni of New Mexico, disparaging the Navajo, call the alcohol treatment centre 'Na Nizhoozhi Center Inc.' or 'Navajo Comfort Inn'.[94] Many jokes deal with the issue of bilingualism. So a Navajo grandmother is ill and goes to the clinic with her young bilingual grandson to interpret. The doctor says to tell the grandmother to go into the next room, where he will weigh her and give her an injection. The boy tells his grandmother to go into the next room, where she will be hung and shot, the joke being on the translation of English into Navajo, 'hanging' (using hanging scales) for weighing, and 'shot' for injection. Or a grandchild asks a grandfather where he will go when he passes on, and he says the burning place, that is hell, but it also means the place of forest fires, where for Navajo firefighters the pay is good.[95] This humour is self-directed and Native-based and is similar, for instance, to that of the Inuit. So Rebecca Veevee in a stand-up routine holds up a toilet roll and says the Inuit are rich because they now have toilet paper.[96] Often, Inuit jokes, like Navajo ones, are subsistence-based, such as the one about a musk ox calf that keeps getting up when it is about to be butchered, so the hunter threatens to shoot it.[97] But much of the outside Eskimo, rather than Inuit, humour is intra-group and largely racist, with an astonishing media acceptance of images and attitudes that would be unacceptable in reference to the Middle East or Africa, largely about stupidity, physical types, ice, snow and the temperature.

Other Languages

Joking language is only one of many different types of communication laid down before contact with proto-writing systems. Related to Plains ledger art is Plains sign language, a universal system of communication used from Alberta south and east to the Gulf of Mexico, a visual lingua franca that sat alongside the Chinook jargon mischiff and smoke signals, that near-apocryphal phenomenon that developed in the nineteenth century an imaginary presence of its own. Native North American peoples possessed and used numerous systems of proto-writing, expressive codified systems of symbols, widely understood through single and closely related societies. For instance, in Plains societies the war record, describing actual events pictographically, different for different peoples, shared general principles to do with counting coup – touching or taking from an enemy rather than killing – and the depiction of individuals by characteristics developed on paper into ledger book art. Similarly, the totem system of the Anishinaabe used the clan system to provide a codified means of explaining identity through introduced wampum belts and later in treaty documents, where leaders were required to sign away territory. *Nindoodem* (clan) identities were inherited from the father and usually zoomorphic: sturgeon, catfish, pike, bison, caribou, turtle, snake, though some were botanical and mythic figures. These appear in rock art, on birch-bark and on weapons and probably trees and functioned, it has been suggested, like European armorial seals rather than as individual signatures.[98] In contrast winter counts, in which each year in a calendar is symbolized by weather and intertribal and celestial events, are general, whereas war records celebrate individuality. In the north, and especially in northwest Alaska among the Inupiat, a highly systematized form of pictography – engraving on ivory – was used into the early twentieth century to record life and hunting, showing, for instance, the seasonal condition and gender fur colouring of caribou, housing, whaling, bird-hunting and the arrival of Europeans, in narratives, which, while certainly not writing, assert, like Anshinaabe *nindoodem*, a degree of permanence and immutability, of the kind which characterizes literate and written narrative. Personal narratives are told on Woodland war clubs, with records of encounters, of clan, and a portrait of the owner. Equally, the clan stories told on totem poles, on dance screens in the Pacific Northwest, on paintings in the southwest or in rock art break down the dichotomy that often characterizes the comparison of oral literature and textuality.

Deep Time

Related to proto-writing, and especially narrative art which brings together multiple symbols to create near-text, is the issue of deep time and the 'carrying capacity of oral tradition': whether or not ancient legends, like material remains, extend back thousands of years. Whether oral history has been passed down unchanged since time immemorial, remembered by all, or has been altered over time without any note of the changes, the broader reality is that storytelling is an aspect of everyday life which helps provide a context for comprehending and appreciating current social, cultural and political issues. For instance, Greenlanders retained into the nineteenth century deep-time memories of the Vikings, to whose extermination they contributed in the fifteenth century, and Canadian Inuit continue to tell stories in the twenty-first century of the Tuniit, or Paleo-Eskimos, whom the first Inuit encountered maybe 1,000 years ago, and from whom they may have learned much ice technique, for instance in the building of snowhouses. Even older may be the oral histories, *adawx*, of the Tsimshian, Gitksan and Nisga'a on the Northwest Coast, with cultural continuity extending back many millennia.[99]

6

Art and Materiality

Clovis projectile point of chert, about 14,000 old, likely to have been hafted on to a pole for use as a lance to kill large animals trapped in water or mud.

The Great Serpent Mound, a coiled snake efigy in the act of swallowing an egg, or the world, in southern Ohio, of the Fort Ancient Culture, eleventh century.

Panel in the Great Gallery, Utah, in Barrier Canyon Style, executed by artists of the Late A

Snow shoes are one of many inventions developed and distanced from their Native American origins.

re, perhaps 2,000 to 4,000 years ago.

Longhouse, Ganondagan State Historic Site, NY. The introduction of the idea of the longhouse from Native America brought about a new understanding of the spatial organization of kinship.

Datsolalee, Louisa Keyser (*c*.1835–1925) (Washoe), Nevada, made the finest coiled baskets for collectors in the arts and crafts era.

D. Y. Begay (b. 1954), fourth-generation weaver, incorporates Navajo philosophy, traditions and designs in her tapestry-weave textiles.

Don Tenoso talking about beadwork with a visitor to the Indian Market, Santa Fe, NM, 2005.

John Deer and family selling beadwork to tourists, mid-nineteenth century.

Dead from the Battle of the Little Big Horn 1876 (1881), by Red Horse (1822–1907) (Minneconjou Lakota Sioux). Although he hasn't named them, the artist has commemorated each person with precise details of clothing, posture and wounds, making them anything but anonymous.

Fresh Trail Apache War Party (1952), by Allan Houser (1914–1994).

David Cusick (*c.*1780–*c.*1831) (Tuscarora) published the first illustrated Indian book, *Sketches of Ancient History of the Six Nations* (1828), which includes this image of Stonish Giants.

Nampeyo (*c.*1859–1942), a Tewa Hopi potter who used ancient designs from Sikyatki in her work.

Beadwork artists Juanita Growing Thunder Fogarty (b. 1969) and her mother, Joyce Growing Thunder Fogarty (b. 1950) (Assiniboine Sioux), attend the opening of the exhibition 'Grand Procession', 2013.

mes Luna (b. 1950) (Luiseño), the conceptual artist who represented the US in the Venice
ennale 2005, celebrating Pablo Tac (1822–41), the Rome-educated Californian.

Les Castors Du Roi (2011), by Kent Monkman (1965–) (Cree and Anglo-Canadian), retelling the story of the French fur trade, of which little imagery survives.

Cultural Crossroads of the Americas (1996), by Bob Haozous (1943–) (Fort Sill Apache), metal billboard installation at the University of New Mexico, Albuquerque, retelling the story of border and immigration.

Indian with a Beer Can (1969), by Fritz Scholder (1937–2005) (Luiseño).

6

Art and Materiality

Embeddedness

This chapter looks at the phenomena of art and material culture in Native North America. Alfonso Ortiz (1939–97), the great Tewa/Puebloan anthropologist, suggested, just before he died long before his time, that an understanding and appreciation of Pueblo Indians as artists may have been one of the many factors which meant that southwestern tribes avoided allotment and destruction by the Dawes Act of 1887: art triumphant over adversity.[1] The intention here is to describe how and why art has a value, including a vital political affect, beyond, on the one hand, aesthetic importance and, on the other, its materiality. So this chapter describes the way in which at different times, and in different places, but especially today and now, objects are created, used and socially embedded, how Native art is about production and consumption surrounding beliefs and the communication and performance of those beliefs.

The ideas of 'art' and 'materiality', or 'material culture', overlap and are not mutually exclusive. Conventional notions of art history, imposed from outside by non-Natives, are useful and work best where there is a coherent body of objects, often but not necessarily by named individual artists, within a recognizable art tradition with a coherent style. But in the case of Native objects and artefacts, even those of great formal and aesthetic quality, whether recovered archaeologically or collected historically from aboriginal people, very often these may be insufficient in number and context to provide, when grouped together, anything more than an impressionistic overview, a meta-narrative through which to understand the past rather than an art

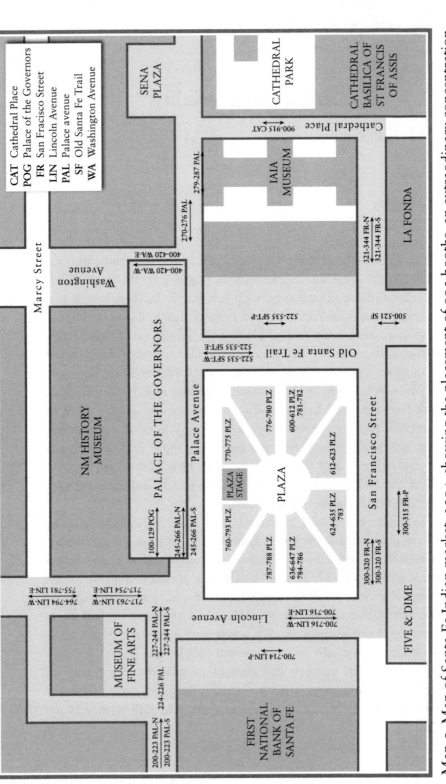

Map 5. Map of Santa Fe Indian market, 2014, showing the placement of 915 booths, an extraordinary concentration of artists in one place at one time.

tradition. Rather differently, contemporary Native art can be seen as a dialogue between the biography and genius of the individual artist and his or her cultural background, mediated by the contributions and demands of the dominant society – whether Anglo, French or Hispanic. Architecture is included in this discussion of art and material culture. Ancient Native art, to expand Rudofsky's telling, seems unforgivably unforgettable, without artists or architects. It is unequalled on the other continents.[2]

Tradition

The term *tradition*, with its idea of development or cultural context, is a reductionist marker used in archaeology to describe an ancient culture as an ideal type often at its maximum extent; the 'Woodland tradition', for example, refers to the pre-contact aboriginal cultures of the east.[3] But the term can be usefully be used to describe what now can be seen as specific moments of creativity, of art production stimulated by and at the same destroyed by Europeans and Americans arriving, providing new technologies, whether the horse or iron tools or Brazilian tobacco, and then passing over Native America, flattening and eliminating Native culture, yet, in a countervailing manner, moving on and providing, in some cases, space for recovery and renewal and innovation, for resistance against the dominant states. Art here, then, is seen, thanks to the anthropologist Alfred Gell (1945–97), as a nexus of social relations, between the artist and the non-Indian consumer, between Indian people and the colonizer and the collector.

Indian Market, Santa Fe

One such contemporary phenomenon, a vital nexus of social relations, is Indian Market, in Santa Fe, New Mexico. Better than anything else, perhaps, this event expresses what Native American art is all about, what artists do, why they do it, how they communicate what they make and how that art is consumed by non-Natives. Indian Market occurs in August each year. Sales of art work are impressive: each of the more than 43,000 visitors in 2001 spent more than $1,500 per group on Indian art as well as $500 on further shopping, adding

$19 million to the local economy. A third of the visitors had graduate degrees, and a third had incomes of more than $100,000. Indian Market, then, is an elite event, which perhaps more than any other occasion emphasizes the importance of American Indians for a certain section of American society.

The market comes indirectly out of the annual fiesta celebration of Don Diego de Vargas' (1643–1704) reconquest of New Mexico in 1692, following the Pueblo Revolt of 1680; that is, the primary celebration of Native creativity commemorates a moment of paramount destruction. This commemoration was reconfigured in 1922 and became a juried event to ensure and impose on Indian people standards of artistry and culture and is the legacy of a group of non-Natives including Edgar Lee Hewett, Kenneth Chapman and Maria Chabot.[4] In August, for two days each year, 100–150,000 people attend the more than 1,000 booths set up; prizes are awarded for different classes of objects, especially jewellery and ceramics; estimates of actual art sales by artists are hard to establish, but they are likely to be in the low millions.[5] Artists from other parts of the continent – Algonquian basketmakers or Dene beadworkers or Alaskan artists – may come, but the emphasis is local. Governed by the Southwestern Association for Indian Arts (SWAIA), the event is independent, charitable and depends on a groundswell of Indian people from nearby, especially the Rio Grande Pueblos, and their interaction and work with non-Natives. Purchasers can view the award-winning artworks the night before at an exclusive and expensive event, and turn up at seven on the Saturday morning and queue to be sure of buying the beribboned winning objects in whatever category, assuming the lusted-after object is actually available. The event then can be constructed as one of sybaritic elitism, one in which wealthy individuals often with only a passing passion (39 per cent of visitors in 2001 were first-time attendees) for Indian art express their own self-worth by purchasing something beautiful. Or it may be that, alternatively, Native art acts as a touchstone of beauty and solace, that it engages with people only able to visit Santa Fe once, people for whom that vacation has permanent meaning. Yet at a more significant level, Indian Market is about the normalcy of Indian art, the successful performance of Indianness in a hybrid occasion, full of absurdities and contradictions, of avarice and greed but above all appreciation. And on the other side there exist and perform a whole range of artists, who achieve annual sales, as well as casual or definite recognition in terms of their own careers, age and ability. For every artist who sells out immediately the production of three months or a year to an immediate queue of art seekers, there are many others for whom Indian Market is just one of many occasions to sit and talk and to hang out with friends, including other artists, and maybe also make sales. While not as old as the Venice Biennale (1895), it is one of the earliest such fairs.

Powwow

Powwow is in a sense the antithesis of Indian Market: its hundreds of celebratory events lasting one or more days, which occur through much of the year, are loosely but emphatically controlled by Indian people for Indian people, who make and use the regalia and costumes. The materiality of the powwow is unobjectified and consumed in use, not by the seeming alienation of a final sale into a non-Indian market. There is no question of powwow celebrating a European conquest. Usually organized within a single tribal nation, powwow competitions will mostly be for performance: for the best fancy dancing, the best Grass Dance or the best costume perhaps; the events will be both communal and individual. The Fancy Dance arose in the 1920s, particularly among the Ponca in Oklahoma, from the War Dance. The costume includes a roach, a great spread ridge of coloured hair attached to the centre of the head, for men, and for women dresses and shawls that can be employed to mimic butterfly movements. The Grass Dance, for men, arose at the same nadir point in the early twentieth century, on the northern Plains, also uses a roach and copious hanging ribbons: the dance may be about the flattening, trampling down of long grass before an event in traditional times. Powwows in their communal aspect may consist of beauty contests or veteran parades; in their private and personal forms, in memorials and giveaways. For instance, at the 2013 Pawnee Indian Veteran's 67th Annual Homecoming the great range of activities included powwow dances: 'Inter-Tribal War Dances, Men's Grass/Traditional, Fancy and Straight Dances and women's Fancy Shawl/Jingle, Buckskin and Cloth'.[6] In

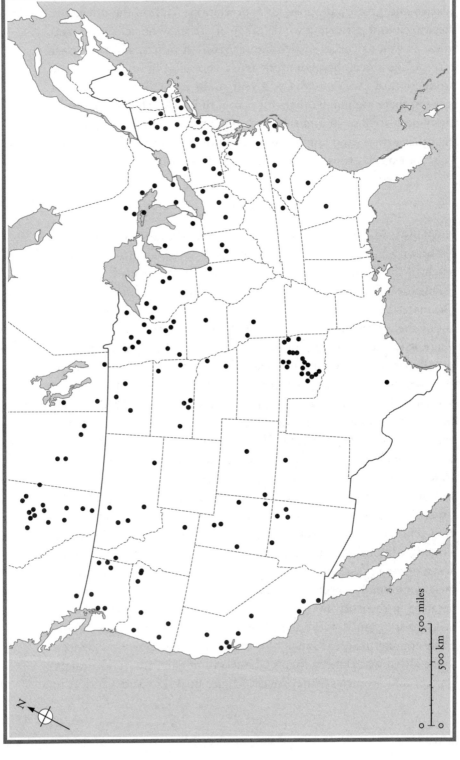

Map 6. The many powwows being held in June and July 2014 across North America.

contrast, in New England the Mashantucket Pequot powwow in 2013 offers a different sort of hybridity, with the Corn Dance, the first fruit ceremony for maize, at the core, but with the same mixture of different elements: 'The Mashantucket Pequot Tribal Nation would like to welcome you to Schemitzun, the Feast of Green Corn and Dance; giving honor to Mantoo (Creator) provider of all things and celebrating our harvest, ancestors, elders, veterans, family and Native American heritage.'[7] In this, of course, the distant bison and the immediate mention of war are absent.

While the clothing and the costume matter, and dancers must dress up and look their best, the material and artistic manifestations of powwow are not the point of the occasion. Indeed, the networks involved in the creation of powwow costumes may include non-Native elements – supply stores, pawn shops, white hobbyists. So Wanbli Charging Eagle (Lakota Sioux and Ojibwe), a leading dancer at the Albuquerque 2010 Gatherings of Nations (a powwow founded in the 1980s), emphasizes respect and individual motivation, without mentioning materiality: 'I try to outdo myself, not the other dancers . . . Grass dance is about movement, footwork, and style – the beat is medium so there are so many things you can do with your body.'[8] One way of looking at the materiality of powwow is through ideas of authenticity: what is likely to matter in a jingle dress worn in a competition is not who makes the dress or the material it is made from. Authenticity is not to do with appropriate and self-referentially respectful costume, but with behaviour and performance.

The potlatch, or 'do', in the Pacific northwest is a flamboyant celebration: of person and family, of individual and clan, band or even, more widely, First Nations identity. Potlaches do seem to be about materiality, an expression of art and wealth, the latter phenomenon being so often tied to the former; they tell inherited stories about mythic encounters, performed with carved, and often complex, regalia. But their materiality is really only incidental to their importance. Common forms of potlatch have to do with marriage, or the memorial of a deceased person, and the transfer of a name, dance song or title from one person, usually one family member, to another, and so share much with the powwow. Unlike the powwow, these events are organized by a specific host who will usually be responsible for raising the cash, organizing the hall, cultural centre, gym or the preferred communal big house. S/he will also require funding to be able to give away money and goods at the end of the event, symbolic acts of largesse celebrating the marriage or remembering the deceased. In the Kwakwaka'wakw potlatch of the 1960s and 1970s new or heirloom masks were used, for instance of Huxwhuhw, the cannibal bird. In organizing the event the host will seek help from those helped previously, borrow money and call in favours. The largest potlatches might be given for a successful leader, maybe a woman who ran the tribal nation and worked at state or provincial level to protect fishing rights or was once a school teacher. Perhaps 500 or more people will attend and need to be looked after during a twelve- or twenty-four-hour event, which includes full sit-down, served meals. Speakers will introduce the performances of specific family groups, with their drummers and singers and ancient performances of stories about their families' mythic origins in contact with the supernatural – an inadequate term which implies too little spirituality and insufficient materiality.

At dos of this kind extraordinary art objects might be used in performance. In Alaska, for instance, these might include ancient clan helmets, of Raven or Killer Whale, Eagle or Frog, from the nineteenth century or earlier, repatriated or returned to clan ownership after a century-long sojourn in an American museum. Coveted by collectors, these artworks may be worth millions of dollars, but this fact and the sublime aesthetics of the piece are irrelevant. Or further south a new mask or more probably set of regalia might be carved by a master carver and used in performance for the first time, representing, say, two Hinkeetsum, or lightning serpents, helpers of the thunderbird, or a new curtain, copied from an ancient model, or perhaps a new Hamatsa mask, representing the cannibal bird with a craving for human flesh, seemingly the largest type of mask. Or perhaps a new dance blanket will be used, a twined goat-wool robe with a crest, woven over a period of months and years, perhaps by a master weaver with her relations. While antiquity of rights and of names and ceremonies are all-important, the actual antiquity of the masks is not so significant: one museum puts the way regalia may be seen very neatly:

all the trappings of ceremony were objects of bright pride, to be admired in the newness of their crisply curved lines, the powerful flow of sure elegant curves and recesses - yes, and in the brightness of fresh paint. They told the people of the completeness of their culture, the continuing lineages of the great families.[9]

At the other end of the spectrum, on the Pacific Northwest Coast, is a rather different sort of memorial potlatch: one where closure is required. Imagine a deceased father, husband and uncle, born, say, in the mid-twentieth century and sent to a residential or boarding school, where, as was too often the case, he was abused, sexually, physically and culturally. In turn he was an abuser, charismatic and big enough, and sufficiently well educated in the white world, after his language was beaten out of him, to be successful for a time, to take up with a whole series of women, to have a number of sequential, or indeed simultaneous, relationships and families, to self-abuse with drugs and alcohol and in turn to abuse his partners and children. And then he dies, leaving conflicted, non-functional, distraught part-families, who hardly knew him, perhaps even in both Canada and the USA. Five years after his death maybe one of his children, for one reason or another, has persevered and pulled away from his or her own story enough to have a perspective and resources and decides to put up a potlatch, and to invite everyone, from the different reserves and reservations, or more likely from their city homes, and have them speak and say who they are and commemorate this man, with dances and regalia, so that all those who worked with him and knew him, those whom he abused and those who helped him and saw the good in him might be assisted and assist themselves in coming to terms with their own situation. A master carver might be commissioned to create a hawk frontlet, or a weaver to make cedar-bark baskets to be given to hardly known half siblings who would be part of such an event. Yet the art aspect, the materiality of the articles used, is of less significance than the relationships created and developed. For instance, Tlingit potlatch oratory may be about words that heal the soul, words which 'simultaneously comfort the mourners, restore order in the social universe and the cosmos, and raise the status of the participating' people.[10] Again, the art of the potlatch, like that of the powwow, lies substantially in the non-material, which the formal materiality acts to sanctify and support.

One other nexus can be discussed: that of the museum, and the archaeological and artistic discourses that delineate the relationships inscribed by collections of material culture. Museums are, supposedly, old school, set up mostly in the nineteenth century to advance knowledge and to protect and make available artefacts to those who needed to work and learn from objects. The Smithsonian Institution, dating to 1848, and dedicated to the 'increase and diffusion of knowledge', has three Native American museums: the National Museum of the American Indian, the better-visited but under-displayed section of the National Museum of Natural History and the George Gustav Heye Center in the old Custom House in New York. To these must added at least a couple of dozen other major museums, in New York and Brooklyn, Cambridge and New Haven, Santa Fe, Albuquerque, Chicago, Berkeley Toronto, Ottawa, Vancouver and Victoria. The major museum period of anthropology, from the 1870s to the great depression of the 1930s, came at the time, to put it politely, of major stress for Native North America: of catastrophic population decline due to epidemics, the final period of the Indian Wars and the programmes of forced assimilation with Christian education, and the stripping of Indian land ownership within US reservations by the Dawes and Curtis Acts. More pernicious is that this was also the period of the formalization of ideas of social evolution, of the assumed disappearance of Native peoples unable to adapt to the industrializing, progressive, colonizing world then in full spate. Anthropology of this period created and then struggled with ideas of race and monogenesis, viral ideas that hybridized and influenced the administrators in Indian affairs and the Christian educators who sought to save Indians and thus ameliorate the Native condition. As ever early theories of race, excised by the academy, left behind a folk memory of difference embedded in the wider society, even as Boas' and Margaret Mead's ideas of culture and personality came to dominate twentieth-century anthropology.

Behind and beyond the museums of this period lay the military engagements of the 1870s, the memory of which remained so vivid well into the twentieth century, and the recovery of Indian goods off battlefields and their sale, as was the practice globally in the nineteenth century. Improving knowledge and disseminating information required the wholesale collecting of Native osteology, especially crania, so that the physical anthropology of Native Americans could be better understood. Collecting from graves was a normal aspect of this, and outwitting unwilling, usually distraught, Native people reluctant to see their ancestors removed to museums was a regular part of this process. Ethnographic collecting worked in a different way: many Native peoples willingly parting with their obsolescent material culture, in, say, Eskimoan Alaska, as part of the business of trading for new technology and opportunity. In other areas collecting occurred in such a way as to remove much of a still usable material culture, as for instance that of the Stevensons in the southwest or Emmons on the Northwest Coast. Yet the Stevensons' removal of so much material culture to Washington, or Boas taking so much Northwest Coast art to New York, preserved objects and communicated the importance of Indian art, the initial primitivizing premise of the early twentieth century ensuring its inclusion in the canon.

Matilda Cox Stevenson (1849–1915), one of the first self-trained anthropologists to work in the southwest from 1879, initially with her geologist husband James, and then by herself, accumulated tens of thousands of objects and nearly a thousand photographs of Zuni alone for the Smithsonian. The transportation of ceramics, for instance, to Washington removed pots from circulation and use, from providing a data base for their continued manufacture. Stevenson wrote extensively about Zuni life and religion and is viewed ambiguously by contemporary anthropologists: as a pioneer and a precise, excellent observer and scholar and yet also as arrogant and pigheaded.[11] In the Zuni Pueblo online timeline only her husband is mentioned '1879 – Col. James Stevenson led a Bureau of Ethnology expedition to Zuni, the first of several which were collecting pottery and other Zuni manufactured items'. Frank Cushing (1857–1900), the anthropologist who worked with the Zuni in the between 1879 and 1884 and became himself involved in religious activities, is mentioned in relationship to his successful advocacy of a Zuni land claim and the visit he organized of prominent Zuni to the president, Chester Arthur, in the 1880s.[12] In this way southwest art was both appropriated and co-opted for rather different projects, enabling survival of a different kind, something beyond the storehouse, that feature of museum mythology often characterized by benign neglect.

In a rare case race remained of interest to museum anthropology. In terms of formal art history one such museum anthropologist, celebrated for his excellent fieldwork among northern Plains Indians such as the Blackfoot, was Clark Wissler (1870–1947). Inspired by field collecting of Indian artefacts during his Indiana boyhood, he wrote *Mythology* (1908) and *Bundles* (1912). Wissler succeeded Boas as curator at the American Museum of Natural History in 1905 and disagreed with Boas' insistence on monogenesis. The institution in the 1920s and 1930s mostly promoted eugenics, and Madison Grant, the saviour of the bison and the redwood and author of Hitler's bible, *The Passing of the Great Race*, was a trustee.[13] In *Man and Culture* (1923) Wissler wrote that the Nordic people were those most likely to advance culture: 'it is theirs to carry forward the lamp of civilization'.[14] Also in New York was the Museum of the American Indian (1922–94), founded and run for much of its existence by that ample figure George Gustav Heye (1874–1957), a successful businessman with a unlimited desire to collect and accumulate Indian artefacts from across the Americas. His museum, containing 700,000 artefacts or more, was underfunded by an impoverished New York City and engulfed by scandals of deaccessioning and of feuding trustees; it was subsequently, to put it bluntly, nationalized by the determined Senator Daniel Inouye (1924–2012), chairman of the Indian committee, and transferred to Washington, DC. Heye, an oil engineer and investment banker, who collected by fair means and foul, symbolizes aboriginal collecting in the age of the robber baron. In Washington this museum, which most symbolized the loss of culture and the presumption of transfer, was turned inside out, to be run by and for Indians, led by Southern Cheyenne lawyer W. Richard West Jnr, who created the new Museum of the American Indian, which opened in 2004 to the fury and regret of fellow Smithsonian employees, the anthropologists in the National Museum of Natural History on the other side of the Mall.[15]

The story of how anthropologists were joined by Indians, then, in museums is seemingly complex, yet can actually be understood quite simply by looking at the writings of Vine Deloria Jnr. Deloria, early on a marine, theologian and lawyer, was during the mid-1960s a reforming head of the National Congress of the American Indians, before activism became an entrenched aspect of Native American politics. His polemic about the way white people see and behave around Indian people and the way anthropologists live off Indians, *Custer Died for Your Sins* (1969), expresses a redemptive attitude to the improvement of the Native situation. Deloria's prestige, for instance as trustee of the Museum of the American Indian from the 1970s, and ability ensured that in the following decades he contributed to the reframing of the relationship between the anthropology and curatorial professions and Native America. This was given expression and force of law in the two Acts of Congress of 1989 and 1990, NAGPRA and the act creating the National Museum of the American Indian, passed into law at the time that Senator Inouye was chairman of the Indian Affairs Committee. In a sense the success of the NMAI and of Indian Market express the same conversion of difficult events, of Heye the robber baron and of Indian Market as celebrating the reconquest, into symbols of Native American success.

Closure and Culture

Of the causes célèbres which more than anything expressed a need, in the third quarter of the twentieth century, for the reform of white behaviour towards Indian remains, most important is that of the Salina burial pit. This was a major tourist attraction in Kansas between its discovery in 1936 and 1989, when it was closed. This site, the resting place of more than 100 Pawnees, became what has been described as a battleground in the recovery of Native authority by Roger and Walter Echo-Hawk. Pawnees scouted for the US cavalry in the nineteenth century, that is, they were friendlies, but were nevertheless removed from Nebraska to Oklahoma, and their burial places disturbed, often excavated scientifically, and their remains appropriated for research purposes. Today the story of this fight is told in *Bones of Contention; Battling for Human Dignity at the Salina Indian Burial Pit*, a video display in the Kansas Historical Society's Pawnee Indian Museum.[16] The bankruptcy of the Heye Foundation and human remains cases, as at Salina, gave rise to two Acts of Congress, and their provisions for the repatriation of human remains, associated grave goods and articles of cultural patrimony to the people from whom they came. American museums were obliged to inventory Native American collections and tell the relevant nations what they held. Different nations reacted differently, and perhaps surprisingly relatively small numbers of objects, whether human or artefact, have been returned. In some cases the returns have been symbolic in extent and outcome, though in other cases, such as Tlingit clan regalia and Seneca wampum belts, more general. Eight unique example of wampum belts, founding documents of the tribe, were listed for repatriation to the Tonawanda Seneca in 2012 following the return of thirty or so in the 1980s. Created from sea shells, for instance the quahog clam, to provide the purple or more valuable form, wampum is used especially by the Iroquoian-speaking Hodenosaunee in upper New York State. The art in wampum comes not from the complexity of manufacture but in the meaning, the abstract ability to communicate treaties and law, which ancient belts possess. However, in Native North America as elsewhere reality often follows fiction. The maintenance of human remains and cultural materials in the anthropology collections at the Smithsonian was explored by Anna Lee Walters's *Ghost Singer*,[17] first published in 1988, a year or two before Congress passed acts relating to the National Museum of the American Indian and to repatriation (NAGPRA).

The history of Native-run American museums goes back to the nineteenth century, with proposals, for instance, for a Cherokee museum before removal and the all-important activities of the Parker family, Senecas from New York. Ely S. Parker or Donehogawa ('He who guards the gate at sunset') (1828–95) was a diplomat collaborator with the first American anthropologist. Lewis H. Morgan, a soldier serving with Ulysses S. Grant in the Civil War.[18] While Parker was not the first Indian person to work with proto-anthropologists, his relationship can be seen as symbolizing scholarly activity through the nineteenth century: mutual respect, with shared aims, resulting in the great dissemination of knowledge, a dissemination not regarded, sometimes, quizzically, as of great benefit.[19] Arthur C. Parker (1881–1955), his great-nephew, was director of what is now the Rochester Museum and Science Center from 1924 to 1955 and wrote a *Manual for History Museums* (1935), as well as numerous publications about Haudenosaunee life and his famous great-uncle. In the second half of the twentieth century pioneering museums were set up on reservations to hold local collections, such as the Malki Museum in 1965 in California; many, like 'Ksan in British Columbia, required long periods of gestation. The Oklahoma Cherokee Heritage Center in Tahlequah, with its interpretative village experience, Tsa La Gi, and museum, was set up in the 1960s by the Cherokee National Historical Society and Colonel Marty Hagerstrand. Most importantly, the heritage centre includes the Cherokee Family Research Centre, where anyone can research their possible Cherokee ancestors.[20] One important feature of museums through the late twentieth century was the migration of control from white to Native curators.

Native American Art History

There are very different contexts, then, for Indian art: in performance, the powwow and the potlatch, where the material may be, frankly, immaterial; in the consumption of art in transgressive circumstances such as Indian Market; and in the vast data bases, run now in tandem with Native people and sometimes exclusively by First Nations. Art history works best in the study and explanation of Native North American culture when there is a great wealth of objects, well preserved and documented and derived from a fully recognized and appreciated culture or nation.[21] This means that there are a dozen or more material cultural traditions with thriving scholarly penumbras, of speaker-specialists usually writing and publishing and buying, selling, exhibiting and collecting objects. These networks are intimately connected with those of creators and artists, and most especially with the people who make and use things to perform and dance, to show respect and to worship. Outside of Asia, Native North America is the only continent with ivory-working and jade-using traditions, and with a full panoply of metal working, from the original use of native copper and meteoric iron to a vast contemporary jewellery market, especially in silver. Then there are the woven objects: twined baskets, the textiles of bark and wool from the Pacific Northwest, the extraordinarily high-quality coiled basketry, especially in California and of birch-bark, a light and tight material for covering canoes, containers and homes, also used in Eurasia, but to a lesser extent. Without the wheel for throwing pots, with virtually no glaze and without domesticated mammals much beyond the dog, achievements in material culture and art were defined in different ways: in painting and the use of skin, the elaboration of basketry not as craft or folk art – in which aesthetic elaboration is pushed to extremes in culturally and politically marginalized communities – but as achievements integrated into the mainstream.

Technology Transfer

Central to understanding the materiality of Native North America is the appropriation of a significant range of artefact types, unique to North America, which have passed into non-Native usage. Most obvious are clothing and costume types, moccasins and mukluks, for instance, and anoraks and parkas. In terms of transportation the toboggan, the bentwood flatbed device for pulling people and prey, has long been manufactured in non-Native circumstances, and in competition with two types of sled, the low, single-membered eastern type, where the runner is also the bed for the crossbars, and the high-raised western type, where the bed and runners are separated by a line of upward-reaching struts connecting the two, the parallel hitch in the west, the fan in the east. Sleds, of course, are a Eurasian form, but developed separately in North America, with perhaps a possible degree of feedback through France.

Much more significant is the canoe and its variant the kayak. Dugout canoes, cut from the trees felled near water, are ancient, at least 5,000–10,000 years old, and are known, of course, in a great swathe of the Old World, the Americas and Africa. In North America birchbark provided a material that is super-flexible, easily available and capable of being stretched and sewn to create water vehicles of an entirely modern utility. Little is written about the first evidence for such items, but that is no reason not to speculate that they may have been first invented in North America as the Archaic ended with increasing hunting and foraging specialization 5,000–3,000 years ago. And given the long-distance trading and travelling interests of Native America, use of such a technology would have spread quickly, irrespective of actual population movement. The kayak takes boat technology to a new level. The problem of canoes in open water is, of course, that of wind, tide and waves and wash from prey, an issue attested for everywhere by the creation of canoe bailers. The best response must be therefore that to cover the canoe with a deck to ensure that spray does not fill and the boat and capsize it. The kayak was invented 2,000 years ago with a series of other technically brilliant ideas around Bering Strait, in an area where driftwood would have been available, well seasoned perhaps because of immersion in the sea, along with materials such as baleen and skin thongs with which to tie the frame together. With usually a single hole for the paddlers, and a double paddle, usefully tipped in west Greenland with whalebone for durability, the kayak is, like the early aeroplanes and violins, a lightly structured article covered with a taut skin, a fragile craft that must be stored on its strongest elements – the gunwales not the keel – and is capable being crated on the head or scooted around on a sled.

The other great invention of the north is the snow shoe, the bentwood frame of wood woven with an elaborate netting of rawhide and caribou skin that enables hunters and trappers to walk over soft snow without falling through it. Although less useful than, and largely replaced by, the European ski, that Sami invention introduced by the French to the Alps in the 1870s, snow shoes are still manufactured, although now mostly of lightweight metal in Asia, and used for sport, having been taken up in the nineteenth century by non-Natives.

Finally and most influential is the ball and stick game, also known as lacrosse, in which teams compete by throwing balls from netted hoop sticks, sometimes in pairs with round nets, and sometimes, as in the Haudenosaunee/Iroquois type, using a single stick with a lenticular shape. This sport, a man's game, was adopted by non-Natives in the mid-nineteenth century, introduced to Europe in the 1880s and taken up in the late nineteenth century as an appropriate girls' game in an empire eagerly receptive of Native North American pursuits in the education of the children of the influential. Lacrosse and these other sports were vital elements of the creation of Canadian identity.

There are, of course, similar inventions from other parts of the world, such as the mancala board, chess, the xylophone, the outrigger canoe and the ski, the overwhelming series of Chinese inventions in paper and cast iron, the rudder and others, but of these only the ski and the outrigger canoe derive from small-scale societies.

One final important technology transfer occurred, probably in the seventeenth century. Basque whalers resumed Europeans hunting in the North American Atlantic. They used an arrow-type projectile, hard fastened into its shaft. In the seventeenth century Dutch whalers, hunting in the David Strait between Greenland and Canada, adopted the toggling or swivelling harpoon on a line from Greenland Inuit, which in a wide variety of forms entered general use from the late eighteenth century.[22]

Tomahawks

One of the uniquely American artefact types is the tomahawk. The term derives from Algonquian and referred originally to clubs used in Virginia both as a weapon and a war record. The device was converted from a ball-headed club into a hatchet or axe furnished also with a pipe – an object for use both in war and in peace. Tomahawks and pipe tomahawks would also be fantastically decorated, with wampum, feathers and scalps, but most importantly with the war records of the owners, with self-portraits engraved into the wood shaft showing tattoos and clan allegiance, with devices demonstrating the transfer of spiritual power from thunderers or thunderbirds to the owners, and then series of images of people, sometimes headless, taken in war. Clubs are essentially a basic weapon form in non-metal, non-firearm societies and so of little consequence in Europe, Asia and Africa, but were particularly elaborate in the Pacific and the Americas. The elaboration of tomahawks in eastern North America was matched in the Pacific northwest, with its entirely different traditions, by clubs carved with crest figures and ancestors and stories of encounters between ancients and mythic personages. These occasionally used a combination of wood and stone, occasionally jadeite, with the club blades forming the tongues of the crest figures, the transfer of spiritual power represented by tongues turned to the bluntly physical. In the traumatic, tumultuous period of colonization tomahawks became personalized instruments of diplomacy, providing a range of meanings across varied Native and non-Native peoples.

Embroidery

One of the embroidery traditions uniquely elaborated in North America is the use of hair and quill for decoration. Dyed, flattened quills from the softer ends of porcupines are used in dozens of embroidery techniques, stitched or woven through with sinew to create elaborate, hard, glossy appliqué panels in three or four colours – natural white, brown, copper-blue and orange – to represent thunderers and lightning and underwater panthers, the binary opposition of the upper and lower worlds in Algonquian thought. Yet the most common quillwork is purely geometric, the black and zigzag lines that adorn belts and pouches from the Subarctic, the great roundels on Plains skin shirts and covers, seams and flaps of moccasins from much of eastern North America. As well as skinny quills from porcupines bigger bird quills were used, differently defined, sometimes with longitudinal depressions to add strength. Other materials are used, for embroidery and decoration, including moose and other cervid hair and turkey beard. Moose-hair was used in false embroidery on twined articles such as pouches and prisoner ties – ties used to hobble but not stop captives from being walked as prisoners into adoption if women or to death by ordeal if men. With pictorial traditions of record keeping and the arrival of new European pictorial forms, hair embroidery adapted and changed uniquely, becoming representational, both of botanical knowledge, which nevertheless used modified European forms, and of scenes, on birch-bark as well as on skin.

Beadwork, Shell and Glass

Beads had a number of uses aside from the decorative function. They were used in a long series of geometric forms, alongside floral and representational narrative ones derived from painting, and also served as units of currency and to create systems of values. In New England Algonquians created wampum, purple and white shell beads that were used as currency in early colonial times. Once changed from flat-bead discs easily pierced with stone tools to long shell beads worked with introduced metal, they could be woven on hemp and skin to create belts used in war and diplomacy to express myths of origins, not so much of Algonquians, but of the interior Iroquoians, and in the foundation of law and the Haudenosaunee. Shell currency was used elsewhere in California, with olivella and abalone shell jewellery, which was traded north in colonial times. So blue abalone from Constanoan necklaces would be preferred to the white abalone available in the waters of the North Pacific, and to this was added dentalium, long tusk-like shells widely used in the Pacific northwest, southern Alaska and eastwards into the continental cordillera.

But of course the familiar beads, the ones seen and used in vast quantity today in clothing for powwows and performances, are primarily small glass seed beads created from tubes of blown glass, broken and rolled smooth and sewn with sinew and later cotton. In the east and north much design is based on floral forms. In the nineteenth century, at tourist spots such as Niagara Falls, vastly productive souvenir traditions incorporated great coils of flowers set on skin or velvet to commemorate and project the presumed disappearance of Indianness, yet actually preserving identity. On the Plains, bolder early traditions based on quillwork embroidery gave way to the more elaborate people-specific traditions of the Lakota and Siouan peoples, with filleted, spiky designs in deep colours on a white ground, heavy blocks incorporating much blue among the Absaroka, Crow, and slender use in the far west and southwest to accentuate leggings and breechclouts in the same way, but with more modest and less dramatic effect, often highlighted with added pigment. Around the Great Lakes, where the use of geometric elements on painted robes and skin costume changed to appliqué ribbon work edging on cloth leggings and shawls, beadworkers took up the geometric elements and applied them to bags and belts and bandoleers for a century and more. But the most important thing in all these traditions is that they were and are only *one* element of art, that beadwork was and is, for instance, combined with the use of hair, for mourning, for skin shirts, for painting war exploits and helper spirits on the same shirts, or used in broad bands in bonnets to hold sprays of feathers, with eagle feather planted in a strip of geometric work of opposing triangles or rimmed elements, both anchoring the moving spray and holding the attention.

Architecture

Of all aspects of material culture in North America, the most interesting in a way is architecture: the great diversity of building types, the time depth in continuity and the hold they have in the public imagination. In a large continent, relatively sparsely inhabited, Indian people created exceptional communities using technically brilliant ideas. It is reasonable to suggest that this diversity and originality is not equalled in other continents, with populations even in the seventeenth century of many tens if not hundreds of millions of people, and with much greater time depth. And the cultural archetypes of other continents, often defined by buildings, do not have such a hold and persistence in the western imagination as Native American buildings. The idea, for instance, of the Haudenosaunee longhouse, which became embedded in literature from the eighteenth century, was fused with that of the longhouse used by the Vikings in Ireland and today has a worldwide reach. The longhouse is a sort of ur-dwelling used in the Neolithic and tribal periods of European history and across the world in small-scale societies, from tropical South America to island Asia. In the eighteenth century it was described in Joseph-François Lafitau's (1681–1746) *Mœurs des Sauvages Amériquains, Comparées aux Mœurs des Premiers Temps* (Paris 1724) and was named by travellers such as Christopher Gist and George Washington when they went out west in the 1750s. Constructed out of bent poles and layered bark, longhouses would accommodate matrilineal members – people related through the female line – of the same clan and might be 25 metres long and house twenty nuclear families. That big houses on the Northwest Coast are often called longhouses and that the pre-Inuit Dorset people built skin-covered longhouses is in a sense irrelevant. The idea of a home much longer than it was broad for multiple occupancy was recorded first in eastern North America.

Tents

Longhouses are simply a form of tent, vastly elongated, a longer-lasting version of a structure used when mobility is not required – by hunters or by the military, for recreation and for protest. So the wigwam, the smaller, mat-covered Algonquian version of the longhouse, known from seventeenth-century Virginia and New England, can also be round and is still used in a casual kind of way by Cree in the Subarctic. A similar dwelling from out west is also known by the generic term 'wickiup', and although of Algonquian origin is found in multiple forms over a vast area. Similar structures are used elsewhere in the world, but it is the American version that defines the various building types; and of course there are huge varieties in materials used, whether for the bent-pole structure or for the matts, skins and withies used to create the cover. Lewis H. Morgan's *House and House Life of the American Aborigines* (1881) was the first account of Native architecture.

The tipi is a different tent form. Dakota in origin, it is X-shaped, with a pouring funnel at the top open to release smoke and a twist of a dozen or more poles counterposed against each other, covered with bison skin or canvas. When the tipi is dismantled the poles are available for use as a travois, the A-framed, sled-like structure pulled by dog and horse. And, like the yurt, the tipi has become ubiquitous.

Pueblos

In the southwest, among the twenty-one Puebloan peoples, multi-roomed, multi-storeyed buildings, sometimes with step-pyramid-like massing, are still used as single-building villages created from stone and adobe, with pine or spruce vigas or beams and flat roofs. These hugely beautiful arrangements of stacked and clustered buildings provided inspiration for the highly derivative Pueblo revival which replaced standardized American main-street architecture from the 1920s and 1930s in the southwest. While this type of dwelling is well known in the Old World and Africa, albeit differently created with use of mud construction, as, say, in the cities of Mali and Nigeria in the Sahel belt, the original forerunners of contemporary ancient pueblos in Arizona,

Colorado and New Mexico were stone-built constructions, often in defensive cliff positions, and date back a thousand years, while adobe was used where water was and is available, along the Rio Grande. And of course there were many other types of accommodation in North America, such as pit houses in the southwest and elsewhere. The use of caves was also important, but not pre-eminent.

Snow Houses

There are some remarkable structures created in the north: for example, tents and semi-subterranean houses built of turf sods and covered using long whalebone beams. But the snow house, the *igluvigaq*, is the one that everyone knows, because it is counter-intuitively the opposite of everything a house should be: temporary and warmed only to freezing point and not much further, because any hotter and the home would melt. Temporary structures built only for a few months, snow houses are often grey rather than white from the soot of seal oil lamps used for heating. Hefted not in a hemisphere but in a parabola, and constructed of heavy, metre-long blocks cut with ivory or iron knives from wind-packed snow, they demonstrate, like the tipi and indeed most building types, a proper understanding of hot air as a fluid, with a tunnel entrance to keep out the cold and a hole in the top to release air. While in a sense the building material, snow, is all around, the right stuff still needs to be found, by testing drifts. The snow house in its exceptional, unique form has also an inverted meaning in common currency. It provides the butt for a continuing stream of racist or near-racist jokes (because for some reason culturally specific humour about Inuit is not considered racist), especially the old saw of the number of words Inuit have for snow, as if this were a badge of incompetence rather than precisely the opposite. The field manual of the US Antarctic Program has a chapter on snow shelters which uses a great range of terms for different types of snow and acknowledges that the snow house, properly built in an ascending spiral, is the most difficult form of snow structure to build. Interestingly, the term used by the scientists for the place from which the snow is cut is 'quarry'; that is, the manual gives the idea of snow bricks a solid permanence which defies their transient reality.

Other house types have obtained regional currency with new usages. The Florida Seminole's temporary *chickee* with palmetto thatch over a cypress log frame became permanent, although homes were always shifting during the Floridas wars of the second quarter of the nineteenth century. Today swimming pools in Florida have chickee bars next to them, for shelter and recreation. Among the Navajo the common *hogan* is a six-sided log cabin with a domed roof, smoke hole and often mud packing. Again it has been reconfigured for modern use, seen as providing important ecological advantages such as insulation and thermal mass, and is made and marketed by Native-owned businesses such as South West Log Homes Inc. Navajo Majority Owned and Operated.

Mounds

The first important cultural climax in North America arose in the riverine heartland of the Ohio/Mississippi drainage, and especially north of the Ohio River in the southern part of Ohio state. Large, probably multipurpose Hopewell mound sites, covering hundreds of acres, used for ceremonial purposes perhaps related to the celestial calendar, were developed between 200 BC and AD 500. Some centres such as Mound City are simple rectangles enclosing burial mounds for the deposition of human remains with an extraordinary wealth of trade goods and art objects; these include copper-based jewellery and ornaments, ear spools and gorgets, cut-out mica forms including hands and raptor claws, elaborately built ceramic vessels incised with zoomorphic forms from the upper and lower worlds and a great wealth, in a couple of places, such as Mound City and Tremper, of carved clay stone pipes, displaying hundreds of superb small realistic representations of birds, rodents, reptiles and amphibians, most identifiable as specific species. Facing the smoker of the pipes, these may have represented helper spirits to the lineage or clan leaders of the descent line interred in the mound. Other exotic goods included freshwater pearls, the teeth of now extinct shark species and beds of large flaked chert tools. The elegantly conceived but poorly expressed Hopewell Interaction Sphere is a means of fixing the idea of the huge trade network in these remarkable materials extending east through the Appalachians, south down to the Gulf, where busycon shells from the sea were traded, and north to what is now Michigan and the Keweenaw Peninsula for Native copper that could be worked by annealing and turned into serviceable status ornaments. The epicentre of the Hopewell tradition (the name comes from that of the settler's farm on which early excavation led to the type site report by Warren Moorhead in the 1890s) is the Scioto Valley round Chillicothe. It was also the Scioto Valley which provided the opportunity for the first systematic archaeology (much beyond Jeffersons' digging) in the United States, that of Ephraim Squier (1821–88) and Edwin Davis (1811–88), conducted in the 1840s before even California and the Puebloan culture area of the southwest had been wrested from the young Mexican republic. Squier and Davis recorded their excavations, used stratigraphic techniques and had the fledgling Smithsonian Institution publish their report, properly defining the scope of their achievements in grandiose terms: *Ancient Monuments of the Mississippi Valley* (1848).

Mississippians

The Mississippians came from a mound-builder-based culture which was widespread across the US heartland in the period AD 800–1500, reached a climax in the early second millennium and declined with climate and other changes before European arrival. Benefitting from introduced maize, beans and squash from Middle America to the south, Mississippians built on and further developed trade networks from the preceding Hopewell culture of the Woodland period. While much of the earth- and wood-based architecture was of bold geometric forms, relating to those from Mexico, some sites with radial networks of mounds are differentially North American, suggesting that much of Mississippian culture was hybrid, original and unique. The flat-topped platform mounds hosted temple-like structures in which depositions were made. A particular feature of Mississippian architecture are ball game courts, perhaps for the playing of the game known in historic contexts as chunkey, played with a rolling stone, if not for the first rubber ball game, *ulama*, because rubber was seldom available in North America (rubber balls have been found at Wupatki, Arizona). Ceremonial complexes were occasionally built on a vast scale, such as that at Cahokia, outside of East St Louis, Illinois. Its main feature, Monk's Mound, so named because of the Trappist foundation created there at the beginning of the nineteenth century, covers fourteen acres and is 100 feet high. While Cahokia's layout is broadly Middle American in concept, that of Moundville, Alabama, consists of an arc series of concentric mounds, situated in a seemingly defensive configuration along the river.

Other centres such as Spiro, Oklahoma, included extraordinary depositions of ceremonial artefacts, while Etowah in Georgia contained two exceptional seated figures, suggestive of divine and possibly hereditary leadership. The best evidence for Mississippian belief systems comes from copiously decorated shell gorgets, adorned with images of falcons/raptors and rattlesnakes associated with the sky and underworld; similar images on repoussé copper plaques; stone figures of priestly rulers; stone sceptres; and portrait-like head pots, maybe trophies, decorated with tattoos. The formulation for this figurative record changed through the twentieth century from the Southern Cult to the Southeastern Ceremonial Complex. Of continuing importance is the relationship between historic peoples and Mississippian ones, the focus being on Muskogean speakers, such as the Chickasaw and Creek in the east, and on the Oklahoman Caddo, who dominated the drainage west of the Mississippi itself.

The Second Great Awakening and the Lost Tribes of Israel

Of great interest is the way in which the American antiquarian view of these early Indian peoples developed in the eighteenth and nineteenth centuries. Originally, antiquarians such as Jefferson used the British term 'barrow' to describe the mounds. Later, these people were termed 'Mound Builders', racially configured as an extinct people not connected to historic Native Americans, being clearly, going by the evidence of their exceptional architecture and grave goods, of much greater sophistication than the supposedly disappearing nineteenth-century savages. One prevalent idea in the early nineteenth century was that the mounds were created by the Ten Lost Tribes of Israel, an idea fostered by the highly successful journalist and racist of the 1830s Josiah Priest

(1788–1851), who published numerous editions of his *American Antiquities* in the 1830s at the time of the ethnic cleansing of the southeast by Jackson. The religious and intellectual milieu from which he came, in upstate New York, gave rise at the same time to the Mormon church, Mormon himself being notionally a Native American who used the learning of the Jews and the language of the Egyptians. Joseph Smith recorded finding the plates on which his religion was founded in 1823:

> He said there was a book deposited, written upon gold plates, giving an account of the former inhabitants of this continent, and the source from whence they sprang. He also said that the fullness of the everlasting Gospel was contained in it, as delivered by the Savior to the ancient inhabitants.[23]

Nephi was the man who brought the Israelites to the Americas: the *Book of Mormon* translates the golden plates, beginning with the explanation of the movements of the lost tribes:

> The course of their travels. They come to the large waters. Nephi's brethren rebel against him. He confoundeth them, and buildeth a ship. They call the name of the place Bountiful. They cross the large waters into the promised land, and so forth. This is according to the account of Nephi; or in other words, I, Nephi, wrote this record.[24]

What is important here is not so much the Mormon church, reconfigured as the Church of Latter Day Saints, and its ambiguities, but that the Mound Builder myth and the success of Joseph Smith arose at the same time as Native American prophets were appearing, that there is a certain unity of religious messianic movements, the Second Awakening, that encompasses both frontier society and Native America.[25]

The Mound Builder misconception was eventually disposed of in the 1890s by Cyrus Thomas (1825–1910) and the Smithsonian, who showed that the Hopewellian tradition and the Mississippians were indeed Native.[26] In the United States the subsequent maintenance, preservation and investigation of these sites has been, and remains, a fraught and difficult business. Cahokia, rescued by state authorities in the mid-twentieth century from a development involving tract housing, a drive-in movie theatre and trailer parks, became a World Heritage Site. Spiro Mound was subject in the 1930s to ownership by a joint stock company for profitable treasure digging. Mound City was flattened for Camp Sherman, a First World War military camp, and rebuilt; it is now a National Park, named for W. T. Sherman (1820–91), the brilliant Civil War general who in 1866 advocated to President Grant the extermination of the Sioux, including women and children: 'nothing less will reach the root of the case'.[27] Perhaps most characteristic of contemporary usage of mound sites is that of the great 200 acre, 1,500-year-old site in Newark, Ohio, where vast structures such as the Great Circle, 1,000 feet across, share an uneasy, but no doubt mutually beneficial, relationship with golf and a country club, somewhat at odds with the original builders' beliefs and commercial intentions.[28]

Art in the Southwest

All of these ideas come together and articulate to their furthest extent in the art complexes of the southwest. Ceramics, textiles and jewellery function as distinct separate entities, yet all derive from ancient traditions, were radically transformed in the nineteenth century and are now articulated with, and an Indian aspect of, the dominant American polity. Yet, while retaining cultural specificity and the authority of the individual creativity of the artist, they are hybridized and speak to and contribute to the identity of tribal nations, and beyond to patterns of wider, near global, consumption. Navajo weaving provides an introduction to this narrative of borrowing, invention and forced context, to adaptation and to the resumption of individual authority and collective identity in the weaving of textiles. Gary Witherspoon in *Language and Art in the Navajo Universe* (1977), describes the dynamic synthesis of the Navajo intellect, of hybridizing and integrating new ideas from divergent cultures. The ancestors of the Navajo arrived, as big-game hunters, in the southwest during the late medieval period or, in American terms, the post-classic, *c.* 1300–1500, from the north of the continent. They borrowed from and were influenced by the Puebloan peoples already in the southwest, where men weave cotton textiles, and by Spanish colonizers, from whom sheep were obtained. Navajo women use tapestry-weave with a continual warp, producing no fringe; the earliest textiles from the beginning of the nineteenth century have bold geometric designs in natural brown (also black, created, for instance, with ash), white, indigo and imported red, from bayeta or ravelled imported textiles. Wearing blankets and ponchos are the idealized types, but the range of nineteenth-century textiles include dresses, belts, saddle blankets and eventually rugs for sale, by the early twentieth century the dominant textile. The geometric designs, beginning with alternating stripes, became through the nineteenth century increasingly complex, with stepped forms seemingly overlaid to create distance and aesthetic tension. Eventually, after the arrival of the railroad in the 1880s, influence from Saltillo and other Mexican textiles, aniline dyes and the development of rugs constituted a new aesthetic, that of eye dazzlers, in which the skilful deployment of contrasting colours and stacked geometrics conveys conflicting movement.

Central to this narrative is the harsh removal of the Navajo in captivity to the Bosque Redondo in the 1860s, the subsequent replacement of sheep species with newly introduced varieties with differing wool qualities. Finally the weaving and marketing of of rugs was reorganized by American traders such J. B. Moore, who issued mail order catalogues in the first decade of the twentieth century. Moore and others introduced new ideas – such as a reduced kelim Middle Eastern- and Caucasus-derived aesthetic – and imposed a need for quality and authenticity as understood by the market in the early twentieth century.

The narrative of sheep farming, of shepherding and wool use provides a historical spine against which to measure that of textiles, a touchstone of identity which through the second half of the twentieth century became ever more conflicted. This arose because of overgrazing by sheep, which resulted from the 1930s in the BIA enforcing flock/livestock reduction among the Hopi, who had earlier adopted sheep husbandry, as well as the Navajo. Overgrazing also created the later dynamics of the Hopi–Navajo land dispute, in which much-contested pasture for Navajo sheep was returned, as birthright land, to the Hopi by Congress in 1974.

Like Pueblo ceramics, but unlike jewellery, the story of Navajo textiles is now often one about consumption and use outside Navajo society. In the early twentieth century the trader–Navajo relationship of Moore and others, one of creative symbiosis, gave rise to a series of now traditional designs: 'Two Gray Hills', 'Crystal', 'Chinle', 'Teec Nos Pos' and 'Ganado'. Excellence is recognized through prize-giving, in which the articulation and development of received designs is judged alongside fineness of weave. In contrast, the much more ancient and originally exceptionally vibrant Pueblo textiles remain to a large extent undeveloped for the non-Native market, though the use of wool, alongside cotton, began earlier.

Southwest jewellery has similar elements but is essentially different in the way in which it connects with dominant society. Jewellery was, and of course to some extent still is, created and used with textiles and pottery, but the dynamics of creativity and production are completely separate. Jewellery incorporated new materials and techniques, as non-weaving or non-jewellery-making peoples adopted these genres, changing producer and gender roles, and took the traditions into tourist and souvenir production and back out into art creation.

The use of turquoise, shell and spiny oyster in southwest jewellery is ancient – around AD 1000 at Pueblo Bonito – and the distribution of raw materials gave rise to long-distance trading networks to the Gulf of Mexico and to Tenochtitlán, the Mexica/Aztec capital, and in return Puebloan peoples received parrots and parrot feathers. So jewellery, unlike wool textiles, was ancient among the Puebloans. From 1519 the Spanish found turquoise from what was to become New Mexico in use in what was to become Mexico City. The use of metals in North America, especially copper, predates European arrival in the sixteenth century, and while definitely present in Ancestral Puebloan sites, its importance and influence in the southwest is limited and debated. What is clear is that Spanish settlement in the seventeenth century brought with it silver, eventually a copious supply of pure high-silver-content Mexican coins, which could be hammered and reworked. In the nineteenth century, following the US annexation of the southwest in 1848, and with the termination of autonomy for the Navajo and around the time of removal to captivity in the 1860s, blacksmithing and jewellery techniques melded and merged to create an exuberant tradition of hammered, beaten, repoussé silver jewellery in bold and emphatic forms including squash blossoms, conchas and the Moorish/Spanish/Arab-derived crescent.

Combination with the ancient use of turquoise resulted in the development of an entirely new tradition, at first for the spectacular use and enjoyment of Navajo, men and women, and then eventually, after the arrival of the railroad and tourists in the 1880s, of non-Natives and increasingly other Native peoples.

While Navajo textiles, originally utilitarian, became largely a rug form for non-Native appreciation, southwest jewellery, which developed among Puebloan peoples such as the Hopi and Zuni in the nineteenth century, grew into something entirely separate. More easily worn, collected and travelled than rugs, jewellery in its southwest Native forms was taken up by American society in the 1930s and 1940s as an expression of both modernism and, more generally, western identity. While the Navajo appreciated bold, heavy designs, the white market required lighter pieces. Uniquely in the United States southwest jewellery broke through the boundaries of the craft/souvenir/art polarization, providing a portable, usable symbol of general Native Indianness, further articulated with ideas of Native American identity, and then with counter-culture in the 1960s, high fashion in the 1970s and environmentalism more recently – turquoise symbolizing water and very much more.

Of the many thousands of jewellers, traders, curators and consumers, some should be mentioned. These include Atsidi Sani (Old Smith c.1828–1918), a blacksmith and then silversmith before the removal of the 1860s; the advocates and marketers of the southwest who created or steered institutions, such as René d'Harnoncourt (1901–68), director of the Museum of Modern Art, who canonized American Indian art with the New York show of 1941, or Mary-Russell Ferrell Colton (1889–1971) and her husband, who founded the Museum of Northern Arizona, one of the pivotal mentor institutions articulating Native artist creativity with American culture. Modernists such as Charles Loloma (1921–92), whose work transcended ethnic barriers, was described in his *New York Times* obituary as having 'changed the look of American Indian jewelry'.

Painted ceramics in the southwest provide a detailed contrast to the indigenous textile and jewellery traditions and indicate how exceptional is the way in which changes in art and material culture developed in Indian Country. Unlike textiles, where techniques and usage hybridized with the dominant Hispanic and Anglo society and evolved quickly, ceramic traditions remain highly stable, eschewing glaze (apart from lead-based glaze paints) and the wheel.

Ceramic traditions in the southwest have much in common with those of weaving: like cotton textiles, pottery is associated with Mexico but in the southwest by the end of first millennium developed in spectacular fashion in traditions which flowered in the dry, sometimes high, desert-like conditions. To the west the Hohokam, increasingly thought to be ancestral to the Tohono O'odham (Papago) and Akimel O'odham (Pima), created between about the seventh and fourteenth centuries large painted ceramic containers and bowls, wonderfully decorated, for instance, in counterposed blocked geometric and scrolled designs in red.

The Ancestral Puebloan (formerly Anasazi) tradition of the four-corner region of the southwest evolved from 3,000 years ago, eventually adopting dry farming in the western Pueblos and river irrigation in the eastern Rio Grande Pueblos. A great variety of painted pottery traditions emerged, which combined with those of the Mogollon. The Mogollon developed in the southern part of the southwest, where the Mimbres culture produced some of the most exceptional black-painted geometric wares, with carefully constructed use of bold geometrics with calibrated positive–negative ratios to ensure maximal visual movement. And the greatest figurative painted ceramics, bold and representational, cartoon-like but with little element of caricature and sometimes a sense of perspective and of narrative, appeared in the eponymous Mimbres Valley.

Two, now recovered, village ceramic traditions of western Pueblos in the middle of the second millennium, the Zuni and the Hopi, are particularly remarkable. That of Hopi Sikyatki is polychromatic, with swirling geometric designs, reminiscent in visual quality of the spinning movement created by the Victorian toy zoetrope, or a stilled kaleidoscope, combined with realistic macaw and feather motifs. Rediscovered in the late nineteenth-century excavations of Jesse Walter Fewkes (1850–1930), the designs were taken up, copied and reconfigured by Nampeyo (c.1860–1942) and then by her family, transforming previously utilitarian ware into an art form which she showed in Chicago and at tourist sites such as the Grand Canyon. The pottery of the Zuni village of Hawikuh, of the same time frame and visited by Coronado in 1540 in his search for gold, is similarly remarkable, using glaze painting, with entirely different combinations of similarly abstracted geometric and realistic elements to create bands of highly eclectic designs. Other traditions flourished into the twentieth century and developed among the Tewa Pueblos as imported enamelware and ceramics eliminated much of the practical use of indigenous ceramics. Instead matt-black and red wares dominated, the most famous of the potters being Maria Martinez (1887–1980) from San Idelfonso, who, with her husband Julian (1879–1943), researched and developed matt black on black burnished ware.

So art the southwest includes an entirely new tradition, among the Navajo especially, of wool textiles, another tradition, jewellery, which is both ancient and incorporative, and a third tradition, ceramics, which, although innovative, changes within strictly defined ancient parameters.

Art and Activism

The business of Indian art is now complicated in the way it is divided between ancient material culture traditions, with contemporary inflections, and contemporary art, which builds on and reflects wider art practice. None of the twentieth-, even nineteenth-century, ideas about new art – modernism, avant-garde, contemporary art, postmodern art – work well in trying to explain what aboriginal American art is now. There are no equivalents of the major moments in twentieth-century western art traditions – while there are many artists abstracting Native traditions – no Pollock-like, symbol-free abstract expressionists, no Duchamp urinals, no Picasso-like appropriation from the ancient Iberian and Africa sculpture. Perhaps more importantly there is no occidental equivalent to Ai Weiwei and few artists with a visceral activist mission to infuriate authority, to transgress and to deal with, say, issues of fracking in the Dakotas, or incarceration in for-profit prisons, or Indian child prostitution in Vancouver's west end. First Nations art, when purveyed by the National Gallery of Canada, often seems just too nice: too consumable, cocktail comfortable, conscience-tickling. Yet activist art creates a context for discussion, and closure. Perhaps activism is much more evident in film making. Especially interesting is that of the Abenaki, Alanis Obomsawim (b. 1932), for instance around the 1990 Oka crisis, about the desecration of Mohawk burials, featured in films beginning with Kanehsatake: *270 Years of Resistance* (1993).

In contemporary architecture pre-eminent is the work of Douglas Cardinal (b. 1931), whose great masterpiece is the Canadian Museum of Civilization of 1988, a group of two highly eroded, contoured structures expressive of the prairie landscape that forms part of Cardinal's Blackfoot and Métis heritage. His work neatly encapsulates, however, the difference between the USA and Canada: in Ottawa-Gatineau his museum was built way over budget, while in Washington, DC, where he was selected to build the National Museum of the American Indian, when differences and delays arose over delivery of the building he was let go and the structure completed by James Polshek in 2004.

The museum, a single, tall, eroded structure, a sort of hoodoo on the Mall, is framed by landscape, and if the business of aboriginal ideas about the contemporary environment is taken as a nodal point, then aboriginal activism becomes securely symbolized in the expressionistic building in front of the Capitol. This is not necessarily seen, of course, in works of art inside, brutally conceived and exquisitely rendered, created by activist artists. Instead more significant than contemporary artworks are the little acts of resistance, the mucky, messy and frankly uncomfortable business of stopping logging on Haida Gwaii and Vancouver Island in the 1980s, selling silk screenprints to raise funds, or of confronting the racist endeavours of sports fishermen in Washington State and Wisconsin and facing and understanding from the inside the dynamics of pipeline pipe-dreams across Alaska, or the Rockies or down to the Gulf of Mexico. In this sense remote acts of activism provide performance art. Or indeed the extraordinary creativity that saw in the late twentieth century the appearance of a hugely expanded idea of Indian law and the performance of justice which resulted in the eventually successful case against the Department of the Interior for misappropriating Indian funds.

Activism and art are usually separate in Native North America, and Native art is sanitized for the gallery. But there are some dozens of First Nations and Native American artists who do confront issues and are activists and express, with cultural and individual genius, their own heritage and language, the bittersweet dialectic of dispossession and of cultural and personal survival. In the Pacific northwest print sales help raise money and awareness for radical movements, for instance that led by Gary Edenshaw or Guujaaw (b. 1953), which resulted in the Morseby Island settlement of 1988, protecting the forest and setting up a sovereign fund for the island.[29] Two or three large-scale works point to the way in which the incorporation or not of the commentator artist, maybe with humour, even rank humour, is a normal process. Bob Haozous' (b. 1943) *Cultural Crossroads of the Americas* (1996) is about the northward migration of indigenous peoples from Middle America. It is a vast billboard iron collage using negative-positive space in a southwest ceramics geometric kind of way, with codex images, and concerns Native and Mexican origins, presages 9/11 with an image of a plane going into a Statue of Liberty-topped high-rise and most usefully is obnoxious on a number of fronts. When installed at the University of New Mexico, it included barbed wire across the top, simulating the barrier between the USA and Mexico, causing outrage. The barbed wire speaks of the violence of Mexico–US border crossings, and in concerning Native America and Mexico, and the artist's own silent, part south-of-the-border origins, grafts categories in a challenging manner. Yet Haozous eschews ideas of the spiritual and religious:

> I don't use those words. I'm trying to inspire people to come up with questions like: What is art? What is the value of art? What is the meaning of cultural art? I chose to be more than a decorator, or illustrator, of Indian themes.[30]

In contrast, in another monument about Indianness and Indian history, the memorial at the site of the Battle of the Little Bighorn, or Greasy Grass, the Native contribution and symbolism are muted. This was originally in the 1940s Custer Memorial, commemorating his death and those of his men, and was constructed by Roybal, a Denver architectural practice, who won the commission in a blind competition. Roybal says of itself that the firm uses a 'disciplined responsive system of project management dedicated to creative architectural and planning solutions that will serve the project well into the future'.[31] The Native part of the monument is a cut silhouette of three people riding, from different nations. The National Park Service (NPS) web page doesn't mention the architectural firm who designed the monument, nor the artist who contributed to the sculpture *Spirit Warriors*, Colleen Cutschall from Pine Ridge: the political importance of the site transcends any creativity associated with the place. Another monument is the Marine Corps Memorial, of 1954, created after a photograph by Joe Rosenthal (1911–2006) of the raising of the American flag on Iwo Jima in 1945. Ira Hayes (1923–55), from the Gila River reservation, was one of those raising the flag. Hayes appeared in the John Wayne film about the moment, *Sands of Iwo Jima*, and was later played by Lee Marvin and then Tony Curtis in two remakes. His ethnicity is not mentioned on the NPS website, because, of course, in contributing to the national narrative, his Indianness is irrelevant.

Folk Art

Perhaps, then, decorative or illustrative art can be considered as folk art. Folk is a European term, from Old German, Dutch, Frisian and Old English; it is used in *Beowulf* and originally meant race, horde or multitude. While in a sense the term comes from Germanic tribalism, in Europe, and particularly when reinvented in the term 'folklore' in England in 1846 by William Thomas (1803–85), it referred to people firmly placed in a subsidiary relationship to dominant society, that of, say, peasantry to feudal lords. Folk art is about encapsulation, about surrounding and situating. And because Native American societies, for instance horticulturalist societies in New York or New Mexico and even more so Plains or Arctic hunters, were very specifically never part of such a divided society, ideas of folklore and folk art may be simply plain wrong when applied to the Native North American context. This does not mean that Native American creativity is never associated with folk matters – the Smithsonian's Folklife Festival involves Native people, and artists may call their work folk art, and musicians Native folk music. The point is that folk implies dependence, and dependence is not something Native

North Americans normally accede to, even though they may be 'domestic dependent nations'. Folk art itself in English is a twentieth-century idea, and one hobbled by ideas of the primitive and unsophisticated, when Native American art works along with both developed material culture traditions and great bodies of language and oral history.

One way, then, of looking at art outside of the folk is through the encapsulated tradition, as in this question: 'To what extent is this or that art phenomenon (a souvenir totem pole, for instance, or an Inuit soapstone piece) part of encapsulated tradition – that is, a tradition which is segregated in some ways from the dominant society and confined in terms of taste and collection to specific institutional and other contexts?' 'Encapsulation' in political anthropology is used to describe villages, tribes within nations, colonial dependencies or sections of urban populations, in order to understand contained and separate entities and their interaction with the larger environment. Because in a real sense Native North American art is encapsulated, self-protected in a non-ideological space, usually separated from mainstream art.

There is, however, one aspect of Native American art that it shares with folklore, and that is that both are non-ideological. Everything Native American is highly political and politicized, but political activity in the United States is very strictly non-ideological. There is no such thing, for instance, as a socialist Native American or, after AIM, a revolutionary Indian. Mass activism, as in the marches of the 1970s, had no text beyond the straightforward nationalist one of the recovery of lost rights. So Russell Means (1939–2012), the actor-activist and occupier of Alcatraz, the BIA, Mount Rushmore and Wounded Knee, did not couch his politics in an imported political discourse but kept the message to strictly Native formulations. Perhaps the point is that the act of remaining Indian, of asserting against overwhelming odds that one is Native or First Nation, is an act of resistance or survival. More potent is the term survivance, survival and resistance, and the fact that Indian artists, performers and writers endure in a world where they are expected to perform, at best, subaltern functions (an expression formulated in Asia), from below and outside non-Native society.

Contemporary Art

Contemporary Native art both places aboriginal identity in a bind *and* transcends the complexities of production, of making art and communicating within and beyond the indigenous community. This is in part because the traditional and the ancient provide a wellspring of authority, oral-based imagery and energy which explains who people are but, in arising from fixed memory, is confined into a traditionalism which can verge on the folk – or enclave art. Bob Haozous puts the issue well:

> What really bothers me more than anything is that Native American art is based on the history, romance, and decoration of the past, or on the art dictates of modern man. Our art isn't dealing with the profound problems or the complex people we are today.[32]

Haozous had a military education, served in Vietnam and went to art school, but his inspiration relates to his father, Allan Houser (1914–94). Houser was taught painting by Dorothy Dunn, the Art Institute of Chicago-educated teacher, who set up the Studio School in Santa Fe and taught there from 1932 to 1937. From this moment emerged a group of exceptional artists, a studio school working in a pictorialist Deco, Jugenstil-related tradition but with clear roots in Pueblo symbolism and vocabulary and southwest aesthetics. In the 1940s Houser turned to sculpture and, influenced by the European stripped-down, streamlined abstraction of Arp, Brancusi, Hepworth and Moore, created *Comrades in Mourning* at the Haskell Institute 1948, the first of a long series of important commissions which inserted Indian art into American public life. His style is contemporaneous with the emergence of Inuit sculpture and includes the same elements of abstract realism, in which romantic notions of Indian people, and Inuit hunters, highly reduced in form, were able to communicate a mythic past and proper contemporaneity. What is neat, and to the point of the story of the father–son artistic tradition, is that it both transcends ideas of apprenticeship and confirms that heredity and upbringing is an ordinary aspect of Indian genius.

Dorothy Dunn was one of a number of inspirational figures lodged in Indian educational institutions. Another, rather different, figure was Yale-educated Oscar Jacobson (1882–1966), who was director of the University of Oklahoma School of Art from 1915 to 1954 and who with others fostered the narrative Plains-style pictorialism of the Kiowa Five group of painters during the 1920s. The initiative resulted in an exhibition in Prague in 1928 and a suite of prints published in Paris in 1929. Most significant of all was that Indian artists participated in the great muralist movement of the 1930s and 1940s, Jacobson working with the Works Projects Administration during this period. One of the Kiowas was Steven Mopope (1898–1974).[33] Mopope, from a family which included prominent ledger book artists such as his great uncle Silver Horn (c.1860–1940), was originally taught by a Choctaw nun, Sister Olivia Taylor. He went on to paint one of the murals at the new Department of the Interior building completed in the 1930s, a vast dance, 2 x 20 metres in size. But more modest regional initiatives ensured that other artists of different backgrounds contributed to this repositioning of Native America. Southern Cheyenne painter Richard West Snr (1912–96) was commissioned to decorate the post office of Okemah, Oklahoma, in 1941. Oscar Howe (1915–83) (Yankton Dakota), who attended Dorothy Dunn's school, worked with the line drawings of a ledger book and infused them with a personal dynamic interpretation of cubist forms, both similar to and different from the work of the Kiowa Five. Perhaps most important of his work is, however, the series of WPA worker-realist murals at the Mobridge Auditorium, South Dakota, five of Sioux life and five of life along the Missouri, from the 1940s.

What is interesting here is the seemingly unreasonable comparison with what was happening in Canadian Indian residential schools. In Canada the period of the 1930s and 1940s is seen, from a residential school perspective, as one of British-derived smallness, without American wealth, patronage and imagination, and of unmitigated horror, where teachers abused rather than inspired. Two recent exhibitions touched on the subject. One was the exhibition 'Witnesses: Art and Canada's Indian Residential Schools' in Vancouver in the autumn of 2013, designed to 'illustrate how this issue has become embedded in Canadian art history and to demonstrate the strong social and cultural capacity of art'. The other was 'Speaking to

Memory: Images and Voices from St. Michael's Indian Residential School', which also took place in Vancouver in 2013–14 and is about the Kwakwaka'wakw school in operation between 1929 and 1974, with images of students taken during the 1930s of blown up and projected on the surviving building itself and then at the Museum of Anthropology.[34] The conception and creation of clothing provided a separate portal to art for Inuit women.

Alongside the traditional and the art school stand other North American traditions: photography from the late nineteenth century and glass art from the last quarter of the twentieth century. Few photographers such as Benjamin Haldane, Tsimshian (1874–1941) flourished in the nineteenth century; in the twentieth century Lee Marmon (b. 1925) (Laguna) recorded his own community, while others, such as Duggan Aiglar (b. 1947) (Maidu and Paiute) recorded more widely, in his case California. More recently photography-based Native imaging around nation and personal issues flourishes.

Practitioners working in glass art as well as carving, printmaking, installation, video and cross-over photography are creating visual history, in which production enables the deconstruction and/or the repositioning of Native culture through highly personalized idioms. Such artists include the Tuscarora Jolene Rickard (b. 1956), the Musqueam Susan Point (b. 1952), who monumentalizes the Salish art of urban Vancouver, Michael Nicoll Yahgulanaas (b. 1954) (Haida), who crosses the boundaries of politics and art, using manga to communicate Haida universalism, and Hulleah Tsinhnahjinnie (b. 1954) (Creek-Seminole-Navajo), whose sharp imagination targets the damned awkwardness of Indian history.

Contemporary Inuit Art

Inuit and First Nations Art in Canada received public and, more importantly, private patronage in the 1940s and 1950s. Sales of articles made by Inuit began regularly only in the twentieth century. This developed modestly with an increasing white presence in the north as police and missionary activity contributed to a growing market for souvenirs alongside that already established by whalers and fur traders. Small ivory carvings were, as in Alaska, the principal objects offered through the first half of the twentieth century. Then, as earlier in New Mexico and Oklahoma, a charismatic artist teacher and polymath, James Houston (1921–2005), stimulated and fostered art and Inuit artists. Visiting Port Harrison, now Inukjuaq, Quebec, the Itivimiut community involved in Robert Flaherty's film *Nanook of the North* (1922), Houston brokered Inuit carvings in 1948–9, involving the Canadian Handicrafts Guild, in Montreal, as the venue for gallery exhibitions and the Canadian government for subsidies. These catered to southern tastes, in, for instance, animalier sculpture, such as the polar bears of François Pompon (1855–1933).

Entirely different to the Alaskan situation, in Canada the cooperative movement, starting in the Arctic in 1959, enabled a degree of commercial autonomy to develop in competition with established traders, that is, the Hudson's Bay Company. One arm of the Arctic Co-operatives Ltd, working in more than thirty communities, is Canadian Arctic Producers, begun in 1965 to provide funding for sales and marketing in the south. Houston, after visiting Japan and working with Un'ichi Hiratsuka (1895–1997), a woodcut printmaker, in the late 1950s, introduced print-making to the Inuit community at Kinngait, Cape Dorset, and with the West Baffin Eskimo Co-operative and the marketing arm Dorset Fine Arts brought a rather different Inuit aesthetic to southern collectors. Other communities followed in creating print workshops, and together Inuit experimented with a wide variety of techniques, beginning with drawings and stone cuts, and continuing with stencils, lithography, etching and engraving. The Pangnirtung Print Shop originated in 1969, while Holman Eskimo Co-op, started in 1961, was originally responsible for print-making in that community, now Ulukhaktok, in the western Canadian Arctic. Other arts, such as skin stencils, patchwork, weaving and embroidery, also thrive, but it is graphic art that leads in terms of sourced and sourcing iconography. Much of this imagery, as for instance seen in the work of Dorset artist Parr (1893–1969), can be related to the engraving work of the Thule tradition from which historic Inuit culture, as also Inupiat art, derives. Jessie Oonark (1906–85) worked with images relating to clothing and sewing, including the woman's knife, the *ulu*, while Kenojuak Ashevak (1927–2013) created her own aesthetics in works such as

'Enchanted Owl' (1960), perhaps a joke about an Inuit view of the foolish, rather than wise, owl. The quiet, substantive drawings of Annie Pootoogook (b. 1969) inform and reify domestic life.

Inuit art is extraordinarily successful and in Nunavut alone, as of 2006, provides a contribution of $30 million to the economy, some 10 per cent of total Canadian art sales, with income for more than quarter of the population.[36] At first sight government support for Inuit art replicates that for Native American art under the aegis of Collier's Bureau of Indian Affairs and WPA and stands in contrast to the entirely private-sector initiatives of southwest jewellery or Northwest Coast art, but this is not entirely apposite, since the cooperative movement can be seen as a non-governmental achievement replicating to some degree indigenous communalism.

In the nineteenth and early twentieth century Inuit art contributed to a knowledge-based aesthetic, in which highly skilled Inuit, given often for the first time paper and drawing implements, produced, as it were, instantaneously, maps, portraits and drawings for naval or scientific expeditions requiring guidance and wishing to record animals and peoples. Of these the Greenlander John Sacheuse produced images for John Ross's 1819 published account of his voyage in search of the Northwest Passage of the previous year, George Niagungitok made drawings while touring Europe in the 1820s, and Toolooak created images of William Parry and animals in the same decade. In the early twentieth century the teenage Rose Iqallijuq executed clothing portraits – portraits of specific people, imaged in their clothes, without faces or other identifying marks – for the Fifth Thule Expedition. Canadian Inuit art comes from this tradition, but was entirely reconfigured in the mid-twentieth century.

Other Traditions

Similar traditions arose in other parts of Native North America. Of the first aboriginal artists the Tuscarora Cusicks, uncle David (c.1780–c.1831) and nephew Dennis (c.1800–1824) are important for different reasons. David produced in chapbook style – that is, a cheap disposable form of popular literature sold by pedlars – *The Ancient History of the Six Nations* (1827), the first self-illustrated

American Indian history, with woodcut images that hybridize early American illustration and Iroquois aesthetics, introducing creators and their demons and devils and just maybe providing a source for both Bigfoot and the *Book of Mormon* (1830).[36] Dennis, on the other hand, painted in realistic missionary style – a style with global reach in the nineteenth century – church collecting-box images depicting life scenes. Of other contemporary Haudenosaunee artists, Oren Lyons (b 1930) (Seneca) is one of those uncategorizable multivocal leaders, first a lacrosse player of national significance, then an illustrator and an activist working internationally for indigenous rights.

A separate but analogous tradition arose around the Great Lakes, in the Woodland school of art. A leader in this was the Anishnaabe/Ojibwe artist from Ontario Norval Morrisseau (1932–2007). Educated by his grandparents and at a Catholic residential school, he engaged with the pictographic tradition from birch-bark scrolls and rock art to create bright, vivid pictographic images, informed also by beadwork traditions. Interesting and significant in the recent historiography of Morrisseau, erupting before his death, are questions of authenticity and copyism. This can be taken in different ways, but is best considered in the light of similar problems that surround other artists such as Warhol and Dali – as an aspect of mainstream normalcy. In 2006 the National Gallery of Canada held a Morrisseau retrospective. There is even a Norval Morrisseau Heritage Society, run by experts, but without a proportionate Warhol Foundation-size collection. Daphne Odjig (b. 1919) (Odawa-Potawatomi) takes Woodland imagery in slightly different directions, including abstract imagery of the Algonquian superhero Nanabush, and introduces a cubist inflection to the Woodland school, employing impressionist brushwork on different occasions to speak about, for instance, genocide.

In contrast, earlier contact and colonization of Alaska and Greenland provided environments for very different traditions. In Alaska nineteenth-century mining, trading, revenue and policing activities stimulated the souvenir trade, with an outlet in early twentieth-century Seattle, promoted through events such as the Alaska Yukon Pacific Exposition of 1909. Ivory engravers such as Angokwakzhuk or Happy Jack (1870?–1918) (Inupiat) flourished, as later did self-taught artists such as James Kivetoruk Moses (1900–1982)

(Inupiat), who retained the Inupiat insistence on detail and narrative. He emphasized the importance of his own experience as a hunter over an art school education: 'Young people try to be artists. They come up good artists, very good drawing because they were school. But no experience. Don't know nothing [about] living.' Again the non-material makes Native art.[37] Kivetoruk Moses turned to art in his fifties, following a plane accident. Aron of Kangeq (1822–69) turned to art after suffering tuberculosis and is of a different stature to his contemporaries in the USA or those who contributed to Greenland's souvenir trade in miniaturized forms of carvings and equipment. Aron is perhaps the most famous Eskimoan artist of the nineteenth century. He was taught by missionaries in West Greenland and published exceptional prints, in books and periodicals, which depicted both general oral history and tales of the defeat and destruction of the ancient Norse by medieval Inuit.

Fritz Scholder (1937–2005) (Luiseño), an abstract expressionist, brought modernism to Native America. Working in the figurative de Kooning mode, but with an American Indian imagination and subject matter that gives his work a pop art inflection, like a sort of abstract Warhol, he takes the coyote, the flag or the warrior on horseback, for instance, or Indian stereotypes or kitsch, and visually deconstructs them. What is important historically is that he was taught by Oscar Howe (1915–83), the Yankton Dakota of the Santa Fe school, was educated at art school and projected a universal Indian aesthetic in the idiom of the 1960s; that is, he took Indian art mainstream and so was occasionally rejected by shows for not being Indian enough, like the great Hopi jeweller Charles Loloma (1921–91), who made modernist metalwork that transcended an Indian aesthetic. Rejection for not being Indian enough for Indian shows was in a sense a rite of passage, a stage on the way to universal acceptance. Kay Walking Stick (b. 1935), of Cherokee descent, developed a set of themes similar to Scholder's in her painting with a different aesthetic, incorporating both bead and abstract design, and an especially vivid view of the American landscape, colourizing and reformatting Georgia O'Keefe and the Group of Seven. Jaune Quick-to-See Smith (b. 1940) (Salish and Kootenai) is also of this generation of abstract narrative commentators, working in mixed media, with layered texts, creating an aesthetic focused on Indian identity and history, using war shirts, animals and maps to convey, as in much contemporary Native art, self-deprecating humour, with a Klee-like particularism. Edgar Heap of Birds (Cheyenne Arapaho), born of an aeronautical engineer in Wichita, home of the B29 bomber, in 1954, has taken the business of inscription and of multiples much further, creating public art messages and cloud juxtapositions.

In general terms, however, a number of art practices are not significant in Native North American art. Rigorous abstract painting was generally not a feature of aboriginal art, and neither has objectified land art, it may seem, attracted Native America. However, the modified Native landscape is appreciated aesthetically, as art, especially when altered by vernacular architecture or by hunting and gathering practices such as using fire to clear undergrowth beneath California oaks before gathering, or creating Inukshuit (people figures) and pounds to drive and corral wild species such as caribou and bison. More general abstraction of landscapes, or maps and dreams, of paths and cliffs, of lightning and sky, appears on Ancestral Puebloan or historic ceramics and on painted skin. What is curious is that the importance of this geometric aesthetic, alongside Middle American forms, in contributing to Art Deco design, and to primitivism, is hardly acknowledged. Peformance art, in contrast to land art, flourishes. James Luna (b. 1950) (Luiseño) is one of the exceptional performative artists whose work has been featured at the Venice Biennale (*Emendatio*, 2005). Other artists move in seemingly contradictory directions, for instance combining painting and performance video. Kent Monkman (b. 1965) is engaged with historical North American painters Benjamin West, and the Hudson River school and replicates them with Norman Rockwell realism, introducing sharp deconstructed imagery from Indian life, combining withering scorn and brilliant wit in devastating canvases. The same imperative is also worked in videos, in the sexualized dedemonization of porno-pride, as in *Dance to Miss Chief* (2010), whipping up humour to make sense of the improbable and impossible.

Ceramicists, or rather Native artists who work in ceramics, provide an Indian aesthetic, a medium through which to explore image, narrative and identity. Carl Beam (1943–2005) (Canadian Ojibwe), for instance, took ancient Puebloan ceramics and reworked ideas of Indianness from ravens to Sitting Bull and addressed issues of indigenous whaling, not in only in ceramics, but across the whole range of mixed media, often with incisive inscriptions. Diego Romero (b. 1964) (Cochiti) also started with ancient bowl forms but developed a startling and frankly disturbed and disturbing Indian manga style, with a superhero, Chongo, doing Indian magic, but more often quotidian activities. His work draws on both Puebloan aesthetics and those of Attic ware – red and black Ancient Greek painted ceramics. In contrast, Helen Cordero (1915–94), also from Cochiti, in the 1960s began to model folk-like storyteller pots of mothers and children, while later Roxanne Swentzell (b. 1962) (Santa Clara), among others, subverted Puebloan tradition with larger clay sculptures developed from her personal experience of gender and emotion, of family attachment and cultural connectedness, of mothers, clown figures, and above all of conundrums, and the stillness required to convey resolution.

Labelling

Aboriginal art is also tagged art, in that it is labelled, perhaps quaintly, to guarantee authenticity rather than quality and to limit appropriation by whites and Asian imports. In the early twentieth century southwest jewellery came to be shop-made, then factory-made by Indians and others, as also did Northwest Coast silver. Much was fraudulent. Totem poles were carved of elephant ivory in the east, or fabricated of cheap porcelain, so that Indian art came to need to be protected by the US Indian Arts and Crafts Act of 1935, with fines of $500 and imprisonment of up to six months. The 2012 IACA took this to $5 million and fifteen years' incarceration, but potential prosecutions have foundered in part on the definition of Indian. The Federal Register for the 1990 IACA explains the issues and neatly exposes the conundrum by introducing the term 'Non-Government Enrolled Descendant' and its abbreviation, 'NGED', as perhaps an acceptable definition, when of course the whole point of the act was to exclude the non-government enrolled![38] Appropriation of cultural designs, while questionable, is not illegal, when copyright expires seventy years after the death of the owner. But perhaps more important is the failure of taste, of the regular inability of non-Native designers to make something of an original image, as when, for instance, in 2015 a shaman's caribou-skin parka was reduced to a mishmash of unintelligible symbols, sacred or not, on a $400 sweatshirt.[39]

In Canada the rules are both freer and, with labelling at the marketing and distribution end, more centralized. The outcomes, especially in marketing Inuit graphics and other arts, work well, except when community names such as Holman and Dorset change and confuse the image. Equally problematic is that in the 1960s the tag 'Eskimo Art' appeared under government auspices and used a snow house as symbol. With the replacement of the term 'Eskimo' with 'Inuit' in the 1970s and 'Inukshuk' in the 1990s, with the flag of Nunavut, all of this became rather more difficult. Other tags have appeared that offer protection, such as the 'Authentically Aboriginal' initiative of 2007. The essential point is that, while aboriginal rights are protected in the 1982 constitution and confirmed in the 1997 Delgamukw case, it is very difficult to bring a case to prove communally, or conversely individually, held rights to artist production outside copyright law. And ultimately in the creation and marketing of art, while volume may mean compromise in quality and authenticity, significant work, art that is in the public eye, seldom, to be successful, needs to deceive.

More important is the regular restriction of Native Art to display in overlapping categories, of anthropology and natural history museums, or in regional art museums, largely outside the hallowed halls of American art, less so of Canadian art. That of course is changing so that the National Gallery of Canada does now incorporate aboriginal art in its national narrative, and organizes and collects appropriately.

7
The East

ngraving of the destruction of the Pequot village at Mystic, 1637, by John Mason.

Deyohninhohhakarawenh,
White Head, or King Hendrick,
Mohawk leader (*c.*1680–1755),
ally of the British.

Joseph Brant, Thayendanegea,
Wendat born in Ohio, Mohawk
adopted (*c.*1742–1807), who,
defeated in 1783, took his people
as loyalist refugees to Canada.

Red Jacket, Sagoyewatha (c.1750–1830), so named in the American Revolution, a conservative Seneca leader who fought with the US in the War of 1812.

Six Nations wampum belts, Brantford, Ontario, alienated c.1900 and returned by the Museum of the American Indian in 1988.

Black Hawk, Makataimeshekiakiak (1767–1838), Sauk leader whose defeat in 1832 ended resistance in the Midwest, painted by George Catlin.

Osceola (c.1802–38), Seminole leader, originally from Alabama, who died after fighting Indian removal from Florida, painted by Goerge Catlin.

Demasduit, Mary March (d. 1820), one of the last of the Beothuk, otherwise exterminated in the crown colony of Newfoundland in the early nineteenth century.

John Rollin Ridge, Confederate Cherokee writer (1827–67), whose *Life and Adventures of Joaquin Murieta* (1854) is the first Indian, and first Californian, novel.

CREEK COUNCIL HOUSE 1878

Creek Nation Capitol

AND INDIAN MUSEUM
OKMULGEE, OKLAHOMA

Creek Capitol, OK. When democracy is abolished, new uses are found for legislature buildings. The Creek Capitol in Oklahoma became a museum, here depicted on a 1977 guide.

Elias Cornelius Boudinot
(1835–90), Confederate
Cherokee politician, then
pro-railroad modernizer,
and rogue.

The Revd Peter Jones, or
Kahkewaquonaby (Sacred Feathers)
1802–56), Ojibwe missionary from
Canada.

Deerfoot, Hut-goh-so-do-neh (*c.*1828-97), Seneca runner, was the first Native athlete to receive international acclaim. He is shown here on a music cover *c.*1861.

The Revd William Apess (1798–1839), Pequot writer and leader of the Mashpee Revolt.

Mohawks introduced lacrosse, one version of the aboriginal stick-ball game, to Europe in the third quarter of the nineteenth century.

'Idle No More' movement, founded in 2012 to protest against Bill C-45, which downgraded First Nations rights.

Kinzua Dam. The Seneca lost 10,000 acres due to the flooding of the Alleghany River in the 1960s.

St Kateri Tekakwitha (1656–80) (Mohawk and Algonquin), canonized 2012, painted by Father Claude Chauchetière c.1696.

Ray Halbritter (b. 1951), ironworker and businessman, who remade the Oneida Indian Nation and leads the attack on the use of the Redskin name by the football team.

7
The East

Contradictions

American, Canadian and colonial attitudes to and behaviour towards Native North America originated with first European contacts. On the one hand assistance – help with growing corn, trade in the form of fur and skins and a seemingly inexhaustible supply of land – was offered to the new arrivals. Central to the colonists' motives for immigration was the availability of space, in which beliefs, often unacceptable in Europe, could be practised and developed. On the other hand Indian people, from a European perspective, were not always welcoming, were heathens, did not use the land (by plough farming and animal husbandry) and so were not entitled to occupation, but were well able to form confederations of people in aggressive resistance to intrusion, in which the Haudenosaunee/Iroquois Confederacy in the first two-thirds of the eighteenth century was successful. By the middle of the twentieth it seemed as though Native Americans south of the St Lawrence and Great Lakes and east of the Mississippi were more or less integrated, assuming they had survived disease, the destruction of tribal nations and larger groups and removal west. And so the success of Native North America, especially in the revived nations of the east, in the late twentieth century could not have been imagined during the 1950s, when many peoples, especially those that seemed economically viable, were threatened with termination, the ending of Indian status, the loss of land and above all of the disappearance of community. During the 1950s, as the Civil Rights Movement gained strength with the Brown v. Board of Education (1954) decision, making segregated schools illegal, and when Rosa Parks led the fight against bus discrimination in Montgomery, Indian people were fighting against destructive new policies instituted in the aftermath of the Second World War. Both African and Native Americans had experienced great migrations during the 1940s to northern and western cities for war work. While for African Americans segregation began to be rolled back in the 1950s, for Native Americans in the middle of the twentieth century new measures, especially termination of the reservation system, were still being considered and implemented. Land was still being seized, such as the Cornplanter Tract in Pennsylvania for the Kinzua Dam project, completed in the 1960s. In Canada the St Lawrence Seaway in the 1950s took 1,200 acres from the Mohawk community at Kahnawake and cut the village off from the river.

Eastern Nations Survival

This success in the twenty-first century was led by many, but especially in the east by the Oneida, the Cherokee, the Pequot, the Mohegan and the Seminole. Their rebirth, and the remaking of identity and nationhood through gambling operations, as well as the survival of many others such as Huron-Wendat and the Ojibwe/Anishinaabe/Chippewa, are often seen only in a framework in which the 1940s narrative of dispossession and near-disappearance was in many ways wrong. Yet the negative narrative of the 1940s was in some specific ways correct: most Cherokee *had* been removed during the 1830s, leaving only a small, impoverished minority in the western mountains of North Carolina. Most Seminole did not surrender but were moved out of Florida to Indian Territory by the middle of the nineteenth century, and state-recognized tribes such as the Mohegan and Pequot were reduced to a few families by 1945. Yet if we look at the ways in which tribal nations reconstituted themselves, obtained federal recognition, avoided termination and organized gaming, an extreme form of recreational tourism, the achievements are exceptional, an unparalleled revival. So in 2015 each of the eastern Cherokee received more than $10,000 from the tribe, while each Seminole was said in 2010 to receive nearly $10,000 each *month*.[1]

The cultural history of eastern North America, then, can be told in two ways: as a presentist, deterministic drama in which a series of narratives – about contact with Indian people, about the social and people-based nature of society, about oral history and the founding of the Haudenosaunee and of the United States – led directly to today's gaming nation's success story; or as a less mythopoeic account with a more detailed texture, in which the present is more conflicted, and the future is not well understood, and the seeming certainties of the early twenty-first century can be compared to earlier periods of hope and reconstruction.

The idea of paradise usually relates to a situation now lost. The independent Haudenosaunee in the early eighteenth century, playing off Europeans against each other and dominating Pennsylvania and Ohio, can be seen as one such instance. Bison-hunting horseback Plains society is another paradise destroyed by incomers. Casino-led development may also come to be seen in the future as a paradise, in years to come an extraordinary success story yet to meet its nemesis in the jealousy and acquisitiveness of the greater society. The extraordinary commercial success of Native casinos is indicated by the international reach of the Seminole, with their ownership of the Hard Rock Café, or the Mohegan proposal in 2013 to create the main eastern Massachusetts casino at Revere on the eastern edge of Boston – which when it was blocked was replaced with a vast initiative to build a casino in South Korea.

Early Loss

Of the eastern peoples, designated through much of the twentieth century as Woodland, after the swathes of forest covering most of North America from the Mississippi and Great Lakes east to the Atlantic, a couple of things are important to note. Firstly, ideas from these peoples came early to Europe and contributed hugely to the development of intellectual history, of the visual understanding of ancient Native North America; and secondly, these peoples often strove mightily to modernize and mix with and accommodate Europeans, Americans and Canadians. They suffered much more definite factionalized disintegration and retribution than peoples in other parts of Native North America: early on from disease, and then from rolling land seizure, false treaties and military-backed loss in the early nineteenth century. From the sixteenth century onwards eastern peoples suffered significantly from epidemics and held on to only minute reservations, yet, despite this decimation and disenfranchisement, the recovery of Native North America was disproportionately greater in the east. The fights for federal recognition, for access to gaming opportunities, were fought out in the 1970s and 1980s among the Pequot in Connecticut following the success of the Seminole in Florida in obtaining bingo and then ever more profitable gaming franchises.

Eastern Contributions to the USA

In the nineteenth century the Seneca Parker family contributed to the national story during the Civil War, and to the recording of Iroquois culture and history, which made such a marked, if not entirely benign, contribution to social philosophy, to Marxism, and this followed the early contributions made by the Iroquoians, the Wendat and Haudenosaunee to Lafitau's 1720s account of Native mores, *Mœurs des Sauvages Amériquains*. Of the Algonquian-speaking peoples in the east entirely different, but not less important, contributions can be mentioned. These include, for instance, basic vocabulary introductions to the English language, such as *moccasin, toboggan* and *tomahawk*, and most objectionably *squaw*, which now may mean, in its unacceptable use, 'vagina', though originally referring to women. More interestingly, whole ideas such as wampum, the use of marine shells by Native North Americans based well inland, came from coastal Algonquian-speakers. And it was Virginia and New Algonquians who set up the pilgrims and investors to survive and also accommodated the buccaneering entrepreneurs of Stuart Britain.

Virginia

Seventeenth-century colonization in Algonquian areas of the Atlantic Coast set up the dynamics of later dispossession in what was to become the United States and Canada. In Virginia, friendly relations with the settlement of John Smith (1580–1631) at Jamestown were quickly replaced in 1607 by escalating tit-for-tat outrages, always with excessive British revenge, resulting in a series of more general hostilities, including three wars in which a confederacy of Algonquian-speaking peoples was led by Powhatan, known as Wahunsonacock or Wahunsenacawh (fl. c.1607–18), and then by Opechancanough (fl. 1607–46) (Pamunkeg). In the winter of 1607–8 John Smith may have been saved by Pocahontas, Powhatan's daughter, and adopted, often seen as a romantic interlude rather than the more likely reality of kinship alliance. Her marriage to John Rolfe helped bring to an end the first Anglo-Powhatan War of 1610–14. Each conflict resulted in the deeper penetration of the colonists into Virginia. The second war, in 1622–32, began with an opportunistic attack by Opechancanough, while the third war, in 1644–6, ended the Powhatan Confederacy and resulted in the death of Opechancanough, the most important early leader to fight colonization.

More characteristic of future conflicts of the eighteenth century was the final Virginia war of the seventeenth century, Bacon's Rebellion, in 1676, in which a disgruntled, ambitious frontier planter, Nathaniel Bacon (c.1647–76), was denied access to the fur trade, complained of taxes and of Indian outrages and fought Governor Sir William Berkeley (1606–77). Bacon attacked and destroyed Jamestown, before dying of dysentery, a forerunner of anti-royalist dissent in which friendly Indians, Pamunkeys, suffered from Bacon's attack. One result of the conflict was a more aggressive Indian policy, and another the beginnings of racial discourse to separate poor, indentured whites from African slaves and Indians by providing a pernicious framework of prejudice to avoid the making of common cause in widespread grievances.

New York

To the north, at the same time, the Dutch initiated settlement in Lenape/Delaware territory. The most important of their early voyages was that of the Dutch East India Company undertaken by Henry Hudson (d. 1611) in 1609, in which Hudson, sailing up the New York River to what is now Albany, paved the way for both the beginning of the fur trade and the founding of New Amsterdam/New York. To exploit the fur trade, the Dutch West India Company created the New

Netherland in the 1620s, trading skins for metal tools, and for shell bead wampum, whose development from flat, circular beads to tubular ones was made possible by the arrival of iron drills. The Lower Hudson River was early on, to use a later Hudson's Bay Company term, beavered out, resulting in the marginalization of the Lenape and focus on trade with the Iroquois from what was to become Albany, which became the centre of much enlarged trade leading to the hinterland of the Great Lakes and the Ohio drainage. The most famous piece of Dutch trade was the purchase of Manhattan: purchase of land would have had no meaning for the early Native population, and so a one-sided agreement was concluded. Pieter Shagan, reporting in 1626 to his employers in the Dutch West India Company, noted that '[O]ur people are in good spirit and live in peace . . . They have purchased the Island Manhattes from the Indians for the 60 guilders. It is 11,000 morgens in size.[2] Traditionally this exchange is associated with Pieter Minuit (c.1589–1638), the successful director general of the Dutch colony, but Willem van der Hulst may have been involved. The purchase of Manhattan probably entered national consciousness with the ironic account in Washington Irving's *History of New York* (1809).

Pennsylvannia

Most significant of later seventeenth-century settlements in Lenape country is that founded on the Delaware by William Penn (1644–1718), proprietor of the Province of Pennsylvania from 1681 to 1682. In this original and highly successful scheme a combination of Quaker principles and the determined purchase of Indian lands saw, in a colony without an army, the slow, normally peaceful eviction of Indian people. Notorious in this process was the Walking Purchase of 1737, a seventeenth-century deed enacted by Penn's sons based on the distance a man could walk from the junction of the Delaware and Lehigh Rivers – three runners rather than a single walker being used to increase the land to be transferred. A critic of the colony expressed the general process pithily: 'The land is bought in such lumping Pennyworths of the Natives, [and then] huckster'd out again to the King's Subjects.'[3] The Delaware/Lenape are perhaps best remembered today, like Longfellow's Hiawatha, by an apocryphal text, the *Walam*

Olum, an account of Lenape origins and migration from the deep past. This was not so much a hoax by the French-American autodidact and naturalist Constantine Samuel Rafinesque (1783–1840) as a reconstructed pictographic text, translated from English to Lenape and back again using a mishmash of Algonquian, Egyptian and Middle American symbols. While on the one hand this was simply fraudulent, on the other hand it was also deliberately, and importantly, intended to prove the antiquity and cultural authority of Native America at a time of removal and the rapid development of racial theories.

In New England, the peaceful settlement of the Pilgrims in 1620–21 was aided by Squanto or Tisquantum (d. 1622), a sometime British captive, traveller to Europe and speaker of English, who aided the colonists with explanations of Indian farming. He was later seen as a 'special instrument sent of God for their good beyond [English] expectation. He directed them how to set their corn [and] where to take fish'.[4] Squanto, of the Patuxet, a division of the Wampanoag, despite having been sold into slavery, interpreted for the pilgrims, facilitating co-existence with Massasoit, the war chief of the Wampanoags, later an ally of the British. Massasoit assisted the British in their survival and remained allied to them, ceding land as required. Most importantly, the Wampanoags stayed loyally on the side of the British during the Pequot War of 1637, which, with the siege of Mystic and the burning alive of the Native inhabitants, resulted in the virtual extinction of this powerful Connecticut confederacy.

Metacom

King Philip's War of 1675–6 arose from multiple causes and acts as a coda to the Wampanoag alliance and the overthrow and virtual destruction of that Algonquian people. King Philip or Metacom (d. 1676), son or grandson of Massasoit, after becoming chief made an agreement with Plymouth in 1662 so that the Wampanoags were regarded as subjects of the crown and agreed to uphold all treaties. But this was also a period of increasing rivalry between the three British colonies, Rhode Island, Plymouth and Massachusetts Bay. This was especially so after the granting of a charter in 1663 to Rhode Island, placing Metacom/King Philip's home at Mount Hope in Rhode

Island, rival to Plymouth, thus exacerbating tensions. The war was also about the increasing assumption of rights and regulations by the colony to create and expand towns, such as Swansea in 1671, which Metacom challenged, the consequence of which was that he was forced to yield his arms in a humiliating treaty in which he was also obliged to kill five wolves a year and pay a fine of £100.

This was the period of John Eliot's (c.1604–90) missionary work in translating the Bible and setting up 'Praying Towns', fourteen in Massachusetts Bay Colony in 1675, for Indian believers. Metacom and the Wampanoags were very specifically selected, but they were set against conversion and resisted this intrusion. The actual cause of war was, as tensions rose, the killing of a Christian Indian, John Sassamon, friend of the Wampanoags and witness of the treaty of 1662, in early 1675, by three Wampanoags. Sassamon had hoped, as a man of the cloth, to convert King Philip. The trial of the Wampanoag killers and due process of the law would have it made it clear to Metacom that Indian authority would never recover. After a brutal conflict in which the colonists had no regard for Christian Indians, in the Indian war in which comparatively speaking more American colonists were to die than in any other Native conflict, King Philip was killed in 1676. What is important here is that this foreshadows the story of the Iroquois, allies of the British, traders with the Canadians and British, who, whether they were on the side of the British or later the Americans, even if they were Christian, and however many treaties or concessions were made, always, until rendered near-destitute, possessed land coveted by others.

Wars of the Crown

Indian wars in eastern North America from the 1760s to the 1830s seem to be highly varied and yet have a certain sameness, as part of a general continuity between the policies of the *ancien régime* and those of the young republic. Three wars in the colonial period anticipate US Indian wars. They are more generally framed, especially in the south, by a degree of similarity to Indian relations with the state. These are the Cherokee War of 1759–61, Pontiac's Rebellion or War of 1763–7 and Lord Dunmore's War of 1774. The Cherokee War was caused by increasing pressure by white settlers on the Cherokee frontier in the late 1750s, the Cherokee otherwise being loyal allies of the British, highly important for the trade in deer skins, the southern equivalent of the beaver trade in the north. The siege of Fort Prince George, in South Carolina, in 1753, and of Fort Loudon, constructed near the Cherokee capital of Chota in Tennessee in 1756, during 1760 by Cherokee led by Oconostota (c.1710–83) were followed by swift retaliation, the destruction of well-ordered Cherokee towns, and an eventual peace to avoid the total destruction of the Overhill/Tennessee towns.

The conventional view of British relations with Indians at this period is that they were benign. The British supplanted the French in Indian affections, bought support with better trade goods and, with the Royal Proclamation of 1763, guaranteed non-intrusion by Americans west of the Appalachians. The simpler reality is that the earlier policy of playing off France and Indian peoples against each other strategically, through the allocation of weapons and trade goods, was no longer necessary. This meant that payments to Indian peoples became less important. What mattered on the Cherokee frontier was not which towns were friendly and which were not, but that continued pressure on land produced Indian 'outrages' (better seen as protests) and disputes. With each campaign more destruction was wrought on the Cherokee, the only positive aspect being that, under duress, a degree of common Cherokee identity was forged.

Pontiac's Rebellion

Pontiac's War fits then into a new pattern of direct pro-colonist policies by the British. The conflagration was sparked by the decision by Lord Amherst to reduce payments to Indians, at a time when Pontiac (d. 1769), of Ottawa descent, probably originally from the Detroit region, realized that the British and colonists were not going to go away. Amherst was interested in reducing 'bribes' to Indians, seeing them, prematurely, as unnecessary. Pontiac in this was inspired by the nativistic prophet Neolin (c.1712–69), Delaware or Lenape, from the Ohio country. The Lenape originally dominated the lower reaches of the Hudson and the Delaware Rivers, north to Massachusetts and Mohawk country, including New York City. Devastated, like New England and Virginia Algonquians, by the occupation and rivalry of the Dutch, Swedish and British, they became one of those peoples whose survivors moved north to Ontario, and later went west. They were much adopted into other peoples, although some Delaware moved to Oklahoma in the 1860s, on to Cherokee land, others to Ontario.

Neolin's prophetic, Christian-influenced movement took hold in 1762. He argued that the Great Spirit was angered by Indian adoption of white ways, which should be rejected, with forgiveness possible when Indians returned to hunting and living from the land. Pontiac besieged the great fort at Detroit, part of the forward defensive system in Indian Country, with its connecting network of roads, giving the lie to the British demonstrations of friendship and giving rise to the regularly expressed Native hope that the French would return – a rather similar situation in turn to that which would relate to Native hopes for a British return to the USA held at least until the Black Hawk War of the 1830s. William Johnson, superintendent of Indian affairs, organized peace with Pontiac in 1766, who was murdered shortly afterwards. Little is actually known of him; he can be seen as a pan-Indian leader, or a local menace, a lackey of the French, a romantic, but flawed rebel, but most importantly he may have seen himself in terms of Algonquian country heroes, such as Nanabush, the trickster on the edge of society.[5]

But of course it was not only the Europeans who encouraged factionalism; the French historian of Canada Claude-Charles Bacqueville La Potherie (1663–1736) noted the great skills in diplomacy of Indian peoples in the early eighteenth century:

The policy of those peoples is so shrewd that it is difficult to penetrate its secrets. When they undertake any enterprise of importance against a nation whom they fear, especially the French, they seem to form two parties – one conspiring for and the other opposing it; if the former succeed in their projects, the latter approve and sustain what has been done; if their designs are thwarted they retire to the other side. Accordingly, they always attain their objects.[6]

In all forms of diplomacy the maintenance of opposing ideas, policies and factions is a reasonable strategy to deal with uncertainty, and this was especially the case in the middle ground, the borderlands between colonies and the confederacies of Indian peoples in the Great Lakes, and Ohio Mississippi drainage. Pontiac, commemorated by the now fading memory of the car manufactured c.1926–2009, and a named trailer park on the site where he died, was one of a series of leaders who, when all else failed, sought to put together an alliance of Native people to remove the intruders from Indian Country.

Lord Dunmore's War

Lord Dunmore's war of 1774 seems an even more straightforward example of a frontier conflict. Action was taken against the Algonquian Shawnee by the Virginia governor on behalf of Virginian colonists and speculators determined to wrest the left or southern bank of the Ohio, especially what is now Kentucky, from the Indians – much ignored in the previous treaty process, the Treaty of Fort Stanwix of 1768, ceding this country to the colonists from the Six Nations overlords, without reference to the original Shawnee or Cherokee inhabitants,[7] or to the Delawares who also used it – for hunting, not simply for food, but for skins required to obtain trade goods. With the outbreak of the American Revolution a couple of years later the crown's direst promotion of frontier invasion ceased. Traditional Indian diplomacy, similar to that of the French period, in which Indian allies were encouraged by the British, again protectors, to turn on their tormentors, the now rebellious American colonists.

Although different, these three wars represent types of conflict continued by the USA into the nineteenth century – the prophet- and war-leader-led uprising, the attack on and destruction of a pre-eminent military force, such as that at Fort Loudon, and the US taking-up of arms on behalf of a mixed range of needy, land-hungry frontiersmen. The ending of the 1774 war opened Kentucky to settlement and to the speculations of Virginian Daniel Boone (1734–1820), who founded in 1775 one of the first trans-Appalachian American communities at Boonesborough, Kentucky.

The Cherokee

The central spine of Native history belongs in many ways to the Cherokee, for a number of reasons. The Cherokee speak an Iroquoian language and, like the Haudenosaunee themselves, they lived in the mountainous interior. They were involved in the eighteenth century in the great trade of deer skins. The Cherokee encountered and sought accommodation with the British and sent delegations to London in 1730 and 1762. Embroiled in the American Revolution, they were decimated by internal divisions as a consequence of that fratricidal conflict. Nevertheless the rich resources of their highland community ensured that recovery occurred in the late eighteenth and early nineteenth century, and, as with other nations set on modernization, leaders both came out of mixed-ancestry communities on the frontier and adopted American institutions and state formation as part of their understanding with, and accommodation to, the dominant society. So the Cherokee in the early nineteenth century acquired a constitution, a syllabary and a museum, and plantation owners organized themselves with African American slaves in the long boom time which accompanied the explosive growth in demand for cotton as Britain industrialized. Matrilineal relations in pure Cherokee hands turned to patrilineality in the hands of people of mixed descent. But the transition in the US leadership from the independence generation, often of southern plantation gentry, to the frontier-friendly populists such as Andrew Jackson, known as Old Hickory for his supple toughness, from the 1810s to the 1830s altered fundamental perceptions and lines of authority in the emergent south. The southern myth of aristocracy, and magnolia-white leaders, hid the reality of new money, easily obtained by the plundering of Indian lands, and the consistent frustration of Cherokee ambitions by the state of Georgia. Cherokee used American law and in a series of landmark cases won against the state. In Cherokee Nation v. Georgia (1831) they had the Native situation neatly defined as that of 'domestic dependent nations'. Yet it is the Cherokee especially who suffered from the removal policy, the resettlement of Indian peoples, which marks so neatly the way that, as throughout Native American history, liberal, accommodationist

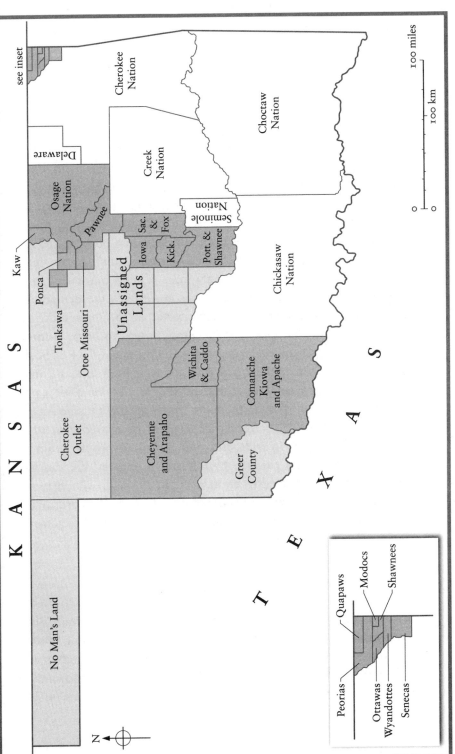

Map 7. The Tribes and Nations of Oklahoma and Indian territories, 1890's.

progress has been subverted and then inverted, creating an end result which is entirely opposite to that intended by the seemingly well-intentioned proposals for removal.

Indian Territory

With the victory of the American colonies and Britain in the 1760s, the revivalist movement led by Pontiac with the prophet Neolin frightened the crown. The proclamation of 1763 confined Americans to a line east of the crest of the Appalachian Mountains and allowed the vast lands to the west to be the preserve of Native peoples. But of course without frontiers the line was immediately porous, and the colonies had in any case long claimed territory running west from the East Coast of their original royal grants, a contributory factor to the American Revolution. By the 1810s and 1820s the demand by American plantation owners, scarcely affected by the abolition of the slave trade, meant that Georgia, backed as it was to be by Andrew Jackson, the ruthless militia leader who had decimated the Red Sticks and then the Creek, would fight what would have been seen as Cherokee pretensions to nationhood. 'Indian Territory' – set aside as all territory west of the Mississippi, apart from Canada and the American colonies – provided a simple concept to be moved around in imaginary Washington worlds, into which Indian people could be forced, packed off and paid off by a hustler Congress. The descriptions of the removal, the destruction wrought by the division between different factions, is well captioned in the congressional records of the period. The records show, in excellent detail, great Cherokee achievements, indicating what was left behind.

Woodlands Achievements

Early studies of the remnant communities marooned in the United States produced important ideas central to the understanding of society and the way it works: ideas of matrilineality, the incest taboo and kinship emerged from a study of the Huron Wendat in Canada and of the Haudenosaunee/Iroquois proper in New York and Canada. The initial study of Iroquoians was undertaken during the great thrust of the counter-reformation by Jesuits in eastern Canada, especially Ontario, where the Huron then lived. Over 200 years, annual reports were sent from New France/Canada back to Europe, where they were considered, edited and published. They provided the basic context for what is often considered the first work of ethnography, by the Jesuit Joseph-François Lafitau.

Lafitau was a missionary for nearly six years in Canada during the second decade of the eighteenth century, and he summarized Jesuit knowledge of native cultures in his *Mœurs des Sauvages Amériquains* (1724). Lafitau's achievements are many, but his most important is that he looked at and described Huron society from within, as Hurons saw it, and made 'savages' real people for the first time. He used ethnographic observation as a methodology for illuminating and reconstructing antiquity. In a sense he used his American ethnography both to understand Indians and as a heuristic device, an experience-derived technique for problem-solving and learning about history and culture. While in a sense his comparative method came from André Thevet's (1502–90) work on Canada and the Brazilian Tupinamba and José de Acosta's (1539–1600) work on the Mexica and Incas and relates to compendia of Asian religions, as for instance by his contemporary Bernard Picard (1673–1733), or earlier Marc Antoine Muret (1526–85) in comparing funerals, Lafitau is the first to insist that heathen savages are to be differentiated from each other and are remarkable for their own knowledge and belief systems. He explicitly tells people that 'one must never take it upon oneself to describe the manners and customs of a country on which there are no systematic studies unless one knows the language'.[8] So, for instance, he treats dreams, so vital in making decisions, as a serious aspect of Indian belief systems determining behaviour and treats tobacco as a spiritually important substance used to show respect. He argues also about the importance of ecology in determining material culture: the way elm-bark canoes were made and used only when the smoother, lighter northern birch was not available. But most remarkable, beyond his understanding of the role of women, is Lafitau's respect for religion. His description of the search for a personal spirit is modest, factual and to the point:

The Huron, Iroquois and Algonquian tribes also have their initiations
which they still celebrate. All I know about them is that they are begun at
the age of puberty; they retreat into the woods . . . In particular they pay
careful attention to their dreams and report them exactly to those in
charge of them . . . To determine what they should take for their *Oïaron*
or Manitou on whom the future happiness of their life must depend.[9]

What is striking is how important, in cross-cultural terms, this
study was in comparing Iroquoians with the ancients and the Asians.
While they were an extremely small group of peoples or nations,
numerically insignificant in comparison to the other cultures mentioned, they loomed large on the frontier in comparison to the slight
populations of European colonists at that time.

A Mohawk Prophet

The Haudenosaunee/Iroquois contribute to the national narrative in
many other ways. St Kateri Tekakwitha (1656–80), the Algonquin-
born Mohawk saint, from New York, but who lived in Kahnawake,
has been claimed as the aboriginal American of the seventeenth century about whom most is known. From the Mohawk Valley she was
adopted by her father's people when her mother died and brought up
in a period of endemic warfare between Algonquian-speaking peoples
and Iroquoian ones and of commercial competition and warfare
between the Dutch and the French. She became a Catholic and for the
last years of her life lived as an abstemious penitent. After her early
death she was sometimes associated with miracles; for instance, a
piece of her coffin cured someone of smallpox, from which Tekakwitha had suffered as a child. Interest grew in her life and lessons through
the late nineteenth century. In the USA, her story, as a Catholic American, was fused with the traditional use of Native American culture
and historiography to symbolize the republic. So she became a focus
for the rolling-back of late nineteenth-century Protestant prejudice
against poor Catholic immigrants from Ireland and southern Europe – the medium being Ellen Walworth's *The Life and Times of*
Kateri Tekakwitha (1891), a biography which described Tekakwitha's
life with a light fictional gloss. Walworth was led to this project by her

uncle Clarence, a converted priest who fought for Tekakwitha's memory. The canonization process began with the Council of Baltimore in 1884, but it took until 2012 for sainthood to be conferred. The second miracle, required in the process, took place in 2006, when a young Lummi boy, Jake Finkbonner, in Washington State, was saved from a flesh-eating disorder by prayer to Tekakwitha.

The more general background to the canonization of Kateri Tekakwitha is the rapprochement of indigenous Americans with the Catholic church organized by John Paul II in the aftermath of the development of liberation theology during the 1960s and 1970s and the need to redefine and revive the Papacy in the Americas. First among indigenous American saints was St Juan Diego Cuauhtlatoatzin (1474–1548), who saw a vision of the Virgin Mary four times in 1531 in the Valley of Mexico and was only canonized in 2002. So far the story is a conventional one, of hemispherical renewal of the church and of Native America. But Tekakwitha's narrative also fits into other narratives, one of which is that of nativistic revival, of a syncretic Christian/Native American prophet who combined rejection of sin, of the white world, in an attempt to obtain redemption and freedom from oppression by the colonizers, with self-mortification. In this sense Tekakwitha is a prophet alongside Handsome Lake, with his revitalizing code after the American Revolution, and with Wevoka of the Ghost Dance after the disappearance of the bison. The use of relics to bless photographs of Tekakwitha for sale is related to the use of medicine bundles, containers filled with esoteric relics relating to personal and/or clan spirits. The mortification of the flesh also relates to the visionary piercing of humble bodies as in the Sun Dance. On the other hand, this is an unusual history of a female prophet, who, instead of being dismissed as a near-mad heathen, was drawn very slowly over the centuries into the arms of Rome, just as two others – Joan of Arc (in 1920) and St Bernadette of Lourdes, the nineteenth-century mystic (in 1933) – were canonized.

League of the Iroquois

The League of the Iroquois, the Haudenosaunee, plays an important part in US and Canadian history. Their territory was recognized by the mid-eighteenth-century colony of New York and lay to the east of Lake Erie, south of Lake Ontario, with the Mohawk in the east, the Seneca in the west, the Oneida, Tuscarora, Cayuga and Onondaga between, across the drainages of the Mohawk-Hudson in the east, the Allegheny and Susquehanna in the south, and the Genesee and other rivers and lakes in the centre and flowing to the Great Lakes.

Speaking related languages, the Iroquois were hunter-horticulturalists, in the eighteenth century inhabiting both bark-covered longhouses and log cabins and numbering less than 20,000 people. (There are more than 100,000 now.) Incoming Europeans regarded their vast hunting territories, tens of thousands of square miles, as scandalously underused, as far as farming was concerned. Their society was organized, as everywhere in Native North America, according to the rights of kin and relations, real and socially configured, matrilineal and matrifocal, and the centre of kin relations was the longhouse, the place of responsibilities, rights and obligations, divided by cooking fires. The expression 'Longhouse Religion', to refer to the nativistic movement of Handsome Lake, neatly expresses the way in which the home is the place of being and belief, the place of clan mothers who elect the men of the Grand Council, and through whom status and descent is reckoned.

The League of the Iroquois came out of the Great Peace in the fifteenth century, founded on the idea of a unanimity of purpose to ensure that rivalry, revenge killings and witchcraft were avoided. The Haudenosaunee, the 'People of the Longhouse', developed out of negotiations between Deganawida, Hiawatha and other chiefs and gradually gained acceptance, especially from the Onondaga chief, Thadodaho, at a great council, a meeting to be repeated annually at Onondaga, the most centrally placed settlement of the Iroquois peoples. Government was organized by fifty council chiefs or *sachems*, raised by their clans, that is by women, following condolence ceremonies, nephew following uncle in the maternal line. *Sachems* were (and still are) empowered to discuss issues until unanimity was achieved, other leaders being appointed, for instance, war chiefs, as circumstances required. The original Five Nations – Mohawk, Oneida, Onondaga, Cayuga and Seneca – were joined by the Tuscarora, originally from North Carolina, around 1722.

Towards the end of the seventeenth century the Iroquois took centre stage in complex tribal politics which evolved after New York was taken by the British in 1664 and when, from 1701 to 1768, the Iroquois held the balance of power between the French and the British – losing much of their authority after the Treaty of Paris in 1763, and especially with the Treaty of Fort Stanwix of 1768. This treaty, in recognizing new colonists' rights in what is now west Virginia, Kentucky and Tennessee, adjusted the Indian frontier far further west than the boundary proclaimed in 1763. It foreshadowed the loss to the Iroquois not just of their remaining land in Pennsylvania and the Ohio watershed, but eventually much of their New York territory. Essentially, still in colonial times, it was these treaties that undermined the Royal Proclamation of five years earlier and the original idea of Indian Territory.

The League and the USA

Outside of the Haudenosaunee themselves, the League is important as a national symbol, expressing American difference and freedom, a means of resolving the need for an idea of liberty, as expounded by John Locke, which was settled away from the fundamental elements of democracy that existed in the thirteen colonies. In the middle of the eighteenth century Benjamin Franklin and Canasatego (fl. 1740–50) urged the colonies to combine against the French, the League providing a model for cooperation and unity. At the Treaty of Lancaster negotiations (1744) leading to the secession of the Shendandoah Valley, Canasatego is recorded as saying:

> We heartily recommend Union and a good Agreement between you our Brethren. Never disagree . . . We are a powerful Confederacy; and, by your observing the same Methods our wise Forefathers have taken, you will acquire fresh Strength and Power.[10]

But this insistence on agreement and a league was radically different from the idea of election to colonial assemblies by propertied freedmen, property and the idea of freedmen remaining central to the young constitutionally formed United States and irrelevant in most Native societies. For the Iroquois recruitment of outsiders was based on adoption and marriage; in the young republic recruitment included, as in earlier European colonies, indenturing and chattel slavery, in which the presence of traded, transported slaves played an important role. League governance was not adopted by the USA; instead the idea of Iroquoian-derived unity became a touchstone of American freedoms, an encompassing metaphor, throughout the nineteenth century, with both white and Indian historians converting parallel structures into one of seeming derivation. In a sense the more important Native idea is that of confederacy, that is, of loose federations of peoples coming together on occasion, when necessary, at a time of war, with war and spiritual leaders. In that way the mid-nineteenth century American confederacy in the south, a loose, opportunistic, failing group of entities, which coalesced and was destroyed in the Civil War, could be said to be more symbolic of an Indian political form than the federal USA.

Joseph Brant and Red Jacket

The history of the eighteenth- and nineteenth-century conflicts can be read through the complex, difficult and often tragic biographies of aboriginal leaders in the United States and Canada, which form a coherent theme in Native history. Between the mid-eighteenth-century colonial wars and the ending of the Civil War in 1865, a series of remarkable people, usually men, engaged with European America, often very successfully, and were then betrayed. In part they were abandoned by their white friends and allies, but above all they were destroyed by the fast-moving circumstances in which white greed and the need for Indian land took precedence over loyalties and the sanctimonious expressions of good intentions in treaties. For the Iroquois, in the centre of the process, the story is set in the borderlands of what are now New York, Ontario and Quebec, or with their westward extensions' middle ground, with frontiers that were once fluid and malleable, but became fixed boundaries, dividing nations. In particular the waterways, the Great Lakes and rivers such as the Niagara, once a focus of trade and communication, came to symbolize difference and division, an extreme form of inversion or perversion of cultural and economic realities.

Of the British allies the most interesting of the First Nations leaders is Joseph Brant or Thayendanagea (1742/3–1807). He was born in Ohio, of Huron-Wendat origin, descended from people adopted into the successful Mohawk following one of the Iroquoian movements westwards, part of the story of Native survivance, the stubborn endurance of a people much sinned against by incoming colonists. Brant was educated, after teenage military service in the French and Indian War, by Eleazar Wheelock, the founder of Dartmouth College, who described him as 'of a Sprightly Genius, a manly and genteel Deportment, and of a Modest and benevolent Temper, I have Reason to think began truly to love our Lord Jesus Christ Several Months ago'.[11] After further education he was appointed (war) chief in 1774, and then, by the British, chief interpreter for the army, because of his linguistic skills. He travelled to England to complain of land loss and then with war worked ceaselessly to support the crown, believing this course in the best interests against patriots who would cheat Indian people 'of the small spots we have left for our women and children to live on'.

Having been persuaded to fight with the British through the American Revolution, First Nations were ignored at the Treaty of Paris and then taken up again in the unrealistic pursuit of an Indian confederacy beyond the American frontier in the USA. At the same time 14,000 or so loyalist Indians were given a huge tract at Grand River, Ontario, only partly in fact purchased from the indigenous Mississauga. Britain's silent but mischievous plans, of supporting an Indian confederacy on the US frontier, were dropped with the conclusion of the Jay Treaty of 1794, and again Indian interests were ignored. At that time the British retreated from frontier forts, such as Detroit, in what had been since 1783 American territory.

As a Christian translator of biblical texts, Brant believed in education, the private ownership of land and the importance of white involvement in Indian affairs, while passionately objecting to double standards in the administration of law.

In 1778 Mohawks and Senecas, including Joseph Brant and Red Jacket or Sagoyewatha (c.1750–1830), took part in a frontier campaign under Colonel Butler in eastern Pennsylvania, fearing that the French who had entered the war after British defeat at the Battle of

Saratoga would retake the western frontier. In June and July various patriot forts were destroyed by the Iroquois, and the defeated patriots were killed and scalped, some tortured to death. While women and children were spared, the description of the Battle of Wyoming on 3 July and its aftermath brought down American wrath on the Iroquois villages to the east in New York, and in 1779 Washington, known as 'Town Destroyer', authorized Sullivan's Expedition, which methodically eliminated forty Iroquois villages. Brant was not at the Battle of Wyoming, but he features in Thomas Campbell's 1809 poem *Gertrude of Wyoming; A Pennsylvanian Tale* as the 'foe – the Monster Brandt – with all his howling desolate band . . . he left of all my tribe nor man, nor child, nor thing of living birth'. The popularity of the poem may have resulted in the naming of the territory, and then state, of Wyoming in 1868 and 1890.

Red Jacket or Sagoyewatha ('he keeps them awake' or 'keeper awake Seneca'), Brant's contemporary and rival, was also a great orator. Of Americans he said:

> You are a cunning People without Sincerity, and not to be trusted, for after making Professions of your Regard, and saying every thing favorable to us, you . . . tell us that our Country is within the lines of the States.[12]

Red Jacket rejected Christianity and was scorned by Brant as a cow killer rather than warrior: in the 1770s, Brant said, he had represented a bloody axe as from battle rather than animal butchery. A supporter of the British during the American Revolution, he remained in western New York, fighting against land cessions, a constant gadfly reproaching American hypocrisy:

> Brother, our seats were once large and yours were small. You have now become a great people, and we have scarcely a place left to spread our blankets. You have got our country, but are not satisfied; you want to force your religion upon us.[13]

The land cessions continued in any case: by the 1797 Treaty of Big Tree, which made good the holding of the Holland Land Company, 1,500 Senecas were to receive $100,000.

Handsome Lake

The ending of the revolutionary war did not, then, resolve the situation of the Iroquois in New York, nor did it effectively guarantee their access to their former hunting and trading territories in the Ohio Valley. While Britain waited, in vain, for the young republic, without a constitution until 1788, to collapse, and continued to occupy frontier forts, America embarked on a process which began by confining the Iroquois as much as possible to New York and ended, once the Seneca and others had conceded frontier territory, in the disingenuous spectre of Indian removal, seen by America as a humanitarian gesture designed to save Indians from frontier farmers. The treaties made by the Iroquois through the 1790s closed off the west and the waterways to them. Recovery by the Iroquois from war and loss of land came in part through the teachings of Handsome Lake, who was a signatory of the (Pickering) Treaty of Canandaigua of 1794, with President Washington, guaranteeing Iroquois rights. An alcoholic, Handsome Lake had a series of visions when he was about sixty-five at the end of the eighteenth century, which led him to proclaim the 'Good Way', *gaiwaiio*, in the form of a codified speech taught by him until his death. This forbade alcohol use and abortion, advocated traditional values, especially those of the family and emphasized the importance of children. Initially unpopular because of an emphasis on witchcraft, which he later prohibited, during the troubled time of the War of 1812, Handsome Lake's teachings later became popular.

After his death, at the instigation of female elders, Handsome Lake's grandson, Jemmy/Jimmy/James Johnson, who was about forty at the time, became responsible for the annual recital of the Code, as recorded by Lewis Henry Morgan in 1851: Johnson 'was appointed his successor, the first and only person ever "raised up" by the Iroquois, and invested with the office of supreme Religious Instructor'.[14] After Johnson's death, and the settlement of the reservation issue in 1857, when the Seneca were allowed to buy back land illegally removed with the funds originally intended to assist in their removal, a degree of stability returned, with the Code regularly pronounced in the autumn for all to hear and acknowledge. The general importance of Handsome Lake, his Code and the revival of the Longhouse religion comes from its use by Alfred Wallace to create a theoretical framework for revitalization movements in the 1950s, building on Ralph Linton's earlier typology of nativistic movements so defined: 'Any conscious, organized attempt on the part of a society's members to revive or perpetuate selected aspects of its culture'.[15] Linton had outlined the difference between millennial movements and nativistic ones, millennial movements being new creations, whereas nativistic ones, such as the Code of Handsome Lake revitalization movements, employed ideas and teachings from the past.

The Parkers

Ely Samuel Parker was the first aboriginal person after the American Revolution to achieve national importance. Highly educated as a lawyer, but debarred as a non-citizen, he became an engineer with the help of his friend and collaborator Lewis Henry Morgan, to whom he acted as a consultant. He was befriended by Ulysses S. Grant, through whom he was enabled to contribute to the Union during the Civil War as a successful engineer, for instance at the Siege of Vicksburg (1863), the capture of which divided eastern and western confederate forces. Subsequently Parker was appointed adjutant and military secretary to Grant and attended Lee's surrender at Appomattox, helping to draft the surrender document of the Confederacy. After the Civil War he was appointed to the Southern Treaty Commission, which replaced the treaties made with southern Indian nations transplanted to Indian Territory. The commission negotiated largely with Union leaders, but the Cherokee delegation included Stand Watie (1806–71), the Cherokee principal chief and only Indian also to become, like Parker, a brigadier general – in fact, the last Confederate general to surrender. Grant, when president, appointed Parker the first Native commissioner of Indian affairs (1869–71). Exceptionally talented and determined, Parker acted at an early age as interpreter in seeking to reverse land transactions and introduced Morgan to Iroquois culture, setting up perhaps the most important consultant–informant relationship in the early history of anthropology.

Morgan was a lawyer and anthropologist from Aurora in upstate

New York, from a family working former Cayuga land. Like many Americans and Europeans, he was affected by the romance of the recent history of the Native occupants of New York and with his fellow students and associates as a young man was involved in creating a succession of societies, part literary and part fraternal. Like many non-Native vernacular scholars – autodidacts and hobbyists who come to study American Indians on their own and who play Indian – Morgan dreamed of being Indian and then became something authentic: a researcher, who placed the Haudenosaunee centre stage. In Aurora Morgan joined a secret society called the Gordian Knot, later renamed the Grand Order of the Iroquois or the New Confederacy of the Iroquois. Morgan researched Iroquois history to add authenticity to the society, collecting names and ceremonies. His first interviews were conducted in the spring of 1844, after he had bumped into Jimmy Johnson and two other Tonawanda Seneca chiefs visiting the state capital, Albany, while browsing in a bookshop. Parker, then aged sixteen and a mission-educated bilingual, acted as an interpreter, and then over the next six years as an informant in what is reasonably considered to be the first anthropological fieldwork.

In total Morgan may have made half a dozen visits of one to two weeks, supplemented by discussions with Parker, whom he fully acknowledges in *The League of the Ho-de-no-sau-nee* (1851). The initial interest in the ethnography of the Iroquois, fed by collecting material culture for the newly founded New York State Museum, branched out in two directions of research: into kinship through philology and the evolutionary development of social structure. Morgan characterized the Iroquois system of kinship as classificatory, rather than descriptive. From this grew a far wider understanding of kinship, including aspects such as matrilineality and cross-cousin marriage, something which Morgan researched with further field visits and interviews with Algonquian-speaking informants, especially in Michigan, where he worked as a lawyer, and beyond, eventually publishing *Systems of Consanguinity and Affinity of the Human Family* (1871). From America his ideas spread elsewhere, immediately to Australia and to the study of aboriginal kinship. Morgan's ideas about the evolution of society based on encounters with Iroquois clans in the 1840s and 1850s were expressed in *Ancient Society*

(1877), which describes the change of society organized by social relations to one organized by property, in three stages, each defined by technologies: savagery, barbarism and civilization. What Morgan did was to take original information obtained with Parker, among the Iroquois and other Native peoples, and create two syntheses, using the three-age system – stone, bronze and iron – introduced by C. J. Thomsen and J. J. A. Worssae from Denmark in the 1840s to develop the first fieldwork-based explanations of societies. These were very influential, especially with Marx and Engels: Engels relied on Morgan for his evolutionary view in *The Origin of the Family, Private Property, and the State* (1884). So Native America provided key ideas in the development of European Marxist ideology. *The Origin of the Family* is organized in a series of comparative chapters in which prehistoric peoples, early families – the Greeks, Romans, Celts and Germans – are compared in terms of social organization and state formation, with the Iroquois centre stage: 'The Iroquois League represented the most advanced social organization attained by Indians that had not passed the lower stage of barbarism.'[16] As in the case of Lafitau, then, a minute Native American people, numbering maybe 20,000 people, was given a role alongside vast ancient empires.

Morgan's career and achievements contain within them the ambiguity inherent in the study of Native North America: he came to it as an outsider, wanting to use the Iroquois League for his fraternity, on the one hand, and on the other became involved with campaigning against the Ogden Company to impose fraudulent land deals on the Seneca. Morgan recorded Iroquois culture, made the Iroquois well known and in his business life was a lawyer working for the westward expansion of railroads, though he did fight the monopoly interests of Vanderbilt, understanding their consequences for democracy. In his political life tried and failed to become Commissioner of Indian Affairs.[17]

Borderlands

Brant had actually encouraged white settlement on Six Nations reserve, the Canadian land allocated to First Nations loyalists who had left the United States after the Revolution. Much of the reserve was alienated through the nineteenth and early twentieth centuries, in part, as ever, because of a lack of unity. Levi General, known as Deskaheh (1873–1925), rose to prominence in the post-war turmoil of the early 1920s, when the Six Nations were divided between the adherents of the Longhouse religion, Christian more assimilationist elements and ex-servicemen who wanted both an elected council and land on the reserve. Enforced enfranchisement, with the amendment of the Indian Act in 1920, and the removal of Indian status, radicalized Deskaheh, who took these grievances to London and to the League of Nations in 1923 in the form of lobbying for recognition of Six Nations as an independent nation. The British successfully insisted that this was an internal Canadian matter, and the following year the first council was elected, but this year-long campaign was the first time that First Nations issues drew international attention.[18] Deskaheh died on the Tuscarora reservation, but at the end of his life asked Clinton Rickard (1882–1971) to campaign on Native issues: the Indian Defense League, founded in 1926, was the result, with campaigns for the implementation of treaty obligations. Rickard was also successful in keeping open the border between the USA and Canada, as it came to be affected from the 1920s onwards by immigration as well as citizenship legislation.

The Marginalized Oneida

A more recent activist, Doug George-Kanentiio, has documented the misplaced round of activities of the last three governors of New York. Mario Cuomo (governor 1983–94) worked to improve Iroquois–New York relations, but from a strategic viewpoint determined by self-interest. He organized an Office of Indian Relations but packed it with former state police, so that it was ignored in Indian Country. As ever New York, like other states, wished to tax and extend authority over reservations: Cuomo determined to do this by permitting casino development, selecting the smallest group for this initiative, a splinter of the Oneida, with only 32 acres left in 1920, and one which did not take part in the Confederacy and so was not bound by the anti-gambling rules of the Iroquois. Turning Stone Casino and Resort opened in 1993; now there are many Native casinos. George Pataki (governor 1995–2006), in 1996–7 organized a Trade and Commerce Pact with the confederacy, which was derailed by violence. One of the main organizations fighting Indian land rights is Upstate Citizens for Equality, founded in 1997, which proclaims that the Iroquois are, like Americans, incomers, true in a very limited sense but irrelevant to the land claim issues, which are about illegal land deals. UCE is regarded nationally as a hate group but campaigns on the basis that it is ordinary citizens who are being discriminated against. This is in respect of taxation and other privileges accorded Native Americans, for instance around the success of the Oneida and their claim and that of the Cayuga to take back land lost with treaties unratified by Congress.

Oneida Gambling

The Oneida casino is a huge success. Who should benefit from this success is a major issue, and the possible beneficiaries might simply constitute those tribally enrolled, a thousand people at just one (the Oneida Indian Nation or OIN) of three Oneida reservations. The historian Josh Gerzetich in 2010 explained neatly how to be Oneida you had to be a quarter-blood, that there were two ways of being an Indian: according to federal guidelines, or according to tribal nation guidelines. In the Oneida case the federal and the tribal guidelines coincide. Gerzetich goes on to say he doesn't understand why the blood quantum is used to determine membership of OIN, describing it as a European idea, whereas in fact today it is uniquely American, and pointing out, eloquently, that Iroquois traditionally adopted in captives or tribal remnants decimated by war and disease. This is particularly important in the case of Ray Halbritter, the Oneida who resurrected Oneida fortunes with the casino. As a highly successful and innovative entrepreneur – his original enterprise was a petrol station, SavOn – he is very combative and selects issues strategically and deliberately. One such is the long-standing battle to stop the Redskins, the often unsuccessful American football team now located in Washington, DC, from using a racial epithet as their name. This is an old battle, dating back decades, and which is dependent for its venomous quality on deep-rooted racism. In Canada, in the capital Ottawa, there is also a team called Redskins, and the national chief in 2013 was fighting to have the name changed, but the chair of the local Ottawa Aboriginal Coalition, Marc Maracle, said he didn't think the club was being deliberately malicious: 'we've taken the issue in a more positive light'.[19] The issue seems to be the same in Canada, but the context and discussion are slightly different. In the USA the Oneida, under Halbritter, who has close connections to the White House, are pursuing a symbolic issue of major interest to a great swathe of fans. So Halbritter has been attacked as a non-legitimate leader of the Oneida, on two counts: that he is not recognized by the Iroquois Confederacy, that is by his own Native government, and that it was for the marginality of the Oneida that Cuomo selected the OIN to have a casino. Halbritter has also been attacked by a New York assemblywoman, Claudia Tenney, because he is not, she says, really Oneida. The 1885–1940 Indian census roll shows Halbritter's great-great-grandmother Lucy Carpenter was a non-Oneida Indian resident on the Oneida reservation – that is, she was from one of those peoples, other Iroquoian or Algonquian, adopted into the Oneida. Adoption is perfectly legal and appropriate both in Native practice and in western and US Indian law, but in New York blood lines are said to trump practice and legality, an extraordinary situation in which politicians and newspapers can be permitted to openly offer nineteenth-century racial interpretations as normal discussion.[20]

Another criticism of the OIN is that it pays so little in the way of an annual dividend in per capita terms. Gerzetich for the Oneida has outlined neatly the benefits of the Oneida way of retaining much of the casino profits and spending them on development, saying, for instance, Oneida didn't need affordable care, and indeed Indian people have been excluded:

> Any Oneida can go to our health center and be treated. If they can't do it here they will refer you out to somewhere else, to someone who can get it done. That's already here. All Oneidas have to do is go there, and they can get treated. We have a school system – K through 12 – that we pay for with our gaming revenue. It pays for this museum. We also have a nursing home and programs for the elderly. We also buy a lot of houses that elderly and low income families can live in at a reduced rate. We have a police force.[21]

On the other hand, per capita payments by tribes can be seen as returning to a cultural norm in which leaders redistribute wealth as it becomes available. As put for the Seminole, per capita payments 'reinforce longstanding norms and practices of political leadership that are grounded in the redistribution of wealth, as several Seminole explained by comparing dividends to the redistributive rituals of the annual Green Corn Dance'.[22]

Land Claims

Another aggressively fought case, led by the Oneida, Oneida Indian Nation v. County of Oneida (2010), has already had a rather strange and disturbing result, a change in the law about what in the USA is called laches, or unreasonable delay in pursuing a legal claim, which in Europe or in criminal law is termed the statute of limitations. This particular unreasonable delay resulted in the rejection of Oneida land claims, with a consequent general effect for Indian land claims. After the final British–US and Iroquois–US settlements of the mid-1790s private interests such as the Holland America Company successfully removed much of the land base of the Haudenosaunee nations of upstate New York. The Oneidas lost 250,000 acres and in the early 1970s sued for rent. Over the next forty years various claims wound their way through the court, and while occasionally settlement may have been possible, this came to be upset by disagreement between the three Oneida nations.

The OIN increased their claims from one for rent to a much more general one and began to attach the names of individual landholders to the claim. One of the defendants was the flatware/cutlery company also called Oneida, and it filed an effective brief. This had the result that the Oneida claim began to be seen as in bad faith, and it was argued that the damage done to the Oneida in the nineteenth century could only be rectified by ejection of long-standing landholders from their possessions in the twenty-first century: two wrongs do not make a right. Having taken on major foes, the Oneida are for the time being defeated. No claims will be upheld. It was put like this: 'New laches, a pernicious defense not properly called "equitable," denies all relief for any land claim, putting a court solution out of the hands of tribes.'[23]

The Seminole

Most interesting of the now highly successful nations are the Seminole in Florida. While much movement of Native people in the USA was to the west, and particularly to the midwest and then to Oklahoma, though some Californian peoples such as the Modoc were moved eastwards, separate migrations happened in Florida. The original Native inhabitants of the sixteenth century were devastated by disease and enslavement by the British, French and Spanish,. The last Florida Indians may have been sent to Havana when the British took over at the time of the French and Indian War. During the American Revolution most Indian peoples sided with the British, and in the south this was paralleled by the opportunistic semi-emancipation of slaves. In 1775 Lord Dunmore (1732–1809), governor of royal Virginia, promised liberty to slaves who fought with the loyalists, an idea extended by the general, and sometime commander-in-chief, Sir Henry Clinton (1730–95), alienating slave-holding loyalists in the south and New York from Britain. On the southern frontier, between plantation colonies and what had been Spanish Florida, African Americans fled slavery into independent existence along the Gulf Coast and Florida, creating Maroon villages, settled communities of escaped slaves. There they were joined particularly by Creek Indians after the revolution and into the nineteenth century. The two groups traded, intermarried and coalesced, the Maroon communities acting as satellites to Indian villages and remaining for American plantation owners a source of contention and fury (for harbouring escaped slaves), and for the British a factor in frontier politics to be manipulated when politically convenient and ignored when peaceful relations with the USA resumed central importance.

Red Sticks

In 1783 Florida, the current state plus the original West Florida extending to the Mississippi River, was returned by Britain to Spain, which was unable to control much of the colony, particularly after the outbreak of hostilities with France and alliance with Britain in the

1790s. For Britain Florida was part of an informal trading empire, run from the West Indies, and particularly associated with Scottish traders and with the Bahamas. During the War of 1812, Britain, interested in retaining trading access to the centre of the continent, was allied to Native peoples, in particular supplying them with weapons. In 1813–14 tensions between the Upper Creek, on the Alabama River system, away from the Gulf Coast, and the lower Creek villages, on the Flint and Chattahoochee river system, led by plantation-owning mixed-descent Indians, strongly connected in a matrilineal society to their Native relations, developed into civil war. The Upper Creek, the Red Sticks, defeated the Lower Creek at Burnt Corn and massacred them with British arms at Fort Mims. This led to the rise of Andrew Jackson, who created state militias outside of federal control to defeat the Creek, supported by Pushmataha (c.1760–1824) and the Choctaws, at Horseshoe Bend in 1814 and to drive the fleeing Creek southwest into Florida. While the emergence of leadership outside of the southern squirocracy and the use of informal troops were significant features of such wars, their most important effect was the dispossession, as was to happen almost everywhere through the nineteenth century, of both the nativist and the patriot Creek regardless, at first of half their lands and then, with removal to Indian Territory in the 1830s, of all the rest.

Seminole Slaves

Seminole enslavement was different to plantation chattel slavery as practised elsewhere in the USA or British West Indies. The slaves of Seminole lived apart in separate villages, and little was demanded of them apart from rent. Two descriptions of Maroon life, in 1813 and 1823, give an idea of this difference. The Seminole Maroon village near King Bowlegs or Bolek (d. 1819), the principal chief, had 386 houses, 1,500–2,000 bushels of corn, 300 cattle and 400 horses, apparently not a community of impoverished slaves. The African Americans belonging to the next principal chief, Micanopy (c.1780–1849), lived apart in the 1820s at Pilaklikaha, 12 miles from his village at Okahumke, a distance suggesting a high degree of independence. Micanopy was to lead the Seminole in the second war of the

1840s and in its aftermath move west with associated black Seminole.[24] It was the three Seminole Wars, over a thirty-year period from 1817, and the associated treaties which saw the destruction and removal of most of Indian communities of West Florida with their African American elements, and conversely the survival of the free and undefeated minority in central Florida.

Summary Execution

The First Seminole War in 1817–18 provided a significant moment in America history, one which in 2011 provided specific grounds for comparison between the twenty-first-century War on Terror and the early nineteenth-century wars on Indian nations. In a case against a Guantanamo Bay suspect, United States v. Al Bahlul, it was said that the trial and summary execution by Andrew Jackson of two Scots in Spanish Florida, traders with the Seminole, was legal and correct and provided precedent for contemporary behaviour by the USA in the war against Al-Qaeda. The Scottish traders had been supplying weapons to terrorists. In a non-ironic manner the Seminole were themselves compared to Al-Qaeda. The prosecution put it this way:

> Ambrister and Arbuthnot, both British subjects without any duty or allegiance to the United States, were tried and punished for conduct amounting to aiding the enemy. Examination of their case reveals that their conduct was viewed as wrongful, in that they were assisting unlawful hostilities by the Seminole and their allies. Further, not only was the Seminole belligerency unlawful, but, much like modern-day al Qaeda, the very way in which the Seminole waged war against U.S. targets itself violated the customs and usages of war. Because Ambrister and Arbuthnot aided the Seminole both to carry on an unlawful belligerency and to violate the laws of war, their conduct was wrongful and punishable.[25]

The National Congress of American Indians took exception to this comparison and replied appropriately:

> General Jackson was ordered by President Monroe to lead a campaign against Seminole and Creek Indians in Georgia. The politically

ambitious Jackson used these orders as an excuse to invade Spanish-held Florida and begin an illegal war, burning entire Indian villages in a campaign of extermination. The Seminole efforts to defend themselves (with arms from the Scots) from an invading genocidal army could be termed an 'unlawful belligerency' only by the most jingoistic military historian.[26]

Or, to put it another way, in 2011 US prosecutors used a genocide of 1817–18, aimed at obtaining the return of slaves to their owners in the USA, as a justification for misbehaviour in the wider world in the twenty-first century. And to make a more general point, it was that US strategy and behaviour against Indian nations that helped determine US behaviour in dealing with other twenty-first-century pestilent terrorists; and of course what was specifically obnoxious to the NCAI in 2011 was that there were around 24,000 Indian people serving in the military that year, and approximately 383,000 American Indian veterans.

Chief Jim Billie

The renaissance of the Seminole began in the 1970s and 1980s under the charismatic leadership of James Billie, born in 1944 of a white father off to war, but in a matrilineal society what matters was his mother people and clan – Bird in his case. A Vietnam veteran, Chief Billie learned, early on, alligator wrestling and took over the Seminole Indian Village attraction at Hollywood, outside of Miami, made it a success and started up bingo. In 1977 the Seminole opened the first smoke shop, selling cheap cigarettes. In Florida bingo was legal, with a prize limit of $100, increased by Chief Billie to $10,000, resulting in raids and disputes with non-Indian authorities. The Seminole nation, alongside the Cahuilla, eventually won the final legal challenge in California and fought off threats to their gaming (Seminole Tribe of Florida v. Butterworth 1983). In 1979 the Seminole turnover of $9 million was government derived; by 1986 $5 million came from bingo, and $2 million from smoke shops.[27] One of Chief Billie's great stories is about the setting-up of the reservation police force, initially consisting of himself and other veterans, who took on airborne drug smugglers given to landing their planes in the Everglades – which would in the early 1980s be seized or destroyed, Billie being an accomplished pilot – and then buying in training and expertise from existing police. He is also a Grammy-nominated folk singer.

High-stakes Gambling

But the modest success of bingo was to be transformed by the 1987 challenge of California v. Cabazon. The Cabazon Cahuilla Indians, like the Seminole close to resort country, in their case Palm Springs, had a modest bingo operation. In 1953 California had claimed jurisdiction over reservations through Public Law 280 and so maintained that it could prohibit gambling. The 1953 act had been clarified in a seemingly minor court case which had gone to the Supreme Court in the 1970s; this case, Bryan v. Itasca County, was brought for an Ojibwe couple who owned a trailer on reservation land by legal aid volunteers. The state of Minnesota had initially billed Helen and Russell Bryan for $29.85 in unpaid taxes. The Supreme Court ruled that that the 1953 act was about criminal jurisdiction, and that in general terms the interpretation of laws had to favour the Indian nation, so Minnesota could not bill the Ojibwes for their trailer on tribal land, meaning, inter alia, that states could not regulate gambling. In the 1987 case the Supreme Court ruled in the Cabazon's favour, saying that, since California had a state lottery, it regulated rather than prohibited gambling.

In consequence, since other states had also loosened regulations to allow charity lotteries, it became necessary to regulate gambling throughout the country. The Indian Gaming Regulatory Act (1988) recognized that Indian gaming would survive and expand, but stated that it had to be controlled for the benefit of states. The brilliant compromise reached ensured the explosive growth of Indian casinos: they would be legal provided that Indian nations sign a compact with the state, a necessity which would ensure regular payments from Indian nations to states. 'Gambling', as a term, was replaced by 'gaming'; the difference is very neatly, and ironically, explained by the OED definition of 'gaming':

> In early use almost always with pejorative connotations of extravagance, immorality, etc. Now typically used more neutrally with the

implication that games played involve skill and a player's rewards and losses can be largely managed strategically (sometimes with implicit contrast with *gambling*).[28]

More importantly gaming, having lost its pejorative connotations, was divided into three categories, the third category, Class III, including slot machines, the most profitable form of gambling.

The spread of Seminole casinos, on reservation and to Oklahoma, transformed the modest success of Indian bingo into a business with a billion-dollar-a-year turnover, all under Chief Billie's chairmanship, until the beginning of the twenty-first century, when a series of lurid scandals engulfed him, and he returned to making chickees, palmetto-thatched buildings. He later re-emerged, eventually to be elected chief of the tribe. While Billie was on his break, the Seminole bought the London-based business Hard Rock Café for $965 million in 2007, making Indian businesses international for the first time. With an investment-grade BBB rating, they were able to issue $500 million in bonds to finance the deal. Ray Osceola Jnr, a tribal spokesman, made a series of jokes, one of which went that the Seminole knew about hard rocks, the kind his mother used to use for washing; and that with cafés around the world they would become like the British in days gone by: an empire on which the sun never sets.[29]

The Kickapoo

The Seminole are descended from the Creek, defeated by the USA in the southern states along the frontier of Spanish Florida. Fleeing south and east, they re-emerged in Florida. The ability of Indian peoples to merge and move, and to retain identity and culture, is illustrated in different ways by the movement of peoples south and west, and the survival in that process. Most extreme of these national histories is that of the Kickapoo, an Algonquian-speaking people from Indiana, horticulturalists and band hunters, first contacted by the ex-Jesuit French explorer Robert de La Salle (1643–87). From around the Great Lakes, and then living along the Wabash, they were part of a confederation which included other Algonquian peoples, including the Wea, the Miami and the Piankashaw. Involved with the resistance of Tecumseh in the War of 1812, the Kickapoo moved west to Missouri, then to Kansas, Texas, on to Indian Territory, and then under the influence of the Seminole to Coahuila, Mexico, where they survive, building the only authentic mat-covered wigwams and making dolls dressed in Great Lakes ribbonwork costumes. Yet even in Mexico they were subject to American depredations, instituted perhaps, like the measures taken against the Seminole in Spanish Florida at the beginning of the nineteenth century, to protect frontier property in Texas. In 1873 General William T. Sherman sent Ranald Mackenzie across the border to destroy Kickapoo settlements, to stop raids on Texas and to persuade Kickapoo to return to the USA.

The Kickapoo had been led, before the final series of upheavals in the second half of the nineteenth century, by an unusual nativist leader, Kenekuk (c.1790–1852), the prophet who promoted 'acculturation without assimilation'.[30] Originally a drunken ne'er-do-well, he was taken up by a Catholic priest and developed his own redeemed identity. From Illinois, Kenekuk espoused a nativistic religion that was based on ideas of alcohol-free purity, and the possibility of fulfilment expressed in Catholic beliefs, evangelical determination and Algonquian prayer and performance. Having neither the Bible nor written materials, Kenekuk created prayer sticks, engraved handy prayer boards incised with symbols that no doubt acted as mnemonic devices to enable the prophet to remember the songs and prayers he had received from the great spirit or Manitou, and which he used to pray to God and to the Virgin Mary. Sinners had to confess and repent, and be whipped and give thanks for the punishment. As well as advocating the pure life, Kenekuk retained his language and thwarted, after removal to Kansas in the 1830s, all attempts to convert the Kickapoo to mainstream Christianity and to make them surrender their lands. Of the missionaries who tried to convert the Kickapoo, most bizarre was the millenarian Harriet Livermore (1788–1868), who believed that Napoleon was resurrected as the anti-Christ.

Kickapoo Medicine

While there is little connection between the Kickapoo prophet and medicine, it is for patent medicine that the Kickapoo are best remembered. Quack medicines have a long history in Europe going back to the seventeenth century and in the USA were firmly established by the early nineteenth century. Indian medicine shows, entertainments used to sell patent drugs, that is, concoctions protected by trademarks rather than actual patents, took off especially with the coming of the railroad. Most successful was the Kickapoo Indian Medicine Company of Connecticut, founded around 1880 by John Healy and Charles 'Texan Charlie' Bigelow. They developed a brew called Sagwa, followed by others such as Kickapoo Indian Oil, Kickapoo Buffalo Salve, Kickapoo Indian Cough Cure and Kickapoo Indian Worm Killer. Worm Killer consisted of pills containing dried fibres, which, on passing through the bowels, expanded, to become what appeared to be dead worms in faeces. Buffalo Bill's name was used to promote Sagwa: 'Kickapoo Indian Sagwa . . . is the only remedy the Indians ever use, and has been known to them for ages. An Indian would as soon be without his horse, gun, or blanket as without Sagwa.'[31] Medicine shows passed from community to community, with performances on platforms, fake Indians mixed with real Indians, including Mohawks from Kahnawake, or contract Indians furnished by Indian agents off US reservations, using all the regular tricks such as shills, that is stooges in the audience who talk up the product. The original Sagwa had, it was claimed, saved Texan Charlie (Bigelow) as he lay dying in the wilderness, through the intervention of an Indian chief who was carrying some. This neatly contains the paradox of Euro-American attitudes to Indians: fear and hatred on the frontier, combined with exaggerated interest in Native health and wellbeing, and in homeopathic heroes, represented on the medicine stage by strongman performances proclaiming success. In the late nineteenth century maybe up to 100 Kickapoo shows would be on the road at any one time.

Kickapoo medicines emerged out of the creative chaos of late nineteenth-century pharmacy, which included Bovril, named after Vril, the magic substance used by Bulwer-Lytton's master race in *The Complete Race* (1871), Coca-Cola and tonic water. The association of entertainment with health remained: Anadin was marketed with serial radio shows into the 1930s. In 1905 S. H. Adams published an account, the 'Great American Fraud' in *Collier's* magazine, that led to the passage of the first Pure Food and Drug Act, 1906, which insisted on proper labelling rather than the banning of alcohol or narcotics in medicine. Nevertheless Indian medicines continued into the 1920s. And of course the eruption of Indian cures in the 1880s coincided with the closing of the frontier and the dispossession of Indians of reservation land following the 1887 Dawes Act.

Today in matters of medicine and pharmaceuticals use has diverged in two totally opposite directions, neither of them entirely perfect. On the one hand, a substance such as echinacea, from a species of Plains daisy, is sold in hundreds of forms, especially in Germany, as an analagesic, a mild booster for the immune system; the Indian cone flower, used by Pawnee and others as a specific, was grown on the Mall outside the Museum of the American Indian. On the other hand, powerful psychotropic drugs, cosh cures, are used by the medical profession to calm the ill and incapacitate the unhappy. So while on the one hand the Mexican Kickapoo have managed to maintain their culture against on all odds, on the other hand they are remembered for entirely inauthentic medicine.

8

The West

Ancient *kiva*, Bandelier, New Mexico. These chambers are used by Pueblo people for ceremonies invoking *katsinam* or spirit beings.

Hopi women preparing maize flour. Photograph by Edward Curtis, early twentieth century.

Preparing acorns, the California staple food, requiring leaching of tannin before consumption, Upper Lake Pomo. Photograph by Edward Curtis, *c.*1924.

Feast day at San Estevan del Rey Mission, Acoma Pueblo, New Mexico.

Southern Plains delegation in Lincoln's White House, 1863; within eighteen months the four leaders at the front (the middle two are War Bonnet and Standing in the Water) would be dead, at Sand Creek, 1864.

Manuelito Ch'ilhaajinii, Black Weeds (1818?–93), who resisted Navajo removal then signed the Treaty of Bosque Redondo, 1869, enabling Navajo to return home.

Little Crow, His Scarlet People
(1812?–1863) (Taoyateduta), Dakota
leader in the War of 1862, Minnesota,
only buried in 1971.

Curly (c.1856–1923), Crow/Apsaroka
scout for Custer who survived and
reported the Battle of the Little
Bighorn/Greasy Grass River, when
Lakota and Cheyenne repelled an
attack on their summer encampment.
Photographed here c.1885.

Execution of thirty-six Sioux, authorized by Lincoln, in the aftermath of the 1862 revolt. Detail from an 1883 print. It is not clear what the motives would have been for purchasers of this print to hang it in the home or office.

Chief Joseph (1841–1904) (Nez Perce), leader in the war of 1877, poses with a decorated sash, Bismarck, North Dakota.

After the North-West Rebellion, 1885, loyal leaders including Mekaisto or Red Crow (c.1830–1900) (Kanai), *centre*, toured eastern Canada.

In the aftermath of Wounded Knee, 200 to 300 starving Lakota were killed after surrender by drunk soldiers fearful of the Ghost Dance, 29 December 1890.

Diane Humtewa (b. 1964), the first Native American woman federal judge, appointed in 2014.

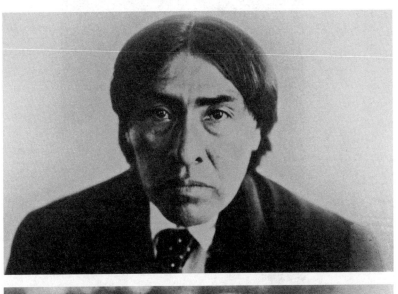

Ishi (*c*.1860–1916) (Yahi), dubbed 'the last wild Indian', was taken to jail in 1911, and then lived at the University of California, Berkeley.

Cahuilla man, Palm Springs, CA, *c.*1924. The Morongo Band of Mission Indians led the introduction of gaming with a bingo parlour, 1983.

Robert Doucette (b. 1961), head of Saskatchewan Métis, leads the campaign for redress for the 20,000 people of Native descent forcibly adopted out during the 1960s.

Passport photograph, 1935, of Chief Yowlachie, born Daniel Simmons (1891–1966) (Yakima), a Hollywood actor who played Sitting Bull in the 1927 movie.

Hopi religious items were returned from Paris in 2013. Sam Tenakhongva (*second right*) led the campaign: 'They're not masks, they are friends.'

Navajo women learning to drive, 196

Peter MacDonald (b. 1928), Navajo
code-talker and tribal chairman, 1979.

8

The West

An Idea

The history of the American west is sometimes seen as a single story: one of tragedy and the triumph of the USA. More satisfyingly, it is better conceived of as a series of highly interconnected stories of separate processes, played out among fundamentally different Native peoples: on the Plains, buffalo hunters, originally on foot, who remade themselves as horsemen in the eighteenth century; in the southwest, dry farmers, on to whom was imposed aspects of Spanish civilization and Christian culture, protecting a few dozen peoples and permitting them to survive at home in Pueblos, without war (with the important exception of the Taos revolt of 1847) or removals, after US annexation. In much of California, the last lunge of the Spanish enterprise, the violent and misguided Franciscan corralling of Indians into missions was out of time. The missions fell, in independent Mexico, to the land hunger of the newly minted liberals, who dissolved them just as Pueblos and new synthetic identities were forming. California and the Pacific northwest supported great populations in managed environments – where fire was used to help plant harvesting, and weirs to collect and kill fish.

Western Languages

As mentioned, North America had extraordinary linguistic divesity at contact, especially small language families and language isolates. The West Coast is where this diversity is concentrated. Perhaps the most threatened, and the most endangered, are the languages of California, most of which are now already extinct: in the middle of the twentieth

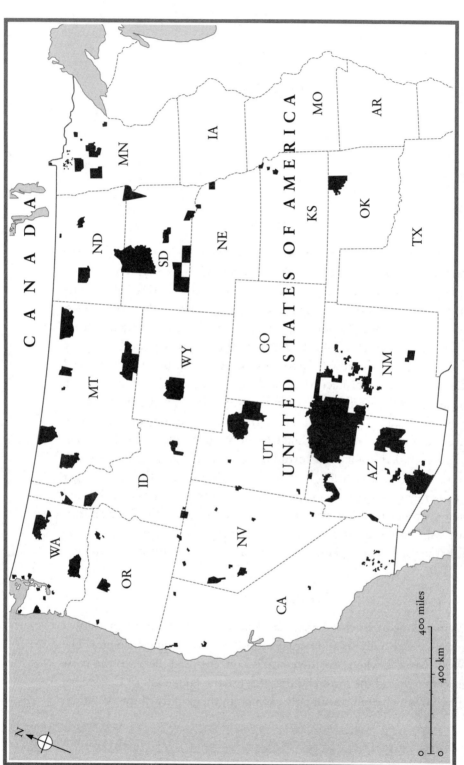

Map 8. Western US reservations. The only reservation in Oklahoma is that of the Osage, coterminous with

century a couple of dozen languages survived with a few speakers. Linguists do not agree as to how many languages existed in California at European contact in the eighteenth century, but there were at least sixty-four and perhaps as many as eighty. The study of languages without written records depends on basic systems of recurrent sound correspondences to determine the relationship of languages, and this has been achieved for a small number of languages. Most Californian languages come from two major language stocks, Hokan and Penutian, but some languages, Wiyot and Yoruk, relate to Algonquian in the east, and a few relate to Athapaskan in the north and Uto-Aztecan in the south. Many of the tribes or grouped peoples spoke related but very different languages; so for instance the Chumash, who occupied the coast and offshore islands between Malibu and San Luis Obispo, spoke at least three generally unintelligible languages which became extinct in 1965.[1]

Another important group is the Pomoans, who lived north of San Francisco Bay, Sonoma and Napa counties, in redwood and wine country. With seven languages and around ten thousand people today, they are perhaps the largest Californian people. Those Pomoan languages are less closely related to each other than Navajo and the varieties of Apache are to each other and relate to each other around as much as Navajo is related to the languages of the same Athapaskan group in Alaska, such as Tanaina. Pomoan languages differ as much from each other as do the Germanic languages – German, English, Dutch and the Scandinavian languages. As so often the grouping is one imposed from outside, highly shaded and indeed fugitive in meaning and characteristics. As it was put in 1939:

> what we call Pomo – the Indian had no word for it – refers to no definable cultural entity but only a sort of nationality . . . there was a series of highly similar independent but never quite identical Pomo cultures, each carried by one of the independent communities or tribelets.[2]

Each people had its own land, the amount of land being determined by the food required rather than anything else. But they shared a common belief system and religion, centring on the culture hero Kuksu or Guksu.

Where oaks provided the main food source, today among the

hundreds of wineries of northern California there is the first Native winery, the Pomo Nation Wine Group, started by two Pomoan people, Gary Ray Cordova (Dry Creek Band) and Ben G. Ray III (Big Valley Band), who have fifty years' experience of working in tribal economic development between them. Starting in the new millennium, they have produced award-winning wines including 'Bi Du (acorn) red, which is a blend of Cabernet Sauvignon, Syrah, Merlot and Petite Sirah', and 'Bi Si (wispy clouds) white, a blend of Sauvignon Blanc, Riesling, Vognier and Semillon'. These wines are served appropriately at events such as American Indian film festivals and at Native-owned casinos including the Pala Casino Spa and the Marongo Casino Resort Spa in Southern California.

California

California is important in the story of Native North America because of its size – it is slightly larger than Germany – its exceptional linguistic diversity and its recent, and in the early stages catastrophic, history. Even today there are more unrecognized tribes – fifty-five – in California than in any other state. In various important ways treatment of Californian Natives was more abusive than elsewhere in North America.

'California' was named in the sixteenth century, like the earlier Ethiopia and the Amazon, after a pagan mythical character, the Muslim Queen Califia – from the Arabic 'caliph' or religious head of state, California suggesting therefore the 'Land of the Caliph'. It was only at the end of the eighteenth century that land expeditions led, quickly, to the extension of Spanish rule northwards from New Spain into territory claimed but not occupied from the sixteenth century. Gaspar de Portolá de Rovira (1716–86), a Catalan soldier, mounted the first expedition to Alta, or Upper, California and established Franciscan missions, twenty-one in all, from San Diego (1769) in the south to Sonoma (1823) in the north, eventually with four military districts. Spanish settlement of Upper California, without the trading basis of other empires, and without the immigrant population from France or Britain, depended on Indian labour; the missions provided an economic means of establishing a Spanish presence in an area long claimed. The settlement of California was organized by militias and a mendicant order. Together, pacification and conversion of Indians would, in an ideal world, provide a compliant peasantry, creating peons from gentiles or pagans, situated in Pueblos. Once Indians had been brought in and converted, priests established a highly ordered regime. This would stipulate where people lived, when they worked (unpaid) and when and how they married. Mission society was organized, and disciplined, by *alcaldes*, magistrates, from the Arabic word meaning judge. And inevitably the Spanish movement into California was accompanied by the same virgin soil epidemics which decimated populations elsewhere and which radically reduced population numbers from that at occupation which may have been perhaps 300,000 people. Some 90,000 of these were included in the mission system at its termination in the 1830s.

In the early nineteenth century California attracted traders, especially Russian and Canadian, active in the fur trade. Fort Ross, in Russian California, was a short-lived trading and agricultural experiment north of San Francisco in Pomo territory. Lasting only thirty years, 1812–42, it was designed to harvest sea otter fur for the Asian market but, as with the Hudson's Bay Company's extermination of the beaver in the interior, effectively killed off the sea otter within a decade. Fort Ross brought down from Alaska Aleut and Alutiiq hunters, who mixed with Kashaya Pomo and tried also to develop an export economy growing wheat for use in Alaska. This too failed, resulting in closure of the fort and its sale to John Sutter (1803–80), the Swiss Mexican, then American, whose Fort Sutter was the centre of the California Gold Rush from 1848, and whose son founded the capital Sacramento.

While Spanish and Mexican occupation of California was brief, and left no body of inquiring scholarship equivalent to that of the Jesuits in seventeenth- and eighteenth-century New France or of Native Protestant clerics such as Occom, Apess and Copway, there are nonetheless important Native records from the eighteenth and nineteenth centuries. From the church perspective there is one exception: Padre Felipe Arroyo de la Cuesta, who came to California in 1807 and recorded at San Juan Bautista the grammar and lexicon of Mutsun (Costanoan), and material from twenty other languages. Aboriginal narratives do survive; best known is that of Pablo Tac (1822–41)

(Luiseño), from San Luis Rey de Francia, now in Oceanside in southern California, who was sent to Rome to be educated in the 1830s and as a boy wrote an autobiography. This became part of a collection put together by the linguist and Vatican librarian Cardinal Giuseppe Caspar Mezzofanti (1774–1849). The autobiography includes a diagram of the mission and a drawing of people and notes both the extent of depopulation that occurred, and at contact the demand of a chief to the Spanish that they be gone. Recently the Luiseño conceptual artist James Luna (b. 1950) created an installation on behalf of the National Museum of the American Indian for the 2005 Venice Biennale, *Chapel for Pablo Tac*, as a means of looking behind the superficial aspects of Californian missions, with church and Native symbols. Luna is from La Jolla, the reservation recently remembered for being burned down in a catastrophic 2007 fire. Californian Natives from the pre-contact period were renowned for managing the landscape and resources with fire, avoiding such events.

Mexican California

The Franciscans were dispossessed by Mexico in 1834–6, in the post-French Revolutionary orthodoxy of the time, and the lands ceded in grants to Californios, born gents becoming instant aristocrats, dons and *hacendados*, comparable with, but not similar to, the plantation owners who also took over Indian, mostly Cherokee and Creek, lands in the south at around the same time. The behaviour of the Franciscans, and their dispossession, is the subject of another Native autobiographical record, that of the sometime neophyte Lorenzo Asisara, originally from Mission Santa Cruz, just south of Silicon Valley, situated in Costanoan (Ohlone) territory. Asisara was later a soldier at the Yerba Buena presidio, now in San Francisco. His accounts, the first recorded when he was fifty-seven, in 1877 describes, unusually, the behaviour of the priests and of the Mexicans who took over the missions and his own role in these events. Asisara begins by describing the cruelty of the Spanish priest Ramon Olbés (b. 1786) administering beatings to the stomach. In particular, Asisara describes in detail the punishment of a childless couple, complete with physical examinations: fifty lashes and punishment of the woman by being forced to carry round a doll to be treated as a baby and presented in church over nine days. The birth rate of Native Californians, with new diseases and circumstances, had suffered a catastrophic decline; abortion was suspected and the infertile were punished, as was separately reported by a Scot, Hugo Reid, married to a Native Californian, at San Gabriel:

> When a woman had the misfortune to bring forth a still-born child, she was punished. The penalty inflicted [included] having to appear every Sunday in church, on the steps leading up to the altar, with a hideous painted wooden child in her arms![3]

Olbés was succeeded at Santa Cruz by another Spaniard, Luís Gil Y Taboada, whom Asisara said, in contrast, was much liked by the Indians. He stopped the punishments and had sex with Indian women, until syphilitic eruptions appeared; eventually his syphilis became so bad that he could only conduct mass sitting down. Asisara also described the secularization of the Santa Cruz Mission by Mexican Ygnacio Ramón de Jesus del Valle (1808–80), later granted the 100,000 acre Rancho El Tejon in Kern County. Asisara observed the priest remove all the valuables from the mission, with Valle's connivance, before handing over what was left to the Indians. Valle kept for himself 5,000 head of cattle and other animals, which again should have been distributed locally. Asisara should himself have received lands but ended his days as a ranch hand.[4] Californian missions were highly successful and without dissolution would no doubt have become stable Pueblos, protecting if not Indian languages then perhaps aspects of Indian belief systems, subsistence practices and even a degree of family life.

Resistance in California

Asisara's father was involved in the probable assassination, in 1812, of Padre Andrés Quintana of Santa Cruz. Military rule in Spanish and Mexican California provoked acts of resistance and revolt, such as this killing, the Chumash revolt of 1824, and that of Estanislao, of mission San Jose, who defeated earlier attempts at subjugation and who was eventually brutally chased off by Mariano Guadalupe Vallejo (1808–90), frontier soldier, politician and historian, in 1828/9.

The Californio Vallejo eventually parlayed his success as a soldier into a ranch of 66,000 acres and is warmly remembered as a founder of Anglo-California. Estanislao was reconciled with the mission of San Jose and became himself a skilled hunter-down of escaped neophytes, as resistance followed by accommodation was a frequent character-izing feature of the behaviour of Californian peoples. Two Chumash women left oral records of the 1824 revolt; one of them, Luisa Ygna-cio at Santa Inés, said that the Indians were warned by a page boy that the priests were going kill them, and that the boy had had his tongue cut out and his feet chopped off, and his body was burned by the Spanish.[4] Following the revolt the Chumash looted Spanish posses-sions but were persuaded by Jaime, an Indian doctor, singer and teacher, who came with Spanish soldiers, to return to the mission.

American California

The snuffing-out of Native land rights in California, after annexation in 1848 and statehood in 1850, came in three parts. California Indi-ans had been made Mexican citizens in 1824 and theoretically were citizens according to the Treaty of Guadalupe Hidalgo, signed in 1848 outside Mexico City at the site of the shrine to the Virgin's apparition to the first indigenous American saint, San Juan Diego Cuauhtlatoat-zin (1474–1548). The American war effort in California was assisted by Indians, but they were not properly paid off by the USA and returned to raiding, subsisting on the cattle that should have been theirs with the ending of the mission system. Under the treaty Mex-ican rights, for those on mission lands actually less than twenty years old, were recognized, while the ancient rights of Native Americans, even though they were theoretically citizens, were ignored. In 1850 a vagrancy law in the new state was enacted, enabling Indians to be declared vagrants, put in jail and their labour sold, serf- or slave-like, to the highest bidder, without pay. Further, in 1851 the Land Claims Act stipulated that land claims had to be registered, and of course Indians were less likely than Mexicans to be literate and able to regis-ter their land claims. No Indian tribe registered any claims, and so subsequent cases, often taken to the Supreme Court, repeatedly affirm that aboriginal title in California was extinguished in the 1850s.

California in the 1850s adopted two notable racial epithets. 'Diggers' was the term used for Indian people; a seventeenth-century term used for low church dissenters and also for miners, in reference to aboriginal people it suggested a low level of civilization, a people so primitive as to rely for subsistence on root crops. The actual reality is that some Indians did use wild roots – at least fifty-eight species of plant, including wild onions, mariposa lillies, yampah and yellow nutsedge – but root foraging was only important much further north, and other forms of hunting and gathering took precedence in California.[6] The other epithet was 'Greaser', a term applied to Mexicans.

California Treaties

Prior to this in the immediate aftermath of statehood, Congress also recognized the importance of organizing treaties. Commissioners were dispatched, and eighteen treaties were signed with 139 signatories, applying to 8.5 million acres reserved for Indians. Under pressure from the state legislature, which did not wish to compromise gold-mining claims, the treaties were never ratified, and the Senate placed them under seal, so that they remained secret until 1905. Further, Congress did not tell the signatories that the treaties had not been ratified, and so the signatories may even have reasonably felt that their land claims had been properly recognized. In 1864 four reservations for the whole of California were authorized by Congress. Subsequently California Natives were organized without treaties by the BIA and by presidential order: around forty reservations for the 10–20,000 people on a mere half a million acres were set up by the early twentieth century. In 1905 knowledge of the unratified treaties was made public, and the Rancheria system of small, uneconomic land grants for Indian peoples was implemented, marginal lands that sometimes in the late twentieth century could be used for casino enterprises. These in turn were terminated in the 1950s, although some were restored in the 1980s.

None of this should be unexpected. Early American California was founded on very explicit genocide, the same sort of genocide, killing for the sake of extermination, that took place in British Newfoundland and Tasmania in the nineteenth century and in German southwest Africa in the early twentieth century. Most prominent of the exterminationists was Peter Burnett (1807–95), a southerner from Tennessee and Missouri, the first governor of California (1849–51). In his second address to the legislature in Sacramento, the state capital, in which he had operated as real estate promoter, on 7 January 1851, he was explicit in his intentions:

> That a war of extermination will continue to be waged between the races, until the Indian race becomes extinct, must be expected. While we cannot anticipate this result but with painful regret, the inevitable destiny of the race is beyond the power or wisdom of man to avert.[7]

The Indian wars of the 1850s were conducted by militias, supported by the state, the right to bear arms cognate in California with the right to exterminate at this time. In particular militias were empowered to carry out the protection of livestock, raided for essential subsistence, by the extermination of Indians. Some $1,293,179.20 was claimed from the state of California for wars between 1851 and 1859. The official report on the Mendocino War of 1860 recorded:

> The conflict still exists; Indians continue to kill cattle as a means of subsistence, and the settlers in retaliation punish with death. Many of the most respectable citizens of Mendocino County have testified before your committee that they kill Indians, found in what they consider the hostile districts, whenever they lose cattle or horses; nor do they attempt to conceal or deny this fact. Those citizens do not admit, nor does it appear by the evidence, that it is or has been their practice or intention to kill women or children, although some have fallen in the indiscriminate attacks.[8]

The essential point is that, deprived of their own territory, and not provided with reservations, there was little other choice for Indian people except to kill livestock, following the over-running of lands for acorn and plant gathering.

Indentured Indians

Another aspect of the Mexican and Spanish periods was the indenturing Indians, and indeed the buying and selling of people, under the vagrancy law, something close to slavery. Because of the shortage of labour, Euro-Americans in California employed near-slavery as a means of obtaining a sufficient workforce, for instance in Northern California, as reported in the press in an article 'Lo, the Poor Indian,' from *Alta California*, 7 April 1855:

> One of the most infamous practices known to modern times has been carried on for several months past against the aborigines of California. It has been the custom of certain disreputable persons to steal away young Indian boys and girls, and carry them off and sell them to white folks for whatever they could get. In order to do this, they are obliged in many cases to kill the parents, for low as they are on the scale of humanity, they [the Indians] have that instinctive love of their offspring which prompts them to defend them at the sacrifice of their lives.[9]

Californian Novels

The rapid romanticization of Mexican California in the nineteenth century coincided with the disappearance of a Native narrative in the origins of California. Two highly popular novels tell this story. The first is by John Rollin Ridge, the Cherokee Cheesquatalawny or Yellow Bird (1827–67), who published the first Californian and indeed Native American novel in 1854: *The Life and Adventures of Joaquin Murieta: The Celebrated California Bandit*. This was popular and much pirated and may be related to the later stories of Zorro. Based on the life of a gold miner, the story's protagonist is a much-abused Mexican in American California, marginalized in the same ways as Ridge would have been and felt as an Indian unaccepted in Indian Territory. Murieta is eventually killed, and his head displayed as an exhibit. The Cherokee Ridge had however little time for Native Californians:

> Were these Indians like the genuine North American red man in the times of the bloody frontier wars of the United States, brave, subtle, and terrible in their destruction, it would be a different matter. But they are a poor, humble, degraded, and cowardly race.[10]

For Yellow Bird killing California Indians is such a simple business that it is entirely unheroic:

> And however much military or any other kind of men, may strive to make [Native Californians] appear like dangerous or even respectable antagonists with their bows and arrows against muskets and Colt's revolvers, it remains nevertheless a fact, that it is no credit for a white man to kill a Digger, or even fifty of them. It requires no heroism at all, no more than to slaughter the deer in the hills, or the coyote in the plains. It is pitiful to think of so cowardly a contest

The wronging of Mexicans in American California, by limiting their ability to mine, by seizing land, also frames the romance *Ramona* (1884) by the activist novelist Helen Hunt Jackson (1830–85). In this novel the orphaned Indian girl, of mixed Scottish descent, is adopted by a fierce Mexican woman. She first marries an Indian, Alessandro Assis, then, after he is murdered for taking a horse, marries her foster mother's son, Felipe, to provide a happy ending in which the Mexican trumps the Indian. In this story the deracinated heroine is treated romantically and sentimentally as a means of capturing the reader and empowering the Native:

> Part of her was dead. But Ramona saw now, with infallible intuition, that even as she had loved Alessandro, so Felipe loved her. Could she refuse to give Felipe happiness, when he had saved her, saved her child? What else now remained for them, these words having been spoken? 'I will be your wife, dear Felipe.'[11]

Ramona, like *Uncle Tom's Cabin*, in framing the debate around slavery, told the whole story of Native dispossession and helped underwrite the Dawes Act, sponsored by Jackson's eponymous friend, which served to dispossess reservation Indians of land while seeming to empower them. *Ramona*, in sentimentalizing the Indian story in a frame of Mexican California, where Felipe's family lost their land to Americans, and where Mexicans, in contrast to Americans, are noble and right-thinking, helped create a new Californian identity cleansed of the earlier historic reality of the state. Numerous films were made of the story, and since 1923 every summer a pageant play is performed, the oldest of its kind. And since 1893 there has been a Ramona band of Cahuilla Indians, in traditional territory, Riverside County north and inland of San Diego, east of Los Angeles. One of the favoured places visited by Jackson, and a possible location for the novel, is Valle's Rancho Camulos in Ventura County. Ramona has been portrayed on film by Mary Pickford, Dolores del Rio and Raquel Welch. Ramona's fictional beauty was compromised in one of the near-contemporaneous accounts of the possible model for the Indian heroine. The disreputable journalist David A. Hufford (1858–1941) put it like this in 1900, employing the racialized idiom of the time:

> Mrs. Jackson's Ramona lives today about the same as she did sixteen years ago, with the exception of course that she is older and not so trim and spruce as all young Indian girls like to be when under good influences. There never was an Indian girl with fine features such as are being painted and lithographed and sold on the market today as Ramona. She is now like all other Indian women become as they grow older, greasy and slovenly, with no thought of cleanliness or tidiness. The Indians of the Southwest show their age earlier, and Ramona is no exception to the rule. She is just as haggard-looking and lazy as the other squaws.[12]

Recovery in California

It is the Cahuilla and Luiseño bands who have led much of the move to gaming, and to economic recovery, in California, and indeed in the wider United States, after termination in 1958. Riverside is basically desert country, where in marginal lands reservations were established without disturbing agriculture. In the early 1980s two bands, the Cabazon and the Morongo, established bingo parlours, and then card clubs where poker could be played. As we saw earlier, the state tried to have gaming closed down as a criminal activity but was unsuccessful. Indian gaming became regularized by the 1988 Indian Gaming Regulatory Act (IGRA), which set up a commission to organize it. In a sense then what happened is that Jackson and *Ramona*'s legacy provided a context, a blank space from which many aspects of ethnicity had been peremptorily removed, in which Indian nations could be enabled to take control of their own lives. The Cahuilla, living on marginal lands, were fortunate to be close to large urban areas interested in gaming, and which, as the submission in 1986–7 pointed out, could support few other industries apart from gambling and tourism.

Puebloans and Hunter Herders in the Southwest

Pueblo society in the southwest had also earlier played a central role in the recovery of Native North America in the early twentieth century. This arose through the confluence of a number of different trends. As ever, the determined absorption, appropriation and above all appreciation of southwest life both endangered Indian survival and in a countervailing way provided a context and form which would protect these surviving nations in Arizona and New Mexico. In contrast to the first transcontinental railroad of the 1860s, boosters for the Atchison Topeka and Santa Fe Railroad of the 1880s worked with Fred Harvey Company to create tourism. That rare businessman a successful British restaurateur, Harvey created regionally and Indian-themed restaurants and hotels throughout the southwest to cater for visitors, giving an ornamental view of Arizona and New Mexico. At the same time the journalist Charles Fletcher Lummis (1859–1928) promoted the wider southwest and fought for Indian rights and historic preservation from Los Angeles and founded the now defunct Southwest Museum in 1914. His work provided context for designer-architects such as Mary Colter (1869–1958), who built and decorated hotels in a variety of Hispanic and Pueblo styles. At the same time the protection of monuments and the creation of museums provided the cultural infrastructure necessary to provide for tourists' interface with Native peoples. In this Edgar Lee Hewett (1865–1946) was paramount, as a teacher and museum founder (the Museum of New Mexico and the Maxwell Museum) at the School of American Research and as instigator of the Antiquities Act (1906), which, though providing less status and fewer resources than a National Park, exists under presidential rather than congressional authority, enabling easier site protection. Hewett also drew on and supported the work of the San Idelfonso potter Maria Martinez (1887–1980) and the ethnologist and Dawes Act protagonist Alice Fletcher (1838–1923). Hewett acted as skilled lobbyist, if not politician, for the promotion of a unitary, somewhat imaginary identity for the southwest in which adobe architecture, Catholicism and Pueblo ritual, ruins and ranches would

exist together, if not free of tension then in productive synthesis, enabling economic development and cultural survival.

Indian Dance

But of course this period was also that of the nadir of the Native
population and the height of the assimilationist movement, of the
provision of boarding schools to eliminate Indianness and ensure
Natives would have the opportunity of becoming good Americans.
For Puebloan peoples the absence of children away at boarding
schools fundamentally interfered with their own system of education,
of initiating young people into Pueblo institutions and belief systems.
Their religious practice required an oral society performing highly
socialized learning over long periods, as well as solitary seclusion.

This attack on one aspect of religion was combined with another in
the early twentieth century, that of the role of dancers and dancing in
maintaining religion in a very formalized calendar. In both Canada
and the USA Indian ritual and performances, especially with directly
religious overtones, were increasingly prohibited from the 1880s. In
Canada the revised Indian Act of 1884 prohibited potlatches and revivalist movements. In particular, both the Ghost Dance and the Sun
Dance aroused fear, both in a military and a religious context. In the
southwest much of the fear of Indian dances in the 1910s and 1920s lay
in the portrayal of gender roles and in their sexual expression.

There were persistent anti-dance movements in the early twentieth
century on the part of white assimilationists, who were convinced that
they were immoral and degrading. In fact the dances are humorous,
satirical and most importantly normative. The real significance of these
dances, and especially of the role played by clowns, was in education and
boundary maintenance, and the business not so much of incorporating
outside influences, but of reverse contextualizing, if not assimilating,
white behaviour and incorporating an understanding of whites into
Pueblo society. In the view of Martin Vigil from Tesuque in 1970:

> our dances are not wicked like you people . . . You come down to any
> Pueblo, visit our dances, we don't hug each other when we dance . . . We
> dance about five feet apart, not like you people.[13]

Attendance at boarding schools and Christian conversion both stimulated Native opposition to traditional dances, and provided the education essential for leadership in a rapidly changing United States.

The movement against Pueblo dance at the BIA gathered testimonies from Christian Indians and white educators documenting what they saw as inappropriate behaviour and satirical performances representing prostitution, sexual desire and intimate public behaviour on the part of white people. Evidence was collected over many years from Christian Natives, administrators and non-Native white advocates of assimilation such as Mary Dissette and Clara True. This was all gathered together in a 'Secret Dance File' in the 1920s, which served as part of the necessary evidence for Commissioner Charles Burke (1861–1944) to issue Circular 1665 and its supplement in 1921/1923, prohibiting some dancing. It was put like this:

> The dance, however, under most primitive and pagan conditions is apt to be harmful, and when found to be so among the Indians we should control it by educational processes as far as possible, but if necessary, by punitive measures when its degrading tendencies persist. The sundance and other similar dances and so-called religious ceremonies are considered 'Indian Offences' under existing regulations, and corrective penalties are provided.[14]

The evidence that was gathered from Christian converts served to polarize and fracture Indian communities, precipitating the emergence of new villages, depending on acceptance or not of Americans ways. Hopis were caught between an America that respected traditional values and another which promoted prosyletization. One Christian Hopi, K. T. Johnson, or Tuwaletstiwa, expressed his view, kept in the 'Secret Dance File', like this:

> To begin with, as I know myself as no one else knows me, I consider that I was a very bad man before I became a Christian. My life was unspeakably evil. You see me as I am now: I was formerly very different, morally speaking. While groping in this immoral life, I heard of the Crucified One, faith in Whom saved me. By becoming a Christian I have forsaken the evil ways that I once followed . . . When a Hopi

becomes a Christian he quits attending these dances. He knows the evil of them to be so great.[15]

The dance controversy ran parallel to the alienation of Pueblo land. By the Mexican Treaty of 1848, article VIII, property belonging to Mexicans was guaranteed. In 1876, in the Supreme Court case the United States v. Joseph, it was decided that Puebloans were civilized and not Indians in the sense of existing US law, so that land was held by fee simple and could, as in Taos in this case, be alienated by sale. But following statehood in 1912, when Indian Country and communities were recognized as dependent on the government, the 1913 case US v. Sandoval confirmed that the government determined policies such as the sale of alcohol, as at San Juan. This inadvertently put into play the legality of land sales to non-Indians, an action that under the non-intercourse acts had been prohibited.

The Meriam Report

In the wake of the granting of American citizenship to Indians in 1924, the new high-profile interest of modernists in Native culture and the campaigns of the Society of American Indians, the secretary of the interior appointed in 1926 Lewis Meriam (1883–1972) to investigate Indian affairs. His 1928 report *The Problem of Indian Administration* criticized allotment, education and a host of other issues, which were addressed by Roosevelt's administration of the 1930s through the Indian Reorganization Act (1934). This was led by the new commissioner, the social reformer John Collier (1884–1968).

John Collier, whose tenure as commissioner was to change Indian history in the 1930s, devoted his early professional life to housing projects in New York, and then in accordance with his radical but conservative view of society in protecting and developing community-based networks and ties. In the early 1920s he went to Taos, at the invitation of Mabel Dodge Luhan (1879–1962), and became convinced that here was a model for successful community relations. This was how he put it:

> The discovery that came to me there, in that tiny group of a few hundred Indians, was of personality-forming institutions, even now

unweakened, which had survived repeated and immense historical shocks, and which were going right on in the production of states of mind, attitudes of mind, earth-loyalties and human loyalties, amid a context of beauty which suffused all the life of the group.[16]

Collier was hired by the Indian Welfare Committee of the General Federation of Women's Clubs to investigate Indian affairs, and a number of new organizations emerged: the New Mexico Association on Indian Affairs, the Eastern Association on Indian Affairs and the American Indian Defense Association, with John Collier as its executive secretary, in 1923, following the fight against both the anti-dance orders and the Bursum Bill. This was the bill designed to retrospectively allow non-Indians to obtain title to Indians lands alienated illegally. This process, of politicians seeking to permit illegal land transactions, goes back, of course, to colonial times. The muddle which had arisen in the 1840s, because it was felt that Puebloan Indians were civilized and so not Indian for the purpose of alienation of the land, was resolved in 1913. The 1848 treaty confirmed thirty-five land grants totalling 700,000 acres.[17] For a decade 3,000 landholdings, obtained from Pueblos by non-Indians, and now belonging to 12,000 non-Indians, were placed in jeopardy. Senator Holm O. Bursum put forward the bill. It failed, though it was supported by fellow New Mexican Albert Fall, the minister of the interior and an illegal recipient of moneys from oil companies in the Teapot Dome scandal of the 1920s. While some of the land claims were those of poor farmers, the bill's passage would have had a generally devastating effect for a number of reasons. First the Pueblo lands that had been alienated were often those best suited for farming: so San Ildefonso had 12,500 acres of original land grant, of which only 1,250 was irrigated, and of this San Ildefonso retained only 248 acres. One of the white claimants to San Ildefonso lands was Clara True, an Indian activist, so as ever factionalism prevailed. While True may have been interested in subsistence farmers, other lands were held by corporations such as the Denver & Rio Grande Railroad. With the granting of citizenship Indian people would be expected to survive on their own.[18] Further, the Bursum Act was designed deliberately to ensure that all disputes to do with internal affairs and government were to be settled by local state courts, notoriously hostile to Pueblo interests. In the decade of manoeuvring over the white land claims, violence remained a threat, for instance at Tesuque in 1921.

The Luhans

Mabel Dodge Luhan (1879–1962) was perhaps the most influential of the modernists. Her championing of the southwest contributed to the situating of the Pueblos as the pre-eminent Indian trope, the rolling back of the assault on Pueblo society in the 1920s becoming in the 1930s the rolling back of assimilationist assault on Indian society. She rejected the mores of her rich Victorian parents and found early fulfilment, and an identity defined in terms of the 'other', like so many, in Paris and Florence before 1914. In 1917 she moved to New Mexico to escape the war and illness and remade herself as a champion journalist, occidentalizing and romanticizing the southwest. She settled in the village of Taos, where the Taos Society of Artists had been founded in 1915. In marrying Tony Luhan in 1923 from Taos Pueblo, she both liberated herself from romantic notions and burdened herself with a false relationship that, in a sense, inverted the more regular association of white men and Indian women. Luhan's friend John Collier's romantic notions were no less vivid than hers, and he was well able to express them in a passionate idiom in an article about the rebirth of 'Red Atlantis':

> The Pueblo is not dying; on the contrary, it is alive, pregnant and potentially plastic; potentially an inheritor of the future and a giver to the future of gifts without price, which future white man will know how to use. The white man, tacitly and also officially, has condemned it to die: to die not by sudden execution but through proscription and slow killing. This is the drama and the huge social significance of Taos.[19]

Collier the social activist was to fight against the determined assaults on Indian America.

Taos

Taos in a sense remains a significant emblem of success through the twentieth century for a variety of reasons. One is the successful resolution of the dispute of 1906–70 around Blue Lake in the mountainous watershed and hunting area of the Pueblo, the source of water for farming, a place of shrines and annual pilgrimage and sacred land. While only 46,000 of the 300,000 acres of traditional land, the area was appropriated to form part of Carson Forest in 1906 by Teddy Roosevelt, at a time when no one really would have appreciated what this in effect meant – the managed exploitation of the area for forest resources and tourism. For more than sixty years Taos Pueblo, and activists such as Collier, fought for the return of the lake, arguing successfully that ownership underpinned the survival of the Pueblo. The 1970 act returning Blue Lake was the first successful application to restore Native American land based on religious freedom. This was initiated by Fred R. Harris (b. 1930), the Oklahoma senator married to the Comanche activist LaDonna Harris (b. 1931). Taos leader Juan de Jesus Romero testified before Congress and made it clear that the victory was a general one: 'A new day begins not only for the American Indian, but for all Americans in the Country.'[20] What victory means is that that Blue Lake is not available, unlike Devils Tower, to tourists; that the *kiva* religion remains secret; that language competency is very high; that white people can visit the Pueblo from Taos village, can play at the smoke-free casino and contribute to the buy-back of other lands; but they are only permitted to do so during working hours. And finally, of course, just as Christianity thrives alongside Pueblo religion, so the powwow is also part of the Taos calendar, but is strictly separate from the ritual calendar.

The Horse

Pueblo and other societies were transformed by the arrival of the horse. The lives of foot-based nomadic hunters were overturned, creating rapidly, and without precedent, an immediate horse culture, with instant, variously replicated tribal formations appearing and dominating different areas of the Plains depending on ecology and other circumstances. The use of horses, driving the Spanish invasion of the Americas, enabled the Spanish to become established in New Mexico at the beginning of the seventeenth century. Indians in and around Santa Fe were enslaved by the Spanish to look after horses and given the name *genízaro*, a Spanish term adopted from the English word 'janissary', which derives in turn from the Ottoman Turkish word *yeniçeri*. There was no opportunity for an independent existence outside of the colony. Two groups, the Jumanos and Apache, obtained horses in small numbers by the mid-seventeenth century. This changed with the Pueblo revolt and the capture in 1680 of large quantities of all forms of livestock.

Horse use developed through the opposing but symbiotic mechanisms of war and trade: war, absconding slave stealing horses; and trade, for slaves and skins. Over the next century horse use spread in two directions: northwards, west of the continental divide, up into what is now Canada and across the northern Plains with the Blackfoot; and eastwards, fanning out into Texas and then northeast through Oklahoma eventually up into the eastern Plains. In a sense the northern movement of horse use mimicked and reversed the southwards descent of the Athapaskan-speaking people a few hundred years earlier, when they came south to become in the eighteenth century the Apachean (Nde, Ndeh) and Navajo (Diné) peoples, though not necessarily along the same routes. And the Lakota, in the northeastern Plains, fixed in the imagination as the greatest of the Plains warriors, most effective in the defeat of the United States in the 1860s and 1870s, were among the last peoples to obtain the horse. Use of the horse required a new way of being, and in providing easy and unlimited opportunities for hunting enabled the creation of additional wealth, in terms of horse herds and movable chattels. It altered the relationships between the genders, freeing up people, especially women, and dogs from transportation, enabled successful hunters/traders/warriors to accumulate wealth and prestige, and so by the nineteenth century had altered the formerly egalitarian form of Plains society. Bison could be killed with thrilling ease, travel to trade and for war was endlessly extended, and horses could reproduce to an infinite extent on the bountiful grasslands.

The repeated misunderstandings of this region, especially the High Plains, by Americans, is exemplified by the misnaming of the bison-covered region as the 'Great American Desert' by the formidable surveyor and locomotive engineer Major Stephen Long in the 1820s. This was equalled later in the century by the opposite, but bizarrely wrong-headed, belief of Cyrus Thomas that 'rain follows the plough', that is, with the extension of cultivation rain would follow. The actual development of farming depended much more on the Ogallala

Aquifer, centred on Nebraska and extending south to the New Mexico/Texas borderlands, one of the world's great water resources, now rapidly depleting. Abundant buffalo obscured this reality.

Hunting buffalo was in a way simple: it could be undertaken by stealth, by stalking and picking off the young beasts for tender eating and mature animals for robes. Pounds could be created for the driving of herds into carefully constructed enclosures, where trapped animals could be finished off; or herds could be driven over cliffs to create a mess of the dead and dying, indiscriminate killing to produce unlimited meat, requiring effort only to dry and pound and preserve it. Plains bows, made for instance of Osage orange, a dense, fine-grained wood, of necessity became shorter for use on horseback and necessitated an entirely new dimension of skill: to pull back a bow through the vertical to release the arrow requires strength and coordination of a different order to that employed on the ground while undergoing slow manoeuvres.

Horse-backed archery developed quickly. It was an innovation in a tradition of bow use stretching back 4,000 years, when bows were first imported across Bering Strait from Asia by the peoples known by the unwieldly epithet 'Arctic Small Tool tradition', who used them initially to hunt caribou. A number of different bow types are known historically, including sinew-backed bows again pulled through the vertical to power the release, especially from California, but also on the Plains, where antler or bison ribs might be backed for bows, to provide a short, powerful weapon.

It was not the bow that near-exterminated the bison, nor the arrival of the horse and then cattle, which provided competition for the grass; it was the demand for bison products. In Canada bison were hunted for meat, for the dried, ground pemmican, from the Cree word for 'fat', sometimes mixed in a ratio of one to one with berries and used by *voyageurs* in the fur trade. Much more significant was the demand for robes, which could only be taken at the end of the summer from animals with thick coats in preparation for winter, and then the demand for leather, for belts to drive industry in the eastern United States. Allied to this was the easy understanding by Americans that extinction of the bison would destroy the Indian way of life, so that the extermination of the buffalo would destroy the Indian as well. The development of railroads from the 1860s to the 1880s provided an easy way to transport skins, and additional demand contributed to the demise of the great herds. The effective end of the bison hunt on the northern Plains can be attached to the arrival of the Northern Pacific Railroad, from St Paul, at Miles City on the Yellowstone River in 1881. The collapse of the trade was recorded by a Minneapolis dealer, who shipped 200,000 skins in 1882, 40,000 in 1883 and the one and only box car full to go east in 1884.[21] The professional hunting of bison on the Canadian Plains did not occur in the same manner, but bison just about disappeared in the same way, the near extinction also driven perhaps by the effective use of the horse, creating an unsustainable hunting culture for which there was never to be any steady-state equilibrium.

Railroads

It was the railroads which brought about the swift, if expensive, means to exploit both buffalo and land in western North America. And it was Lincoln, the railroad lawyer, who insisted during the Civil War on the building of the Central Pacific Railroad section of the Union Pacific in 1862–9, the first transcontinental route. This was achieved with government-funded railway bonds, Chinese labour in the west, Irish in the east, and lavish land grants, construction taking place in the decade of Indian wars. In Canada exploitation of the west was driven rather differently, by the Hudson's Bay Company's monopoly rather than more complex crony capitalism.[22] And it took place against the plight of the rural Scottish and Irish. The first major initiative of the Hudson's Bay Company was the Selkirk Settlement of 1811, for the Scottish made landless by the Highland Clearances, where slow agricultural development was set against the building of fur-trading communities, French and Catholic as opposed to Protestant and often Scottish. This enmity fed also by the infusion of Irish to Canada, most famously of 2,000 people from the Irish estates of the prime minister, Palmerston, during the 1840s, the decade of the Irish famine. Just as Canada followed the USA with the process of surveying and selling land, so the building of the first railway, the Canadian Pacific, followed American practice and with an American executive, William Cornelius Van Horne (1843–1915), although promoted by the one-time fur trader Donald Smith, Lord Strathcona (1820–1914), who drove in the final spike in 1885. In contrast with the American situation, where there was no unified body of Métis or people of mixed descent, and there had been a long series of significant wars, there were virtually no major conflicts in nineteenth-century Canada following the War of 1812. The major exception involved the settlement of Métis in what had previously been the Selkirk lands and the creation of Manitoba after confederation in 1867. Following the Red River Rebellion of 1869–70 and the founding of Manitoba by its leader Louis Riel (1844–85), curtailment of what were seen as protected rights led to the North-West Rebellion of 1885. In this the Métis were supported by Cree and Assiniboines, and the rebellion ended with the execution of Riel on his defeat at the Battle of Batoche.

War on the Plains

War on the northern Plains is too often remembered as a white–Native business, when long before European contact warfare was endemic to the Plains. Hostilities arose around personal prestige or status and perceived slights, over hunting grounds, women and the capture of equipment such as bows, as well as the desire for revenge for perceived threats. Highly important in the historic period was the idea of counting coup, of touching the enemy and gaining prestige through an abstract act of war. Two lines of evidence suggest the antiquity of warfare. One is the pictographic record in Montana and Alberta, such as the Pictograph Cave, and writing on stone on the Milk River, in the Gulf drainage, which shows foot soldiers hefting huge rawhide shields for protection. Then in the river flatlands along the Missouri in the Dakotas horticultural peoples – the Mandan, Hidatsa and Arikara, with others, the Pawnee in Nebraska on other tributaries – all lived in earth lodges in defensive situations, the archaeological evidence extending back many centuries before contact. All of this changed from the late seventeenth century as the use of horses percolated north from Spanish territory, by raiding and trading, encouraging mountain and woodlands people on to the Plains and engendering a new dominant form of warfare: horse raiding of villages and settlements, where animals were rounded up and removed.

Warfare in the early historic period was conducted around alliances, in the northeast most importantly the ebb and flow of Siouan peoples, especially those known as the Sioux or Nadoessi ('enemies' in Algonquian), who were divided into three groups: the Dakota or their allies the Santee in the east; the Yankton; and the western Sioux, or Lakota. In the far northwest was the Blackfoot Confederacy of Algonquian-speaking peoples in Alberta and Montana. To the east was the Assiniboine and Cree alliance, and across the Plains were the Crow, allied with the Mandan and Arikara. During the nineteenth century alliances changed; peoples moved and some became allied with the United States, the generalized enemies of Native people.

Little Crow's War, or the Dakota War, of 1862 contains many of the basic elements of nineteenth-century resistance and dispossession. Also known as Taoyateduta, His Scarlet People or Little Crow (c.1812–63) was an eloquent warrior of a line of leaders formerly involved with the British. A realist, he participated in the major treaty negotiations of the period and travelled to Washington to negotiate when the treaty obligations were not fulfilled. At the Treaty of Mendota of 1851 a 14 million acre strip of land along the Minnesota River was ceded to the USA in return for about $3 million, to be paid in annuities. The Bureau of Indian Affairs, in thrall to local business, regularly dispensed treaty moneys directly to the traders, for payments of debts in arrears with falsified elements. In 1858, a further northern strip of land was ceded. During the summer of 1862 the treaty payments were reduced, and starvation threatened. In August Little Crow warned his people of the consequences of revolt against the US in no uncertain terms, and then led the war:

> if you strike at them they will all turn on you and devour you and your women and little children just as the locusts in their time fall on the trees and devour all the leaves in one day. You are fools . . . your ears are full of roaring waters.[23]

The year following the defeat, Little Crow was ambushed and killed, and his cranium, a scalp and some long bones were displayed in the

Minnesota Capitol, eventually being buried in 1971. Alexander Ramsey (1815–1903), first governor of Minnesota territory and a treaty signer, called for the extermination of Indians. It was Lincoln who acted, in a limited sense leniently, to end the hostilities. He claimed, during the difficult year of 1862, that the attacks were unexpected and suggested that large numbers of people were killed by Indian people; in his Second Annual Message of 1 December 1862, he put it like this:

> the Sioux Indians in Minnesota attacked the settlements in their vicinity with extreme ferocity, killing indiscriminately men, women, and children. This attack was wholly unexpected, and therefore no means of defense had been provided. It is estimated that not less than 800 persons were killed by the Indians.[24]

His speech also dealt with the continued development of the transcontinental railroad, with the importance of the Homestead Act for settling people and the likely expansion of the population of the USA, to around the same size as that of Europe, about 250 million people, in 1925, in fact the year after Native Americans would receive US citizenship. At a time when the Civil War was gradually turning in the Union's favour, the president was looking ahead, laying out the future of the great country, with the emancipation proclamation and in other ways that indicated that he regarded the future was only marginally affected by consideration of Indian people.

After defeat in September, more than 300 Dakota were tried and sentenced to death at Mankato. Many of the sentences were eventually commuted by Lincoln, with thirty-eight in the end being hanged, and their cadavers removed after burial for medical use. One of the main engagements was the siege of New Ulm; in 2011 John LaBatte, descended from two of the Dakota whose sentences were commuted, said in an interview: 'I'm part Dakota and when I moved to New Ulm I didn't list my phone number because I heard rumors that people at New Ulm didn't like Indians.'[25] In an important sense the challenge of the Civil War to US identity ensured more extreme responses to Indian issues of the period.

The process of the disenfranchisement of the Western Sioux, that is the Yankton and the Lakota, was very different and no less bloody,

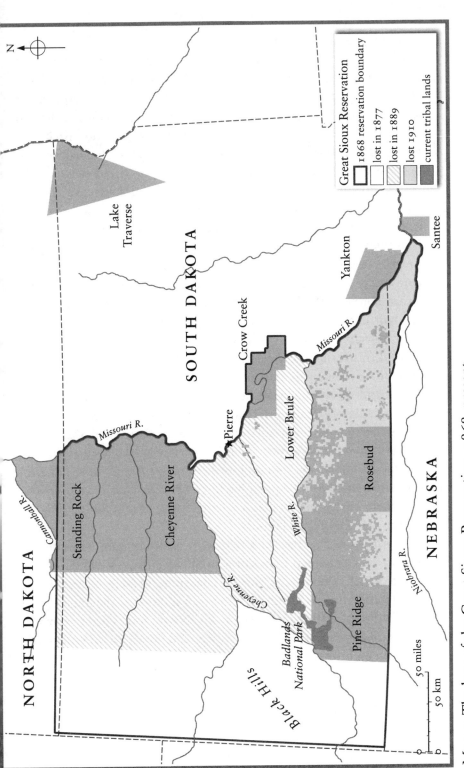

Map 9. The loss of the Great Sioux Reservation, 1868–present.

and yet lasted longer. It is remembered for perhaps the two most famous encounters between US forces and Native America, the Battle of the Little Bighorn in 1876 and the massacre at Wounded Knee in 1890. The first large-scale penetration of the west by Americans took place in the 1840s during the California Gold Rush. Trails – in the south the Santa Fe, and in the north the Oregon and Bozeman – provided expeditious routes to the fabled riches of what was to become the golden state. Clashes inevitably occurred between the Native inhabitants and the incomers, in part, of course, to do with hunting and access to bison herds. The federal response was to create a great series of forts along the routes to protect the trails. An initial framework for peaceful coexistence was put in place with the two Treaties of Fort Laramie, in 1851 and 1868, by which Western Sioux lands were protected, especially with the creation in 1868 of the Great Sioux reservation. This constituted rather more than the western half of what is now South Dakota west of the Missouri River. Crucially it included the Black Hills, a great area of spiritual resource, first taken over by the Western Sioux in the late eighteenth century, with new access made possible by the use of the horse. In the early 1870s gold was found in the Black Hills, which were then invaded by gold speculators, leading to clashes with Sioux. George Armstrong Custer (1839–76), the headstrong and charismatic Civil War leader, was sent to defeat Native resistance. Eschewing the normal practice of cautious manoeuvring into hostile territory, Custer took unnecessary risks and was killed and his force destroyed by a confederation of loosely allied warriors led by Red Cloud, Sitting Bull and Crazy Horse, defending their families.

This occurred as the United States was celebrating its centenary year at the Centennial Exposition at Philadelphia, a shocking coincidence which empowered mixed coalitions of self-interested and disinterested parties to consider finding a solution to the Indian problem. Military retribution came quickly. Native forces fled to Canada, where they were spurned by the crown, and, as usual, the great reservation was broken up. Ten years later the Dawes Act enabled the selling off of supposedly surplus lands to homesteaders and set up homesteading for Indian people, with disastrous results. The destruction of the bison herds ensured the end of mobility for Indians, with one final moment of false hope, the Ghost Dance movement of the 1880s, resulting in the misapplication of force at Wounded Knee in 1890, when hundreds of people were killed, more from fear than in response to any properly constituted military threat.

The Black Hills

The continued dispute around the Black Hills, Paha Sapa in Lakota, seems superficially eminently easy to settle, yet has proved intractable. Guarantees in the Treaty of Fort Laramie of 1868 were removed in 1877, after Custer's demise. The Lakota were the last Native occupiers, but for them and numerous others the Black Hills are a living, mythic landscape, whose importance is well recorded in oral and written history and in records such as Amos Bad Heart's map from the turn of the twentieth century. For the Lakota the hills are associated with the Falling Star, who is part star person and part human, immortalized by Black Elk and associated with the seven villages of the Pleiades or the Big Dipper/Plough. For the Cheyenne Bear's Butte is a place of prayer and renewal, as is Devils Tower in Wyoming, also known as Bear Lodge. The immediately previous occupiers of the Black Hills, the Kiowas, called them Sadalkani K'op, meaning 'Entrails Mountains', because a girl when chased by a bear told a small hill to turn into bison entrails to stop him.[26] The Arikara, Mandan and others are also involved with the Black Hills, and it is likely that ideas about the sacred landscape were shared and transferred from people to people through time.

Moves to return the Black Hills (so called because of its trees, that is, a similar etymology to Black Forest), which lie in an area surrounded by the Cheyenne and Belle Fourche Rivers, began in the 1920s. The claim was begun by a Lakota soldier and lawyer, Richard Case, from the Cheyenne River reservation, but took more than fifty years to reach the Supreme Court. In 1980 a lower court awarded $106 million. This was rejected on the grounds that the Sioux were not represented at the award and wanted the return of the lands seized in 1877. Subsequently disagreements broke out as to whether the moneys should be used, and in 2010 the Lakota writer Tom Giago pointed out that the award had now grown to more than a billion dollars, and that the use of the money had become more problematic rather than less, in that some Indian people thought the money should only go to full bloods, and that in the end it was the younger generation who would decide on the form of settlement, particularly in view of the poverty of northern Plains people. President Obama has since spoken up in favour of the return of the lands to the Lakota.

Perhaps the most important points are the very simple ones: that the Black Hills have meaning, to a large if not exclusive extent, because of Native use and custodianship of the hills; that the most appropriate use for the hills is that they be curated in the broadest sense for tourists, and for Natives by Native custodians. This huge area is sparsely populated, and the National Park sites, Devils Tower, Mount Rushmore and the Crazy Horse Memorial, as well as historic towns such as Deadwood, are best observed through a Native lens, one in which religion acts as a penumbra rather than a driving force for change. After all, Native people shared the hills before the arrival of white people, and they are not suddenly going to desecrate Mount Rushmore, notwithstanding a brief occupation in the 1970s. Nor are they able, beyond voluntary agreements, to prevent climbers for ascending Devils Tower.

Plains Confederations

Two confederations dominated the northern and southern Plains. In the north the peoples of the Blackfoot Confederacy are thought to have moved on to the Plains in the second half of the eighteenth century, being Algonquian-speakers. Adopting the horse, they dominated the vast area of northern Montana and southern Alberta. With an analogous but very different history are the Comanche, Shoshonean speakers from Wyoming, who dominated a vast area of eastern New Mexico, West Texas, Oklahoma and moved into Colorado and Kansas. The Blackfoot consist today of four separate peoples: the southern Piegan/Blackfoot in Montana, the Piegan, the Kainai/Blood and the Siksika. The Comanche similarly consist of several separate peoples, who came together in the eighteenth century, adopted the horse, muskets and textiles and dominated the Spanish frontier at the end of the century. Successfully they maintained autonomy in the face of the disintegrating empire of New Spain and stopped Mexican consolidation in the decades immediately before the US-Mexican War; it was only after US annexation that Comanche power was destroyed by American forces. In this the Comanche can perhaps be compared to the Iroquois in the northeast, who also unsuccessfully sought after the American Revolution to maintain themselves beyond the American frontier. The Comanche were confined to a small proportion of Oklahoma – some 3 million acres in the Fort Sill area – by the first Medicine Lodge Treaty of 1867. These rich grasslands were threatened not by gold-miners or farmers but by Texan cattlemen driving beasts to market.

Quanah Parker (d. 1911), born of a white mother captured in the 1830s, assisted in the settlement of his band on the reservation in 1875 and became leader and advocate of the Comanche, as well as a founder of the Native American Church. A rancher, he is associated with Texas cattlemen, and at the end of his life knew Teddy Roosevelt, who nevertheless was unwilling to assist him in ensuring the retention of Comanche lands. Devastation came in the aftermath of the Dawes Act, which had not included the dispossession of Indian Nations in Oklahoma. This changed in the 1890s, with the Cherokee Commission appointed to sign agreements for further homesteading in the new territory of Oklahoma. In an agreement of 1892–3 the Comanche agreed to permit the development of severalty, and in 1901–6 individuals were allotted their 160 acres, and the rest of the lands were sold off. Headquartered today in Lawton, Oklahoma, there may now be 15,000 Comanche. The best-known representation of Comanche identity is the John Ford/John Wayne movie *The Searchers* (1956), where Nathalie Wood plays a kidnapped white person, one of the best westerns, based on Quanah Parker's mother. Among other modern representatives of the Comanche identity are the code-talkers, soldiers who bamboozled the Germans, though, as a recent exhibition points out, they were landed on the wrong D-Day Beach. Also promoted on the Comanche Nation website is the Comanche 'Fighter Boy', George Tahdooahnippah (b. 1978), keeping the warrior tradition alive and to the point.

An Indian Bank

A different sort of battle was fought on the northern Plains. Elouise Cobell, Inokesquetee Saki or Yellowbird Woman (1945–2011), arranged for the Blackfoot to have their own National Bank in 1987, starting with $1 million in capital. This first Indian bank, it was renamed the Native American Bank and in 2013 had assets of $82 million. Cobell went further: she took the USA to court for misman-agement of Indian funds. From 1820 payments to Indians were handled centrally, eventually by the Bureau of Indian Affairs. Already by 1828 Indian agent and anthropologist Henry Schoolcraft (1793–1864) in Michigan noted that the financial side of the bureau had been admin-istered with a pitchfork. With the Dawes Act of 1887 and alienation of treaty land the scope for maladministration widened considerably, and of course receipts included moneys from minerals as well as land. In the 1970s Indian moneys were used to bail out New York City and Chrysler. During the Clinton years banker Paul Homan was appointed to look into the matter. He found 238,000 accounts: 16,000 were without documents, 50,000 were without account addresses (so that money couldn't be paid), and 118,000 were missing documents. He resigned when obstructed in 1999. The eventual settlement of 2010, two years before Cobell died, provided $3.4 billion, an average of $1,800 per account, part for payment and part for sorting out the problem of fractionated land. From an early age Cobell had been ridi-culed in her requests for figures; attached to her computer when she died was a note which said: 'First they ignore you, Then they laugh at you, Then they fight you, Then you win.' While others believed that there were still tens of billions of dollars at issue, Cobell herself believed it was time for a settlement.[27] One important aspect of the settlement is that nations have funds to buy back minute parcels of fractionated (and so otherwise useless) land and take them back into tribal ownership.

9
The North

nuit whaler and beluga, the skin rich in vitamin C, c.1870. The Inuk is holding the
arpoon head, the foreshaft pointing vertically downwards from the shaft. This technology
vas introduced to Europe in the seventeenth century.

An Alaskan carrying a sealskin-covered kayak, the bow pierced to reduce the side impact of
waves, and wearing a sea mammal rain parka, c.1900.

Rachel Uyarasuk (Igloolik), measuring skin for tailoring, 1990s. Few images exist of these informal but accurate ways of measuring, many millennia old.

Cree fur traders, James Bay, c.1865. The York boat derives from the Viking longship, via the Orcadian youl. The man is wearing a white capote or trade blanket.

amily on a sleeping platform in a snowhouse, 1950s, breath condensing in the cold air.
. photograph by Guy Mary-Rousselière, prominent priest and anthropologist.

'he last prophets, *c.*1931. Eastern Arctic Inuit converted themselves to Christianity
ising publications in syllabics. Here they are wearing parkas decorated with ladders to
ieaven and large halos across their shoulders.

'Exorcising Evil Spirits from a Sick Boy': posed image of a shaman curing a boy, Nushagak, *c.*1906–8, Alaska.

Inuit and the Hudson's Bay Company ship *Nascopie*, 1939. Annual supply visits to the eastern Arctic began in the early twentieth century.

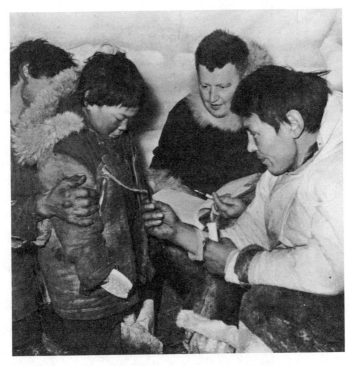

Taking the 1950 census. In a snowhouse an Inuk examines the child's Eskimo identification number, as used in the military, the census-taker behind, the child holding a pilot biscuit.

Gabriel Stepetin (b. 1911) (Aleut). In 1942, under attack, Aleuts were removed from island Alaska to internment camps; later, Stepetin fought against the 1974 ban on sealing imposed by conservationists.

William E. Beltz (1912–60), president of the first Alaskan Senate (after statehood), pointing out his Inupiat home, Unalakleet, 1959.

Alaska Native Danny Hugo working on a rescue dig for the Alaska Pipeline, posing with an early point, thousands of years old, 1972.

'In his case it was self-defence.' Uluksuk (c.1887–1929), an Innughuit shaman in 1916, was one of two Inuit who killed two missionaries, ate some of their livers, was tried and convicted, but freed.

Queen Margarethe of Denmark, with Prince Hendrik, holding their two sons, wearing elements of Greenlandic national dress, from a recent visit, 1970.

Zebedee Nungak (b. 1951) (Kangirsuk), who signed the 1975 JBNQA agreement, at the Smithsonian Institution.

Welcome of the first two Greenlander MPs, 1953, after the granting of Home Rule.

Inuit helping build the US Cold War radar Distant Early Warning line at Kuujjuarapik, Quebec, 1956.

Ray Mala, Inupiat actor (1906–52), starring in *Eskimo* (1933), with poorly designed Inukshuk or landmark for hunting and wayfinding.

'Dogs aid crash probers', 28 January 1968. A B52 bomber had crashed a week earlier, causing a dirty explosion from 4 H-bombs. Most of the plutonium remains isolated on the seabed in Bylot Sound, Greenland.

The late Paul Apak Angilirq (1954–98), snacking on young walrus, Foxe Basin, 1994. Apak wrote the screenplay for *Atanarjuat: The Fast Runner*, which won the Caméra d'Or at Cannes in 2001.

9
The North

First Peoples

Northern North America, covering around 4 million square miles, is a vast region. Including Greenland, the north, an area large as all of Canada or the USA, was probably never populated, aboriginally, by more than a few hundred thousand people. The division between the Arctic – without trees, with permafrost and shoreline – and the Subarctic – with timber – is the tree line, which approximates to the isotherm (or temperature contour) for a 10°C average through the warmest month of July. The Arctic Circle (66° 33' N) is the limit of the polar night and midnight sun and is the home of radically differing hunting cultures, mostly originating around Bering Strait in the last few thousand years. Around 8,000 years ago populations in the interior were originally Na-Dene or more generally Amerind, dependent on hunting mainly caribou, but also other large mammals, fish and birds. On the coast, new cultural patterns regularly appeared in the Eskimoan area, where altering climatic conditions changed fauna availability, whereas in the forested interior hunting patterns remained relatively constant for many thousands of years. Although all aboriginal populations entered the Americas through the funnel of the Bering Strait region, their cultural response to the changing patterns of northern cold differed.

Asia

The idea that America was not totally disconnected from Asia was first proposed by the Spanish Jesuit José de Acosta (1540–1600), in his *Historia natural y moral de las Indias*.[1] Migration of peoples to the

Americas occurred during glaciation, from possibly more than 40,000 to more probably 14,000 BP, when Siberia and Alaska were joined to a variable extent by a land bridge across Bering Strait. Glaciation caused up to 20 per cent more terrain to be exposed. The earliest inhabitants, Paleo-Indians, are known from a small number of often contested sites in deep time, such as Monte Verde in Chile *c.* 15,000 BP and, even more controversial, Pedra Furada in Brazil, as well as from a well-established horizon of big game hunters in North America, the Clovis culture from around 11,000 years ago. The people of the Clovis culture used large, lanceolate, flaked and fluted (concave, scarred) Folsom and Clovis chert or flint points to hunt bison and mammoth. Large animals were probably driven into swamps and water to slow them down, or over cliffs: kill sites of bison and other animals were first identified in the USA in the 1920s. Interestingly, there are no archaeological equivalents in Asia.

We are thus presented with the question of how and where the Clovis culture evolved. If, as is likely, the Clovis people developed their unique hunting weapon in the Americas, why is there no acceptable evidence for their antecedents? One would expect to find evidence in Alaska and North America in particular, for instance, of much earlier people using chopping tools – crudely knapped choppers made out of pebbles or similar – or of a culture which used some antecedent projectile point leading to the beautifully fluted spear head of the Clovis. There is no ready explanation for this absence, unless it is posited that the first Americans arrived in such small numbers and their remains are so scarce that no reliable sites have yet been discovered. Occasionally sites such as that at the Bluefish Caves, Old Crow, Yukon Territory, yield animal bones of great antiquity perhaps modified by humans, yet these finds are seldom regarded as acceptable evidence of Clovis antecedents. The conventional explanation is referred to as the Clovis-First theory, which proposes that the Clovis people are the first known inhabitants of the Americas, who followed big game from Alaska down through the two continents of the Americas. While the Clovis-First theory is the one that currently prevails, it is regularly – and appropriately – challenged in many areas.

There are three other strands to this debate about how the Americas were first inhabited: (1) What route was used to go south from

Alaska? (2) What do human remains tell us about the DNA of the first Americans? (3) How do these separate theories relate to language and the controversial theory of glottochronology, that is, the length of time required for the differentiation of American languages?

What were the possible routes south from Alaska approximately 10–50,000 years ago? One route would have led along the western coast of the Americas, providing a relatively simple pathway to Tierra del Fuego, and might allow for the approximate 14,000 BP date of Monte Verde with its hearths and huts. Since during much of this period central Alaska was glaciated, alternative routes would have involved travel across northern Alaska and then south, either through central British Columbia, or more likely down the Plains through Alberta, along the eastern edge of the Rockies.

As for the second question, a 2013 study of mitochondrial DNA, led by Alessandro Achilli, suggests that an earlier model positing three waves of immigrants to the Americas is correct. The first occurred around 15–18,000 years ago, along the Pacific coastal route, enabling rapid diffusion south and then eastwards. This first group, usually called Amerinds, constitute the ancestors of most aboriginal peoples in the Americas. The lack of physical evidence from archaeological sites along their route south is due to flooding as a result of rising post-glaciation water levels – at the time of migration the islands and archipelagos of Pacific North America, Vancouver Island, Haida Gwaii, the southeast Alaskan archipelago, Kodiak and even the Aleutians would have been joined to the mainland. This ties in neatly with the Clovis-First theory: that the first great florescence of aboriginal culture in the Americas arose around hunting with spears or lances, and that Clovis culture developed from a narrow population base, probably in situ in North America, and in South America changed and adapted rapidly to local hunting and gathering opportunities.

The first immigration, of Amerinds, into the Americas was followed a few thousand years later by another wave of people from Siberia. Instead of moving down the coast, these people moved southwards but inland, around and through the Rockies. This population, according to the DNA record, is ancestral primarily to the aboriginal peoples who speak Na-Dene languages, that is, the group which includes the interior Subarctic peoples of western Canada and Alaska. The Na-Dene group also includes the breakaway peoples who migrated to the southwest of the United States around 1,000 years ago, and are ancestral to the Navajo and Apaches, who also called themselves Diné/Dene and Nde/Ndeh.[2] However, this breakaway group shares genetic markers with other aboriginal peoples in North America, making a simple association of the migration with a single language group impossible. Much later, sometime after about 7–4,000 years ago, people from Alaska moved eastwards to Arctic Canada and Greenland, and westwards through Beringia to Siberia, to form probably the historic Eskimo-Aleut population. Achilli and his co-authors suggest that 'the first American founders left the greatest genetic mark, but the original maternal makeup of North American Natives was subsequently reshaped by additional streams of gene flow and local population dynamics, making a three-wave view too simplistic'.[3] Understanding Native American DNA continues to evolve quickly: in 2015 one paper suggested that the Americas were settled in a single wave around 20–23,000 years ago, with divergence of populations 13,000 years ago and later arrivals from Asia and Australia-Melanesia; another relates genes from the second peopling of the America also to Australia-Melanesia, and this time specifically to Amazonia.[4] Alas there remains a profound problem with the reception and use of DNA research; in a society in which racism is given pre-eminent normative value, the results of gene tests may act as a catalyst validating prejudice and sidelining culture. This has been explored in Kim TallBear's *Native American DNA* (2013).

Time and Language

A greater time depth for the population of the Americas, as far back as 50,000 years ago, has been suggested both by controversial finds from doubtful archaeological sites, and even more controversially by glottochronology, the time depth required for the linguistic diversity that existed at the time of contact with Europeans. The latter comes from the work of two linguists, Joseph Greenberg and Johanna Nichols, working with the meta-classification of languages and other ideas. During the 1980s Greenberg reworked the original theory that the Americas were first inhabited mainly by peoples of a single migration – the Amerinds, with a single language, Proto-Amerind, associated with the Clovis culture – and then by the Paleo-Arctic, associated with the Proto-Na-Dene speakers. Nichols did not agree with this – in fact most historic linguists entirely disagreed – and suggested that the time depth required for the differentiation of languages might be tens of thousands of years, maybe as much as 50,000 years. Later Nichols suggested that the ancestors of the inhabitants of Monte Verde (14,500 years ago) must have entered the Americas before the glacial maximum (26–19,000 years ago), at which time their path south through North America would have been blocked by ice.[5] What matters is not that the historical linguists studying single languages or language groups do not agree with the archaeologists, who may not agree with the geneticists, and who may not agree with the meta-data big-picture linguists. Rather, what is important is that they all propose models which, though more or less fallible, enable the discussion of how and when people entered the New World to take place.

The problem here is that while the first Paleo-Indians must have passed through Alaska, they left no remains there. There is some suggestion that some of the earliest archaeological cultures of the Paleo-Arctic period, from the Nenana Valley (around 11,000 years ago), may possibly be ancestral to the Clovis, but the absence of a clear hypothesis as to where the finely made, thin projectile points found there came from has led to one extreme theory. This was proposed by Bruce Bradley and Dennis Stanford and suggests that the earliest population of the Americas came from the European Solutrean period, around 19,000 years ago, from northern Spain and France. The theory suggests that 4,000 years earlier a maritime adaptation of this culture moved across the North Atlantic sea ice, hunting sea mammals (with a cold-climate technology for which there is no evidence) and using heat derived from (technically unlikely) mammal-oil-filled ice basins. Better grounded in reality is the theory that the first Arctic populations, designated Paleo-Eskimo, developed the Arctic Small Tool Tradition from approximately 4–5,000 years ago, for which there is copious evidence across the top of North America. Using flaked micro-blades for composite arrows or spears, they were probably the first to introduce the bow to North America, along with microblade, core and lithic technology from Asia. There are many exceptional aspects of the Paleo-Eskimo and later traditions: the great variety of hunter tool kits; the way these tool kits overlap, appear and disappear; the manner in which the prey focus changes in various successive and geographically specific cultures; and the way in which prey choice and availability was affected by periods of cooling and warming in the Arctic. Technologies kept changing: the use of the throwing-stick and/or bow, the use or lack of the drill, the extent of the use of dogs and sleds and of boats are all discussion points about Arctic occupation over the last five millennia. Arctic peoples were also influenced by their Indian neighbours, whether Northern Archaic in Canada for the early habitation of the north, Dene in the west or Algonquian-speaking in the east.

The Arctic Small Tool Tradition spread rapidly eastwards to Greenland and was replaced in Canada and Greenland by the Dorset culture. Whereas the earlier Paleo-Eskimo hunters, called Inuit Tuniit, were dependent on land animals, especially the caribou, and on anadromous fish, the Dorset people (c.500 BC–AD 1500) in Canada and Greenland were sea-ice hunters of sea mammals, using an elaborate series of whaling harpoons and small sleds. They developed belief systems related to the hunt which they expressed in exquisite carvings of animals and people. They possessed neither bows nor drills, but instead were dependent on the careful use of flaked burins and small tools for all their carving. What is spectacularly impressive is the development of a high level of skill to gouge out, without drilling, the eyes of the myriad needles required for the creation and maintenance of clothing on a daily if not hourly basis, using such a minimal tool kit. The Dorset people survived into late medieval times in Canada. Much of their technology was probably taken over by people of the Thule tradition, the immediate ancestors of historic Inuit, who maintained an important oral history about their predecessors. The Tuniit, they believed, were people of great strength and calm, able to pull a walrus home alone.

In Alaska the development of the Thule culture, people of the modern Eskimoan tradition, can be traced back 2,000 years and earlier to the Old Bering Sea culture, but its relationship to other Alaskan cultures and traditions remains a matter for discussion. One lineage sees the Arctic Small Tool Tradition developing into the Norton tradition, around 3,000 years ago, moving from caribou hunting to sea mammal hunting, and gradually, by about 2,000 years ago, developing many if not most of the components of Old Bering Sea culture. With warming, new opportunities for hunting large sea mammals developed, and whaling became an important feature of pre-Thule culture. It was taken across the Arctic as people of this tradition spread eastwards. Two sites in Beringia have been excavated to yield well-articulated accounts providing the preferred sequencing of Eskimoan culture. The first was that of Ipiutak, at Point Hope in northwest Alaska. The people of Ipiutak were sea mammal hunters (ringed seal and walrus), caribou hunters and, in spite of a village settlement lasting approximately 200 BC–AD 800, did not possess the Old World characteristic of making pottery. On the Siberian side of Beringia 100 burials have been excavated at Ekven, from the same date but of the Old Bering Sea culture. The inhabitants of both villages possessed elaborate but different art styles, with animal beings expressed in both geometric and realistic forms, related in origin to earlier shamanistic cults in Siberia.

The Old Bering Sea culture was succeeded differentially by the Punuk and Birknik cultures, which replaced Ipiutak. They incorporated open-sea whaling and by about AD 1000 had become the ancestral Thule culture, available to move rapidly eastwards. Thule hunting culture meshed knowledge of the environment seamlessly with a belief system in which everything had its own spirit. The technical features of the culture include the toggling harpoon, which separates from the harpoon shaft like a two-stage missile and swivels sideways beneath the skin of the prey; the sled and later the dog sled; snow goggles – wood, ivory or skin spectacles with eye slits which radically reduce spring ice and snow glare; and a great range of tools and skills that exploit the technical qualities of the cold. Most important of these, perhaps is the use of sea mammal oil to heat the home or iglu (*igluviga* being the word for a snow house) in lamps which produce light and heat but virtually no smoke; in contrast, wood fires in tents in the Subarctic, a conventional heating strategy, require large smoke holes.

The Kayak

Central to northern culture is the learning of practices and beliefs required to be a successful hunter. For ancient Eskimoans at the Bering Strait, and for Inuit into the twentieth century and beyond, the kayak was essential to the hunt. A light-framed boat with a covered deck and a hole for the hunter, it is constructed out of driftwood and covered (usually) with sealskin, meticulously prepared and carefully sewn with an internal double-covered seam. The kayak is both highly complex in its design and construction and, seemingly, super-simple in its function. For instance, because a smooth flow of water must be maximized, the de-haired skin would be orientated as on the seal, head to toe, so that the remnant hair follicles would cause minimal disruption to water flow and avoid alerting prey. The elegant form, designed to be a weapons platform as much as transportation device, varies geographically across the Arctic. In Alaska it might be equipped with a bifid or pierced bow, so that, when hit with a side wave, the kayak would dissipate the energy rather than capsize. As it lacks a pronounced keel, a high degree of skill is required to maintain balance with the (usually) double-bladed paddle, worked in a contra-rotating rowing technique. The hunter would be clothed in a pullover or parka-style sealskin or sea mammal gut clothing, tied tight over the hole of the vessel with sinew cord. While balancing and paddling, the hunter would also need to be able to launch a harpoon with a throwing stick, *atlatl* or *narsaq*. Thus he would silently balance the boat, then pick up and lever-launch the harpoon with a flick from over his shoulder on one side of the boat. He might also use bird darts, bows and lances, or knives for stabbing caribou. And in himself the hunter would need also to be connected to the animal spirit.

The knowledge base and the development of the multiple skills required for this procedure are exceptional and unteachable in the abstract, requiring mastery through practice in situated learning. This involves preparation through early socialization, from infancy, using songs in which the child, rocked in a boat-like motion by his mother, would be primed to throw an imaginary harpoon. Later, rock outlines of kayaks set up on dry land would be used for the practice of harpoon use. This would be followed by early use of a kayak on water, the testing of skills, strength and fitness through sport, practising the kayak roll and the accumulation of the whole panoply of knowledge about currents, ice, weather conditions, wind and the heavens for purposes of navigation. All of the actions of a kayaker have to be embodied intuitively in behaviour, to be deployed instantly: reaching for hunting gear, understanding the environment without thinking. This practice has also to be effective in teamwork – done noiselessly and with visual communication only, for example when pursuing walrus in a group.

An interesting psychosis of the late nineteenth century, reported only in Greenland, indicates both the centrality of kayak use and the effect of colonization-induced stress. Kayak-fear, a psychosomatic illness, appeared in the 1860s. It was a phenomenon in which hunters in calm seas would experience dizziness and distress. Similar terms were used from the 1860s of middle-class Americans who were diagnosed with neurasthenia, or stress in the booming city, and late Victorian and Edwardian colonials, diagnosed with tropical neurasthenia, self-induced disorders to do with living in a hot and unfamiliar climate. A wide variety of explanations have been provided for kayak-fear: excess consumption of coffee, race weakness (i.e. the supposed primitive nature of the Eskimo brain) and shamanism. More likely, kayak-fear was to do with a general cultural implosion brought about in the colonial situation, with its emphasis on hunting for the market in sea mammal products, which disappeared in the mid-twentieth century with the move in Greenland to the use of larger boats for the emergent fishing economy.[6] Kayak-fear is a neat example of the mimicking and internalization of parallel colonial psychoses.

So this complex learning process, of how to use the kayak, has been given a phrase of its own by Tim Ingold: 'enskilling', derived from the Marxist debate of the 1980s around the effects of computerization in factories. Learning and socialization are probably sufficient sobriquets to describe the long-term process of developing skills in hunting and trapping; on the other hand, the rapid business of deskilling, a slightly earlier mid-twentieth-century term also used to refer to factory work, has real application in the north. Learning about the land, about weather and environment, and about using dogs or kayaks, requires significant early learning, skill sets that can only be acquired in situ from elders and by constant application, listening to people talk night after night. With the introduction of the school year, television and other distractions and – for the fortunate minority – paid employment, the opportunity for everyday learning is lost. What has happened, then, through the twentieth century is that northern aboriginal peoples, while taking charge of their affairs, have too often become deskilled. In part, of course, this has been due to the fluctuating fortunes of the fur and sealskin trade: there is no point, apart from the cultural value, in spending time on the trap line or the floe edge hunting seals if the price for skins is too low. And in the destruction of hunting the European Union played an important role, yielding to the animal rights movement in 1983. The law (Council Directive 83/129/EEC) banned imports of certain seal products, except those taken by Inuit, but consumers were not able to make the distinction.

Whaling

Whaling enabled the move eastwards from Alaska of the Thule culture and remains central to Alaskan culture. Whaling is conducted from open boats rather than closed kayaks. In northwest Alaska, among the Inupiat, the whaling captain or *umialik*, the closest thing to a chief, is the boat owner and leader. He steers and organizes, traditionally leading with songs, and contributes with the power of his whaling amulets: whale skulls or dried raven or the tip of a fox's tail. Whaling takes place from his *umiak*, or open boat, and his family will take part. He will receive the most prestige, organizing the distribution of meat. Traditionally whaling was hedged about with definite taboos, to maintain distinction between land and sea and to avoid death. Taboos particularly affected women; Asatchaq (1891–1980) from Point Hope put it like this: 'While the men are on the sea-ice, the women stay home. They sit in their iglus. They do nothing.' This is their way of helping[7] the hunting. In the 2013 spring whaling season, Point Hope was, in contrast to Barrow, to the northeast, very successful, the various teams killing six whales, with one captain, Michael Guzroyluk Snr, taking two. Among the Inupiat and Yup'ik, whaling would be celebrated in winter with the Messenger Feast. Today the feast, Kivgiq, thrives among the Inupiat, having been revived in 1988.

Traditionally, a highly successful *umialik* (the term including the sense of boss and rich man) would send two messengers (*kivgak*) to a neighbouring village, who would discuss gift exchanges, all of which would take place in the *umialik*'s men's (ceremonial) house or *qargi*. The meetings would involve trading, dancing and performance, and affirmation of kinship.

The original feast went into decline and disappeared in the 1910s, with the collapse of commercial whaling and consequent widespread destitution, followed by the flu epidemic of 1918, which, when combined with missionary hostility, ensured its disappearance. The revival took place in 1988, at a cost of $200,000 provided by Native and non-Native sponsors. This project was initiated in 1987 by the North Slope borough mayor, George Ahmaogak Snr, along with research on its origins and the best way of organizing it in modern times. The revival was seen as an aspect of healing, with ancient elements of purity, including avoidance of alcohol and drugs, and a return to traditional values, strikingly analogous in this aspect to the nativistic or revivalistic movements of the nineteenth century. In 1994 Ahmaogak put it like this:

> Our Iñupiat people have seen tremendous change over this past century – as much in the last two decades alone as mainstream America experienced over two centuries . . . We can enjoy western food, but cannot satisfy our physical or spiritual needs . . . There is a social and spiritual need inside us as Iñupiat which can only be satisfied by our own traditions. This is why we revived Kivgiq.[8]

The language used in a newspaper report of the 2013 Kivgiq festival is specifically religious in tone without mentioning religion – in a sense, if belief systems are fully incorporated into everyday life, religion as an idea becomes a heuristic device and a simplistic label. This is how Kivgiq was described:

> what stood out to me wasn't the continuous stream of dancers, drummers and singers who took the stage over the four-day festival in Barrow . . . But it was the flowing crowd around me that really caught my attention. More than once, I was seated a few feet away from an elder. These men and women took their spot among the crowd and

waited – waited for the throngs of people who would come to them, thrust a baby into their hands, hug them, and wish them well. Time and again, I saw teenagers, young parents, older adults, stream up to these elders and offer them recognition and love . . . it was impossible not to feel the roots of their knowledge spreading out from the dance floor.[9]

In northwest Alaska, the end of the spring whaling season is celebrated with the whale feast, Nalukataq, called after the blanket toss which characterizes the celebration. Whaling captains and wives are tossed first, and they throw out candy instead of the more traditional goods once distributed in this way. The drumming, dancing, blanket toss and other sports are maintained and are included in the biennial international Arctic Winter Games since 1970 and the World Eskimo-Indian Olympics in Alaska since 1961. Two other important sports are the high kick – how high can you kick a target with one or two feet – and the head pull, where opponents face each other, stomach to the floor, and pull each other with a strap round their heads.

The Spread of Arctic Sports

The most important sports to have travelled beyond Eskimoan communities are kayaking, which outside the north has lost all its Inuit inflection, and dog sledding. 'Mushing' (from the Canadian French 'Marchez!') goes back perhaps to the seventeenth century and was adopted in English by the nineteenth century and celebrated in the USA by the Arctic scientist Robert Kennicott (1835–66) from working with the Hudson's Bay Company. Today dog mushing in Alaska, for instance the Iditarod race between Nome and Anchorage, is an Indian/Eskimoan hybrid, with hybrid dogs and hybrid sleds, and is dominated by non-Natives. It has even been won by non-Alaskans, for instance Libby Riddles (1985). What is interesting is that dog-driven sleds, whether Greenlandic, as used for Robert Peary's travels towards the North Pole, or Canadian and Greenlandic, as used by Amundsen towards the South Pole, are a form of transport which have assumed a general life separate from aboriginal people. Of course, outside Greenland, dogs have been pretty much displaced by snowmobiles/snow-machines, except for sport and tourism. This has had the effect of reducing pressure on mammal populations, especially walrus, a favoured dog food.

Canoe racing, which was once a way of life, also seems ubiquitous in the non-aboriginal world, as it once was in the Subarctic, though the birch-bark canoe may be superior in its lightness and economy of design for inland water to the more robust dugouts used through time round the world. Few if any other cultures have contributed in this way to global sports.

Whaling and Conservation

The original belief systems involved in activities such as whaling, expressed, for example, in the drumming and singing that act as a prelude to whaling or as a celebration afterwards, are often disregarded outside aboriginal North America. Yet the belief systems – similar in character but entirely different in their features – which surround Asian martial arts find ready acceptance in the West. Arctic hunting – and whaling in particular – is seen as a rather more controversial act of cultural expression.

The idea, however, that whale saving and whale hunting are antithetical activities, and that advocates of animal welfare and those of aboriginal society are in opposition, is perhaps rather mistaken. The Alaskan Eskimo Whaling Commission (AWEC), founded in 1977, described itself in 2012 as:

> a tax-exempt non-profit corporation whose purpose is to preserve and enhance a vital marine resource, the bowhead whale, including the protection of its habitat, To protect Eskimo subsistence bowhead whaling, To protect and enhance the Eskimo culture, traditions, and activities associated with bowhead whales and subsistence bowhead whaling, To undertake research and educational activities related to bowhead whales.[10]

The commission appeared in the 1970s because suddenly, without any reference to the Alaskan Native whale-hunting community, the USA signed up to the first restrictions on the number of bowhead whales that Eskimos could hunt, along with the International

Whaling Commission, which had been founded in 1946 to regulate commercial whaling. As ever, the dominant society, having threatened a significant resource by destroying the whale populations visiting Alaskan waters in the nineteenth century, then sought to impose restrictions on those Native people who had only ever used that resource for subsistence. The issue came to the forefront in the late twentieth century because of an unrealistically low estimate of bowhead whales, with a suggested figure of 600–2,000 in 1977, down from a pre-contact figure of 11,700–18,000 in, say, the eighteenth century. So today there is agreement that bowhead whales, and Inupiat hunting, seem not to be under any threat. Yet in the broader picture the Arctic Sea remains a major area for oil exploration, and whales are highly sensitive to intrusions by survey vessels, as well as to any more substantial threats that might arise from *Exxon Valdez* type wrecks or Deepwater Horizon blowouts.[11] New oil exploration, as encouraged by the US government, remains highly contentious in Alaskan and Arctic waters for this reason.

The AEWC had its problems in the 1990s and 2000s, when it was operated without supervision, so that its directors were able use it for personal gain. In 2012 two successive directors pleaded guilty to theft, the first of $400,000 over a seventeen-year-period between 1990 and 2006, and the second to stealing $100,000 in 2007 and 2008. The first of the directors, Maggie Ahmaogak, was indicted as her husband, the politician and whaling captain responsible for reviving the Messenger Feast, George Ahmaogak Snr, was running for a new term as mayor of the North Slope borough in 2011. At that time he called the charges 'baseless'.[12]

Geese

A similar story can be told about the hunting of migrating geese. The rights of people to hunt, whether whales or birds, are part of a complex network of obligations, regarding giving and receiving, which radiate out from multigenerational social groups and encompass non-human animal persons – in this case the spirits of geese which require respect. Leaders in hunting communities are selected for their skills, and this practice reflects widespread reciprocity, spiritually, socially and in the material sense of providing food. Animals are included and are indeed identified with. This reciprocal respect is expressed in Lynn Whidden's 'Essential Song' (2007). Another song, by, the Cree George Pepabano in Chisasibi in 1982, explicitly compares the partridge with its feathered feet and the hunter on his broad snowshoes – perhaps the snowshoes are even woven with a bird-foot design to make explicit the imaginative association between hunter and hunted:

This song is about the partridge bird.
The partridge, and how he runs through the snow.
His feet are able to carry him through the snow on top, without sinking.
The hunter compares himself to this bird, to a partridge.
When he has on his snowshoes he is able to run
Like the partridge on top of the snow.

Other forms of respect are also important: the hunter 'smokes to the game' (*pwaatikswaau*), in a sense blessing the animals of the air with air, when sitting in the blind waiting for the geese to pass overhead, singing to them.

The first-fruits ceremonies in the spring include sharing the geese killed on the first day, and then keeping further geese so that they may be shared out evenly through the camp for a feast in which reciprocity is celebrated, and the geese beings invited; the cartilage windpipes of the geese are placed in trees, so as to beckon more geese. The decoy sounds are employed with model decoys, the Canada geese ones both in alert postures and feeding, accompanied by honking, while the snow goose is attracted by colour alone, white buckets or rags serving to bring the birds in. To attract other animals, physical and aural decoys are used: the beaver will be attracted by the sound of a beaver eating branches; the fox and the muskrat will be attracted to the kissing, lip-smacking sounds of a mouse. This mixture of technical, knowledge-based skill – how to call animals – is seamlessly integrated with the performance aspects of beliefs and with social behaviour, as well as with attitudes towards scarcity and conservation – limiting the taking of animals for reasons of respect and to avoid the anger of the species. The naive western dichotomy of nature and man, vital though it is a heuristic device, is avoided at all times. For the Wemindji Cree hunting in autumn or winter, hunting spots will be rotated so that at any one time geese will be respectfully left in most areas to feed unmolested. And if a hunter kills too many geese, is greedy instead of leaving younger hunters the opportunity to succeed, then his death may be expected.[13]

Alaskan Twentieth-century Settlements and Corporations

Both Indian and Eskimoan peoples in Greenland, Canada and the USA suffered precipitous decline, through disease and intrusion, from the seventeenth or eighteenth century onwards. Yet even though chronic epidemics spread through communities during most of the twentieth century, northern communities have recovered a high degree of autonomy, paradoxically because, for the most part, none of the colonial powers ever bothered to 'make treaty', as Canadians put it, with northern aboriginals. In the late twentieth century governments throughout the north became obliged to reach virtually self-governing settlements with aboriginal peoples.

Of all the contemporary settlements, the most important is the Alaska Native Land Claims Act (ANCSA) of 1971. It is thoroughly modern in most of its provision and neo-liberal in its outcomes and achievements. It successfully provides a corporate-based future for Alaskan Natives, who had not, of course, been consulted during the process of the creation of the state of Alaska in 1958–9. The need to come to a settlement was recognized in the late 1960s with the discovery of oil, the largest field in the USA (25 billion barrels, found by ARCO, and run by BP). Alaskan Native politics had hitherto been centred on southeast Alaska, led by Tlingits and Tsimshians, who founded the Alaska Native Brotherhood in 1912. In the 1940s the civil rights leader was Elizabeth Peratrovich (1911–58), who opposed public racial discrimination against Natives, organizing the 1945 Alaska Equal Rights Act a decade before civil rights issues emerged in the southern United States. From an Alaskan point of view, the settlement of land claims was promoted by the liberal Republican governor of the late 1960s, previously a campaigner for statehood, Walter Hickel (1919–2010), later secretary of the interior under Nixon. He brought in Morris Thompson (1939–2000) (Koyukon), who did much to promote ANCSA and went on to become commissioner for Indian affairs in Washington in the mid-1970s, signalling the north's new-found importance.

The Alaskan settlement, which created share-based restricted companies in Native-only ownership, was entirely different to those of the treaty process, which had stopped exactly a century earlier. The corporations were set up in 1971 to work 'without establishing any permanent racially defined institutions, rights, privileges, or obligations, without creating a reservation system or lengthy wardship or trusteeship, and without adding to the categories of property and institutions enjoying special tax privileges'.[14] Twelve regions were created, with a thirteenth for non-resident Alaskan Natives, along with 200 village corporations. Settlement included 44 million acres (of 375 million), $462.5 million paid over an eleven-year period and a royalty of 2 per cent up to a total of $500 million on mineral development in Alaska. Each Native received 100 shares in the regional corporation, while village corporations had to be set up community by community (of more than twenty-five inhabitants) to receive and invest settlement, mineral and forestry funds, either as profit or non-profit corporations.

It was estimated in an article explaining the flaws in the act that each Alaskan Native would receive about $900,000, made up of equal annual payments for the first eleven years, and moneys from mineral rights over an indefinite period,[15] insufficient to make proper investments for long-term purposes and a paltry sum for the extinguishment of title. The consequence of this was that many corporations rapidly went into deficit, including the Koyukon Coporation, which was turned around by Morris Thompson from 1981. In 1987 amendments were made to the act to avoid the alienation of shares to non-Natives, a provision of the original act enabling this to happen from 1991. One of the major inequities was the difference between those regional corporations with mining interests and those without. Sealaska Corporation, which had timber rather than mines, was one so disadvantaged. In the 1980s the tax code used was altered to allow for non-operational losses – the decline in the value of timber – to be declared and sold to successful corporations, such as the Carlyle Group, requiring measures to alleviate the tax burden of the purchasing corporation.[16] Problematically this sale of the tax losses

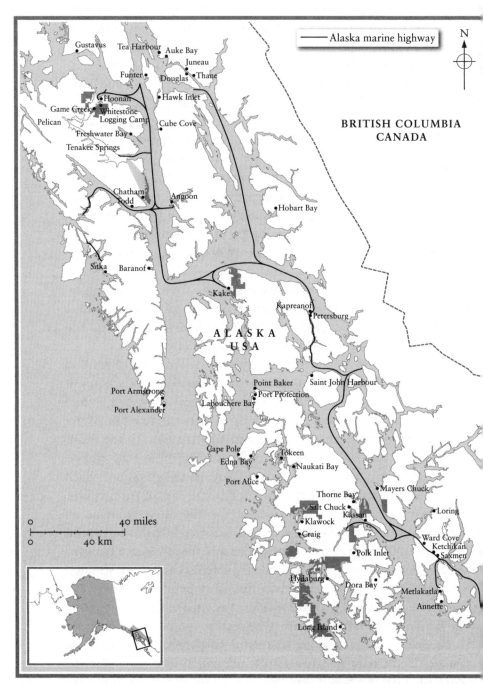

Map 10. Sealaska Timber Corporation, Southeast Alaska, 2015 the dark areas indicating corporation lands.

required clear cutting of the timber, such as might be found around Alaskan villages such as Hoonah. In 2013 Tlingits put their continued resentment at this process to the Senate Energy and Natural Resources Committee, one saying:

> Taking land around Native towns, Sealaska became one of the richest Native Corporations in the state. To do so, they mowed down the trees for tens of square miles in a row. Their own shareholders in Hoonah screamed, and still scream, about the legacy of devastation they saw.[17]

But the situation in Alaska is anomalous: on the one hand, the twelve public corporations are independent entities owned by Native shareholders who cannot sell their shares and must eventually transfer them to other shareholders. On the other hand, Alaskan communities rich in land and shares have less sovereignty than many Indian reservations with curtailed land base. Public Law 280 was enacted in 1953, at the time of termination and elimination of trusteeship, to extend federal and state law enforcement jurisdiction over Indian people on reservations, a process which continued with Alaskan statehood in 1958–9 and ANCSA in 1971. Crucial to the elimination of tribal sovereignty in Alaska was the court case Alaska v. Native Village of Venetie Tribal Government (522 U.S. 520, 1998). The village of Venetie, in the interior of Alaska, is one of a small number inhabited by the Gwich'in, caribou hunters over many millennia, who are spread across a vast area of Alaska, the Yukon and northwest Canada. The Gwich'in wished to tax non-Natives doing business in their community, but the Supreme Court ruled that they were not situated in Indian Country, that the prerogative of taxing was for the federal and state government and that ANCSA in 1971 had eliminated sovereignty, that lands held in fee simple rather than in trust no longer had the rights of nations. In other words Alaskan Natives, endowed with the benefits of a land settlement, are less independent than Indians on reservations in the Lower 48. With no authority over non-Natives, any idea of self-government by Natives in Alaska is limited, though practically speaking it is very circumscribed elsewhere.[18] Almost immediately after the 1971 act was passed, disadvantages were noted, particularly in the loose definitions of Native and reservation resident, and in the transfer of funds from one corporation to another. But the main disadvantage was that in cash terms each village shareholder would receive theoretically around $40,000 a year over a period of upwards of eleven years. More important would be the 44 million acres transferred to Native ownership in two respects – as a capital resource in itself and as a resource to be exploited, whether for timber or for mineral wealth. In a way ANCSA had some similarities to the vast land transfer treaties of the nineteenth century when annuities were provided to Indians. But for some Native peoples the Alaskan settlement has been extremely propitious.

The Eyak story is one of destruction, recovery and retribution. Living along a 300 mile coast in southern Alaska, between the Tlingit and the Eskimoan peoples, the Eyak were traditionally a rich Indian hunting people, with a stratified society, including slaves, when first contacted by Russians in the late eighteenth century. Linguistically and culturally they were related to the Tlingit, but without a major carving tradition of creating, for instance, totem poles. In the late nineteenth century, when the herring and salmon had been fished out, a railroad was constructed through Eyak territory to serve the developing town of Cordova. As De Laguna put it, the Eyak were debauched by alcohol and ravaged by epidemics, and the children were shipped a thousand miles to boarding school at Chemawa, Oregon, few returning.[19] Michael Krauss estimated that in 1985 there were five Eyak speakers left; yet in 1973, when the Eyak Corporation was set up under the ANCSA of 1971, in the Cordova area there were 326 Native shareholders, the Eyaks outnumbered by the other Native Alaskans eight to one. In 2015, there were 504. Eyak shareholders, according to their website, are mostly of Aleut descent, but the corporation was so named to commemorate this Indian people by the founder Cecil Barnes, who was of Alutiiq descent. This is now a highly successful Native corporation, with shareholders of Eskimoan and Indian origin, and run in 2010 by the Tlingit businessman Rod Worl. No monies were distributed until after the *Exxon Valdez* disaster of 1989, when the corporation sold half of its landholding of 76,000 acres back to the state of Alaska for $25 million, each shareholder receiving $77,000, because Eyak Natives were much affected by the collapse of traditional subsistence in the wake of the oil spills.

But because these corporations are not sovereign nations, following the Venetie decision, unlike tribes in the Lower 48 states, the Eyak Corporation received a tax bill for $16 million. This would have bankrupted them.

The tax bill was settled following a new initiative. In 2002 Eyak-Tech was set up by Eyak Corporation to engage non-competitive contracts for defence-related spending in the aftermath of 9/11 in the beltway at Dulles, Virginia. This process was encouraged by the Small Business Association, under a remit called the '8a Business Development Program'. This is a federally mandated programme designed to help disadvantaged business people and stipulates that 'the firm must show that one or more socially and economically disadvantaged individuals serves as the highest officer, controls the board [and] makes long-term decision'.[20] In the summer of 2013 Harold Babb, the head of contracts at EyakTek, was sent to prison for seven years. EyakTek had received contracts totalling $1.5 billion since October 2001. The fraud scheme worked around the Tiger (Technology for Infrastructure, Geospatial, and Environmental Requirements) Program. This enabled Homeland Security, NASA and the Coast Guard to acquire information technology services and physical and infrastructure security. Fraudulently inflated invoices for subcontracts were submitted to EyakTek, the contract fulfilled, and the planned criminal surplus, $30 million, was to be returned to the conspirators, the principals including a manager in the US Corps of Army Engineers, Kerry Khan. When arrested in 2011, they were beginning to organize a further programme, called CORES (Contingency Operations Readiness Engineering and Support), worth $1 billion. In 2010 it was said that EyakTek had returned over $29 million in benefits to the Eyak Corporation's Alaska Native shareholders, including payment of tax bills. This process of successfully taking on government projects has enabled the company to completely retire the IRS levy derived from the sale of aboriginal land back to the state, payment of which was finally completed in 2009. In total, the Eyak Corporation and its Alaska Native Settlement Trust have paid $35 million in dividends to its Alaska Native shareholders since inception. This is equal to more than $108,000 per shareholder (holding 100 shares). Since overbilling is endemic in US health care and in the US military-security complex, one has to ask why a small Native corporation should be targeted for a fraud investigation, and part of the answer may be that a marginal business may simply be an easier target than a multi-billion-dollar public corporation.[21] It can also be reasonably argued that the resurrection of the Eyak is a contemporary version of the process in which, particularly in the Midwest and Oklahoma, Native peoples remade themselves by adopting in survivors from dislocated or destroyed Nations swept aside by the colonizing process.

Eastern Canada

Further east, recent history is rather different. The territory of Nunavut, the greater part of Arctic Canada, is about 725,000 square miles, 20 per cent of Canada and comparable in size to Greenland and Alaska, but with a population of 37,000 in 2015, representing less than 10 per cent of the Alaskan population. The movement towards self-government began during the 1970s, after the Calder case, 1973, from British Columbia was taken to the Supreme Court, which affirmed that underlying aboriginal rights to land can exist. The setting-up of Nunavut followed two acts, one extinguishing aboriginal rights, and the other providing for the three branches of territorial government – legislative, administrative and judicial – with a premier and a commissioner to represent the crown. Some 140,000 square miles were transferred to Nunavut, 13,500 with mineral rights. Compensation of $1.1 billion was payable from 1993, and a training fund of $13 million was allocated; most importantly animal harvesting rights were protected. On the other hand, Inuit agreed to surrender 'any claims, rights, title and interests based on their assertion of an aboriginal title',[22] as in Alaska. The Nunavut Development Corporation, from 1999, has investments especially in fishing and in art production but does not have the high-profile airline interests of aboriginal Quebec (First Air) or the long-standing extractive industries of Greenland and certainly none of the southern business profiles of Alaskan Native corporations. The companies involved are small-scale. The Nunavut Arts and Crafts division turns over $1.8 million in Ontario each year; in 2014 Pangnirtung Fisheries had a turnover of $2.9 million and had twenty-eight employees. It was sold in 2015.

In contrast, in Alaska the Eskimoan Chenega Corporation, in a village with a population of seventy-six in 2010, had a thirty-year head start on Nunavut and bills itself as the most successful Alaskan village corporation, boasting:

> Well known in the industry as a socially and ethically responsible enterprise, Chenega's corporate culture is steeped in the values and ethics that flow from its Alaska Native leaders. Those values distinguish Chenega as 'a corporation for a higher cause', where a substantial portion of profits are dedicated to elevating the Chenega Community and its people to lives of self-sufficiency and a sustainable, productive future. The Corporation also leads the way among Alaska Native Corporations in providing consistent dividends and in supporting comprehensive cultural, social, religious and community, initiatives, programs and projects.[23]

Chenega sits on an island at the entrance of Prince William Sound. Named by Captain Cook on the first European expedition in southern Alaska in 1778, the community was devastated, moved and rebuilt following the 1964 earthquake. Chenega Corporation was recently subject, with other Alaskan Native Corporations, to a Senate investigation into no-bid contracts, which reported on Chenega's partnership with the security firm Blackwater, notorious for its mixed record in Iraq. The report said that Chenega had more than 5,300 employees, and in 2000–2008 revenues of $5.8 billion. The brief and rather curt conclusion of the report is very tactful, neither denying nor affirming fraud, in a sense condemning by omission; it finished with:

> In recent years, federal auditors and academics have raised concerns that the preferences granted to Alaska Native Corporations create the potential for waste, fraud, and abuse in government contracting. The record before the Subcommittee shows that the Alaska Native Corporations are multi-million or billion dollar corporations that rank among the largest federal contractors. The Subcommittee's investigation shows that the ANCs have taken advantage of their 8(a) contracting preferences, receiving large no-bid contracts and passing through much of the work to other contractors. The record also shows that ANCs provide some benefits to their shareholders.[24]

In 2004 Chenega was already distributing $1 million a year to 142 shareholders.[25] As ever with allegations of corruption, what is crucial is the moral authority of the accuser, the identity of the beneficiary of any allegations and the extent to which the accuser may or may not be involved in similar practices.

One of Chenega's recent contracts was to provide security to the US Atlantic (Trident programme nuclear) submarine fleet base, Kings Bay, Georgia. In his change-of-command farewell speech on 16 July 2012, Captain John O'Neill, the retiring commander of the base, expressed 'his sincere appreciation for a job well done' in acknowledging the Chenega Security and Protection Services contribution. His remarks conveyed complete satisfaction with the CSPS team's commitment to the 'First Line of Defence', protecting one of the US navy's most important installations which included the entire Atlantic Fleet's 'strategic submarine assets'. It has to be asked whether, in fashioning ANCSA in 1971, Congress anticipated that, while terminating Native sovereignty, it had also provided vehicles for Native economic success beyond anyone's wildest dreams. Further, much of this wealth is used for cultural projects, publications and language records. One of Chenega's 2013 cultural projects is the 'Development of a Chenega Baidarka Culture Camp'. A *baidarka* is a two- or three-hole kayak developed specifically for the Russian fur trade in sea otter, emblematic if you will, of the near enslavement of the ancestors of the Alutiiq people. Maybe the revival of this ancient practice is a useful symbol, expressing Eskimoan achievement in providing security for a nuclear weapon system, originally designed in the 1970s, to fight the Soviet Union. Perhaps surprisingly one important aspect of Indian policy from the Lower 48 thrives in Alaska: this is the Indian Health Service, which still looks after 140,000 Native Alaskans with a network of hospitals, surgeries and other facilities.

Nunavut

Little criticism is voiced of ANCSA and the corporate autonomy of Alaskan Natives. This is in stark contrast to the situation in Nunavut. The 2013 Caledon report on Nunavut emphasized the high unemployment rate – 22.5 per cent of Inuit older than fifteen – the low level of literacy and numeracy, which prohibits proper participation in skilled employment, and the growing divide of welfare recipients from the educated, working Inuit middle class.[26] The Caledon Social Vision 'sketches out a wide range of social programs in Nunavut in the areas of early childhood development, education and literacy, skills training, regional economic development, affordable housing and income security. The main focus is income security policy.' Thus traditional knowledge and culture has apparently little role to contribute to the improvement of Nunavut society. Of course, literacy, education, the development of skills that may be used in the (albeit highly cyclical) mining industry and limited public sector opportunities are vital. But overarching this is the failure to recognize that the basic resource, of living on the land with low cash income, is actually available to Nunavimmiut. Even more remarkable is that Thomas Berger's 2006 report 'The Nunavut Project' is not mentioned by Battle and Torjman. In this report Berger notes the deficit of Inuit employment in the territorial and federal government, but the significant part of the report is about the failure to deliver competency in the younger generation to speak Inuktitut. He says: 'it has been demonstrated that effective academic use of a child's second language (in Nunavut, this means English) is enhanced through the promotion of the first, indigenous language'.[27] If proper provision of Inuktitut teaching was available, then the cognitive skill acquired – necessary for all language learning – would enhance and make easier the learning of second and subsequent languages such as French, which Berger notes now has an unassailable place in Canadian public life, administration and politics.

Some of the Inuit leaders who led the way to self-government are most critical of the current situation. John Amagoalik is one of them: heading a succession of Inuit organizations including the Inuit Tapirisat of Canada and the Nunavut Implementation Commission (1993–9), which set up Nunavut. Amagoalik quoted a Price Waterhouse report on the project of Nunavut, a cost to the federal government of '$65 million annually to maintain a "fly-in, fly-out" public service'. Yet he is less critical than some journalists, such as Patrick White, who dwell on abuse and suicide instead of articulating the ways in which a hunting society, only a couple of generations off the land, has achieved an important high degree of autonomy. In contrast, of course, outsider settlement in Greenland began in the early eighteenth century and in Eskimoan Alaska in the nineteenth century, rather than, for Nunavut, the twentieth century. Of course, it would be unrealistic to expect large numbers of people to live in outpost camps, but that need not prevent their growth and positioning as symbolic, if not spiritual homes, places of cultural security and belief, where traditional life continues and reinforces a sense of value and identity in otherwise urban lives.

But the extraordinary aspect of Nunavut's current situation is neither the level of violence and suicide, nor the poverty, but that language, culture and environmental resources for a life if not on the land, then with the land, are there and available. If the Canadian government was willing, a different way forward would be possible: reinforcing, altering and developing the outpost camp programme of the 1970s and 1980s, in which Inuit live on the land, and the young learn the language and how to hunt and survive from their elders. Furthermore, the knowledge base could be spread to southerners, so that they too might know about the Arctic and Inuit, so that all Canadians, even if they never visited Nunavut, have an Arctic identity. Yet despite the problems of education, important innovative initiatives do thrive, such as Nunavut Sivuniksavut, an eight-month college programme in Ottawa, founded in 1985 with a total enrolment of forty to fifty, which trains young people for higher education and careers development. This is the kind of initiative that could be radically expanded to teach *qallunaat*, that is, white people, about the Arctic, and to create a fuller understanding in the south of what the north means. Another important knowledge-based military institution, created in 1947, might also be enlarged: the Canadian Rangers, with Inuit, First Nations and Métis people, patrol the north, with 5,000 or so members, originally on Cold War lookout, and then on a more general duty of guarding the landscape and knowing what's going on.

Colonization in Nunavut was a twentieth-century phenomenon, even though the Hudson's Bay Company had been sailing through Inuit waters, south to the Subarctic, since the seventeenth century. While the increasing importance of the north in the twentieth century was signalled in the 1930s by British air route expeditions recording meteorological information, the actual colonization of the north, that is, the creation of settlements with major all-year transportation hubs, came only with the Second World War. Most important of the new settlements was the USAAF base Crystal II on Baffin Island at a favoured fishing site. It was surveyed in 1941, became Frobisher Bay and then Iqaluit in 1987, and since 1999 has been the capital of Nunavut itself. Another vital base was built on the southern tip of Greenland, Bluie West 1, now Narsarsuaq, through which many thousands of aircraft were flown to Britain in the Second World War. Other projects also contributed to the opening up of the north. Most important was the Alcan highway, 1,700 miles long on completion in 1942, running from Dawson Creek, near the border of British Columbia with Alberta, to the interior road system around Fairbanks in central Alaska. This was presented by Philip Godsell's *Alaska Highway* (1944) as a triumph of American and Canadian frontierism: Native peoples were described as the first invaders from Asia, the second being the Japanese in the Aleutians, in 1942–3. The racial caricaturing extended to African Americans, who were referred to by Natives as *kuskitayweasuk*, or 'black meats', with a tendency to get lost in the bush, or *Tipiskow Inniwew*, 'Midnight Men'.[28]

Pipe Dreams

More salutary, and indicative of fights to come, was the first major pipeline, the Canol Road, constructed during the early 1940s to pump high-grade oil across the Rockies from Norman Wells to a refinery in the Yukon. However, this pipeline was leaky and unsatisfactory and only functioned for a short time in 1944–5. The Canol project did, however, usher in much later an era of pipe dreams, of endless, ever more ambitious plans for pumping hydrocarbons for export, almost always with little aboriginal input. Most famous of the pipelines is the successful Trans-Alaska. Built in 1974–7, with a diameter of 48 feet – twelve times that of the Canol pipeline – it transports oil 800 miles south from Prudhoe Bay, making the 1968 North Slope oil discovery economically viable. But many if not most of the ambitious pipelines have not been built and remain highly controversial. Of the aboriginal battles fought and won, that of the unbuilt Mackenzie Valley Pipe, which was designed to take natural gas from the Beaufort Sea/Mackenzie Delta south, stands out: Thomas Berger's report on the project, more than 280 volumes of evidence issued in 1977, helped delay its construction. Berger argued reasonably that aboriginal people were not an integral part of the pipeline plan. Today in the USA and southern Canada there are still numerous pipeline proposals, some, such as Keystone, now cancelled, many controversial. All are designed to bring northern hydrocarbons to market, but all are environmentally difficult, and their viability is threatened by the cheapness of shale gas. Reserves of shale oil in Alberta are said to amount to a billion barrels, maybe ten times that in the Alaskan North Slope.

The Military

The full construction of the north as a military environment, and an entity in its own right, took place during the Cold War. The spectacular DEW (Distant Early Warning) Line, designed to warn of bombers and missiles, was set up in 1954–7 across the Arctic from Canada to Alaska by Western Electric, at a cost of billions of dollars, with fifty-eight stations along a 3,000 mile expanse. It took just three years to complete. It can be seen, with only mild exaggeration, as a grandiose project comparable in scale and ambition to the building of Brasilia or Abuja, to collective farms, and to hydroelectricity projects. This vastly ambitious US and Canadian initiative, conceived as a binational or, with Greenland, multinational project, was designed to protect western civilization but took very little account of the environment, the local people and millennia of aboriginal knowledge. The creation of infrastructure – roads, pipelines, airfields, radar stations, bombing ranges and the housing and towns required – was expressed in terms of 'defeating the north', as if the environment itself were an enemy alongside the Russians. And in all of this there was little or no benefit to the aboriginal population, who experienced and suffered rapid modernization.

However, the DEW Line was rendered obsolete in the year of completion by the launch of the first ICBM, the Soviet R-7, which was itself also soon to become obsolete, though not before it had instituted the phoney idea of the missile gap. The modernization of the

Arctic, and of Inuit living in northern Canada, which then occurred is best reflected in two studies of the 1960s: John and Inge Honigman's *Eskimo Townsmen* (1965), about Frobisher Bay (now Iqaluit, the capital of Nunavut), and Nelson Graburn's *Eskimos Without Igloos* (1969), about Nunavik or northern Quebec. Both explain the problems in terms of cultural loss and the arrival of the limited benefits of a wage economy in a period of explosive change.

Dog Tags

Most symbolic of this period is the general abandonment of dog teams in favour of snow machines, a process accelerated by the spread of canine epidemics, alongside human ones, and the heavy-handed culling of dog teams by the Royal Canadian Mounted Police (RCMP) to prevent the spread of disease. But another symbol was the introduction and use of numbered discs, card or leather 'dog tags', to make for easy administration of programmes by newly arrived Canadians unfamiliar with Inuktitut names. Dog tags in the military are used to help identify the injured and the dead. Inuit dog tags provided a Christian name, specified east or west division and community and allocated an individual number for the administration of the living. The system was in use from 1941 to 1978, when numbers were replaced with surnames. This project was organized by Abe Okpik (1928–97), who had been the first Inuk to be appointed to the Northwest Territories legislature (1965–8) and who also worked with Thomas Berger on the Mackenzie Valley Pipe Line Enquiry in the 1970s. In 1968–1971 Okpik, whose own name means 'owl', visited communities to encourage and organize the adoption of surnames. Inuit names, often highly inventive, would be given by parents, with new ones regularly bestowed, for instance, on incoming *qallunaat* (white men), joking names reflecting idiosyncrasies. A further feature of Inuit naming is the cross-gender use of names commemorating a deceased relation. Associated with this naming is the referencing and treatment of the young child as though they were the deceased's elder relative, the baby becoming for instance mother or father. So if a male was given his grandmother's name, he would be called grandmother.

The Harnessing of Power

Aboriginal recovery of rights in Canada began, after militarization was complete, with the business of power and electricity generation. Historically the most important power companies are Ontario Hydro (founded 1906) and Hydro-Québec (1944). Ontario Hydro was a monopolistic corporation, whose development in southwest Ontario substantiated the province's imperial status along the umbilical cord attaching southern Canada to the USA. Hydro-Québec was founded to wrest control of power generation from Anglo-Canadian corporations and in so doing became both a symbol of Quebec's successful assumption of economic autonomy and cultural identity and, as a colonizing institution, the dominant agent for change in Northern Quebec/Nunavik (only part of Quebec from 1912) and Labrador.

The involvement of HydroQuébec in Labrador illustrates the final (and in many ways catastrophic in its outcome) mid-twentieth-century northern development that took place without aboriginal input. This development, the Churchill Falls hydroelectric project, took place over twenty-five years from 1947 to 1972 and involved the construction of an enormous dam and an underground electrical generation station in central Labrador. The falls are in Innu or Montagnais/Naskapi territory, the territory of the easternmost (Algonquian-speaking) people in the Subarctic. They were little contacted in the 1940s, except by fur traders and missionaries, as Labrador was part of the crown colony of Newfoundland, only becoming a province and territory of Canada in 1949. A British holding company, Brinco, was set up in 1953 by Rothschild Bank, at the instigation of the Newfoundland premier, Joey Smallwood (1900–1991), the politician who had taken Newfoundland into the Canadian confederation a few years earlier. The project was commissioned in 1971–4. The major issue during development was anchoring sale of the electricity generated, and in the absence of better offers long-term production was sold to Hydro-Québec at 0.25c per kilowatt hour. This is a fortieth of Canada's 2013 energy price of 10c per kilowatt hour (12c in the USA). The price goes down to 0.20 in 2016 for the last twenty-five years of the contract, which ends in 2041. For the Innu, who only in the early

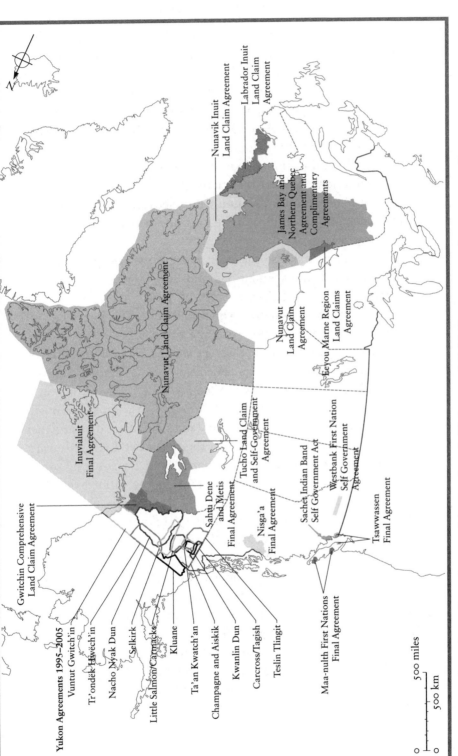

Gwitchin Comprehensive Land Claim Agreement

Yukon Agreements 1995–2005
Vuntut Gwitch'in
Tr'ondëk Hwëch'in
Nacho Nyak Dun
Selkirk
Little Salmon/Carmacks
Kluane
Ta'an Kwatch'an
Champagne and Aiskik
Kwanlin Dun
Carcross/Tagish
Teslin Tlingit

Maa-nulth First Nations Final Agreement

Inuvialuit Final Agreement

Nunavut Land Claim Agreement

Nunavik Inuit Land Claim Agreement

Labrador Inuit Land Claim Agreement

James Bay and Northern Quebec Agreement and Complimentary Agreements

Nunavut Land Claim Agreement

Eeyou Marne Region Land Claims Agreement

Tucho Land Claim and Self-Government Agreement

Sahtu Dene and Metis Final Agreement

Nisga'a Final Agreement

Sachet Indian Band Self Government Act

Westbank First Nation Self Government Agreement

Tsawwassen Final Agreement

500 miles

500 km

Map 11. Modern Canadian Comprehensive Land Claims and Self-Government Agreements since 1975.

twenty-first century started to organize land claim settlements in both Labrador and Quebec, the issue is even more disastrous than for the owners of the Churchill Falls, since they lost forty years of possible development and near-autonomy during the late twentieth and early twenty-first centuries. More generally, the contract makes Labrador financially beholden to Quebec, seemingly to justify Quebec's rejection of the 1927 Privy Council decision which awarded Labrador to the then dominion of Newfoundland, a great swathe of Innu country in the interior of the territory claimed by Quebec. The significance of the failure to empower the Innu with a settlement in the 1970s can be read back into the origins of the fur trade in Gerry Sider's *Skin for Skin* (2014).

Hydro-Québec was also the main agent in the next power project, which was much more ambitious and also largely situated in the Algonquian-speaking Subarctic east of James and Hudson Bays, although this project equally involves the Inuit. The James Bay project, which emerged from surveys in the 1950s, was designed to create a much larger system of dams than the single Labrador one, diverting rivers running into the sea via generation plants. For the first time, aboriginal people successfully challenged the Canadian state, in the form of the ambitions of Robert Bourassa (1933–1996), premier of Quebec and equivalent to Newfoundland's Smallwood as provincial promoter. Six Inuit formed the Northern Quebec Inuit Association (NQIA) under the leadership of Charlie Watt (b. 1941) in 1971–2, while the Cree communities of eastern Quebec formed the Grand Council of the Crees in 1974, creating for the first time province-wide representation, with Billy Diamond (1949–2010) as chief. In the early 1970s the federal government, still with responsibility through the Department of Indian Affairs and Northern Development, began negotiating to terminate the implicit sovereignty held by aboriginal people in northern Quebec, which had been acknowledged by the 1912 agreement extending Quebec territory. The James Bay and Northern Quebec Agreement (JBNQA) of 1975 implicitly followed the Alaska Native Land Claims settlement of four years earlier in providing access to hunting, land and mineral rights, and so enabled the development of the first Canadian corporate aboriginal structures which provided a significant degree of autonomy. However, the James

Bay project was already underway when the JBNQA was negotiated, so there was intense pressure on the participants to reach a conclusion, leaving them with little power to delay the scheme.

In the JBNQA, lands were divided into three types: Category I, 14,000 square kilometres (5,400 square miles), owned by aboriginal people; Category II, 150,000 square kilometres (58,000 square miles), owned by the crown, but with hunting rights reserved for aboriginal people, and other economic rights such as mining and tourism shared; and the remaining 900,000 square kilometres (347,000 square miles) reserved to the crown with limited aboriginal hunting rights. In addition some $225 million was provided for development. The other main First Nation of the region, the Innu, was included in a similar agreement in 1978. The agreement explicitly extinguishes sovereignty with these words:

> the James Bay Crees and the Inuit of Quebec hereby cede, release, surrender and convey all their Native claims, rights, titles and interests, whatever they may be, in and to land in the territory and in Quebec, and Quebec and Canada accept such surrender. (section 2.1)

Worse still, the province was further given a new and explicit role in aboriginal communities specifically: 'the right of Quebec, its agents and mandatories to establish, in addition to the public servitude in favour of public bodies, agencies and corporations . . . servitude for public purposes' (section 5.1.4a).

In contrast the Nunavik Inuit Land Claims Agreement (NILCA) came into effect in 2007. This agreement applies to offshore regions around Quebec, northern Labrador and offshore northern Labrador. Nunavik retain ownership of much of land, without extinguishment of title.

The NQIA developed into the not-for-profit Makivik ('to rise up') Corporation in 1978 in the north, and the Cree Regional Authority was set up in the south. Air Inuit was founded by Makivik in 1978; First Air is also owned by Makivik, and Air Creebec began in 1982. Makivik funds the very successful heritage organization Avataq Cultural Institute (*avataq* meaning 'float', as in a sealskin float for hunting), based in Montreal, which collects and disseminates cultural knowledge – in the form of both artefacts and information.

Emerging from the process was a whole series of public corporations designed to deliver services: for the Inuit these are Kativik regional government (KRG), the Nunavik Regional Board of Health and Social Services (NRBHSS) and the Kativik School Board (KSB). The KRG operates with a council system similar to the Grand Council of the Crees. The important difference from Alaska is that, although Makivik is owned by Nunavik Inuit, there is no privately held share structure issuing dividends, no transfer from one generation to another and no privileged access to federal contracts in the rest of the federation. Instead Makivik acts as the primary interface between the federal and provincial governments, for instance in negotiating further agreements and in providing direct employment to aboriginal people. So Makivik is also a highly successful Inuit economic development corporation, helping to prepare Inuit for eventual self-government and working to control traditional Inuit territory. In 2011 Makivik negotiated the 'Final Agreement on the Creation of the Nunavik Regional Government', which was rejected after a Facebook campaign by 70 per cent of participants in a referendum, because it did not sufficiently protect Inuit rights. Importantly Makivik's governmental mandate is proclaimed implicitly on its website. It is:

> To receive, administer, distribute and invest the compensation money payable to Nunavik Inuit, as provided for in the James Bay and Northern Quebec Agreement; to relieve poverty, to promote the welfare, advancement, and education of the Inuit; to foster, promote, protect and assist in preserving the Inuit way of life, values and traditions; to exercise the functions vested in it by other Acts or the Agreement; and to develop and improve the Inuit communities and to improve their means of actions. Politically, culturally and economically, Makivik has been a leader in building and developing a vibrant region called Nunavik, where, between the dualistic nations of Canada and Quebec, Inuit have established our own distinct place and identity.[29]

This narrative of Makivik success works to counter the alternative and actual narrative of the loss of sovereignty, which combines in turn with two more difficult strands: one relates to the environmental consequences of the damming projects – of the leaching of mercury into the water system, of the alteration of freezing patterns caused by the warming effects of greater water flows, affecting hunting and animal populations – and for the Cree the problems caused by the removal of the people of Fort George to Chisasibi in the 1970s. The JBNQA is characterized, and probably caricatured, as forcing aboriginal people into the liberal-capitalist order instead of along the possibly unattainable path of culturally constructed self-determination. Aboriginal corporations in Canada emphasize the importance of community-based consensus decision-making, particularly associated with leadership from elders, while at the same time they are placed in the contemporary world of accountability through executives and boards of directors. Against this narrative runs a countervailing one, that of the development of a corporate elite, controversially defined by salary payments entirely contrary to traditional Inuit and aboriginal egalitarianism. Yet in Canada the extreme, and usually silent, scandalous behaviour associated with activities on the fringe of Alaskan Native corporations is apparently absent. Furthermore, in Canada the cooperative movement, established before the JBNQA, provides an additional level of successful business activities. 'Eskimo' cooperatives were founded in some communities during the late 1950s, and then in what is now Nunavik during the 1960s. In 1967, La Fédération des coopératives du Nouveau-Québec was established as an umbrella organization bringing Cree and Inuit together. In its first year of operation it achieved a turnover of around $1 million, growing to more than $100 million in 2013. The services it provides include construction, retail stores, internet and a wide variety of land-based help, but without the larger political role of Makivik in the tradition of public corporations.

Western Canada

The corporate model of governance of the JBNQ agreement of 1975 was used as a template for the Inuvialuit Final Agreement of 1984, which covered a region roughly half the size of northern Quebec, approximately 270,000 square miles, in the Northwest Territories and the Yukon. Ownership was established over 56,500 square miles, and the cash settlement included $152 million, with full harvesting rights. Out of this emerged a wholly owned development corporation, the Inuvialuit Development Trust. Annual revenue expanded to more than $200 million from initiation to 2012, with a turnover of $300 million.[30] Investments include logistical provision, and in particular drilling. As in other parts of Canada the Inuvialuit Settlement Region does provide a degree of self-government through overlapping institutional authorities to give representation and services, with programmes associated with autonomy including land use, harvesting, environmental protection and above all employment. Yet progress towards formal and explicit self-government remains an ambition under negotiation.[31]

Greenland

The Nunavut agreement regarding self-government actually followed a non-Alaskan model, that of Greenland Home Rule. Greenland, like Canada during the 1950s, experienced rapid modernization under a paternalistic government and company, the country administered by highly competent professionals intent both on development and on helping Greenlanders, a situation similar to Canada but not to Alaska, which has American militarization.

Greenland was run, like Rupert's Land in Canada and the Hudson's Bay Company, by the Royal Greenland Trading Department (Den Kongelige Grønlandske Handel or KGH) from 1774 to 1908. The major difference is that, instead of fur, the main export was sea mammal products. As in northern Canada, one of the principal vectors of change was mining, of more significance and earlier than in Canada or Alaska. Within a Danish ethos of biculturalism, cryolite mining is explored in Peter Høeg's 1992 thriller *Miss Smilla's Feeling for Snow*. The most famous mine was at Ivittuut, formerly Ivigtût. The cryolite is used as a purifying flux in the preparation of aluminium and was mined for a century (*c.*1887–1987) in an important area of Norse settlement, near the site used by the USAF during the Second World War and the Cold War, Bluie West 7. This community was abandoned, as was the other main mine, the coal town Qullissat (old spelling: Qutdligssat), which was in operation from around 1924 to 1972. After the Second World War, alongside the mines, economic development in Greenland shifted from hunting to commercial fishing, and the total population increased from 24,000 to 50,000, of which the Danish population grew by nearly 20 per cent (i.e. by about 10,000 people). In 1953 the colonial status of Greenland was abolished and the country was integrated with Denmark. During the 1960s demands were made for Home Rule, along the lines of the Faroe Islands, which had obtained it in 1949, and Iceland, which became independent of Denmark in 1944.

As in Canada, Greenland social services, and especially health programmes, were generally highly successful, especially in eliminating TB. But also as in Canada modernization resulted in the closure of settlements (bringing people off the land), a decline in wildlife harvesting and an increase in paid urban employment, all of it highly stressful and very destructive of culture and community. Between 1950 and 1970 the proportion of the Greenland population living in towns grew from 40 per cent to 70 per cent of the total.

The move for self-government was triggered by the closing of the Qullissat mine and the abandonment of the town in the early 1970s, a focus of popular anger; Home Rule came about in 1979. One political focus was on the way in which Denmark had taken Greenland into the EU (then EEC): Greenland itself had voted against joining Europe but had been ignored. Throughout the 1970s Danish colonials lost power to a group of southern-educated bilingual Greenlanders similar to those who came together to oppose HydroQuébec in Canada. Their parties achieved Home Rule in 1979, withdrawal from the EU in 1985 and the nationalization of the Royal Greenland Trading Department at the same time. Economic changes – the move from a hunting to a fishing and mining economy – were accompanied by a degree of enabling of political authority, lastly at municipal level, in 1973. But in the 1970s Danish-educated Moses Olsen and Knud Hertling were empowered by their metropolitan backgrounds to oppose the fractionating process, in which local Greenlandic authority entrenched in municipalities was not matched by new national institutions.

In contrast to the Canadian situation, where political groups were organized by region and ethnicity, along the lines of French Canada, in Greenland political parties emerged. Three important parties were set up at this time: Siumut ('Forward', 1977), Inuit Ataqatigiit ('Inuit Community', 1976) and Atassut ('Solidarity', 1977). Of these Siumut, socialist in outlook, led the Home Rule debate, won the first Home

Rule election and pursued the nationalization of significant institutions. This quickly led to the replacement in the 1980s of Danish office holders with Greenlandic ones, an enormously positive outcome. Enabled by the monolithic nature of the Danish colonial structure, power was transferred at the top. An important degree of Greenlandic self-government was confirmed by Greenland's withdrawal from the European Union in 1985. Denmark, however, retains control of monetary affairs, foreign and defence policy and justice and immigration.

In the 1960s the implementation of social policies and modernization required, Jens Dahl suggests, the creation of 'a group strong enough to implement and protect Danish interests and yet weak enough to be controlled. Today we know that the Danish authorities did not quite succeed, and in the 1970s the élite became considerably radicalized.'[32] Analysis by Dahl of Greenland development suggests that in a counter-intuitive way the decolonization of Greenland through the 1970s acted as a means for Denmark to maintain control of Greenland, which was overturned by Home Rule. This model, with explicit political authority, was the one to be followed in Canada in the creation of Nunavut, though with differing results.

The equivalent moment in Canadian corporate and economic history came in 1974, when Canada's Thomson family took control of the Hudson's Bay Company, funded by the ownership of Scottish Television – 'a licence to print money', as Roy Thomson put it – and gradually transferred the company, its historic archives and collections, to Canada in 1970–74. After that the historic Canadian company transferred or closed down the northern aspects of the business, which eventually became an American corporation. In the same way, in Greenland, the fishing and other aspects of the KGH were transferred out of the company, or became wholly owned subsidiaries of the Greenland Home Rule government.

Different Subarctic Communities

The important early success of Canadian corporation-led governance, in Nunavik in the 1970s and the Northwest Territories/Yukon in the 1980s can be simply compared to the situation without this degree of sovereignty on the other side of James Bay, where treaties prevailed.

At rivers on both coasts live Cree peoples, clustered for centuries on waterways around Hudson's Bay Company posts, both in Quebec on the east side and Ontario on the west. At the beginning of the twentieth century the two provinces were extended north, gifted by the crown with large chunks of Rupert's Land, then still under aboriginal ownership. Ontario was served with one of the crown treaties of the early twentieth century, Treaty 9. This was organized by Duncan Campbell Scott (1862–1947), a prominent poet and Indian administrator, who worked for fifty years to 'save' aboriginal people by sending them to residential schools and terminating their rights at a time of a maximum distress. One poem, 'The Half-Breed Girl' (1916), indicates his romantic contempt for his charges:

> She is free of the trap and the paddle,
> The portage and the trail,
> But something behind her savage life
> Shines like a fragile veil . . .
> She wakes in the stifling wigwam,
> Where the air is heavy and wild,
> She fears for something or nothing
> With the heart of a frightened child.
> She sees the stars turn slowly
> Past the tangle of the poles,
> Through the smoke of the dying embers,
> Like the eyes of dead souls.

Norm F. Wesley, a grandson of Patrick Stephen, a signatory of Treaty 9 in 1905, speaks of his grandfather sitting and listening to the poet-administrator Scott say how the king wanted everyone to be prosperous. He explains further, as sometime chairman of Muskegowuk Council, councillor and chief of Moose Cree First Nation, in the introduction to John Long's *Treaty 9* (2010), that the signatories had no real idea of what the treaty actually meant. In reality the Moose Cree received two small reserves, a few hundred square miles as opposed to the thousands of square miles for each Cree community on the other side of James Bay, and a $4-a-head annuity, as opposed to millions of dollars made available from 1974 by the James Bay agreement.

Scott is also the subject of a film, *Duncan Campbell Scott: The Poet and the Indians* (1995), in which the then national chief Ovide Mercredi (b. 1946) states that you cannot get rid of an Indian culture simply because the Department of Indian Affairs says so; Indian people will always have an identity and that 'when you oppress them that becomes the driving force to maintain that identity'.

Further to the south and east of the Moose Cree is the Attawapiskat Cree First Nation, James Bay, who have a similarly small land base and, with no aboriginally owned industry to provide jobs for the community and to drive economic change, exist in a continual state of crisis. The Attawapiskat joined Treaty 9 in 1930, one of the last of the First Nations to sign up to the historic treaty process. Numbering a few thousand people, the Cree's land base is 27 square kilometres (10 square miles), minute in comparison to the Cree lands held by First Nations on the other side of the Bay. Just as to the east there are huge economic opportunities, in Ontario the wealth is in the form of diamonds; the Canadian Shield is home to numerous Kimberlite pipes, volcanic pipes of the kind that produce most of the world's diamonds. Just over 50 miles west of Attawapiskat is De Beers' Victor Diamond Mine, in which $1 billion was invested in 2006–8 to produce more than 800,000 carats of diamonds in 2011. Aboriginal people are heavily involved in the mine. In 2012 it was said in a promotional release that De Beers was bringing sparkle to the economy of Ontario:

> The Victor workforce includes more than 180 Aboriginal employees, or more than 40% of total employees. In 2011, the company paid total wages and benefits of more than $142 million and about $55.5 million of that total was paid to Victor employees.[33]

In theory this highly successful mine should have enabled Attawapiskat Cree people to take control of their lives, but they do not own or possess any equity in the Victor Diamond Mine and are unlikely to in the future, even if further volcanic pipes in their territory are opened to mining. Instead the community suffers from a long series of disputes – about the chronically inadequate housing, about health issues (2011) – and in 2013 the chief, Teresa Spence, was investigated for inadequate paperwork to do with $100 million received in

2005–11, of which 400 of 500 transactions were found not to be properly documented. When housing supplied by De Beers burned in November 2013, and seventy people had to be evacuated, abusive comments were published in the *Globe and Mail*:

> Oh joy! Treaty 9 . . . I'm sick of it all! Now we are flying them to motels! It's time that the Band and its Chief and Council recognized their addiction to Victimhood and abandoned this failed experiment! As I recall, the Allied forces bombed Dresden and Frankfurt into a 12 foot high pile of rubble during WWII – with massive numbers of innocents losing their lives! Seems that this conquered population got it together – obvious to anyone who has visited these vibrant cities lately. Not a fair comparative [sic] . . . absolute nonsense in my view! Let the Chief and Council demonstrate some leadership in rebuilding.
>
> Geeez, like that has never happened before on a FN reserve! Well . . . off to work I go so my taxes can keep these 'special' interest groups sustainable.
>
> These people burned down their housing after less than two years. Where is their insurance policies . . . oh wait, I almost forgot. The hard working tax-payers are their insurance policy.[34]

With every new crisis, Cree or other, in Canada, aboriginal and non-aboriginal leaders and journalists speak eloquently of the issues: poverty, gender, violence and welfare dependency affecting Native people. Few solutions are proposed, when one neat, if not simple, solution is available. In all the provinces and territories more than 90 per cent of land belongs to federal, provincial or territorial governments. This crown land was, where there were treaties, of course ceded by aboriginal people, in return for minimal benefits. Further , even where there are treaties, these treaties were clearly unequal, unequal treaties being a concept employed in Asia to describe the nineteenth-century arrangements by which, for instance, the United Kingdom obtained title to what was, until 1997, the crown colony of Hong Kong. The return of lands to rural communities, while hardly a foolproof solution, would return significant economic benefits to the original owners of the land. The Nisga'a in British Columbia received title to a small percentage of their original hunting territory. Early similar return of lands to competent aboriginal authorities would permit leaders, in the medium and long term, to take control of micro-economic policies.

Underlying the question of land is a simple point. The issue of balancing Cree society seems straightforward but is actually more complex, in part because if you go to school you don't go out on the land, and even if you finish school there are seldom jobs, and if you finish college or university then the degree is likely to lead to a job away from the community. Thus 40 per cent of Attawapiskat Cree live off the reserve. The problem of subsistence versus education is simply expressed:

> Even *young* women don't know any more how to prepare food or how to smoke food. Or youth doesn't know any more how to cut geese . . . I think, although you do live in the community, but you only go to school . . . that contributes to losing interest in traditional life.[35]

The Fur Trade

The fur trade period, with the unbalanced reciprocity and monopoly provision of stores, is thus seen as, if not a golden age, then one of stability: 'We got money from the furs, but not so much. Only enough. We could buy tea, flour, sugar. But that's all. We lived off wild meat. We only lived off wild game like beaver, moose, rabbit, fish.'[36] The fur trade, one consequence of which is the distress of communities such as Attawapiskat, can be seen as the portal through which colonization occurred. Aboriginal–colonial relations were, for much of the first few centuries of contact, related to the fur trade and its cognates, the trade in deer and bison skin. All of these activities had profound effects on aboriginal culture, beliefs and economics and have given rise to numerous intensely argued debates about trade relations and their economic, cultural and political importance. Until the arrival of the French in Canada in the early sixteenth century and colonization by the French, British, Dutch and Swedes in the early seventeenth century, the fur trade had been dominated by Russia, a country – like Canada – created by the demand for prestige pelts in European lands where animals had been nearly exterminated. In Canada and

American colonies south to Virginia trade in beaver and other furs provided aboriginal people with a wealth of new technology and materials, creating often unrequited demand for metal tools, for imported Brazilian tobacco (known as 'Virginian') and for guns, cloth and tea. A succession of joint stock companies was founded in Europe to exploit these riches, affecting aboriginal life in every respect. In turn Europeans adopted aboriginal knowledge and created a hybrid society which traded with First Nations, from within colonies, for companies.

The changes to aboriginal society in the Subarctic were profound. First, the fur-bearing animals popular in Europe, such as beaver, were used and enjoyed by aboriginal people. They wore beaver robes, made of several skins sewn together, and these used robes were preferred by the traders, since the guard hairs had been worn away, leaving soft under-hair pelts, which were much prized for the making of the lustrous felted covering for hats, a sixteenth-century French invention taken up in Britain. But with the export of beaver aboriginal people needed to change trapping patterns and alter skin usage in clothing. Instead of concentrating on those animals, such as moose, deer and caribou (and other game such as fish and geese), that were primary food sources, hunters devoted ever more time and energy to trapping, that is, following animals which, unlike caribou, for example, might have a non-migratory life style. So a central question – perhaps the central question – about the fur trade is whether European-induced changes to subsistence patterns made aboriginal people more susceptible to hunger and starvation, already a regular occurrence in many hunter-gatherer societies. A second question revolves around the spiritual relationship of Native people to animals as non-human beings, and to the keepers of the game, those belief-system figures who protected and made available animals to those who behaved in an appropriate manner. The question is, with the switch from mostly food-based hunting to fur-based trapping, was the relationship between aboriginal people and their spiritual belief systems broken? If so, did this break mean that the linkage of respect and the need for restraint to ensure preservation of species disappeared? Did the fur trade thus create a new normative behaviour whereby successive areas of North America were denuded, as Europe had been in late medieval times, of fur-bearing animals?

A closely related discussion revolves around the issue of economic man, the imaginary figure who makes decisions motivated solely or primarily by material benefit. On the one hand, in business-based or capitalist societies, and especially in a system organized by trading companies, maximization of profit – buying furs cheaply from aboriginal people and selling them expensively in Europe – is the driving mantra. On the other hand, in tribal societies presentation and gift giving – the generalized offering of material goods, specifically the sharing of food – is normal behaviour, or so it is recorded. Did European traders abuse existing aboriginal systems of gift-giving and sharing for the economic benefit of distant entrepreneurs? Or did they to some extent adopt ideas of presentation, if only in the form of extending credit, to ensure their survival when hunting was bad? Or did the arrival of globalized fur trading alter patterns of behaviour so that aboriginal people moved away from sharing and giving to become more inclined to profit-making? The overall question is whether we can say that aboriginal people were not economic beings, and therefore unmotivated in this respect, perhaps because they did not specify the best in trade goods and did not use their host position to economic advantage. If we imply that aboriginal people were not interested in the best trade goods and maximum gain, are we suggesting that these imagined Natives were noble in their economic behaviour as in all else? In Eric Wolf's *People without History* (1982) aboriginal people involved in the fur trade are, on the other hand, placed in a Marxian narrative, alongside other colonial economic ventures, in silver and cotton, as contributors to the emergence of modern Europe.

From the beginning of contact, fur trading was the basis of relations with aboriginal people. The French explorer Jacques Cartier obtained furs in the 1530s, probably from the Mi'kmaq and from Iroquoians, as did Samuel de Champlain, founder of Quebec and Canada at the beginning of the seventeenth century. Joint stock companies were organized to exploit this commodity, for instance Champlain's Compagnie des Marchands de Rouen et de Saint-Malo of 1614. The Mayflower Pilgrims, founders of the Plymouth Colony of 1620–91, paid stockholders and bought supplies with furs sent to England. Almost immediately, with the extinction of the coastal beaver population, the trade moved inland, with intense competition between Indian peoples and between European rivals. One of the most successful early traders was William Pynchon (1590–1682) of Massachusetts Bay Colony, who founded the city of Springfield and exported thousands of skins from the Connecticut Valley, his success dependent on good, equitable relations with Indian people. The founding of the Hudson's Bay Company in 1670 occurred against a background of competition between Quebec and Boston, between the English and the French, as well as the Dutch in New York

One interesting feature in all of this was the taking-up of aboriginal ways of doing things, especially by the *coureurs de bois*, literally 'runners of the woods', young men encouraged by Champlain to learn aboriginal ways so as to be able to travel and trade, as near outlaws, way beyond the pale of French settlement in the St Lawrence Valley. One such was Jean Nicollet de Belleborne (*c*.1598–1642), who was sent to learn the aboriginal language and ways with the Algonkins up the Ottawa River and who travelled west beyond the Great Lakes into Wisconsin. As the fur trade became more successfully controlled by companies, in the late seventeenth century the dominant figure of the *voyageur* emerged. *Voyageurs* were travellers learned in aboriginal ways, but above all paddlers and *portageurs*, who carried fur bales and canoes between rapids and over watersheds and were celebrated for their fortitude, people who, like the *coureurs de bois*, made their homes and families in the aboriginal north.

One route into the fur-trading riches of the interior continent was up rivers such as the Hudson and the Connecticut, and especially the St Lawrence, and through the Great Lakes to the far west. Another, avoiding competition along the rivers, was to be over the top of the mainland, through Hudson Strait into Hudson Bay and then James Bay. It was two French Canadians, missionaries and *coureurs de bois*, Médard Chouart des Groseilliers (*c*.1618–*c*.1696) and his younger brother-in-law Pierre-Esprit Radisson (*c*.1640–1710), who in travelling together west of New France learned of the great sources of beaver to be found in the north. As a boy Radisson was captured and adopted by the New York Mohawk, during the time of Iroquois wars against the French and their Huron/Wendat allies. In the 1660s Groseilliers and Radisson, trading on their own account and in part illegally, continually changed sides between the French, British and Dutch, parleying extraordinary knowledge of aboriginal culture and landscape into support for court-sponsored trading voyages from London. These led in 1670 to the establishment of the most successful of all trading companies, the Hudson's Bay Company, with Prince Rupert (1619–82), Duke of Cumberland and cousin of Charles II, as governor (the vast drainage into Hudson Bay was for centuries designated Prince Rupert's Land). Designed to take over from the French, the Hudson's Bay Company quickly dominated the southern reaches of both Hudson and James Bays, with the setting up of a succession of posts or factories: York Factory (Manitoba, 1684), Moose Factory (Ontario, 1672), Fort Prince of Wales (Manitoba, 1717). In these factories, supplied annually from summer voyages, factors, often Scottish, would trade for furs brought in by outfitted expeditions and from Indian people. Running the forts and organizing the trade and underwriting were the home Indians, from the various Cree First Nations, the originally inhabitants of Quebec, Ontario and Manitoba round the bay. They would be responsible for supplying the post with food, for negotiating sales with the interior people who brought the furs to the coast in the spring and with outfitting expeditions under trading captains to obtain furs. Relationships began in the seventeenth and eighteenth century as equal, dependent on gift-giving and mutual interdependence, with Indians requiring trade goods and the Europeans fur and food, but changed as populations of fur-trading animals declined. In the late eighteenth century the Hudson's Bay Company set up further posts, for example Henley House, Ontario (1743/1775) and Oxford House, Manitoba (1798), eventually reaching Fort Yukon in what is now Alaska (1847). But the changing pattern away from hunting towards trapping tended to result in a scarcity of nearby game animals, and when the fur-bearing animals became scarce, the First Nations would become debt dependents of the trading post.

With the disappearance of game in coastal colonies in the seventeenth century the trade moved inland, up the Hudson River to Albany, up the St Lawrence to the Great Lakes, and then ever westwards and southwards, culminating in the destruction of the beaver in California (then part of Mexico) during the 1830s, the decade that saw the retirement of John Jacob Astor from fur trading in the United States because of the reductions in animal ranges and the replacement of beaver felt by silk in hats. At a meta-level the fur trade also provides a narrative to do with the founding of colonies and countries, an imperial struggle for continental power, especially in New York and Canada. The trade was highly competitive, and in the late nineteenth and early twentieth century it was its success in providing the best copper pots, axes and awls, tobacco, woollen goods and linen shirts that enabled the Hudson's Bay Company to flourish. This in turn enabled its conversion, around the period of Canadian confederation in 1867, from a trading company to a real estate company, whose former territories formed the new country and whose landholdings along the route of the forthcoming railways would fund expansion into retail stores in the south.

National Narratives

Underlying the twin and often opposed national narratives of Canada and the United States are two highly influential, disarmingly simple, reductionist ideas of nation creation: the 1893 frontier thesis of Frederick Jackson Turner (1861–1932) and the Laurentian or metropolitan thesis of Harold Innis (1894–1952); the latter trained as an economic historian and created the national narrative *The Fur Trade in Canada* (1930), which details the destruction of aboriginal peoples in this process. In contrast Turner suggested that it was the frontier, and the pioneer yeoman farmer, between 1783 and 1890 which created America, fostering a national character of individualism, frontier violence, rough justice and preacher Christianity. But this, of course, downplayed the relationship of land and the dispossessed aboriginal inhabitants, the race-conflicted development of slavery and share-cropping plantations and the finance-dominated business of metropolitan land speculation and denied the essential continuity between colonial and independent America. The Laurentian thesis revolves round the idea that Canada was created, in controlling eastern cities, by the development of primary industries around the exploitation of natural resources – cod and whales, fur, and then water power and mineral extraction. This too crudely reduces highly complex, long-term cultural realities and political history to simplistic phrases. All of the animal extractive industries, in both countries and in Greenland, brought about profound changes to aboriginal society and to the behavioural patterns of whalers and fur traders by encountered by the traders. So initiating the fur trade, determined to maximize profits, required lavish gift giving and non-capitalist behaviour. In unregulated areas this was combined with thievery, the provision of alcohol to facilitate the short-term benefit of immediate sales and monopoly practices. The fur trade sits with mining as the driving force for the colonization of the north, wrapped in the military imperatives of the Second World War and the Cold War, now given expression in the contribution made by Alaskan Native Corporations to the War on Terror. And the study of the fur trade, followed by Innis' studies of communications, contributed to another contemporary trope, that of the central role and importance of communication itself. This was expressed in Marshall McLuhan's phrase 'the medium is the message', from his *Understanding Media* (1964). Innis wrote about the balance of oral and written communication, in and beyond the fur trade, as necessary throughout culture and was McLuhan's teacher, no doubt grounding him in the essence of the oral.

10

The Pacific Northwest Coast

An archaeologist recording seventeenth- or eighteenth-century finds, including two yew paddles pointed for fighting, at Ozette, WA, a unique wet site.

Whale House, Klukwan, Alaska, created by Xetsuwu, *c.*1800, a photograph by Winter and Pond ('Interior of Chief Klart-Reech's house', 1895).

Singing 'God Save the King', Nanaimo Indian School, 1943.

Edenshaw's drawing of Wasgo, used by Boas as the primary image to define primitive art worldwide, from the 1920s. While that term is no longer used, Boas' summary of art in this way led to the re-evaluation of what had previously been termed 'decorative art'.

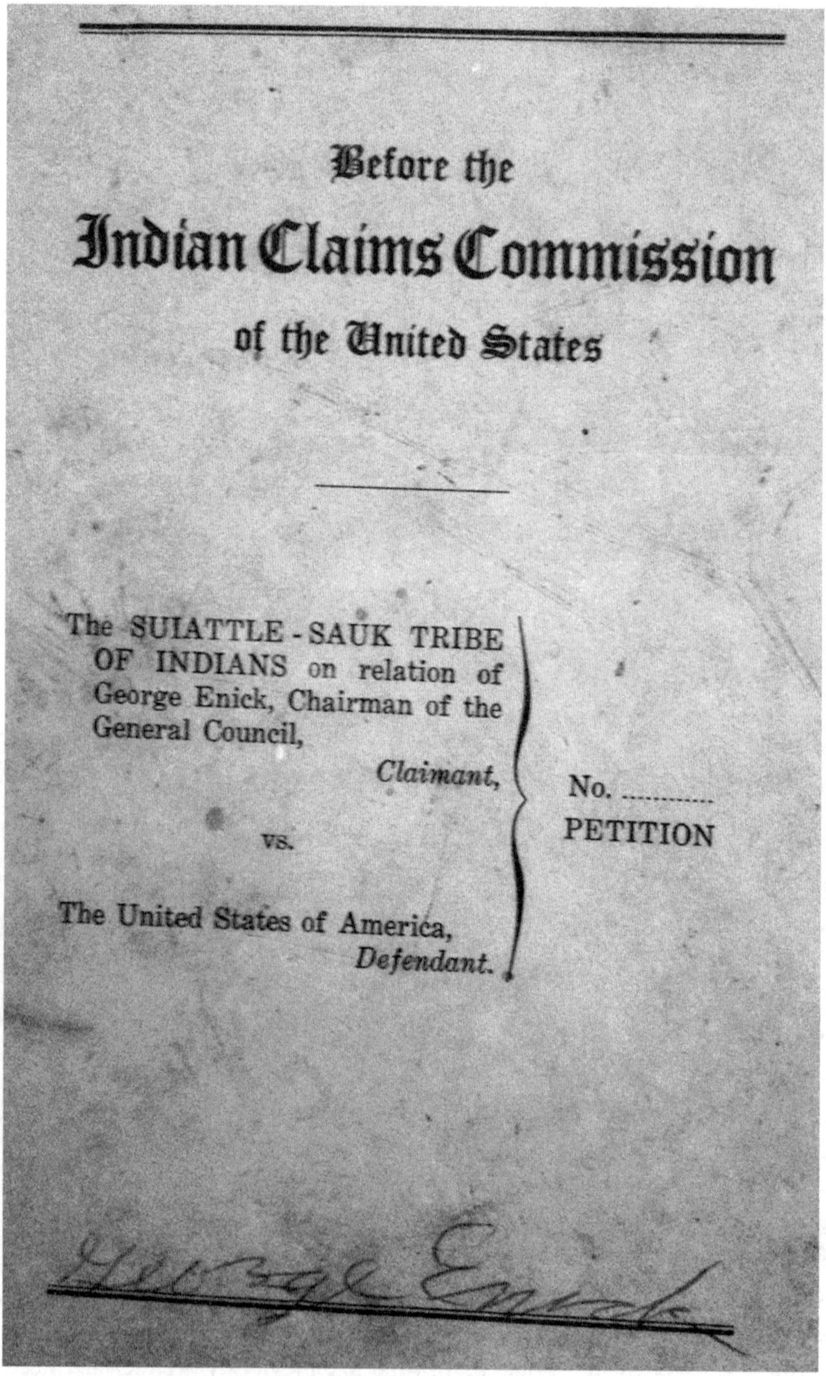

Before the

Indian Claims Commission

of the United States

The SUIATTLE - SAUK TRIBE
OF INDIANS on relation of
George Enick, Chairman of the
General Council,

            Claimant,

        vs.

The United States of America,
        Defendant.

No. ....

PETITION

George Enick

On reservation from 1855, the Sauk-Suiattle Nation in Washington State received federal recognition only in 1855. This 1951 petition, which failed, is signed by the then chief George Enick.

An Edward Curtis photograph of the Hamatsa, a principal performer in the Kwakwaka'wakw winter ceremonies.

Mungo Martin (1879–1962), Kwakwaka'wakw leader and teacher of many mid-century artists, presenting his centenary pole to Queen Elizabeth the Queen Mother, 1958.

Jenny Thlunaut (1892–1986), Tlingit elder who in the late twentieth century kept alive the tradition of creating twined robes.

Rosita Worl, Photographed by Hulleah J. Tsinhnahijinnie.

George Hunt (1854–1933), Kwakwaka'wakw and Anglo Tlingit ethnographer, 1890s.

Bill Reid (1920–98), the Haida artist who embedded aboriginal art in Canadian national identity.

Makah whaling, a highly ritualized activity conducted by privileged leaders, *c*.1910.

Salmon bake, Neah Bay, 1950s. Seven salmon species provided a staple food until the destruction of stocks in the late twentieth century.

Activist poster of salmon and halibut, by Kik-Ke-In, (b. 1948) (Hupacasath) and Nuu-Chah-Nulth, 1980s.

Cover of the 1979 Makah summer celebration programme, canoe racing being one of the traditional activities continuing through the twentieth century.

Shawn Atleo (b. 1968), Nuu-Chah-Nulth national chief 2009–14, here at Ahousaht, 2009.

Byron Mallott, Tlingit politician (b. 1943) appointed lieutenant governor of Alaska 2014, making his inaugural speech.

Jody Wilson Raybould (b. 1971), Kwakwaka'wakw politician appointed minister of justice, Ottawa, 2015.

10

The Pacific Northwest Coast

Raven

Of all the mythic characters on the coast, the best enjoyed is Raven, Yéil in the Tlingit language, borrowed into Haida and often appearing in each language with variants. Known not only in the Pacific Northwest but westwards into Alaska and Siberia, he is man and bird, a person who is greedy and dumb, dupe and creator, thief and trickster, the one who is part buffoon, part leader, the cackling, hopping fool, always doing and in trouble, and always there, eating and messing things up. As a carrion feeder, Raven actually lives with and around people, is uniquely social in calling birds to eat and indeed in attracting predators such as wolves to open up carcasses. Like chiefs, Raven communicates. Beyond the biological details of the bird lies copious oral history. Most importantly, Raven put the sun in the sky. In a prevalent version of the myth he turned himself into a pine needle and was swallowed by the daughter of the chief who has the sun hanging up in his house. The girl becomes pregnant, Raven is born and begs to play with the sun and when indulged seizes the orb and flies into the sky with it, where, of course, he drops it to provide daylight. In much of the crest art Raven is shown with a berry-sized sun in his beak. Raven even created women for men to marry in a Yakutat story, and then decided to create a brotherhood of all creatures, assigning the major crest animals to one side or another, but Wolf would not take part in this scheme, and so Raven doomed wolf to wander for ever, howling for help.[1]

Salmon and Complexity

The peoples of the Northwest Coast constitute the most complex society of hunter-gatherers anywhere. Into the middle of the nineteenth century their society included nobles, commoners and slaves; they numbered a mere 150,000 people at contact with Europeans and Americans in the late eighteenth century and do so again now. The 1,400 mile coast of the Pacific northwest, from northern California to southeast Alaska, where they live, defines much of what Native America is: a highly contested forest riparian environment, once wealthy beyond belief in timber, fish and mammals, now massively depleted and undermined. As a result, it is often hard to find cedar from which to carve the usually termed 'totem' poles, and the beams of big houses may be taken instead from ancient Douglas fir. Salmon runs, the main food source, have been devastated by overfishing, by damming and by the introduction of the farmed Atlantic species. And this environmental degradation occurred long after epidemics and invasion decimated aboriginal peoples from the first European – Spanish and British – contact in the 1770s.

Salmon may have, according to Kenneth Ames, provided the trigger for the development of a complex society: salmon runs last a few days and require immediate cohorts of willing fishermen, as well as (women) workers to dry or smoke the fish as it comes out of the water. Salmon cannot, of course, be stored fresh and require immediate filleting and preserving. The organization of this female force thousands of years ago may have led to the origination of hierarchy and nobility. Whereas in much of North America, except in the southeast, there were no nobles among the noble but egalitarian savages, on the Northwest Coast aboriginal societies were highly stratified. But in the view of the first white people these 'savages' were not noble; instead they were traders, travelling up and down the coast in huge canoes and penetrating deep upstream into the mountains, trading fish oil or grease and currency, keeping and killing slaves and, worse in the white view, destroying wealth in feasts and performing symbolic cannibalism.

Antiquity

Archaeologically speaking, the ancient Pacific Northwest Coast is notable for vast shell middens, as at Namu and Marpole, centres of habitation for millennia, for the extraordinary survivals of wet sites, where wood and organic materials have been well preserved, as at Ozette and Boardwalk, and for the discovery of burials or skeletal material in near-pristine condition. One example is the frozen figure from Tutchone country in the British Columbian Rockies. The other, better-known and much earlier, figure is that of 'Kennewick Man', encountered by chance on the shore of the Columbia River and subject to a long series of court cases as to the acceptability of research and reburial. At the centre of this was the question of whether this man, 'the Ancient One', was ancestral to the contemporary Native population of Washington and Oregon. On the one hand, it is clear that he was a Native American – whatever that meant thousands of years ago – yet importantly the court accepted that he was not directly ancestral to contemporary Native Americans.

In contrast to Ozette, many more purely midden sites, again often thousands of years old, are located in what are now urban areas, near rivers with their salmon runs, and subject to occupation, building and disputed ownership. One of the most important, in the city of Vancouver, British Columbia, is the Marpole Midden, named after an early twentieth-century Canadian Pacific Railway engineer. It is situated, like much of the rest of Vancouver, on lands unceded to the crown, the traditional territory of the Musqueam. Noted first in the late nineteenth century, the site was excavated by local and American archaeologists into the early twentieth century, and finds, often of skeletal materials, were uncovered over a wide area. This and similar sites may be up to 4 metres deep, with good drainage, the lime of the shells neutralizing the acid of the forest environment, enabling bones to be preserved.[2] Dating back 4,000 years and covering more than 4 acres to an average depth of more than 3 feet, the ancient village at Marpole midden was declared a Canadian national historic site in 1933. But development continued, and in 2011–12 the Musqueam First Nation fought a successful battle against a new condominium project. From an artefact point of view, the Marpole phases of development are exceptional and exciting because they are centred on heavy timbered structures and subsistence use of shellfish and salmon from the Fraser River. With these features comes an early phase of Northwest Coast art: the Marpole-phase stone bowls, a series of many dozens of pecked and polished figurative dishes. As symbols of ancient creativity, they sit uneasily with the early theory of one of the main archaeologists, Charles Hill-Tout, about the initial population of the area by a different race preceding the ancestors of the Musqueam. Yet the effect of these discoveries, and the dispossession of the First Nation by the growing city, is in the process of reversal. That reflects the archaeological discoveries, the campaign against further destruction and the buyback of the Fraser Arms Hotel in 1991 by Musqueam First Nation to avoid redevelopment and disturbance of the site, all indicating the way that persistent advocacy may be effective in re-establishing aboriginal authority. The stone dishes, featuring seated figures holding a bowl, may relate to puberty ceremonies and indicate an early origin of the formalized art style and the ancient status of women in what may have been a matrilineal society. A site of similar age in northern British Columbia, the Boardwalk site in Prince Rupert, has in contrast been excavated more recently, and ceremonial weapons have been uncovered which relate to status-differentiated ritualized warfare thousands of years old.

Destruction

The Dalles, from the Canadian French word *dalle*, meaning 'paving stone' or 'drain', is a narrow canyon far inland on the Columbia River where Native people came together to fish salmon for nearly 10,000 years. From the beginning of the twentieth century hobbyist relic hunters have retrieved tens of thousands of stone articles from the enormous salmon middens stretching 25 miles along the river. One such collector was Charles Beckman, 'Arrowhead Charlie', who between 1915 and his death in 1947 may have removed 150,000 arrowheads, making his living by collecting artefacts along the Columbia and selling them to collectors in Portland and New York. But it was not just arrowheads and stone beads, but bowls and carvings and petroglyphs that were recovered and removed. In the first half of the twentieth century national archaeological resources in the USA were limited, with only one Ph.D. programme at the University of California at Berkeley. The Bureau of American Ethnology and the Archaeological Institute of America were both founded in 1879, but the periodical *American Antiquity* began only in 1936, and the Society of American Archaeology was founded only in 1934. Removal of artefacts from federal lands was made illegal in 1906, but this was seldom enforced. Further, during the 1940s, hydroelectrification of the Columbia began, principally for war work and the building of the atomic bomb. This continued after the war with the damming of the Columbia at The Dalles; the Indians received more than $24 million for the loss of their fishing rights, in no sense a recompense for the cultural damage. Much important archaeology was carried out, principally with the Smithsonian's River Basin Survey from 1945, financed by $200,000 of federal funding designed to record all river basins about to be destroyed. The Wakemap Mound, 30 x 20 yards in expanse and more than 20 feet deep, was excavated competitively by archaeologists and relic hunters, who used terms like 'gem point', 'paint pot' and 'picture rock' for their finds and employed a bulldozer with a 13 foot blade to help them in their endeavours. A Yakima woman, Martha Skanawa, protested in the 1950s to a Seattle archaeologist in these terms: 'You make the old woman mad, you make her angry, you kill old woman. When you go away?'[3]

The Ancients

The bones of 'Kennewick Man', the 'Ancient One', were recovered on land administered by the US Corps of Engineers. An almost complete skeleton was gathered together in 1996. It was then subject to a protracted legal case as to whether the skeletal material was Native American, and so subject to NAGPRA 1990, and should be returned to the local Umatilla people for reburial. Eventually, in 2004, a court decreed that the Army Engineers were the rightful owners of the skeleton and that Native Americans could not show any kinship. In the meantime a number of bio-anthropologists had examined the skeletal material and concluded that it was Caucasoid, i.e. white Old World, or

Polynesian and Ainu. In 2012 the most prominent of the anthropologists, Douglas Owsley (who was involved in forensic investigation, for instance, in examination of 9/11 remains and the cadavers from the Waco siege of 1993), announced that isotope analysis indicated that the man had probably not drunk water from the Columbia River and had lived off marine mammals. His age, depending on various scientific evidence, was around 9–10,000 years, and the lanceolate point found in his pelvis was of the type known as a Cascade Point, that is, a lance head known to have been used in the Pacific northwest around that time.

It is useful to compare the recent history of Kennewick Man with that of Kwäday Dän Ts'ìnch, or 'Long Ago Person Found', so named by the local Tutchone, in northern British Columbia, a body that emerged out of an eroding glacier on the border with the Yukon Territory. While not as significant as Kennewick Man for the peopling of the Americas, this scattered body had been completely preserved in the ice with soft tissue and was carbon-dated to the recent Little Ice Age, 500 years ago. After sampling and research, the remains of this teenage trader up from the coast, wearing a gopher and squirrel cloak, were disposed of in a traditional manner. So, without legal battles, the heroic framing of the contestants and polarization of the issues, the Canadian route to research is significantly different from the American. His likely food was saline but probably included venison and vegetable remains. His DNA related him to local people – the descent group for mtDNA being haplogroup A, found particularly among Inuit, Haida, Nuxalk and other Subarctic peoples.[4]

Both finds indicate how very porous the Pacific Northwest Coast is and provide boundaries to one of Alfred Kroeber's early twentieth-century culture areas. They show how the ideal type of a maritime environment, with a long, enduring faith in fishing culture, merges and overlaps with rather different peoples far into the mountain and plateau interior.

Long Ago Person Found ate marine and forest creatures, it is thought, and would have deployed a set of concrete beliefs connected to his subsistence activities. These beliefs are based on an underwater world inhabited by personifications of the food species, spirit species and the crest species – animals to live with and animals to live by. Crest figures and other imaginary beasts are best seen as polymorphic creations, representatives of situation-specific ideas, with varying attributes depending on the house or line, family or feast. Bird and terrestrial species furnish other species, such as deer, for consumption, for thinking with and for creating crests. At the basis of all of this are the salmonid species, the numerous salmon but also trout species, which until recently provided unlimited food for riverine and coastal peoples, such a rich resource that hierarchical, proto-class-based societies were able to develop.

A proviso to the unlimited intake of salmon is the risk of vitamin D intoxication in children; this has sometimes caused death. Lazenby and McCormack have suggested, by looking at carbon isotopes, that this was mitigated by the replacement of a fish diet in childhood with one of land food: mammals and vegetable.[5] So although ill health through overeating is assumed to be a modern problem associated with the consumption of too many saturated fats, sugars and acids, here in the ancient past, several thousand years ago, Native North Americans developed, socially and culturally, behaviour patterns to reduce the over-consumption of fish by children. In adulthood vitamin D toxicity decreases, and so salmon may serve as the staple for adults.

Property

The area of the Pacific Northwest is defined by the series of huge, fish-rich watercourses flowing from the Rockies, extending from Alaska as far south as the Klamath, Trinity and Eel Rivers in northern California. What is distinctive about the Pacific northwest is the ownership by individuals of resources; that is, high-status chiefs owned beaches, fish weirs and village sites and passed these important properties on to descendants, their heirs and relatives, designated in a variety of very different social circumstances. So status, authority and ownership of resources in peoples such as the Hupa, Karuk and Yurok in California were articulated in proto-class-based terms. From a historical point of view, very different political systems have been imposed on coastal peoples at different times: federal authorities in Alaska, British Columbia and the American West Coast states devised completely different treaty, and especially what might best be called 'non-treaty', systems for the control of aboriginal peoples. In British Columbia, apart from the Douglas Treaties of the 1850s, on Vancouver Island, promulgated before unification with British Columbia in 1858, there were virtually no treaties, and First Nations were administered by the Indian Act, an apparatus imposed from thousands of miles away, including in 1927 the provision that it was illegal to fundraise to make a claim to land ownership. This lasted until 1982, with the repatriation of the constitution and the development of case law around the constitutional place of aboriginal people in Canada.

Colonizations

In the United States what had been Spanish California does not really extend as far as the Native communities along the Klamath River, but American behaviour in California in the second half of the nineteenth century was extreme, emphasizing 'labour and lust', slavery and sex, in relations with Indian people.[6] In Washington Territory Governor Isaac Stephens (1818–62) imposed punitive treaties on all Native peoples in the 1850s, grouping them together and defining reservations but guaranteeing fishing rights. In Russian/American Alaska, in contrast, little accommodation was made for Tlingit ownership of land, and the Tlingit population declined substantially, as elsewhere, through disease. Much of this society and material culture survived into the American period, and only then did significant conversion to the Russian Orthodox church occur, as a protest against Americanization. The Russians were unable to effectively subjugate the unruly Tlingit, who were rich both from their own resources and from their abilities as traders, which enabled them to circumvent the Russian-American Company (1799–1867) and to trade goods such as molasses, tobacco and blankets into the interior. In a sense treaty-making became an issue only with the American purchase of Alaska in 1867, to the fury of Indian people, who had never ceded land; but by then in the US the making of Indian nations was about to end. The process was concluded by Dawes in 1871, and Tlingit fisheries were never protected from commercial canneries.

The Canadian view is that occupation of the country occurred with little violence. Yet coastal British Columbia was pacified by the

Royal Navy. As early as 1864, five Tsilhqot'in (Chilcotin) were charged after a violent protest to stop road building.

Candlefish

The subsistence activity that intersects with, and in a sense proves the rule about, ownership of resources, is that of the fishing of eulachon, a small, anadromous fish that inhabits a limited number of rivers, which is prized for its high oil content. As indicated by its nineteenth-century name of 'candlefish', it is suitable for drying and burning to provide light. In a couple of important areas, in Kwakwaka'wakw and Nisga'a territory, people would congregate in their thousands, from great distances, and collectively participate in fishing those few rivers with major runs. While some fish might be eaten fresh, the great trade was in oil. Vast numbers of fish would be caught in nets, not for drying and use as candles, but to be deliberately matured, i.e. rotted by burial, for selling and trading over long distances, for eating and ceremonial use. If you look at the Kiusta bowl collected by fur trader George Dixon in the 1780s, the first bowl known to have been removed from the coast, it is greasy and dirty, in one sense, but rich and glistening with power and meaning, in another. It might, of course, have been boiled up, a technique used by dealers for cleaning feast dishes in the twentieth century to rid them of supposed dirt. While the grease could be sea mammal, it is more likely to be eulachon, because that was what was favoured and traded to Haida Gwaii for high-status use at potlatches, on the islands where there were no eulachon. Tests one day will tell.

One of the sites for eulachon gathering is on the Nass River, where in late spring Tsimshians and Haidas and Tlingits would come together. After the fish had ripened in pits for ten to twenty days they would be boiled, the oil skimmed off, and the fish residue pressed in rough meshed baskets for further extraction. Apart from the Nass River, the Skeena, Fraser, Klinaklini and others had eulachon runs. That on the Klinaklini in Kwakwaka'wakw territory supported a fish camp of several thousand people at Dzawadi (Eulachon Place), where seine nets replaced the traditional ones, and red cedar cooking tanks and 45 gallon oak barrels were used. The oil would be sold on, west to

Vancouver Island and north to the Tlingit and Haida.[7] In more traditional times the oil was used in grease feasts, when large quantities
would be consumed or destroyed (burned), and the trade routes were
known as 'grease trails'.

Raven was seen by some peoples as responsible for creating the
eulachon, in one story by jumping up and down on a gull's stomach
and disgorging an ancestor fish back into the river. But it was more
than that. As William Benyon (1888–1958), a Tsimshian and Nisga'a
chief, put it in the early twentieth century:

> It was the first fish caught and was very often styled the starvation
> fish, as it came just when the people were on the verge of starvation
> before the appearance of salmon and always in great quantities and
> always easy to get.[8]

The participation of disparate groups was possible because it was
the right to fish that was owned, because of cross-cutting marriage
ties between high-status families and because the resources were so
large that exploitation was better effected in this way – even though
on other occasions raiding and war might characterize relations. This
type of focal point existed elsewhere, at The Dalles on the Columbia
River, but also in other seasonal subsistence and trade gatherings, on
the Plains and at Bering Strait, for instance.

Copper and Dentalium

While eulachon grease is a principal form of wealth, other sources of
wealth abound and are expressed in art and performance today. One
such material is copper. The colour of salmon, it symbolically merged
wealth and food and was used as a precious metal inlay and in the
creation of large torso-shaped shields. These 'Coppers', *tina* in Tlingit,
adorned with crests and with the names of their owners, were given
away, on the northern part of the coast, and destroyed publicly as an
expression of position, wealth and conspicuous consumption.

On the southern Northwest Coast small tusk-like dentalium shells
were important as wealth, as a near currency, a unit of exchange,
obtained for instance by the Nuu-chah-nulth with a besom-like brush
thrust into the sea bed on the end of a pole. Tom Saayaachapis, the

Nuu-chah-nulth elder and historian, whose understanding of *tupaati* or rights was recorded in such detail in the early twentieth century, talked of a pre-potlatch taunt spoken to his people. He said that visiting girls would have nothing round their necks when they came; no dentalium equals no jewellery, as it were, for the party and no status for the unadorned females and their male relatives. At these potlatches, much was to do with the crest animals, animals encountered in a mythic world, from whom devolved the right to use that animal as a symbol, to be danced, as often, in a masked performance during the winter season.

Secret Societies

On the southern Northwest Coast, in British Columbia and Washington among Salishan- and Wakashan-speaking peoples, two or three ritual societies, brotherhoods, with dance complexes, lie at the centre of ceremonial life. They are available for high-status individuals, who own rights to membership and performance, which involve performed spirit possession of young male novitiates. The Nuu-chah-nulth wolf ritual the Klukwana, obsolescent by the mid-twentieth century, was one in which masks were worn, but by the owners of the privilege, rather than by the participant initiates. The principal novice would be captured by wolf-like people, taken away and taught songs and dances and returned. Everyone might be included except for the youngest, and people could be inducted more than once. As with other ceremonials, many other performances could be included, for example, the wild-man-of-the-woods, piercing performances and the eating of dogs. Among the Coast Salish peoples the Sxwaywey dance survived much better and remains generally a secluded, private affair.

But best known of these ceremonial complexes is the Kwakwaka'wakw Hamatsa society. As originally told, the young man would seem to disappear even for years to the house of Baxbaxwalanuksiwe, the cannibal spirit, before returning and being pacified in a series of dances by his family. His behaviour would be violent, aggressive and frankly cannibalistic, though probably in a violent play form rather than actual eating, although William Fraser Tolmie (1812–86), the Glaswegian surgeon who worked for the Hudson's

Bay Company in the middle of the nineteenth century, recorded dressing bites, providing grist for the pathologization of the potlatch as cannibal feasts. After four days of dancing and the gifting of other dance privileges, the Hamatsa would reappear dressed in hemlock and gradually be calmed down in a series of successive dances. The visual climax of the ceremony was both in the squatting dance of the bird monster, including Huxhuhw, the bird which cracks open skulls to consume the brain, and in the display of masks. These are important features of the photographer and filmmaker Edward Curtis' (1868–1952) 1914 film *In the Land of the Head Hunters*, an otherwise conventional love story. Interestingly and most importantly the film was shot while potlatching or feasting was banned and illegal, as it had been since the 1884 Indian Act, and was until 1951, when the banning provision was omitted.

Return of Regalia

If cultural continuity was provided for the Makah with the discovery of the buried houses of Ozette and their transformation into a cultural centre combined with the resumption of whaling, and for the Tlingit with the provisions of ANCSA and the creation of the Sealaska corporation, for the Kwakwaka'wakw commumity in the seemingly barren years of the mid-twentieth-century continuity lay in the potlatch, the roll of Kwakwaka'wakw carvers in maintaining their skills – for instance in the pole for the Queen at Virginia Water created for the centenary of British Columbia – and transferring them to other First Nations artists. But cultural survivance also came in the successful campaign for the return of the potlatch regalia seized in 1921 from the family of Chief Dan Cranmer. While potlatching was banned as uncivilized, counter-capitalistic and destructive, very rarely were prosecutions mounted by the police, apart from this singular moment by the zealous agent William Halliday, who confiscated regalia, which was eventually sold to and deposited in museums in the east, with some of it ending up in Europe. More than twenty of the participants received jail sentences. Much of the campaign for return was led by Gloria Cranmer Webster (b. 1931), the first aboriginal graduate from UBC, a great-granddaughter of George Hunt, Boas' research partner, and daughter of the host of the 1921 potlatch, Dan Cranmer. These are displayed at U'mista, the cultural centre opened in 1980. Other materials were returned to the Cape Mudge Museum and, opened a year earlier, the Nuyumbalees Cultural Centre. These precarious institutions require huge fortitude to survive, in one sense existing financially on the margins of the museum world and in another, overarching, sense leading through best cultural practice. They demonstrate how regalia should be seen, used and consumed and how the reality of First Nations art lies in integrated performed heritage, primarily within the community, but also for outsiders.

Whaling

Whaling occupied an important place in the Native world view and subsistence, and today sits in a culturally significant space that is rather different to that of the cultural centre. It was particularly significant among the Nuu-chah-nulth and Makah, the Wakashan-speaking peoples of Vancouver Island and Washington State. The killer whale provides a crest, in many places, and baleen whales the food. Most whales taken and consumed were drift whales, whales wounded or beached for one reason or another – now a regular media feature building on the narrative of uncontrolled environment degradation. These two peoples, however, also hunted whales, and to a very limited extent the hunt has been resumed, in highly controversial circumstances. Importantly, whaling is a high-status activity, a right owned by successive chiefs and passed down through the male line.

The technique involved a toggling harpoon, made with two elk antler valves or barbs and a super-sharp blade made of the giant California mussel, obtained locally. The harpoon shaft, around 12 feet long, would be thrust into a vulnerable part of the whale, such as the pit under the flipper. A succession of graduated floats (inflated sea mammal skins) would be used to slow the whale down, and most whales were wounded and left to die slowly, so that they could be beached.

The blubber was all-important for ritual use, health and wealth. Ritually speaking, the hunter was helped by Haietlik or Lightning Serpents engraved on the elk antler valves. Among the Makah the oil potlatch was the highest-status ceremony: only meat would be eaten, and the host might act the part of the captured whale being hauled into the ceremony by his daughters and granddaughters. A whale song recorded by Wilson Parker at the beginning of the twentieth century goes: 'I have come to see how your house is. Is it prepared for large crowds?' – that is, do people respect you by coming to the potlatch, and will I the whale be properly respected by the large potlatch attendance, if I the singer and the whale allow myself to be killed? Whales, like all animals, are persons.

There are various theories of when the whaling technology evolved. One possibility is that it relates to Inupiat and the Eskimoan whaling complex of northwest Alaska, but the harpoons are different and seem to be large versions of the local harpoons used in obtaining salmon. While from modified bones it is clear that whales have been used for thousands of years, the archaeological evidence from Vancouver Island, and from Ozette and the historic period, suggests that whaling may have originated independently on the Northwest Coast, that in a sense hunting technology was still evolving and developing in a parallel, independent manner in the last thousand years.[9] What is also important to emphasize is the need for ritual and purity in order to be a successful whaler, to be cleaned by freshwater bathing and scrubbing with hemlock greenery, and to celebrate the whale after the hunt. These are all as significant as knowing that the right time to thrust in the harpoon was when the whale was just submerging so that it would turn away rather than upset the canoe.[10]

Ozette

Much of the best evidence for whaling comes from Ozette, the Makah village on the coast of Washington State, occupied until the early twentieth century. Several centuries before, in approximately AD 1400–1600, a clay mud slide occurred, covering and preserving four or five houses in a wet, oxygen-free environment suitable for preserving wood and other organic materials – particularly basketry and bark artefacts. Between 1970 and 1981 excavations took place, revealing the most important wet site in North America, where some 55,000 artefacts were recovered by the University of Washington archaeologist Richard Daugherty (1922–2014) under the aegis of the Makah. While ancestral remains were reinterred, the finds provided a unique insight into pre-contact Northwest Coast life. Most of the objects are utilitarian and to do with buildings, carvings, mats and containers. But a small percentage reveal the complexity of both art and material culture in the seventeenth or eighteenth centuries. Ozette is a shell midden site, with 2,000 years of occupation, with only a small part representing the proto-historic occupation and wet site. What is particularly important is the association of objects with specific activities – such as whaling kit, seal hunting gear and the equipment required for slate-grinding, knife-making and textile-weaving. Interestingly, while no masks were recovered, a number of ceremonial objects were found, including most spectacularly a carved dorsal whale sculpture used in ceremonies, probably celebrating rather than initiating hunting, and kerfed (part cut to enable bending after steaming) and bent wood boxes, as well as a large screen with a Thunderbird. While there are other public museums owned and run by nations on the Northwest Coast, the Ozette cultural centre particularly combines rich pre-contact and contact materials.

Whale Ban

The Makah resumed whaling in 1999 after grey whales had been removed from the endangered species list. The right to hunt was asserted under the (Stevens) Treaty of Neah Bay in 1855, and a single whale was killed, amid much controversy and fury from the environmental movement, relating largely to the issue of the necessity or not of whale hunting, the absence or not of any spirituality involved in the process and the cruelty that undoubtedly occurred in the slow death of the beast. But lingering deaths were historically also a feature of whaling on the coast, wounded whales dying slowly and turning into drift whales washed up on beaches to be claimed by the chiefly owner of the shore. The 1999 whale hunt was repeated in 2007 by the same whaling captain, Wayne Johnson, in even more controversial circumstances. This issue, with the involvement of international whaling politics, especially concerning Japan, opposing accusations of cruelty and racism and eventual prison sentencing, is culturally messy, unpredictable and, in polarizing issues of culture, a moral sump. Most recently governmental agencies have sought to classify, in a hyper-scientific manner, a small group of localized grey whales as a sub-species, separate from the main population of 20,000 grey whales, and so deserving of a permanent whaling moratorium. Science may sometimes in this way act to isolate and disenfranchise Native peoples, here the right of the Makah to hunt whales. As one blogger put it in 2012:

> Its been a whitey and Govt issue since 1492. And yeah THAT part of it has always been about greed. The Makah have every right to hunt whales, including legal rights granted by treaty. Theirs is not some giant factory fleet, destroying everything in its path. Rather, they are a small, unique tribal band and whaling is a defining religious, and cultural activity. The decision to whale or not is theirs to make – not ours, or Greenpeace, or the government.[11]

Northwest Coast Art

The most singular aspect of the Pacific northwest is that of Northwest Coast art, from the core area of coastal British Columbia and the adjacent US. This is because of the antiquity of the decorated objects – stone clubs and bowls, antler combs and other materials – the extraordinary formal qualities of the art. But the art is also powerful because of the place given to (primitive) art in the mid twentieth century, an idea formalized by Boas in his *Primitive Art* (1927), using Northwest Coast material as the central case study, and by the concept of totemism – now in general use. But it is also important because of its success in the imagination, the sheer quantity of materials surviving and the iconic force of animal crest representation. It is important to emphasize again that, for First Nations, in some important respects, the formal qualities of the art, as today practised by aboriginal artists, are largely an irrelevance. Artists carve and design, but in a sense that is not what matters. Whether it is the complexity of design, the excellence of the lines, of the finish, the qualities of the work as being, say, more Haida than Tlingit or the appearance of the crest being more like one sort of mammal or another, none of these things may matter in a cultural sense. Instead what counts is the contextualized oral nature of the physical artworks: the stories, the social position, the networks and the titles that lie behind the masquerade, performance and commemoration, and indeed the big house architecture. These intangible characteristics possess importance rather than the decontextualized mask or rattle, so often in a museum or with flattened meaning adorning a home. In a way the relationship between ability as a carver and the oral history is like that of a hunter who must have hunting skills, but who must also and most importantly possess a relationship with the animal person. And Northwest Coast art, of course, imposes a code, a visual system, through which to impose and understand status and tradition.

From the eighteenth century onwards outsiders commented on and appreciated carved art, performance and oral history. They listened to and observed speeches and dances, marvelled at house fronts and the quality of the art and material culture. From the 1880s onwards concerted professional attempts were made, from Germany and then the United States, to collect Northwest Coast material culture, an effort celebrated in Douglas Cole's 1985 book *Captive Heritage*. Central to this is the career and achievements of the German American anthropologist Franz Boas (1858–1942), whose most important fieldwork took place in Canada, and especially among the coastal peoples of British Columbia. The mainstay of American anthropology was originally a scientist, who brought together in his work two streams of German thought: Kantian rationalism and Herder's ideas of human creativity, answering Wilhelm von Humboldt's eighteenth-century demand for a synthetic anthropology that examines the complete cultural context. Boas conducted his first fieldwork among the Inuit and then in the 1880s became interested in the Northwest Coast following a visit of a troupe of Nuxalk from British Columbia to Berlin for the spectacle of Hamburg showman Carl Hagenbeck. In the 1890s Boas began fieldwork among the Kwakwaka'wakw and organized a performance exhibition at the 1893 Chicago World's Fair. Boas' most important fieldwork took place in the Jessup North Pacific Expedition of 1897–1902, of which he was in charge of research for the American Museum of Natural History. His research in British Columbia aboriginal communities enabled him to refute ideas of

527

social evolution: he demonstrated that matrilineal reckoning might be adopted by non-matrilineal people, and was not simply a stage in evolution. And in studying immigrants in the United States in c.1910, he made the point that peoples who were seemingly different physically tended to converge in generations subsequent to immigration.

Collaboration

Boas obtained huge collections of art and material culture, but as important as the objects themselves and their histories and traditions was working together with aboriginal or local non-trained collaborators such as the part-Tlingit Kwakwaka'wakw-educated George Hunt (1854–1933). Hunt was perhaps Boas' primary collaborator. He had worked for the Berlin Ethnological Museum in the 1880s, met Boas in the 1890s and went to Chicago. He recorded vast amounts of information and made collections, including the Nuu-chah-nulth whalers' shrine, now at the American Museum of Natural History. Hunt's descendants remain the most prominent family from Fort Rupert, at the north end of Vancouver Island, and are engaged as artists and traditional leaders across the world. For instance, Corrine Hunt (b. 1959) created an installation for the 2011 Dresden exhibition 'The Great Potlatch', which partnered the Green Vaults with U'mista, an exchange of extraordinary cultural ambition.

One early historian and leader who did not give up time and stories to Boas was Arthur Wellington Clah (1831–1916), whose life history is recorded in forty notebooks. In his lifetime as a Tsimshian leader he worked with the Hudson's Bay Company, and then with missionaries and gold prospectors in both Alaska and Canada, and witnessed the decline of the land-based fur trade. All of his property was devoted to ensuring his inherited place in traditional systems. In 1868 he assumed the name of Temks and recorded in his diary: 'In this day at home I was spented all My Property. I gave away 6 or 7 hundred in goods give away all they stranger.' Clah's autobiography was acquired by Henry Wellcome (1853–1936), the Anglo-American pharmaceutical entrepreneur who had written an account of the missionary William Duncan in 1887.[12]

From another collaborator, Charles Edenshaw (c.1839–1920), Boas did obtain in the 1890s the drawings of Haida crests that he was to use in his text explaining the formal qualities of Northwest Coast art. While Boas had begun writing about art with his 'Decorative Art of the Indians of the North Pacific Coast' (1897), by 1903 he had started using the phrase 'primitive art'. Northwest Coast art and Edenshaw's drawings and ideas provided the basis of his of monograph *Primitive Art* (1927). In this Boas gave body to a concept which had arisen twenty years earlier, before the interest of Paris painters in the geometric qualities of African masks, decontextualized from their cultural origins, but placed in the harsh binary opposition of the civilized qualities of the West and the elemental qualities of the rest. While the idea of primitive art began to disappear in the middle of the twentieth century, it did contribute to an important understanding that other cultures make art, and art that could be analysed. Boas enumerated those qualities of abstraction and symbolism, of horror vacui and of symmetry, thus placing the Pacific Northwest Coast at the centre of appreciation of art of smaller societies.

Edenshaw was of high birth, early on a carver of argillite shale, a silversmith and a carver whose work is well represented in museums. Among his early titles are: *Da'axiigang*, meaning 'noise in the housepit', and later *Nǝngkwigetklałs* ('they gave ten potlatches for him'). Edensaw's line also remains highly prominent, significant immediately because of his daughter Florence Davidson's role in the community through the second half of the twentieth century, and then through the family school led by her grandson Robert Davidson (b. 1946), who in turn had been tutored by Bill Reid (1920–98).[13] His contribution was celebrated in Vancouver in the 'Charles Edenshaw' exhibition of 2013.

Another of Boas' aboriginal consultants was the Tsimshian Henry Wellington Tate, who died in 1914. He had probably collaborated on missionary projects in the late nineteenth century but in the last decade of his life provided many hundreds of pages of Native texts to Boas, published in *Tsimshian Mythology* after Tate's death in 1916.

The Self-taught

In the USA the idea of the hobbyist seems to demean those who devote their lives to 'outsider' pursuits, such as for instance working with, and especially identifying with Native North Americans. Perhaps a preferable idea is that of autodidact, someone who is self-taught, whose authority derives from his or her own self-belief and determination. In Britain this is in part subsumed in the myth of the amateur, the supposedly non-professional who achieves more than the professional. Someone who transcends simplistic boundaries in this respect is the American artist and anthropologist Bill Holm (b. 1925). Holm was, from the 1960s, in a sense a pivotal figure in the formalization of Northwest Coast art and the development of its enormous international success. A school teacher, originally from Montana, and interested in northern Plains Natives, Holm moved to Seattle and became a supremely knowledgeable, and yet humble, authority on the Pacific northwest. Much of his knowledge was self-taught, and much came from working with British Columbian aboriginals, a great group of carvers who through the difficult decades of the mid-twentieth century, before the lifting of the potlatch ban with the 1951 Indian Act, kept art going. In 1942 Holm became involved with Camp Nor'wester, founded in the San Juan Islands in 1935 as a summer camp for school kids. There, over time, big houses and poles were carved and raised, much of the work being undertaken through and with the Kwakwaka'wakw artist Mungo Martin. Martin designed a big house, and there at the camp people were taught art and Indian ways.

In the 1950s and 1960s Holm was much more than an interpreter of Indian culture. He not simply learned how to carve but analysed the principles of Northwest Coast art. He began, of course, with Boas, but more even than Boas, Holm is someone who does, who makes and who thinks and understands and inspires. The book he published in 1965, which now looks quite unprepossessing but went through many editions, outlined the principles of Northwest Coast art. Holm used as his primary idea that of 'formline', of the swelling, tapering line that surrounds an element of design. He defined it thus:

> formline is the primary design element on which Northwest Coast art depends, and by the turn of the twentieth century, its use spread to the southern regions as well. It is the positive delineating force of the painting, relief and engraving. Formlines are continuous, flowing, curvilinear lines that turn, swell and diminish in a prescribed manner.

They are used for figure outlines, internal design elements and in abstract compositions.

The term 'formline' is a little-known and seldom-used one that comes from contour maps in geography and refers to non-touching lines around a feature, that is, successive contour lines indicating height above sea level that never meet. It is in this very specific and limited sense that Holm adopted the term and imported it into art history. So in Northwest Coast art when an eye or a 'u' form or a salmon trout head is sequestered, roped off, it is surrounded by a formline that does not touch the next formline. Holm's vocabulary and formal analysis received immediate acceptance and use and spread often without demonstrative teaching like the Inuit syllabics introduced by Peck and the Anglican missionaries for teaching Christianity before the arrival of actual teachers. That is, anyone wanting to design or carve could buy a copy of the book, learn the language and start designing and carving. Most interesting of all is the way Holm's text acted as a primer to make rigorous, to intellectualize and define the way art should be done, ensuring that along the coast those people who were already interested in carving could simply turn to art, in an act of confidence, and, if they chose, develop their design and carving skills. But in laying out a vade-mecum in such an accessible manner Holm provided an idealization of Northwest Coast art that allows the tradition to sit across Native and non-Native worlds in a manner unmatched by other traditions. Thus Maori art, Melanesian art, southwest jewellery, West African textiles, Northern Territory aboriginal painting, Cuna mola design or Guyana-Venezuela geometric design do not have the same universality through text – though some may say they are better protected for that reason.

Holm's book was a major contribution to what in the late twentieth century was seen as a revitalization of art, but is now seen as recovery and development. It appeared as things were changing, at around the same time as the Gitanmaax School of Northwest Coast Indian Art ('Ksan) at Hazelton, British Columbia. This began as a library project, the Skeena Treasure House, to protect and store local regalia, initiated by Polly Sargent and aboriginal leaders and developed into what is now the Gitxsan museum of 'Ksan, with a collection of 600 pieces. The then Kitanmax School of Northwest Coast Indian Art was founded as part of the 'Ksan Cultural and Educational Centre in 1970. Other centres and carving sheds developed in Victoria and Vancouver.

Poles and Totems

A separate and rather difficult visual importance is given to aboriginal art of the Pacific Northwest Coast by the prominent but partly false concept of the totem pole. Coming from the Algonquian/Anishnaabe/Ojibwe *ododem*, the totem was perhaps most notably introduced into intellectual life by the Ojibwe missionary Peter Jones in his 1861 *History of the Ojebway Indians*. And before Jones there were Schoolcraft and Longfellow, and perhaps most importantly the Anglo-Canadian fur trader and linguist John Long (1768–91), who in his *Voyages and Travels of an Indian Interpreter* (1791) described languages and the Algonquian and Iroquoian situation through the tumult of the American Revolution.

The actual transfer of the idea of totem from the Great Lakes to the West Coast may have been effected by 1880 in Sheldon Jackson's *Alaska and Missions on the North Pacific Coast*, in which he talks of seeing totem poles at Tongass in Alaska. Jackson's early life was spent further south and east, preaching, and he would no doubt have come across the idea of totem, which was beginning to be discussed in relation to the early structure of the evolution of languages. At that time it was used in its proper sense as an association of clan or individuals with a helper and originator spirit. In the late twentieth century the anthropologist Claude Lévi-Strauss employed it as a fundamental structural idea opposing nature and culture, one that provides a post hoc explanation rather than a core ethnographic concept. What is also certain is that, in terms of visual expression, Northwest Coast art makes material the hybrid idea of totem, more than, say, Algonquian totems or Australian totemism. This is in a sense an appropriate symbolic recognition of the inverted importance of Sheldon Jackson, who from the 1880s, as director of education in Alaska, set up assimilationist programmes for Alaskan Natives.

While the early collections of totem poles were initiated by overseas museums and individuals, by the 1920s the Victoria Memorial

Museum and Royal Museum of British Columbia began to move poles out of villages into public sites, especially those in prominent tourist areas. These include Stanley Park in Vancouver and, in 1941, the precinct of the Victoria Museum; Pioneer Square in Seattle in the nineteenth century; the Grand Trunk Railway in northern British Columbia; and Sitka National Historical Park from the early twentieth century. In British Columbia C. F. Newcombe (1851–1924), of what is now the Royal Museum of British Columbia, and Marius Barbeau (1883–1969), of what is now the Canadian Museum of History, worked to assist pole preservation by removal. Because totem poles have a normal life of seventy-five to 100 years on the shorelines of coastal villages, most outside poles in parks have been replaced, and the historical poles moved inside to museum stores. Poles, along with canoes, began to be shown in major international exhibitions, the first one of which to feature Northwest Coast sculpture being the London International Exhibition of 1862. From the 1950s onwards poles began to be carved systematically for diplomatic purposes and sent overseas or were commissioned by museums or corporations, for instance the 90 foot pole carved by Mungo Martin for the centenary of British Columbia at Wawaditla in Victoria, and that installed in Windsor Great Park. The carving shed at the Museum of Anthropology, begun in 1947, and with a new building opened in 1976, was used by Bill Reid and his amanuenses Guujaaw, Jim Hart and others to create the *Raven and the First Men* (1980), alongside the buildings created earlier.

Elsewhere in the United States Holm influenced non-Native carvers, such as Duane Pasco (b. 1932), who has contributed to public carving in Alaska, and Steve Brown, who is now also an art historian. What happened then is that the public collecting of totem poles provided a context for their survival, for the repair and renewal of monumental sculpture through the middle of the twentieth century, in a manner which ensured skills were not forgotten, in a series of cross-over partnerships between public institutions and public curators. These people included Wilson Duff, Audrey and Harry Hawthorn, Michael Ames and Bill Holm, and more pertinently carvers such as Mungo Martin (1879–1962). Clan symbols and privately held stories entered the public realm while ownership of those properties remained in the hand of families and descent groups: as already indicated, the non-tangible property is that which matters, in art and carving as well as in ownership of the land.

Naming and Nationality

An interesting feature of First Nations in British Columbia is the increasing diversity of identity, of the development of specific names for individual villages and peoples. In an important sense this contrasts vividly with what happened in Alaska after ANCSA in 1971, when the Tlingit and Haida came together in the Sealaska formulation of southeast Alaska. For instance, the Nuu-chah-nulth on the west coast of Vancouver Island developed a strong tribal presence, combining several First Nations, while among the Kwakwaka'wakw individual bands and First Nations have developed strong place-specific band identities with new names. One such people are the 'Namgis, on Cormorant Island off the north end of Vancouver Island, who formerly called themselves Nimpkish. Also among the Kwakwaka'wakw along the east coast of Vancouver Island is the We Wai Kai nation, with their museum at Cape Mudge on Quadra Island, the Nuyumbalees Cultural Centre, which opened in 1979 to receive returned potlatch regalia from museums in the east and which was initially named the Kwaguilth Museum.

The Nootkan-speaking peoples live on the west coast of Vancouver Island and in coastal Washington State. Unlike the Coast Salish peoples in the lower mainland and island, they came together in 1958 and formed the West Coast Allied Tribes. In 1979 they became the Nuu-chah-nulth Tribal Council. Today there are fourteen First Nations in the NTC, but not all of them are involved to the same degree in the treaty process. The Maa-nulth Treaty came into effect in 2011, for five First Nations on the west coast of Vancouver Island, and provides more than 60,000 acres for around 2,000 people. What is striking and extraordinary about this treaty process is the exceptional diversity, that instead of seeking to impose a single treaty on the whole province, as in Alaska in the 1970s, a long, slow and very deliberate process was begun and is still taking place. Critics rightly point out that the awards in terms of land and capital are derisory, but the alternative is frankly nothing, and the seemingly negligible returns provide significant authority of, as already mentioned, enormous symbolic significance.

The Canadian Constitution and British Columbia

Two or three things have driven the treaty process forward. First in importance was the repatriation of the Canadian constitution in 1982. This enshrined the Royal Proclamation of 1763 into law, which states categorically that land not included in Quebec and the Floridas, then British, was reserved to Indians:

> And We do further declare it to be Our Royal Will and Pleasure, for the Present as aforesaid, to reserve under Our Sovereignty, Protection and Dominion, for the Use of the said Indians, all the Lands and Territories not included within the Limits of Our said Three new Governments, or within the Limits of the Territory granted to the Hudson's Bay Company; as also all the Lands and Territories lying to the Westward of the Sources of the Rivers which fall into the Sea from the West and North West as aforesaid; and We do hereby strictly forbid, on Pain of Our Displeasure, all Our loving Subjects from making any Purchases or Settlements whatever, or taking Possession of any of the Lands above reserved, without Our especial Leave and Licence for that Purpose first obtained.[14]

Interestingly this diktat excludes the lands granted to the Hudson's Bay Company, so making the treaty process different in the north, and specifically mentions rivers in the west, more than a decade before actual exploration of the Pacific began. Further rights in Indians' hunting grounds were also preserved in the proclamation. This means that British Columbia is the area of Canada where aboriginal rights were best preserved.

The Calder case, 1973, confirmed these unextinguished rights. This was elaborated by Delgamuukw v. British Columbia; the case was initiated in 1984, and tested in the Supreme Court in 1997. It was brought by the Gitxsan Nation and the Wet'suwet'en Nation, because the treaty process of the period was so cumbersome. This important case concerned 133 territories in relation to 23,000 square miles and

claimed tribal jurisdiction over this land. Seventy-one of the hereditary houses supported it – all of the Wet'suwet'en but not all of the
Gitksan houses (or descent groups). The two First Nations who came
together, a Tsimshian people and an Athapaskan one, neatly symbolize the crumbling and removal of simplistic anthropological-linguistic
categories in the face of actual identity and political realities. Further,
the case was brought in the name of a title, not in the name of a person, and in the course of the case three different individuals
successively held the title Delgamuukw: Albert Tait, Ken Muldoe and
then Earl Muldoe. In the end the actual land claim, the right to aboriginal land, was not decided. Instead what the case did was to define
aboriginal rights:

> Until this decision, no Canadian court had so directly addressed the
> definition of aboriginal title. Other cases had dealt with aboriginal
> rights in terms of the right to use the land for traditional purposes
> such as hunting. Aboriginal title is a property right that goes much
> further than aboriginal rights of usage.[15]
>
> Consequently since 1997 'courts must recognize lineage-owned
> oral histories as manifestations of indigenous legal systems that prove
> aboriginal title and govern an attachment to the land'.[16]

Such a process did not arise without a background and history.
One of the main participants and instigators of the process was the
house of Wii Gaak, the head of which as Neil Sterritt Snr, who sued
on his own behalf and on behalf of all the members of the House of
Wii Gaak. Neil Sterritt Snr, was involved in the claims process and
has written and published about the significance of the case, in Australia as well as Canada. John R. Cove wrote about Sterritt in 'The
Gitksan Traditional Concept of Land Ownership.' in 1982.[17] Cove
had begun in the 1970s with a grant to study rights in the Skeena
Valley. This he was not allowed to do by the First Nations there. He
was inveigled into returning the funding and taking aboriginal
employment to work on the land claims. He worked in the 1970s and
1980s especially with British Columbian archaeologist and founder
director of the Canadian Museum of Civilization, now History,
George MacDonald. That is, the early twentieth-century authority
process, with an anthropologist in control, was reversed to enable the

evidence for the Degamukuukw case to be gathered together. Sterritt has written briefly about Albert Tait, the chief in whose name the case was begun, though he died in 1987, before the first hearing. He says particularly that, apart from being a 'horseman and packer, carpenter and logger on the upper Skeena River, and a successful commercial fisherman', he epitomized the Gitxsan saying 'Sdinhl Xpaawhl Simoighet' ('the chief's jaw is heavy, don't flap your mouth and say nothing').[18]

A main part of the explanation for the success of land claims lies in the need to secure title for agreement on the exploitation of extractive resources, just as in Quebec and Alaska in the early 1970s. So in 2013 agreement is needed to enable the development and transportation of energy from the northern interior of North America. Early in the Second World War an only partly successful oil pipeline named Canol was constructed from Norman Wells in the Northwest Territories to the Whitehorse Yukon. Today twelve projects compete to build outlets for liquid natural gas to Asia; the one that is actually being built, by Shell, is organized in partnership with the Haisla First Nation at Kitimat, British Columbia.[19] While this is partly supported by aboriginal people, the northern gateway proposal, to create two huge pipelines to export oil from Alberta tar sands, is controversial, for reasons of pollution and politics. On the one hand, the northern gateway to Kitimat would lessen Canadian dependence on US oil exports; on the other hand, it might, like the second trans-Canada railway, the Grand Trunk, which also finished at Prince Rupert in northern British Columbia in Edwardian Canada, turn out to be a white elephant. The Haisla, like the Tlingit, the Haida and the Kwakwaka'wakw, have been successful in expressing the continuation of their beliefs and traditional culture with the return of a totem pole in 2006 from the Etnografiska Museet in Stockholm. Thus economic development and confident modernization are closely related to cultural heritage, which acts as badge of authenticity and authority for Native people crossing into the white domain, while actually being something more.

Tribal councils in British Columbia vary in size, complexity and the roles they assume for member bands. One example is provided by the main Canadian section of the Haida Nation, on Haida Gwaii, in the Pacific, 50 miles out from the mainland, just below Alaska, and

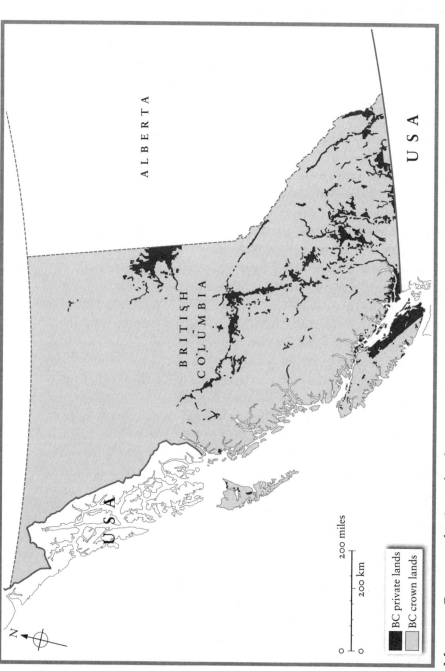

Map 12. Crown and private lands in British Columbia: only 5 per cent is privately owned.

divided from the American part of the tribal nation on Prince of Wales Island, named after George IV. Speaking a language that either represents an isolate or is one from the Na-Dene language family which separated from the nearby Tlingit and other Athapaskans perhaps 5,000 years ago, today the Canadian Haida are constituted in two bands, Skidegate and Masett, to which during the period of population collapse and consolidation in the late nineteenth and early twentieth centuries people moved from outlying villages. In the 1970s the neologism Haida Gwaii, 'islands of the people', appeared and was made manifest by Bill Reid's canoe sculpture *The Spirit of Haida Gwaii* (*c*.1986–91), installed in three versions, in Vancouver, Ottawa-Gatineau and Washington, DC, and then on the Canadian $20 bill. In 2010 the Haida Gwaii Reconciliation Act officially renamed the Queen Charlotte Islands in this way, superseding the original name derived from George III's queen, and more specifically from the *Queen Charlotte*, one of the ships of the fur trader George Dixon in the 1780s. The constitution of the Haida Nation, of 2003, outlines the duties of the Council of the Haida Nation, of 1974, which brought together the two federally constituted reserves, Old Massett Village Council Skidegate Band Council and the Hereditary Chiefs. That is, the gradual development of institutions was paralleled by the changes in the legal situation of the Haida people, itself interacting with and developing from aboriginal activism around forests.

On Haida Gwaii from 1979 Gary Edenshaw/Guujaaw, initially a carver working on Reid's 1980 *Raven and the First Men*, took the forestry minister to court, claiming that title to the forest had not passed to the crown. With the Lyell Island movement against clear cutting in 1988, Gwaii Haanas National Park Reserve was created. In 2002 Guujaaw, the elected president, and the Council of the Haida Nation prepared a land claim for the Supreme Court of British Columbia.

Here again is an example of leaders who are both artists and politicians, in the secular 'real world', except that of course for First Nations the real world includes the production and consumption of art, both for traditional performance and commemoration, and as part of the major contribution made by Inuit, Métis and First Nations to the continued construction of national/Canadian identity. An alternative trajectory, of the politician becoming an artist, is that of the Haida artist Michael Nicoll Yahgulanaas (b. 1954), who, before becoming a full-time artist and creator of Haida manga, was mayor of Massett. In 1993 the Haida entered the treaty process and in 2005 had completed stage two of six, that of declaring that Canada, British Columbia and the Council of the Haida Nation would start negotiating a treaty. But in a sense the treaty process is now running parallel to the constitutional process, in which case law, and the implicit recognition of ownership of land and resources by First Nations, renders in some sense the treaty process irrelevant.

This contrasts with the situation on the northern mainland among the peoples who speak dialects of the Tsimshian languages, on the coast and inland on the Skeena and Nass Rivers. Five coastal communities are joined together in the Tsimshian First Nations Treaty Society, which is still negotiating land claims. Originally consisting of seven bands, this was reduced to five. One Tsimshian-speaking people, the Nisga'a, agreed the first British Columbia treaty or settlement since 1899, in 1998–2000, whereby they received title to 800 square miles and rights to more than 150,000 salmon a year for a population of 2,500 in the Nass Valley, and a total population of 5,500, and health and education budgets administered by the Nisga'a government. Some claims overlapped with neighbours'. While in one sense the Nisga'a lost most of their land rights, in another sense they established themselves along the Nass with an economic and moral presence which matched their cultural position: nothing can now happen in or around their traditional territory without their involvement, even though 95 per cent of their land was ceded. The symbolic importance of treaty-making, then, is much greater than the limited practical benefits. The other inland people, the Gitxsan, are still negotiating final settlement of the land claims. A union of five bands began the treaty process in 1994 and claims more than 11,000 square miles. Their treaty process has, as with all British Columbia treaty negotiations, six parts: intent to negotiate, readiness to negotiate, framework for negotiation, agreement in principle, finalization and implementation, a long and expensive series of negotiations, explaining why, in twenty years, this one people, the Nisga'a, of the approximately sixty, has successfully achieved agreement, although more than half have now achieved the fourth stage of AIP, agreement in principle.

Alaskan Corporations

The situation in Alaska is very different. The primary institution is the private corporation, Sealaska Inc., founded in 1971, on the back of the Alaska Native Land Claims Settlement Act, with about 16,000 eligible shareholders, today operating successfully primarily in timber and in plastics, with significant swings in economic performance and over the last thirty years insignificant growth in turnover and profits. It is owned primarily by Tlingit and Haida people and during the 1980s, for instance, suffered the seemingly normal ups and downs of the business cycle. So in 1982 Sealaska lost $28 million following a botulism scare after a Belgian died from canned salmon. But in 1986, as a result of increased demand for timber, profits at Sealaska grew to $23.9 million, on a turnover of $237 million. In that same year a financier, R. Michael Crowson, was convicted of mail and wire fraud, tax evasion and defrauding Sealaska at the beginning of that decade.[20] In a sense, then, Sealaska is simply a working commercial corporation delivering profits to its shareholders in the best traditions of free market business practices, subject to white fraud, the history of which goes back to the beginning of European contact. In May 2013 Sealaska announced a turnover of $312 million and net profits of $11.3 million for 2012. It remains, however, very dependent on timber and, having taken possession by conveyance of rights to 290,000 acres in 2011, has cut 199,500 acres as of March 2013.[21] Sealaska is entitled to a further 70,000 acres under ANCSA. A controversial bill, HR 740/S340, was passed by Congress in 2014. This provides old growth timber, in part from outside the original area agreed by treaty, for possible felling. Again this is simply part of normal business.

At the village level something similar happens. The Tlingit village-for-profit Huna Totem Corporation is responsible for 22,000 acres of timber, of which it cut 10,000 acres in the 1980s and 1990s, and had, it was reported in 2011, received $88,900 in subsidy for replanting. This is a private corporation with forestry interests providing economic and cultural benefits, but of course it is only one of many such corporations with privileges of this kind. So in a sense the writing-off of losses against tax in this way is an everyday practice, one which emphasizes the new normalcy of Native corporations.[22] Finally, in 2014, the everyday success of the Tlingit is seen in the campaign of Byron Mallot (b. 1943), the Democrat lieutenant governor of Alaska from 2014, having been a founder director of Sealaska in the 1970s, and later chairman. In Canada First Nations politicians have achieved similar success: Stolo chief Steven Point (b. 1951) was appointed lieutenant governor of British Columbia 2007–12, that is, the queen's representative, rather than an elected officer, after a complex corporate and public career. Point is also well known as a judge reviewing the long series of botched investigation of murders of young First Nations women in Vancouver.

Tlingit involvement in felling timber is in stark contrast to the situation in Canada, where so much was made in the 1980s and 1990s of avoiding clear cutting of forest; that is, much of the recovery of First Nations position in the province was associated with timber preservation rather than exploitation. On the other hand, the continuing profitability of Sealaska also contributes in a major manner to heritage maintenance and development through the Sealaska Heritage Institute. This was founded as a not-for-profit institute in 1980, following a conference at which the late Tlingit elder George Davis, from Angoon, said:

> We don't want what you did here to only echo in the air, how our grandfathers used to do things (i.e. by speaking empty words) . . . Yes. You have unwrapped it for us. That is why we will open again this container of wisdom left in our care.[23]

The president of the Sealaska Heritage Institute, sponsored by the corporation from 1981, is the Harvard-educated anthropologist Rosita Worl, who also serves as vice chair of the board, where she is responsible for shareholders' relations and for lands. Most importantly, she has many Tlingit positions. Her names include Yeidiklats'akw and Kaaháni, and she is an Eagle of the Shangukeidí (Thunderbird) clan from the Kaawdliyaayi Hít (House Lowered from the Sun) of Klukwan.[24] One way again of seeing this confluence of culture and commerce is that in traditional terms it is exactly right, that Worl is simply doing what her ancestors did: working in a commercial world and promoting culture.

As well as language work in preserving, recording and publishing materials and ensuring a degree of both symbolic and significant language competence in all areas of Tlingit life, the Sealaska Heritage Institute also assists with the return of clan regalia and treasures, for instance assisting with the overseeing of new poles by Nathan Jackson to go to the Burke Museum, Seattle, to replace two returned to Alaska. One repatriation story involves Louis Shotridge (c.1882–1937) from Klukwan. Of high birth, he was, of course, in a matrilineal society, from a different clan to his father. He was well educated and worked for the University Museum, Philadelphia, collecting Tlingit materials between 1915 and 1932, the first Northwest Coast Indian to be a curator and to publish Native artefacts on his own account. Some of these items have been returned; others are now subject to a possible shared arrangement between the traditional owners and the University of Pennsylvania. Again, what is striking here is the difference with the Canadian situation: in Alaska clans have reclaimed materials, while in Canada First Nations museums are society-run and -involved, in association with the original family owners.

Another important expression of pan-southeast Alaska identity is the series of celebrations occurring every two years and bringing together Tlingit, Haida and Tsimshian. It can be suggested that the biennial celebrations in southeast Alaska are akin to Native events, including powwows, in the Lower 48 (mainland USA), in which people come together to be close and to celebrate family and culture, and that there is no equivalent south of Alaska. But this is misleading, since potlatches, especially when memorial events for the diseased, or for the passing-on of names, fill a similar social space and involve diverse groups from up and down the coast. Further, some people organize their own events, such as Makah Days, with canoe races, dancing and games, as do for instance the Squamish in North Vancouver, and other Coast Salish people on and around Vancouver Island.

Cities and Settlements

Elsewhere there are tribal nations with little recognition. In contrast to Vancouver, where the federally recognized Musqueam are involved in continued negotiations for rights, including those around archaeological sites, the Duwamish, the Salishan people of Seattle, are not federally recognized by the US government. Chief Seattle (c.1780–1866) (Duwamish and Suquamish), who as a boy may have seen Vancouver's expedition in Puget Sound in 1792, signed the Point Elliott Treaty in 1855, which guaranteed his people's rights, but no reservation was ever created for the Duwamish. Seattle himself is remembered for his size and presence – the Canadians called him 'Le Gros' ('Big Man') – and for a much-discussed speech advocating environmental responsibility, recorded and remembered in his name, and for the help given the incoming American settlers in the 1850s. In the aftermath of the city' s 150th anniversary the Duwamish were able to acquire land to build a cultural centre, a longhouse available to the wider community. One member of the Native community, Thomas Scranton, from Mukilteo (Point Elliott), a smart Seattle suburb, expresses the minimal identity of the Duwamish like this: 'What does it mean to be a Duwamish? It's like it's there, but you see I'm only sixteenth, and so it's like a tangent touches a circle.'[25] The contrast with the Suquamish people, to whom Seattle was related through his mother, is striking: they have a reservation, a casino, self-government and, since 2012, a museum. They celebrate their village across Puget Sound from Seattle as Chief's Seattle's winter village.

The non-provision of reservations to those signing treaties in 1855 has only been slightly mitigated by the federal recognition of treaty tribes of the 1850s, such as the Samish (Skagit) and Sauk-Suiattle in the late twentieth century. Of more general importance than the occasional obtaining of federal recognition was the spread of the civil rights movement in the late 1960s and early 1970s to include fishing rights in Washington State, with the presence of Marlon Brando at a fish-in, an act of 'illegal' fishing. The Boldt decision (United States v. Washington, 1974), fought over through 1974–9, reaffirmed that Indian tribes were entitled to half the harvest. Consequently, the Northwest Indian Fisheries Commission (NWIFC) was set up and now looks after the fishing rights of western Washington treaty Indians. This was led by Billy Frank, Jnr (1931–2014), the Nisqually fishing activist of the 1960s, who emphasized cooperation with non-Indian fisherman and conservancy. Frank campaigned in a highly sophisticated manner against pollution. So, for instance, permitted water pollution depends in part on how much fish a month each individual is said to eat: the less fish that is eaten, the fewer toxins are ingested, and so the level of water purity can be lower, allowing polluters to pollute more. Therefore in 2013 Billy Frank was campaigning for an increase in the supposed amount of fish eaten by a Washington State resident, up from the unrealistically low one meal a month, to an amount something more realistic for fish eaters, simply so that water purity could be improved.

An alternative view, of privileged access to fishing and the skewing of benefits to recognized tribal nations, was voiced after a little more than ten years of the Boldt decision. This court case 'appears to be encouraging the creation of a wealthy class of offshore, capital-intensive, treaty-tribe fishermen who are intercepting much of the resource before it reaches the traditional estuary and river fisheries of the tribes'.[26] The benefits Indian rights were said to have devolved to a small group of rich people. In a sense, however, that is culturally appropriate, since these fishing peoples have always been class-based societies, with a definite sense of the haves and the have-nots, even if this was defined in terms of relationship with the mythic worlds of animals and oral history rather than ownership of boats.

Jargon and Trade

In the nineteenth century, Pacific Northwest commerce and culture was unified by a trade language, Chinook, the jargon used up and down the coast for more than 600 miles, which originated pre-contact and was used with Captain James Cook and by later explorers and by writers such as Jack London. Originating on the Columbia River, with a liberal admixture of Wakashan from British Columbia, and then after European contact of English and French, it became the lingua franca – so that for instance the Stephens Treaties of the 1850s in Washington Territory were negotiated in Chinook. Vocabulary survives in English: *tyee* for chief, *tillicum* for people or family, *cheechaco* for newcomer, *skookum* for big or strong, *klootchman* for woman, *cultus* for bad, and *siwash*, from the French *sauvage*, the derogatory term for a Native, especially a drunk Native. *Potlatch* from the Nuu-chah-nulth for giving. Just as Nootka Sound and the Mowachaht

Nuu-chah-nulth were for the British and Spanish the central place and people in the late eighteenth century, so the Chinook-speaking people at the mouth of the Columbia, at Fort Clatsop, were for the Americans the centre of power and the origin of the US presence on the Pacific. Clatsop, 'place of dried fish', was where Lewis and Clark, the first Americans to cross the continent, wintered in 1805–6 and where John Jacob Astor built Fort Astoria, the failed fur trading post immortalized twenty-five years later by Washington Irving. Chinook was the language used in the Klondike Gold Rush, after gold had been discovered by the Tlingit Tagish Canadian Jim Mason, known as Skookum (c.1855–1916).

Northern California

Further to the south, while basketry thrives, there is no formal Northwest Coast art. Culturally speaking, the outsider view would suggest that California, even northern California, is a rather different place from the Pacific northwest. Yet the Native reality is that the group of coastal peoples in northwest California shares much with the people further to the north. These Californian peoples cluster along the Klamath, Trinity and Eel Rivers, just as others live along the Columbia, Fraser, Skeena and Nass to the north; and the great main resource remains salmon. In contemporary terms the central issue here is also Native rights to salmon fishing. One difference between northern California people and those of, say, coastal British Columbia and southeast Alaska was the presence of starch in their diet. Starch was easily available from acorns, perhaps the primary Californian food, which, once ground up and leached of toxins, provided an easily storable food. The three to five peoples of northern California share a common social stratification, with vigorous articulation of ideas about wealth and currency and the ownership of resources, and a belief in the inviolable nature of the dance, with its emphasis on family descent, wealth and spirituality. Apart from the display of treasures at dances, similar technologies including the canoe, the toggling harpoon for fishing and the use of maidenhair fern in twined basketry and sharp bright bear grass for decorating hats and other articles.

Perhaps the most fundamental feature of these people, which they share with those up the coast, is that they come from very diverse language groups; that is, they moved into northern California at very different times and quickly adopted local characteristics, with notable convergence in most things apart from language. Some of the northern peoples speak Athapaskan or Na-Dene languages, that is, languages related to the interior of Alaska and the Northwest Territories and to one or two peoples of the Northwest Coast such as the Tlingit, and to the Navajo and Apache. Arriving perhaps 900 to 2,000 years ago, the Hupa on the lower Klamath River share much with the upstream Karuk and Yurok, including subsistence and performance patterns. The Hupa acknowledge these connections in a matter-of-fact way and say:

> Much of the Hupa language, although complex in linguistics, is relatively easy to improve once you have mastered the basic principles of word formation. If you want to learn more look out for the Hupa Language Dictionary Second edition or contact the Hoopa Tribal Office.[27]

Further north, the river and fish issues are to do with commercial fishing, that is, who is entitled to what fish and whether they are to be used for subsistence or business. On the Klamath River two different issues converge: one is, as on the Columbia, about hydroelectricity, and the four dams on the river, and the ways they impact on salmon migration and breeding; the other is the vexed business of irrigation for farms. In 2010 it was announced that agreement had been reached between then Governor Arnold Schwarznegger and the tribes and river basin authorities to remove the four dams, but this would not happen for ten years and would require huge amounts of money for congressional approval ever before the funding actually required for removal.

Of particular importance are the dance and ritual complexes, to do with the first salmon, the harvest of the tan (preferred species of) acorn, the Deer Dance and the Jump Dance; the circulation of currency – dentalium shells – also used up the coast into Alaska; and valuables made of local obsidian, volcanic glass. Other wealth items include white or coloured deer skins and horizontal band headdresses decorated with woodpecker-feathered skin. The Hupa have the largest reservation in California and are rich from timber, 12 million board feet being taken each year. In their class-based society traditionally slavery was to do with debt, rather than, as further north, a feature of warfare.

But there is another aspect to tribal self-government for the Yurok, Karuk and Hupa, and this is that northern California is ideal for growing marijuana. Though semi-legal now, the trade is dominated by drug producers willing and able to set up plantations on Indian land, where regular state jurisdiction does not operate. In a sense, where the landless invaded the Plains for Indian land after 1862, and the Black Hills for gold in the 1870s, so in Klamath country now the landless invade Indian Country to grow weed. A new argot has grown up with the extensive marijuana fields. Police say they counted 400 'grows' in a single flight, and locals say people must be mad to have a nine-to-five job instead of 'growing'.[28] This is all very twenty-first-century and yet entirely in keeping with the core historical perspective of land seizure by non-Natives. Yet, conversely, growing marijuana may become an increasingly important ambition of tribal governments.

Of the similarities of the northern Californians with the northern coast peoples, the most important is the sense of aristocratic identity, and the way this is expounded in terms of great houses and great dances. Lowana Brantner, one of the great woman of the Yurok, said in 1983:

> I am considered one of the rulers from the dances of the Yurok country. I am from the four great houses of the whole territory: the house of the fish dam at *sa?a*; the house here at *metah*; the house of the lady doctors at *murekw*. I am from the house of *caspaw*, the killers.[29]

One of the duties of the great women of the tribe is to ensure that the salmon run smoothly. For the Klamath River one of the issues is the sand bar which forms over the river mouth and which annually is broken through in winter to allow the salmon upstream. The contemporary cry is 'Undam the Klamath', advocating the removal of the numerous dams built in the twentieth century for hydroelectricity and water transfer south. In 1934 the sand bar was not broken through in the seasonal manner, and commented at the time: 'It was the mean old ladies of that house who let people starve.' Of course, most interesting today in the discussions about the removal of the dams is that what for earlier generations was corrected with a medicine ritual has with concrete dams become a political and cultural issue. While the dams are removable, the rivers are only recoverable with the expenditure of great wealth. And if the dams are removed they may yield vast amounts of stored up sand, recreating in any case the ancient problem of seasonal sand bars. Other aspects of ecologically sound, culturally ancient behaviour relate to forest management: Native Californians always used fire to help clear brush below oaks for acorns. Now it is recognized that clearing forest areas with controlled fires avoids major fires, so much a troubling feature of the US states. In all of these things the changing balances and checks in this very diverse area bring unexpected developments.

Notes

PREFACE

1 Russell Thornton, 'Native American Demographic', *American Studies*, 46(3/4) (Fall–Winter 2005), pp. 23–38; *Indigenous Studies Today*, 1 (Fall 2005/Spring 2006).

2 In the US today the BIA delivers services to 1.9 million Indian people and Native Alaskans. However, the 2010 US Census identified 2.9 million as American Indian and Alaska Native alone, and a further 2.3 million were partially Native. In Canada in 2011 there were 637,660 registered Indian people and 1.4 million people of aboriginal identity (including Métis and Inuit). So 2.5 million – 1.9 plus 637,600 – is a minimal figure. See: http://www.census.gov/prod/cen2010/briefs/c2010br-10.pdf; https://www.federalregister.gov/agencies/indian-affairs-bureau; http://www12.statcan.gc.ca/nhs-enm/2011/as-sa/99-011-x/99-011-x2011001-eng.cfm, accessed 3 September 2015.

INTRODUCTION

1 Gambling Impact Study (Spectrum Gaming Group, 28 October 2013), p. 210, available at http://www.spectrumgaming.com/reports/, accessed 26 February 2014.

2 Ibid., p.12.

3 Gambling Impact Study (Spectrum Gaming Group, 28 October 2013), p. 12, available at http://www.leg.state.fl.us/gamingstudy/docs/FGIS_Spectrum_28Oct2013.pdf, accessed 24 November 2015.

4 David Hume, 'Of Interest', chapter II.IV.7, available at http://hermetic.com/93beast.fea.st/files/section1/hume/extras/Essays,%20Moral,%20Political,%20and%20Literary.pdf, accessed 5 September 2015.

5 William Norman Grigg, 'The Cliven Bundy Standoff: Wounded Knee Revisited?', 12 April 2014, available at http://www.ronpaulinstitute.

org/archives/featured-articles/2014/april/12/the-cliven-bundy-standoff-wounded-knee-revisited.aspx, accessed 5 September 2015.

6 *Gentleman's Magazine* 8 (1738), p. 285.

7 Both quotes from: 'The Works of Israel Zangwill: The Melting Pot', np, available at http://www.gutenberg.org/files/23893/23893-h/23893-h.htm, accessed 5 September 2015.

8 Quoted by Kevin Washburn, 'Felix Cohen, Anti-Semitism and American Indian Law', review in *American Indian Law Review* 33(2) (2008/9), pp. 583–605, at p. 604.

9 Geoffrey Dunn, 'Palin's Latest *Rogue* Gaffe', 18 March 2010, *Huffington Post*, available at http://www.huffingtonpost.com/geoffrey-dunn/palins-latest-emrogueem-g_b_373453.html, accessed 5 September 2015.

10 Quoted by Stephen W. Silliman, 'The "Old West" in the Middle East: U.S. Military Metaphors in Real and Imagined Indian Country', *American Anthropologist* 110(2) (2008), pp. 237–47, at p. 239.

11 Khaled Ahmed, 'The Foaming Margins', *Newsweek Pakistan*, 16 March 2014, available at http://newsweekpakistan.com/the-foaming-margins, accessed 29 April 2014.

12 Deborah A. Rosen, 'Wartime Prisoners and the Rule of Law: Andrew Jackson's Military Tribunals during the First Seminole War', *Journal of the Early Republic* 28(4) (2008), pp. 559–95.

13 Benjamin Runkle, 'The Truth about Geronimo . . . and Osama bin Laden', *Washington Post*, 6 May 2011, https://www.washingtonpost.com/opinions/the-truth-about-geronimo--and-osama-bin-laden/2011/05/04/AF7USTBG_story.html, accessed 6 September 2015.

14 Wilcomb E. Washburn, 'A Fifty-Year Perspective on the Indian Reorganization Act', *American Anthropologist* NS 86(2) (1984), pp. 279–89, at p. 283.

15 For a discussion see Jessica Bardill, 'Tribal Sovereignty and Enrollment Determinations', available at: http://genetics.ncai.org/tribal-sovereignty-and-enrollment-determinations.cfm, accessed 6 September 2014.

16 Washburn, 'A Fifty-Year Perspective', p. 287.

CHAPTER 1: SUCCESS

1 Tim Giago used 'smidgen' in 2012, 'Claiming Indian Heritage Does Not Make It Right', 17 September 2012, http://www.indianz.com/News/2012/007097.asp, accessed 9 January 2015.

2 Russell Thornton, *American Indian Holocaust and Survival* (Norman: University of Oklahoma Press, 1987), p. 160.

3 http://www.cdc.gov/minorityhealth/populations/REMP/aian.html.

4 http://www.statcan.gc.ca/pub/91-552-x/2011001/ana-eng.htm.

5 For a historical treatment of Métis status see J. Sawchuk, 'Negotiating an Identity . . .', *American Indian Quarterly* 25(1) (2001), pp. 73–92. Definition is by blood and descent: 'Métis are persons of mixed blood – European/Aboriginal blood (Indian ancestry); Someone who is distinct from Indian and Inuit, someone who has genealogical ties to Aboriginal ancestry. Note: There is no specified blood quantum.' From the Canadian Métis Council, http://www.canadianmetis.com/Qualifying.htm, accessed 13 October 2014.

6 However, similar complexities exist in references to the Spanish equivalent to Métis, Mestizo, and especially Chicanos, an originally generally abusive term used to refer to Nahuatl speakers from the Mexican state of Morelos, and to Latinos, Hispanics and so on, for which see http://www.mexica.net/chicano.php, accessed 6 September 2015.

7 http://www12.statcan.gc.ca/nhs-enm/2011/as-sa/99-011-x/99-011-x2011001-eng.cfm, accessed 24 November 2015.

8 N. Shoemaker, 'How Indians Got to Be Red', *American Historical Review* 102(3) (1997), pp. 625–44.

9 Quoted by Paul Spruhan, 'A Legal History of Blood Quantum in Federal Indian Law to 1935', *South Dakota Law Review* 51 (2006), pp. 1–50, at p. 4; see also Ryan W. Schmidt, 'American Indian Identity and Blood Quantum in the 21st Century: A Critical Review', *Journal of Anthropology* 2011 (2011), available at: http://www.hindawi.com/journals/janthro/2011/549521/, accessed 6 September 2015.

10 The Indian reserve or territory lay west of the Appalachian mountains. The proclamation states: 'it is just and reasonable, and essential to our Interest, and the Security of our Colonies, that the several Nations or Tribes of Indians with whom We are connected, and who live under our Protection, should not be molested or disturbed in the Possession of such Parts of Our Dominions and Territories as, not having been ceded to or purchased by Us, are reserved to them, or any of them, as their Hunting Grounds'. Available at http://avalon.law.yale.edu/18th_century/proc1763.asp, accessed 22 September 2015.

11 http://millercenter.org/president/speeches/detail/3450.

12 See D. A. Rosen, *American Indians and State Law: Sovereignty, Race, and Citizenship, 1790–1880* (Lincoln: University of Nebraska Press, 2007), p. 68.

13 D. A. Rosen, 'Colonization through Law: The Judicial Defense of State Indian Legislation, 1790–1880', *American Journal of Legal History* 26(1) (2004), pp. 26–54.

14 Frell M. Owl, 'Who and What Is an American Indian?', *Ethnohistory* 9(3) (1962), pp. 265–84, at p. 274.

15 Jonathan Hughes, 'The Great Land Ordinances: Colonial America's Thumbprint on History', in David C. Klingaman and Richard K. Vedder (eds.), *Essays on the Economy of the Old Northwest* (Athens: Ohio University Press, 1987), pp. 1–13, at p. 9.

16 Article 7, http://digital.library.okstate.edu/kappler/Vol2/treaties/che0008. htm#mn7, accessed 22 February 2015.

17 Quoted by G. C. Anders, 'The Reduction of a Self-Sufficient People to Poverty and Welfare Dependence: An Analysis of the Causes of Cherokee Indian Underdevelopment', *American Journal of Economics and Sociology* 40(3) (1981), pp. 225–37, at p. 228.

18 Robert D. Aguirre, 'Picturing Tropical Nature', *Victorian Studies* 45(4) (2003), pp. 731–3, at p. 732.

19 Claudio Saunt, 'The Paradox of Freedom: Tribal Sovereignty and Emancipation during the Reconstruction of Indian Territory', *Journal of Southern History* 70(1) (2004), pp. 63–94, at p. 63.

20 Ibid., p. 68.

21 Ibid., p. 73.

22 Ibid., p. 75.

23 Ibid., p. 78.

24 Ibid., p. 83.

25 'Bad Medicine for the Klan: North Carolina Indians Break Up Anti-Indian Meeting', *Life* 44 (27 January 1958), pp. 26–8.

26 D. E. Wilkins, 'Breaking into the Intergovernmental Matrix: The Lumbee Tribe's Efforts to Secure Federal Acknowledgment', *Publius* 23(4) (1993), pp. 123–42.

27 T. Moore, 'Congress Decree: Only Two North Carolina Tribes Can Have Gaming', *Indian Country Today*, 28 December 2013, http:// indiancountrytodaymedianetwork.com/2013/12/28/congress-decree-only-two-north-carolina-tribes-can-have-gaming, accessed 22 February 2015.

28 See Joseph M. Prince and Richard H. Steckel, 'Nutritional Success on the Great Plains: Nineteenth-Century Equestrian Nomads', *Journal of Interdisciplinary History* 33(3) (2003), pp. 353–84, at p. 354.

29 From an interview published in 1986, available at http://www. heritage.nf.ca/articles/politics/1918-spanish-flu.php, accessed 24 September 2015.

30 See for instance: http://www.gi.alaska.edu/alaska-science-forum/villagers-remains-lead-1918-flu-breakthrough, accessed 24 September 2015.

31 Svenn-Erik Mamelund, Lisa Sattenspiel and Jessica Dimka, 'Influenza-Associated Mortality during the 1918–1919 Influenza Pandemic in Alaska and Labrador: A Comparison', *Social Science History* 37(2) (2013), pp. 177–229, at pp. 208–9.

32 These quotes come from the discussion by Philip Ranlet, 'The British, the Indians and Smallpox', *Pennsylvania History* 67(3) (2000), pp. 427–41.

33 The issues of genocide and holocaust are dealt with at length in Ward Churchill, *A Little Matter of Genocide: Holocaust and Denial in the Americas 1492 to the Present* (San Francisco: City Lights Books, 1997); and in Lilian Friedberg 'Dare to Compare: Americanizing the Holocaust', *American Indian Quarterly* 24(3) (2000), pp. 353–80. Churchill's controversial work on Indian identity and AIM activism is a fraught issue, complicated by his dismissal by the University of Colorado in 2006, for which see D. Eron and S. Hudson, *Report on the Termination of Ward Churchill*, Colorado Committee for the Protection of Faculty Rights, 2011, at https://www.scribd.com/doc/71999087/Mitchell-Churchill-Report.

34 Paul Kelton, 'Avoiding the Smallpox Spirits', *Ethnohistory* 51(1) (Winter 2004), pp. 45–71, at p. 45.

35 Ibid., p. 58.

36 As concluded by H. Jay Paulsen, 'Tuberculosis in the Native American: Indigenous or Introduced?', *Reviews of Infectious Diseases* 9(6) (1987), pp. 1180–86.

37 M. Lux, 'Perfect Subjects', *CBMH/BCHM* 15 (1998), pp. 277–9.

38 M. Trenk, 'Religious Uses of Alcohol among the Woodland Indians of North America', *Anthropos* 96(1) (2001), pp. 73–86, at p. 82.

39 Kathryn A. Abbott, 'Alcohol and the Anishinaabe of Minnesota in the Early Twentieth Century', *The Western Historical Quarterly* 30(1) (1999), pp. 25–43.

40 http://www.dailymail.co.uk/news/article-3273346/Deformed-mother-s-alcoholism-Indian-territory-hundreds-children-suffering-fetal-alcohol-syndrome-pregnant-moms-won-t-stop-drinking.html#reader-comments, accessed 15 October 2015.

41 Quoted by I. Ishii, 'Alcohol and Politics', *Ethnohistory* 50(4) (2003), pp. 671–95, at p. 675.

42 Ibid., p. 687.

43 M. T. Baker, 'The Hollow Promise of Tribal Power to Control the Flow of Alcohol into Indian Country', *Virginia Law Review* 88(3) (2002), pp. 685–737.

44 http://america.aljazeera.com/articles/2013/8/15/pine-ridge-indianreser vationvotestoendalcoholban.html, accessed 23 November 2015.

45 S. Neuman, 'Pine Ridge Reservation Lifts Century-Old Alcohol Ban', National Public Radio, 13 August 2013, available at http://www.npr.org/ blogs/thetwo-way/2013/08/15/212272144/south-dakota-reservation-lifts-century-old-alcohol-ban, accessed 24 February 2015.

46 P. F. Molin, 'Training the Hand, the Head, and the Heart. Indian Education at Hampton', *Minnesota History* 51(3) (1988), pp. 82–9, at p. 85.

47 David Wallace Adams, *Education for Extinction: American Indians and the Boarding School Experience, 1875–1928* (Lawrence: University of Kansas Press, 1995).

48 D. Davis, *Showdown at Shepherd's Bush* (New York: Thomas Dunne, 2012).

CHAPTER 2: RECOVERY

1 Some Indian people had already become citizens: the Stockbridges in the 1840s, the Pueblos under the Mexican treaty of 1848 and those choosing allotments under the Dawes Act of 1887.

2 Quoted by Kevin Bruyneel, 'Challenging American Boundaries: Indigenous People and the "Gift" of U.S. Citizenship', *Studies in American Political Development* 18 (2004), pp. 30–43, at p. 34.

3 Quoted in ibid., p. 34.

4 Clinton Rickard, *Fighting Tuscarora*, ed. Barbara Graymont (Syracuse: Syracuse University Press, 1973), p. 53.

5 *'Citizens Without Proof' Stands Strong* (New York: New York University School of Law Brennan Center, 2011), np, available at https://www.brennancenter.org/analysis/citizens-without-proof-stands-strong, accessed 15 September 2015.

6 Quoted in Bradford J. Vivian, 'Up from Memory', *Philosophy and Rhetoric* 45(2) (2012), pp. 189–212, at p. 195.

7 Washburn, 'Felix Cohen', pp. 594–5.

8 John W. Lederle, 'The Hoover Commission Reports', *Marquette Law Review* 33(2) (1949), pp. 89–98, at p. 89.

9 Charles F. Wilkinson and Eric R. Biggs, 'The Evolution of Termination Policy', *American Indian Law Review* 5(1) (1977), pp. 139–84, at p. 147.

10 Ibid., p. 150.

11 Roger Daniels, 'Myer, Dillon Seymour', *American National Biography Online*, February 2000, http://www.anb.org/articles/07/07-00216.html, accessed 21 September 2015.

12 Wilkinson and Biggs, 'The Evolution of Termination Policy', p. 159.

13 Stephen J. Herzberg, 'The Menominee Indians: Termination to Restoration', *American Indian Law Review* 6(1) (1978), pp. 143–86, at p. 151 n. 43.

14 Quoted by Susan Hood, 'Termination of the Klamath Indian Tribe of Oregon', *Ethnohistory* 19(4) (1972), pp. 379–92, at p. 381.

15 Quoted in ibid., p. 389.

16 Quoted by Angela Gonzales, Judy Kertész and Gabrielle Tayac, 'Eugenics as Indian Removal', *Public Historian* 29(3) (2007), pp. 53–67, at p. 64.

17 Katarzyna Bryc et al., 'The Genetic Ancestry of African Americans, Latinos, and European Americans across the United States', *American Journal of Human Genetics* 96(1), pp. 37–53, at p. 48.

18 Elizabeth Snell, 'Churchill had Iroquois Ancestors', nd, np, available at http://www.winstonchurchill.org/resources/myths/churchill-had-iroquois-ancestors, accessed 15 September 2015.

19 Jane Lawrence, 'The Indian Health Service and the Sterilization of Native American Women', *American Indian Quarterly* 24(3) (2000), pp. 400–419, at p. 411.

20 Ibid., p. 401.

21 Karen Stone, 'The Coercive Sterilization of Aboriginal Women in Canada', *American Indian Culture and Research Journal* 36(3) (2012), pp. 117–50, at p. 131.

22 Ian Mosby, 'Administering Colonial Science', *Histoire sociale/Social history* 46(91) (2013), pp. 145–72, at p. 147.

23 Ibid., p 169.

24 The first brief occupation had occurred in 1964.

25 Richard Nixon, '*Special Message* on *Indian Affairs*, July 8, 1970', available at http://www.epa.gov/tribal/pdf/president-nixon70.pdf, accessed 16 September 2015.

26 Quoted by Claire Palmiste, 'From the Indian Adoption Project to the Indian Child Welfare Act: The Resistance of Native American Communities', *Indigenous Policy Journal* 22(1) (2011), pp. 1–10, at p. 7.

27 B. J. Jones, 'The Indian Child Welfare Act', nd, np, available at https://www.americanbar.org/newsletter/publications/gp_solo_magazine_home/gp_solo_magazine_index/indianchildwelfareact.html#content, accessed 16 September 2015.

28 Palmiste, 'From the Indian Adoption Project to the Indian Child Welfare Act', p. 6.

29 http://pages.uoregon.edu/adoption/topics/IAP.html.

30 Jones, 'The Indian Child Welfare Act'.

31 Raven Sinclair, 'The '60s Scoop', available at http://www.originscanada. org/aboriginal-resources/the-stolen-generation/, accessed 8 February 2014.

32 Allyson Stevenson, 'Vibrations across a Continent', *American Indian Quarterly* 37(1–2) (2013), pp. 218–36, at p. 233, n. 9.

33 Dean J. Kotlowski, 'Alcatraz, Wounded Knee, and Beyond: The Nixon and Ford Administrations Respond to Native American Protest', *Pacific Historical Review* 72(2) (2003), pp. 201–27, at p. 211.

34 Quoted in G. St Germain, *First Nations Elections*, Senate Report, Ottawa, 2010, p. 6, available at http://www.parl.gc.ca/Content/SEN/ Committee/403/abor/subsiteMay10/Report_Home-e.htm, accessed 5 January 2015.

35 See 'Joseph Blasts Study', available at http://www.canada.com/story_print. html?id=d1b94299-ee31-4287-9535-4ef55dd02369&sponsor=, accessed 21 September 2015.

36 Quoted in St Germain, *First Nations Elections*, p. 22.

37 Ibid., p. 18.

38 *A Review of the Kahnawá:ke Membership Law*, 2007, www.kahnawake. com/org/docs/MembershipReport, accessed 5 January 2015.

39 Melissa L. Meyer, 'American Indian Blood Quantum Requirements: Blood Is Thicker than Family', in Valerie J. Matsumoto and Blake Allmendinger (eds.), *Over the Edge: Remapping the American West* (Berkeley: University of California Press, 1999), pp. 231–44, pp. 241–2 .

40 Shakopee Mdewakanton Sioux Community v. Acting Minneapolis Area Director, Bureau of Indian Affairs, IBIA 94-37-A, 94-38-A, www. oha.doi.gov/IBIA/IbiaDecisions/27ibia/27ibia163, accessed 5 January 2015, accessed 5 January 2015.

41 http://www.nytimes.com/2012/08/09/us/more-casinos-and-internet-gambling-threaten-shakopee-tribe.html?pagewanted=1&ref=us&src =me&_r=0, accessed 5 January 2015.

42 'The Harper Government Has to Consult on Changes to the Indian Act October 19, 2012', http://www.fsin.com/index.php/media-releases/ 829-the-harper-government-has-to-consult-on-changes-to-the-indian-act-october-19-2012.html, accessed 5 January 2015.

43 Joe Friesen 'Surge in Newfoundland Native Band has Ottawa Stunned, Skeptical', *Globe and Mail*, 14 April 2014, available at http://www.theglo beandmail.com/news/politics/ottawa-moves-to-tighten-aboriginal-membership-criteria/article17954032/, accessed 9 September 2015.

CHAPTER 3: LAND

1 Hobbes and Locke are discussed by Benjamin B. Lopata in 'Property Theory in Hobbes', *Political Theory* 1(2) (1973), pp. 203–18.

2 Both quotes from Noel Malcolm, 'Hobbes, Sandys, and the Virginia Company', *Historical Journal* 24(2) (1981), pp. 297–321, at p. 305.

3 Stuart Banner, *How the Indians Lost Their Land: Law and Power on the Frontier* (Cambridge, MA: Harvard University Press, 2005), p. 53.

4 Lawrence Kinnaird, Francisco Blache and Navarro Blache, 'Spanish Treaties with Indian Tribes', *Western Historical Quarterly* 10(1) (1979), pp. 39–48.

5 Quoted by Christian B. Keller, 'Philanthropy Betrayed: Thomas Jefferson, the Louisiana Purchase, and the Origins of Federal Indian Removal Policy', *Proceedings of the American Philosophical Society* 144(1) (2000), pp. 39–66, at p. 44.

6 B. A.Watson, *Buying America from the Indians* (Norman: University of Oklahoma Press, 2012).

7 Russell Thornton, 'Cherokee Population Losses during the Trail of Tears: A New Perspective and a New Estimate', *Ethnohistory* 31(4) (1984), pp. 289–300, at p. 289.

8 Senate/Department of War/Treasury/Document 403: 190, 1836.

9 http://www.nps.gov/mnrr/historyculture/upload/Standing%20Bear. pdf, accessed 2 October 2015.

10 Wilcomb E. Washburn, *The Assault on Indian Tribalism: The General Allotment Law (Dawes Act) of 1887* (Philadelphia: Lippincott, 1975), p. 9.

11 US Department of Interior Office of Inspector General, 'Coordination of Efforts to Address Indian Land Fractionation', Washington, DC, 2011, p. 3.

12 Department of Interior, Coordination of Efforts to Address Indian Land Fractionation Report No. WR-EV-BIA-0002-2010, p. 1, available at https://www.iltf.org/sites/default/files/ILCP%20Inspector%20General %20Evaluation%201-4-11.pdf, accessed 24 November 2015.

13 http://www.indiantrust.com/important, accessed 8 January 2015.

14 Leonard A Carlson, 'The Dawes Act and the Decline of Indian Farming', *Journal of Economic History* 38(1) (1978), pp. 274–6.

15 The papers written to commemorate the 250th anniversary in 2013 are at http://activehistory.ca/papers. See for instance /the-royal-proclamation-in-historical-context/, accessed 18 November 2014.

16 http://www.cbu.ca/mrc/treaties/1725, accessed 2 October 2015.

17 Uttered famously by Sir Henry Wotton (1568–1639); see Ian Ousby, *English Literature* (Cambridge: Cambridge University Press, 1996), p. 431

18 Quoted in OED definition of diplomacy from T. C. Grattan, *Beaten Paths* (1862), vol. 2, p. 223.

19 D. Jones, 'Canadian Court Expands Aboriginal Rights', at http://www. factsandopinions.com/dispatches/justice/canadian-court-expands-abo riginal-rights/, accessed 18 November 2014.

20 http://www.digitalhistory.uh.edu/disp_textbook. cfm?smtid=3&psid=727, accessed 2 October 2015.

21 http://www.commerce.state.ak.us/dca/logon/plan/planning-ancsa.htm, accessed 2 October 2015.

22 Paul Ongtooguk, *The Annotated ANCSA*, nd, available at http://www. alaskool.org/projects/ancsa/annancsa.htm, accessed 12 January 2013.

23 http://www.blm.gov/ak/st/en/info/newsroom/2012/november/NPR-A_oil_ and_gas_lease_sale_generates_898_900dollars_in_revenue_11072012. html, accessed 2 October 2015.

24 http://www.nytimes.com/2014/10/27/opinion/the-land-grab-out-west. html?hpw&rref=opinion&action=click&pgtype=Homepage&version =HpHedThumbWell&module=well-region&region=bottom-well&WT. nav=bottom-well&_r=0, accessed 27 October 2014.

25 Jered T. Davidson, 'This land is your land . . .', *American Indian Law Review* 35(2) (2010–11), pp. 575–619, at p. 582.

26 G. Malcolm Lewis, *Cartographic Encounters* (Chicago: University of Chicago Press, 1998); Mark Warhus, *Another America* (New York: St Martin's Press, 1997).

27 Lewis, *Cartographic Encounters*, pp. 11–13.

28 Anne Henshaw, 'Pausing along the Journey: Learning Landscapes, Environmental Change, and Toponymy amongst the Sikusilarmiut', *Arctic Anthropology* 43(1) (2006), pp. 52–66, at p. 56.

29 Claudio Aporta, 'Routes, Trails and Tracks: Trail Breaking among the Inuit of Igloolik', *Études/Inuit/Studies* 28(2) (2004), pp. 9–38, at p. 13.

30 Henshaw, 'Pausing along the Journey', p. 53.

31 John MacDonald, *The Arctic Sky: Inuit Astronomy, Star Lore, and Legends* (Toronto Royal Ontario Museum / Nunavut Research Institute: Royal Ontario Museum, 1998), p. 163.

32 Ibid. pp. 186–7.

33 George Copway, *The Life, History, and Travels of Kah-ge-ga-gah-bowh (George Copway), a Young Indian Chief of the Ojebwa Nation* (Philadelphia: J. Harmstead: 1847), pp. 19–20.

34 http://www.atns.net.au/agreement.asp?EntityID=2026, accessed 2 October 2015.
35 http://www.irc.inuvialuit.com/about/finalagreement.html, accessed 2 October 2015.
36 Paul Raynard, ' "Welcome in, but Check Your Rights at the Door": The James Bay and Nisga'a Agreements in Canada', *Canadian Journal of Political Science / Revue canadienne de science politique* 33(2) (2000), pp. 211–43, at p. 241.
37 These include: Milton Freeman (ed.), *Inuit Land Use and Occupancy Project: A Report.* (Ottawa: Ministry of Supply and Services, 1976); T. R. Berger, *Northern Frontier, Northern Homeland: The Report of the Mackenzie Valley Pipeline Inquiry* (Ottawa: Ministry of Supply and Services, 1977); Carol Brice-Bennett (ed.), *Our Footprints Are Everywhere: Inuit Land Use and Occupancy in Labrador* (Nain: Labrador Inuit Association, 1977).
38 See Darcy S. Bushnell, 'American Indian Water Right Settlements', 2013; available at uttoncenter.unm.edu/pdfs/American_Indian_Water_Right_Settlements, accessed 22 October 2015.
39 Ibid.
40 See http://www.international.gc.ca/trade-agreements-accords-commerciaux/topics-domaines/disp-diff/sunbelt.aspx?lang=eng, accessed 2 October 2015.
41 *California Law Review* 84(6) (1996), pp. 1573–655.
42 'Review of Jerry Brotton, *A History of the World in Twelve Maps*', *The Times Literary Supplement*, 12 October 2012, pp 8–9). For the story see Jorge Luis Borges, 'On Exactitude in Science', *Collected Fictions*, translated by Andrew Hurley, available at http://www.sccs.swarthmore.edu/users/08/bblonder/phys120/docs/borges.pdf, accessed 2 October 2015.

CHAPTER 4: OTHERS: BEINGS, BELIEVING AND THE PRACTICE OF RELIGION

1 R. A. Brightman, 'The Windigo in the Material World', *Ethnohistory* 35(4) (1988), pp. 337–9.
2 R. A. Brightman, 'Field Notes, Pukatawagan and Granville Lake, Manitoba, 1977–9', quoted in 'The Windigo in the Material World', p. 352.
3 Jack D. Forbes, *Columbus and Other Cannibals: The Wetiko Disease of Exploitation, Imperialism and Terrorism* (New York: 7 Stories Press, 1978/2008).

4 For which see S. D. Gill, *Mother Earth* (Chicago: University of Chicago Press, 1987).

5 See https://indiancountrytodaymedianetwork.com/2014/03/14/yellowstone-bison-slaughter-over-controversy-remains-154018, accessed 25 October 2014.

6 L. Burton, 'Birthing the Woolly Cow', in *Worship and Wilderness* (Madison: University of Wisconsin Press, 2002), pp. 170–93.

7 Two Makah were imprisoned for whaling in 2008; the need for a permit to hunt was said to override the 1855 treaty right to hunt. K. Alexander, *The International Whaling Convention (IWC) and Legal Issues Related to Aboriginal Rights*, p. 11, http://fas.org/sgp/crs/row/R40571.pdf, accessed 24 October 2014. The World Wildlife Fund says there are 15,000–22,000 grey whales: http://wwf.panda.org/what_we_do/endangered_species/cetaceans/about/gray_whale222/, accessed 24 October 2014.

8 D. B. Shimkin, 'Siberian Ethnography', *Arctic Anthropology* 27(1) (1990), pp. 36–51.

9 'Médecins' is the term used by Louis Nicholas for Algonquian specialists in the 'Codex Canadensis', from his missionary activities of 1664–75. See G. Hamel and W. A. Fox, 'Rattlesnake Tales', *Ontario Archaeology* 79/80 (2005), pp. 127–49.

10 The title of Carl Jung's monograph (London: Kegan Paul Trench Trubner, 1933).

11 L. Aldred, 'Plastic Shamans and Astroturf Sun Dances', *American Indian Quarterly* 24(3) (2000), pp. 329–52.

12 www.newagefraud.org, accessed 8 October 2015.

13 http://www.angelvalley.org/, accessed 8 November 2015

14 N. Riccardi, 'Self-help Guru Convicted in Arizona Sweat Lodge Deaths', http://articles.latimes.com/2011/jun/22/nation/la-na-sweat-lodge-trial-20110623, accessed 27 May 2014.

15 'Piers Morgan Live, Rewind: An Exclusive Interview with James Ray, the Man Convicted of Three Deaths Following a Sweat Lodge Tragedy in Arizona', http://piersmorgan.blogs.cnn.com/2013/11/26/piers-morgan-live-rewind, accessed 11 November 2014.

16 Kenn Harper, 'February 10, 1922: A Circus of Formality', http://www.nunatsiaqonline.ca/archives/50225/opinionEditorial/columns.html, accessed 8 October 2015.

17 Quoted in Hans Christian Gulløv, 'The Revival at Pisugfik in 1768: An Ethnohistorical Approach', *Arctic Anthropology* 23(1/2) (1986), pp. 151–75, at p. 152.

18 Ibid.

19 F. de Laguna, 'Atna and Tlingit Shamanism', *Arctic Anthropology* 24(1) (1987), pp. 84–100.

20 N. J. Turner, 'Use of Devil's Club', *Journal of Ethnobiology* 2(1) (1982), pp. 17–38.

21 J. D. Bloxton, A. Der Marderosian, 'Bioactive Constituents of Alaskan Devil's Root (Oplopanax horridus, Araliaceae)', *Economic Botany* 56(3) (2002), pp. 285–7, at p. 286.

22 J. Oosten, F. Laugrand, C. Remie, 'Perceptions of Decline: Inuit Shamanism in the Canadian Arctic', *Ethnohistory* 53(3) (2006), pp. 445–77, at p. 471.

23 R. S. Michaelsen, ' "We Also Have a Religion": The Free Exercise of Religion among Native Americans', *American Indian Quarterly* 7(3) (1983), pp. 111–42.

24 S. S. Harjo, 'The American Indian Religious Freedom Act: Looking Back and Looking Forward', *Wicazo Sa Review* 19(2) (2004), pp. 143–51.

25 S. Michaelsen, 'Ely S. Parker and Amerindian Voices in Ethnography', *American Literary History* 8(4) (1996), pp. 615–38. L. T. Scales, 'Revolutions in Nat Turner and Joseph Smith', *American Literary History*, 24(2) (2012), pp. 205–33.

26 C. L. Eisgruber and M. Zeisberg, 'Religious Freedom in Canada and the United States', *International Journal of Constitutional Law* 4(2) (2006), pp. 244–68, http://icon.oxfordjournals.org/content/4/2/244.full, accessed 29 September 2013.

27 Frank v. Alaska, 604 P.2d 1068 (Alaska Sup. Ct., 1979), http://law2.umkc.edu/faculty/projects/ftrials/conlaw/frank.html, accessed 8 October 2015.

28 F. Boas, 'Origin of Totemism', *American Anthropologist* 18(3) (1916), pp. 319–26, at p. 319.

29 C. Lévi-Strauss, *Totemism* (London: Pelican, 1969). R. Riddington, T. Riddington, 'The Inner Eye of Shamanism and Totemism', *History of Religions* 10(1) (1970), pp. 49–61. W. Shapiro, 'Claude Lévi-Strauss Meets Alexander Goldenweiser', *American Anthropologist* 93(3) (1991), pp. 599–610.

30 Takao Abé, *The Jesuit Mission to New France* (Leiden: Brill, 2011), pp. 115–16.

31 J. Axtell, *The European and the Indian* (New York: Oxford University Press, 1981), pp. 45–6.

32 J. Axtell, 'The Scholastic Philosophy of the Wilderness', *William and Mary Quarterly* 29(3) (1972), pp. 335–66, at pp. 337–8.

33 Ibid., p. 360.

34 Ibid., p. 361.

35 For this period see, for instance, B. C. Peyer, *The Tutor'd Mind* (Amherst: University of Massachusetts, 1997).

36 J. P. and J. Ronda, 'The Death of John Sassamon', *American Indian Quarterly* 1(2) (1974), pp. 91–102.

37 H. J. Viola, *Thomas L. McKenney, Architect of America's Early Indian Policy: 1816–1830* (Chicago: Sage Books, 1974).

38 D. M. Nielsen, 'The Mashpee Indian Revolt of 1833', *New England Quarterly* 58(3) (1985), pp. 400–420, at p. 416.

39 D. B. Smith, *Mississauga Portraits* (Toronto: University of Toronto Press, 2013).

40 George Copway, *The Life, History, and Travels of Kah-ge-ga-gah-bowh*; D. B. Smith 'The Life of George Copway, or Kah-ge-ga-gah-bowh (1818–1869): And a Review of His Writings', *Journal of Canadian Studies* 23(3) (1988), pp. 5–38.

41 For whom see: http://www2.mnhs.org/library/findaids/P0823.xml, accessed 15 November 2014.

42 A. G. Eastman, *Pratt, the Red Man's Moses* (Norman: University of Oklahoma Press, 1935).

43 R. F. Engs, *Educating the Disfranchised and Disinherited: Samuel Chapman Armstrong and Hampton Institute, 1839–1893* (Knoxville: University of Tennessee Press, 1999).

44 D. B. MacDonald and G. Hudson, 'The Genocide Question and Indian Residential Schools in Canada', *Canadian Journal of Political Science / Revue canadienne de science politique* 45(2) (2012), pp. 427–49.

45 S. Kan, 'Orthodox Christianity and the Tlingit Mortuary Complex', *Arctic Anthropology* 24(1) (1987), pp. 32–55, at p. 47.

46 W. K. Powers, 'Sixth Grandfather: Black Elk's Teaching Given to John G. Neihardt by Raymond J. DeMallie', *Ethnohistory* 33(1) (1986), pp. 121–3.

47 See Arnold Krupat, 'Chief Seattle's Speech Revisited' *American Indian Quarterly* 35(2) (2011), pp. 192–214.

48 C. Bierwert, 'Remembering Chief Seattle', *American Indian Quarterly* 22(3) (1998), pp. 280–304, at p. 281.

49 E. B. Tylor, *Primitive Culture* (London: John Murray, 1871), vol. 1, xi, p. 384.

50 G. Harvey, *Animism: Respecting the Living World* (New York: Columbia University Press, 2006), pp 36–9.

51 L. Sundstrom, 'Mirror of Heaven: Cross-Cultural Transference of the Sacred Geography of the Black Hills', *World Archaeology* 28(2) (1996), pp. 177–89.

52 Voice of America, 2003, 'Crazy Horse Memorial Generates Mixed Feelings', http://www.voanews.com/content/a–13–a–2003–09–13–7–crazy–66325922/543925.html, accessed 8 October 2015

53 G. Goodwin, 'White Mountain Apache Religion', *American Anthropologist* 40(1) (1938), pp. 24–37, at p. 27.

54 K. R. Fletcher, 'The Road to Repatriation', 25 November 2008, http://www.smithsonianmag.com/specialsections/heritage/the–road–to–repatriation.html#ixzz2eT1zEvew, accessed 10 September 2013.

55 J. R. Welch, 'White Eyes' Lies and the Battle for dził nchaa si'an', *American Indian Quarterly* 21(1) (1997), pp. 75–109.

56 P. W. Lackenbauer and M. Farish, 'The Cold War on Canadian Soil: Militarizing a Northern Environment', *Environmental History* 12 (2007), pp. 921–50.

57 W. N. Fenton, *The False Faces of the Iroquois* (Norman: University of Oklahoma Press, 1987).

58 W. N. Fenton, 'The Seneca Society of Faces', *Scientific Monthly* 44(3) (1937), pp. 215–38, at p. 216.

59 W. La Barre, *The Peyote Cult* (Norman: University of Oklahoma Press, 1989). J. S. Slotkin, *The Peyote Religion* (Glencoe: Free Press, 1956). O. Stewart, *The Peyote Religion* (Norman: University of Oklahoma Press, 1987).

60 H. W. Hertzberg, *The Search for an American Indian Identity* (Syracuse: Syracuse University Press, 1971).

61 People v. Woody, 394 P.2d 813, Sup. Ct. Calif. 1964.

62 G. De Verges, 'Constitutional Law: Freedom of Religion: Peyote and the Native American Church', *American Indian Law Review*, 2(2) (1974), pp. 71–9. For the church see, for instance, http://Nativeamerican–churches.org/, accessed 8 October 2015.

63 R. Linton and A. I. Hallowell, 'Nativistic Movements', *American Anthropologist* 45(2) (1943), pp. 230–40.

64 A. F. C. Wallace, 'Revitalization Movements', *American Anthropologist*, New Series, 58(2) (1956), pp. 264–81, at p. 264

65 F. L. Owsley, 'Prophet of War', *American Indian Quarterly* 9(3) (1985), pp. 273–93.

66 See: M. Angel, *Preserving the Sacred* (Winnipeg: University of Manitoba Press, 2002); L. W. Gross, 'Cultural Sovereignty and Native American Hermeneutics in the Interpretation of the Sacred Stories of the Anishinaabe', *Wicazo Sa Review*, 18(2) (2003), pp. 127–34; E. Benton-Banai, 'The Great Flood', http://nrd.kbic–nsn.gov/PDF/Cultural/The–Great–Flood.pdf, accessed 23 November 2014.

67 A. A. Cave, *Prophets of the Great Spirit* (Lincoln: University of Nebraska Press, 2006), pp. 183–229.

68 S. Neylan, 'Shaking Up Christianity', *Journal of Religion* 91(2) (2011), pp. 188–222.

69 J. Blackeslee, 'The Origin and Spread of the Calumet Ceremony', *American Antiquity* 46(4) (1981), pp. 759–68.

70 A. C. Fletcher, 'The Hako: A Pawnee Ceremony', 23rd Annual Report of the Bureau of American Ethnology, Washington, 1904, p. 176.

71 W. N. Fenton, 'The Iroquois Eagle Dance', *Bureau of American Ethnology Bulletin* 156,Washington.

72 C. Vecsey, 'Pueblo Indian Catholicism: The Isleta Case', *U.S. Catholic Historian* 16(2) (1998), pp. 1–19, at p. 7.

73 Peter Whiteley, 'Re-imagining Awat'ovi', in R. W. Preucel (ed.), *Archaeologies of the Pueblo Revolt* (Albuquerque: University of New Mexico Press, 2002), pp. 147–66.

74 Ibid, p. 13.

75 http://bloggerpriest.com/2013/07/15/the–flying–padre–fred–stadtmueller/, accessed 8 October 2015.

76 Vecsey, 'Pueblo Indian Catholicism', p. 18.

77 J. Shapiro, 'From Tupã to the Land Without Evil: The Christianization of Tupi–Guarani', *American Ethnologist* 14(1) (1987), pp. 126–39.

78 J. B. Richland, 'Hopi Sovereignty as Epistemological Limit', *Wicazo Sa Review*, 24(1) (2009), pp. 89–112.

79 http://www8.nau.edu/~hcpo-p/, accessed 8 October 2015.

80 T. Mills, 'He Arrived a Skeptic', http://indiancountrytodaymedianet work.com/2012/02/22/he–arrived–skeptic–left–believer–power–and–wisdom–hopi–rain–dance–99005, accessed 8 October 2015.

81 James A. Sandos, 'Junípero Serra's Canonization and the Historical Record', *American Historical Review* 93(5) (1988), pp. 1253–69, at p.1255.

82 James A. Sandos, *Converting California* (New Haven: Yale University Press, 2008), pp. 175–6.

83 The use of the term 'horticulture', as opposed to agriculture, has been taken as demeaning of the scale of Mississippian farming; it is preferred here because agriculture implies the use of mechanical devices such as the plough and animals such as oxen, absent, of course, from the Americas before European contact.

84 A rolling stone disc game in which is a stick is thrown, the winner being the one whose stick is closest to the stone when it falls over.

CHAPTER 5: LANGUAGE AND LITERATURE

1 Franz Boas first introduced the question of terms for snow in 1911, which in the late twentieth century became an *idée fixe*, a trope and a means of caricaturing, objectifying and 'othering' 'Eskimos'. But in other non-hunting societies similar elaboration of terms are important: the pastoralist Nuer in South Sudan have hundreds of different terms for cattle, used also to structure kinship relations, and the Hanunoo in the Philippines have ninety-two names for rice. See John Steckley, *White Lies about the Inuit* (Peterborough: Broadview Press, 2008), pp. 132-3). Against this, in the middle of the twentieth century, with the Whorfian rise of linguistic relativism, the Sapir-Whorf hypothesis, which suggested that culture follows language, linguists wished to show that culture and language possessed separate autonomous structures; while popular culture and Native self-presentation preferred the close association of language and culture. Martin expostulated against this 'vitality beyond university walls' as though only academics might have the right to determine the life of ideas. L. Martin, 'Eskimo Words for Snow', *American Anthropologist*, 88(2) (1986), pp. 418-23. What matters in this is the vitality of the discussion, as a source of understanding, rather than any overarching sense that one point of view is 'correct'.

2 Review by Keren Rice 'The Languages of Native North America by Marianne Mithun', *Language* 77(2) (2001), pp. 356-60.

3 Edward J. Vajda, '*The Languages of Native North America* by Marianne Mithun, Review by Edward J. Vajda', *Journal of Linguistics* 36(3) (2000), pp. 608-12.

4 J. Nichols, 'Language Spread Rates and Prehistoric American Migration Rates', *Current Anthropology* 49(6) (2008), pp. 1109-17.

5 W. Labov, S. Ash and C. Boberg, 'A National Map of the Regional Dialects of American English', http://www.ling.upenn.edu/phono_atlas/NationalMap/NationalMap.html, accessed 16 December 2012.

6 See J. A. P. Wilson, 'Material Cultural Correlates of the Athapaskan Expansion', PhD thesis, University of Florida, 2011, pp. 53-4.

7 L. J. Murray, 'Vocabularies of Native American Languages', *American Quarterly* 53(4) (2001), pp. 590-623, at p. 592.

8 See Peter Stephen Du Ponceau Collection 1781-1844, Mss.B.D92p, American Philosophical Society, Philadelphia.

9 H. J. Viola, *Thomas L. McKenney: Architect of America's Early Indian Policy, 1816-1830* (Chicago: The Swallow Press, 1974).

10 Algonkin, 'real people', was an early version of Algonquin and refers especially to the First Nation north of Ottawa on the Ottawa River.

11 See Richard C. Trexler, 'Making the American Berdache: Choice or Constraint?', *Journal of Social History* 35(3) (2002), pp. 613–36. Gregory D. Smithers, 'Cherokee "Two Spirits"', *Early American Studies* 12(3) (2014), pp. 626–51.

12 E. Vajda, 'A Siberian Link with Na-Dene languages', in J. Kari and B. A. Potter (eds.), *The Dene-Yeniseian Connection*, Anthropological Papers of the University of Alaska, New Series, 5(1–2) (Fairbanks: UAF Department of Anthropology and the Alaska Native Languages Center, 2010), pp. 33–99.

13 J. H. Greenberg, 'In Defense of Amerind', *International Journal of American Linguistics* 62(2) (1996), pp. 131–64.

14 B. Adler, 'Echoes from the Past', http://sciencenotes.ucsc.edu/9901/echoes/echoes.htm, accessed 8 August 2014.

15 M. Swadesh, 'Archeological and Linguistic Chronology of Indo–European Groups', *American Anthropologist* 55(3) (1953), pp. 349–52.

16 K. Bergsland and H. Vogt, 'On the Validity of Glottochronology', *Current Anthropology* 3(2) (1962), pp. 115–53.

17 Roger Blench, 'Accounting for the Diversity of Amerindian Languages: Modelling the Settlement of the New World, Presented at Archaeology Research Seminar, RSPAS, Canberra November 21, 2008', available at http://www.rogerblench.info/Archaeology/New%20World/New%20World%20archaeology%20opening%20page.htm, accessed 14 October 2015.

18 Michael R. Waters, Steven L. Forman, Thomas A. Jennings, Lee C. Nordt, Steven G. Driese, Joshua M. Feinberg, Joshua L. Keene, Jessi Halligan, Anna Lindquist, James Pierson, Charles T. Hallmark, Michael B. Collins, James E. Wiederhold, 'The Buttermilk Creek Complex and the Origins of Clovis at the Debra L. Friedkin Site, Texas', *Science* 331 (2011), pp. 1599–1603.

19 http://www.ethnologue.com/region/Americas, accessed 19 September 2014.

20 M. Paul Lewis, 'Sustainable Language Use 2014', http://www.ethnologue.com/ethnoblog/m-paul-lewis/sustainable-language-use#.Vh5sYHpViko, accessed 14 October 2014.

21 U. P. Gad, 'Post-colonial Identity in Greenland? When the Empire Dichotomizes Back – Bring Politics Back In', *Journal of Language and Politics* 8(1) (2009), pp. 136–58, available at polsci.ku.dk/arbejdspapirer/2008/ap_2008_06.pdf/, p. 13.

22 http://aboutworldlanguages.com/irish-gaelic, accessed 14 October 2015.

23 Anthony Mattina, Peter J. Seymour and M. DeSautel, *The Golden Woman: The Colville Narrative of Peter J. Seymour* (Tucson: University of Arizona Press, 1985).

24 https://portal.ehawaii.gov/, accessed 9 September 2014; and http://labor .hawaii.gov/ola/about-us/, accessed 14 October 2015.

25 J. Crawford, 'Seven Hypotheses on Language Loss Causes and Cures', in G. Cantoni (ed.), *Stabilizing Indigenous Languages*, revised edn (Flagstaff: Center for Excellence in Education, Northern Arizona University, 2007), pp. 45–60.

26 http://www.census.gov/prod/2013pubs/acs-22.pdf, accessed 9 September 2014.

27 T. Korte, 'How Effective Was Navajo Code? "One Former Captive Knows"', http://www.yvwiiusdinvnohii.net/articles/navcode.htm, accessed 13 June 2014.

28 Other peoples also contributed code-talkers: Cherokee, Comanche, Hopi and Choctaw, the first in the First World War.

29 *Aboriginal Languages in Canada*, Census of Population (Ottawa: Statistics Canada, 2011).

30 M. L. Aylward, 'The Role of Inuit Languages in Nunavut Schooling: Nunavut Teachers Talk About Bilingual Education', *Canadian Journal of Education* 33(2) (2010), pp. 295–328.

31 Ibid., p. 311.

32 http://langcom.nu.ca/node/400, accessed 14 October 2015.

33 'Between 2001 and 2006, the proportion of Nunavummiut who reported using Inuktitut or Inuinnaqtun most often at home declined from 57 to 54 per cent, and while 26 per cent of Nunavummiut identified English as their only mother tongue in 2006, it was the language spoken most often at home by 44 per cent of the population.' 'Our Primary Concern: Inuit Language in Nunavut 2009/2010. Annual Report on the State of Inuit Culture and Society', Nunavut Tunngavik Inc., Iqaluit, p. 5, www.tunngavik.com, accessed 20 October 2015.

34 L. Wyman, P. Marlow, C. F. Andrew, G. Miller, C. R. Nicholai and Y. N. Rearden, 'High Stakes Testing, Bilingual Education and Language Endangerment: A Yup'ik Example', *International Journal of Bilingual Education and Bilingualism* 13(6) (2010), pp. 701–21.

35 O. Alexie, S. Alexie and P. Marlow, 'Creating Space and Defining Roles: Elders and Adult Yup'ik Immersion', *Journal of American Indian Education* 48(3) (2009), pp. 1–18.

36 L. T. Wyman, 'Youth Linguistic Survivance', in L. T. Wyman, T. L. McCarty and S. E. Nicholas (eds.), *Indigenous Youth and Bi/Multilingualism* (London: Routledge, 2013), pp. 90–110.

37 http://www.edu.gov.on.ca/eng/aboriginal/fnmiframework.pdf, accessed 20 October 2015.

38 http://www.cde.ca.gov/be/st/ss/documents/histsocscistnd.pdf, accessed 20 October 2015.

39 http://www.aicls.org/, accessed 20 October 2015

40 In D. Hallett, M. J. Chandler and C. Lalonde, 'Aboriginal Language Knowledge and Youth Suicide', *Cognitive Development* 22(3) (2007), pp. 392–9.

41 A. Calkins, *Ten Years After* (Juneau: Sealaska Corporation, 2013).

42 There was no equivalent politician to Inouye in Canada in the last third of the twentieth century to fight for aboriginal rights and promote legislation, perhaps because of the different structure of Canadian politics.

43 L. Warhol, *Native American Language Policy in the United States* (Washington, DC: Alliance for the Advancement of Heritage Languages, Center for Applied Linguistics (CAL), 2011).

44 Robert Yagelski, 'A Rhetoric of Contact', *Rhetoric Review* 14(1) (1995), pp. 64–77, at p. 69.

45 Quoted in T. J. Maxwell, 'Pontiac before 1763', *Ethnohistory* 4(1) (1957), pp. 41–6, at p. 41.

46 OED, 1642, T. FULLER *Holy State*, II.vii.73: 'Some condemne Rhetorick as the mother of lies.'

47 Yet American writers were suspicious of too much rhetoric: See 'On Puffing', *American Magazine and Historical Chronicle* 1 (1743–4), pp. 249–51, which speaks of: 'A satirical survey of the various species of Puffers, or those full of themselves and willing to put on rhetorical displays. Among the most noteworthy and infamous puffs, says the writer, are the clergy and members of the bar, whom the author calls "Puff–rhetoricians".' Quoted by J. M. Farrell and J. M. Noone, 'Rhetoric, Eloquence, and Oratory in Eighteenth-Century American Periodicals', *Rhetoric Society Quarterly* 23(2) (1993), pp. 72–80.

48 R. Wheeler, 'Hendrick Aupaumut Christian-Mahican Prophet', *Journal of the Early Republic* 25 (2) (2005), pp. 187–220, at pp. 205–6.

49 A hilarious portrayal of Cooper's caricaturing of Indians was published by Mark Twain in 1895: *Fenimore Cooper's Literary Offences,* in which he suggests the 'leather stocking' tales should be renamed the 'broken twig' tales, for the way in which Cooper's Indian trackers follow broken twigs.

50 Brother Jonathan was loosely based on a Washington catchphrase, 'We must consult brother Jonathan', speaking about his quartermaster, royal and then American governor Jonathan Trumbull (1710–85). By the end of the nineteenth century this heroic American trickster had morphed into the much less funny Uncle Sam as the personification of the United States.

51 Cadwallader Colden, *The History of the Five Indian Nations of Canada* (London: T. Osborne, 1747), np, available at http://www.gutenberg.org/files/35719/35719-h/35719-h.htm, accessed 20 October 2015.

52 Francis Jennings, 'Logan, James', *American National Biography Online*, February 2000, http://www.anb.org/articles/01/01–00530.html, accessed 20 October 2015.

53 Arnold Krupat, *'That the People Might Live': Loss and Renewal in Native American Elegy* (Ithaca: Cornell University Press, 2012).

54 B. A. Meek, 'And the Injun Goes "How!" ', *Language in Society* 35(1) (2006), pp. 93–128.

55 See J. Brooks, *The Collected Writings of Samson Occom, Mohegan* (Oxford: Oxford University Press, 1982); B. C. Peyer, *The Tutor'd Mind* (Amherst: University of Massachusetts Press, 1997).

56 B. O'Connell (ed.), *On Our Own Ground: The Complete Writings of William Apess, a Pequot* (Amherst: University of Massachusetts Press, 1992).

57 D. B. Smith, *Sacred Feathers: Reverend Peter Jones (Kahkewaquonaby)* (Lincoln: University of Nebraska Press, 1987).

58 D. B. Smith, 'Kahgegagahbowh', in *Dictionary of Canadian Biography*, vol. 9 (Toronto: University of Toronto/Université Laval, 2003), available at http://www.biographi.ca/en/bio/kahgegagahbowh_9E.html, accessed 20 October 2015.

59 'Jane Johnston Schoolcraft' (2004), at http://voices.cla.umn.edu/artist-pages/schoolcraft_jane.php, accessed 6 October 2014.

60 Elisabeth Tooker, 'The League of the Iroquois: Its History, Politics, and Ritual', in William C. Sturtevant (ed.), *Handbook of North American Indians*, vol. 15: *Northeast* (Washington, DC: Smithsonian Institution, 1978), pp. 418–41, at p. 432.

61 Sherman Alexie, *The Absolutely True Diary of a Part-time Indian* (London, Andersen Press, 2008).

62 *Honouring the Truth, Reconciling the Future*, p. 93, available at http://www.trc.ca/websites/trcinstitution/File/2015/Findings/Exec_Summary_2015_05_31_web_o.pdf, accessed 25 November 2015. See also http://www.cbc.ca/news/aboriginal/huge–number–of–records–to–land–on–truth–and–reconciliation–commission–s–doorstep–1.2617770, accessed 20 October 2015. A. Smith, 'Soul Wound', 2007, http://www.amnestyusa.org/node/87342, accessed 20 October 2015.

63 Sarah Winnemucca Hopkins, *Life among the Piutes* (Boston and New York: Cupples, Upham, Putnam's, 1883), p. 231.

64 Marilyn J. Rose, 'Johnson, Emily Pauline,' in *Dictionary of Canadian Biography*, vol. 14, (Toronto: University of Toronto/Université Laval, 2003), http://www.biographi.ca/en/bio/johnson_emily_pauline_14E.html, accessed 28 September 2014.

65 A. L. Ruoff, 'American Indian Literatures: Introduction and Bibliography', *American Studies International* 24(2) (1986), pp. 2–52.

66 S. L. Smith, 'Francis LaFlesche', *American Indian Quarterly* 25(4) (2001), pp. 579–603.

67 N. M. Clark, 'Dr. Montezuma, Apache: Warrior in Two Worlds', *Montana: The Magazine of Western History* 23(2) (1973), pp. 56–65.

68 R. Spack, 'Dis/engagement: Zitkala-Ša's Letters to Carlos Montezuma, 1901–1902', *MELUS*, 26(1) (2001), pp. 172–204.

69 D. B. Smith, 'Jones, Peter Edmund', in *Dictionary of Canadian Biography*, vol. 13, (Toronto: University of Toronto/Université Laval, 2003), http://www.biographi.ca/en/bio/jones_peter_edmund_13E.html, accessed 6 October 2014.

70 Gayle M. Comeau-Vasilopoulos, 'Oronhyatekha', in *Dictionary of Canadian Biography*, vol. 13 (Toronto: University of Toronto/Université Laval, 2003), http://www.biographi.ca/en/bio/oronhyatekha_13E.html, accessed 6 October 2014.

71 For a church and freemason view of Philip Deloria, see: J. E. Bennett, 'Prince of Dakota Sioux', at http://lodge141.tripod.com/indian.htm, accessed 20 October 2015; and for a Native and family view, see: V. Deloria Jnr, *Singing for a Spirit* (Santa Fe: Clear Light Publishers, 1999).

72 P. C. Braunlich, 'The Oklahoma Plays of R. Lynn Riggs', *World Literature Today* 64(3) (1990), pp. 390–94, at p. 392.

73 C. S. Womack, 'The Cherokee Night and Other Plays by Lynn Riggs', *Studies in American Indian Literatures* 17(1) (2005), pp. 114–21, at p. 115.

74 See R. Velikova, 'Will Rogers's Indian Humor', *Studies in American Indian Literatures*, Series 2, 19(2) (2007), pp. 83–103; A. M. Ware 'Unexpected Cowboy, Unexpected Indian: The Case of Will Rogers', *Ethnohistory* 56(1) (2009), pp. 1–34.

75 C. Hunter, 'The Historical Context in John Joseph Mathews' Sundown', *MELUS* 9(1) (1982), pp. 61–72.

76 D. F. Littlefield, *American Indian and Alaska Native Newspapers and Periodicals* (Westport, CT: Greenwood Press, 1984).

77 Arthur C. Parker (1881–1955) was one of the leading intellectuals of the first half of the twentieth century. Seneca and Scottish, he was an

anthropologist, advocate and the first president of the Society for American Archaeology (1934). See, for instance, H. Hertzberg, 'Nationality, Anthropology, and Pan–Indianism in the Life of Arthur C. Parker (Seneca)', *Proceedings of the American Philosophical Society* 123(1) (1979), pp. 47–72.

78 T. Giago, 'What Is the Truth About the Murder of Anna Mae?', 30 August 2007, at http://www.huffingtonpost.com/tim–giago/what–is–the–truth–about–t_b_62521.html, accessed 20 October 2015.

79 T. Giago, 'The Tea Party Took Its Name Based on an Act of Deception', *Huffington Post*, 29 June 2014, np, http://www.huffingtonpost.com/tim-giago/the-tea-party-took-its-na_b_5541662.html, accessed 20 October 2015.

80 Ruth Arrington, 'Muriel Hazel Wright,' in Barbara Sicherman, Carol Hurd Green, Irene Kantrov and Harriet Walker (eds.), *Notable American Women: The Modern Period* (Cambridge, MA, London: The Belknap Press of Harvard University Press, 1980).

81 For a Native appreciation and obituary, see A. Ortiz, 'D'Arcy McNickle, 1904–1977', *American Anthropologist* 81(3) (1979), pp. 632–6.

82 'Albert White Hat, Preserver of Lakota Language, Dies at 74', *Washington Post*, 23 June 2013, http://ww.washingtonpost.com/local/obituaries/albert–white–hat–preserver–of–lakota–language–dies–at–74/2013/06/23, accessed 26 September 2014.

83 B. Stonechild, *Buffy Sainte-Marie* (Calgary: Fifth House, 2012).

84 A. Dundes, 'The American Concept of Folklore', *Journal of the Folklore Institute* 3(3) (1966), pp. 226–49.

85 In Edmund Leach (ed.), *The Structural Study of Myth and Totemism* (London: Routledge, 1967).

86 A. Dundes, 'Structural Typology in North American Indian Folktales', *Southwestern Journal of Anthropology* 19(1) (1963), pp. 121–30.

87 Lili Cockerille Livingston, *American Indian Ballerinas* (Norman: University of Oklahoma Press, 1999). There are other biographies of Tallchief, for instance, Paul Lang, *Maria Tallchief* (Springfield: Enslow, 1997).

88 E. Cook-Lynn, 'The Broken Cord by Michael Dorris', *Wicazo Sa Review* 5(2) (1989), pp. 42–5.

89 C. Covert, 'The Anguished Life of Michael Dorris', *Star Tribune*, 3 August 1997, http://www.startribune.com/local/83838677.html?refer=y, accessed 12 July 2014.

90 M. Dorris, 'Shining Agate', *Ploughshares* 19(2/3) (1993), pp. 87–104.

91 *The Economist*, 8 August 2014, p. 25.

92 K. Lincoln, *Indi'n Humor* (New York: Oxford University Press, 1993), p. 318.

93 Keith H. Basso, *Portraits of the Whiteman* (Cambridge: Cambridge University Press, 1979), p. 55.

94 daybreakwarrior at https://www.youtube.com/watch?v=TVzRQsO6Kvo, accessed 20 October 2015.

95 https://www.youtube.com/watch?v=IkQL3syloPc, accessed 20 October 2015.

96 http://www.nac.nu.ca/Special/001_e.htm accessed 27 8 14, accessed 20 October 2015

97 http://www.nunatsiaqonline.ca/stories/article/65674did_you_hear_the_one_about_the_muskox_read_on_in_inuktitut/, accessed 20 October 2015.

98 H. Bohaker, 'Reading Anishinaabe Identities', *Ethnohistory* 57(1) (2010), pp. 11–33.

99 Susan Marsden, 'Adawx, Spanaxnox, and the Geopolitics of the Tsimshian', *BC Studies* 135 (2002), pp. 101–35.

CHAPTER 6: ART AND MATERIALITY

1 A. Ortiz, 'The Dynamics of Pueblo Cultural Survival', in R. DeMallie and A. Ortiz (eds.), *North American Indian Anthropology* (Norman: University of Oklahoma Press, 1995), pp. 296–306; T. J. Wenger, *We Have a Religion: The 1920s Pueblo Indian Dance Controversy* (Chapel Hill: University of North Carolina, 2009).

2 B. Rudofsky, *Architecture Without Architects* (New York: Doubleday, 1964).

3 R. W. Yerkes, 'The Woodland and Mississippian Traditions', *Journal of World Prehistory* 2(3) (1988), pp. 307–58. Other examples are the Maritime Archaic Tradition, the Paleo-Indian Tradition, etc.

4 B. Bernstein, 'From Indian Fair to Indian Market', *El Palacio* 98(3) (2007), pp. 14–19; and *Santa Fe Indian Market* (Albuquerque: University of New Mexico Press, 2012).

5 See http://swaia.org/Indian_Market/Indian_Market_2014_FAQs/, accessed 1 December 2014.

6 Toni Hill, 'Pawnee Indian Veteran's 67th Annual Homecoming', 2013, p. 1, available at: http://www.pawneenation.org/files/veterans/Homecoming-2013-Final.pdf, accessed 20 October 2015.

7 Pequot, 'Schemitzun', 2013, p. 1, available at http://www.mashantucket.com/uploadedFiles/Schemitzun_2013.pdf, accessed 20 October 2015.

8 ICTM Staff, 'Origins of the Grass Dance', 2011, np, available at http://indiancountrytodaymedianetwork.com/article/origins-of-the-grass-dance-26738, accessed 20 October 2015.

9 http://www.burkemuseum.org/totempoles/totem.swf, accessed 20 October 2015.

10 Sergei Kan, 'Words That Heal the Soul: Analysis of the Tlingit Potlatch Oratory', *Arctic Anthropology* 20(2) (1983), pp. 47–59, at p. 47.

11 Gwyneira Isaac, 'Re-Observation and the Recognition of Change: The Photographs of Matilda Coxe Stevenson (1879–1915)', *Journal of the Southwest* 47(3) (2005), pp. 411–55.

12 See http://www.ashiwi.org/ChronologicalHistory.aspx, accessed 20 October 2015.

13 J. P. Spiro, *Defending the Master Race* (Burlington: University of Vermont Press, 2009).

14 E. B. Ross, 'The Deceptively Simple Racism of Clark Wissler', *American Anthropologist* 87(2) (1985), pp. 390–93, at p. 391.

15 For a general account, see J. A. Shannon, *Our Lives* (Santa Fe: SAR Press, 2014).

16 http://www.kshs.org/p/pawnee–indian–museum–exhibits/11893, accessed 29 November 2014.

17 Anna Lee Walters, *Ghost Singer* (Albuquerque: University of New Mexico Press, 1988).

18 Biographies of Parker have been written, for instance the dissertation of John Robert Siegel, 'Two Cultures, One Cause' (Purdue, 1993) and Joy Porter, *To Be Indian: The Life of Iroquois-Seneca Arthur Caswell Parker* (Norman: University of Oklahoma Press, 2001).

19 S. Michaelsen, 'Ely S. Parker', *American Literary History* 8(4) (1996), pp. 615–38.

20 http://www.cherokeeheritage.org/cherokeeheritagegenealogy–html/cherokee–family–research/, accessed 29 November 2014.

21 For art history see, for instance, a recent summary: M. A. Herzog and S. A. Stolte, 'American Indian Art', *Wicazo Sa Review* 27(1) (2012), pp. 85–109. In a field now led by women of crucial importance has been Mary Hamilton's *American Indian Art Magazine* from 1975; see http://www.aiamagazine.com/.

22 William Fitzhugh, personal communication, 31 October 2014.

23 http://freebookofmormon.wordpress.com/testimony-of-joseph-smith/, accessed 20 October 2015.

24 https://www.lds.org/scriptures/bofm/1-ne/1?lang=eng, np, accessed 20 October 2015, p. 5.

25 T. S. Kidd, *The Great Awakening* (New Haven: Yale University Press, 2007).

26 R. Silverberg, *Mound Builders* (Greenwich: NY Graphic Society, 1968).

27 W. T. Sherman, in [various authors], *Wild Life on the Plains* (St Louis : Pease Taylor, 1891), p. 119.

28 The nineteenth-century Lost Tribe formulation is still used in the name 'Mound Builders Country Club' see: http://www.moundbuilderscc.com/, accessed 20 October 2015.

29 I. Gill, *All That We Say Is Ours: Guujaaw and the Reawakening of the Haida Nation* (Vancouver: Douglas & McIntyre, 2009). The Gwaii Trust was established in 1991 and is geographically based, rather than exclusive to the two Haida First Nations. http://www.gwaiitrust.com/about/history/, accessed 20 October 2015. In this respect the people of Haida Gwaii, like those of the Labrador Coast, are developing generalized identities including incomers.

30 Bob Haozous, 'Straight Talk with Bob Haozous: Interview by Guy Cross', 2003, np, available at http://www.bobhaozous.com/media.html, accessed 20 October 2015.

31 http://www.roybalcorp.com/firm/firm-index.htm, accessed 25 November 2015.

32 http://www.bobhaozous.com/media.html, accessed 11 November 2015.

33 http://digital.library.okstate.edu/encyclopedia/entries/M/MO017.html, accessed 20 October 2015.

34 See http://moa.ubc.ca/portfolio_page/speaking-to-memory/, accessed 20 October 2015.

35 http://www.authenticnunavut.com/data/UPLOADS/fck/file/Sanaugait_ eng. pdf, p. 5, accessed 20 October 2015.

36 See Paul Royster at http://digitalcommons.unl.edu/libraryscience/24/, accessed 20 October 2015.

37 David Mollett, 'James Kivetoruk Moses, Inupiaq Folk Artist', available at http://www.nps.gov/akso/beringia/projects/Products/2009/2009-Kivetoruk-Moses-presentation-text.pdf, np, accessed 20 October 2015.

38 'Department of the Interior Indian Arts and Crafts Board 25 CFR Part 309 RIN 1090–AA45 Protection for Products of Indian Art and Craftsmanship', p. 5455, at http://www.iacb.doi.gov/pdf/1990_fed_register_notice.pdf, accessed 20 October 2015.

39 In other countries, such as Australia, protection is offered. For the shaman's parka see: http://www.cbc.ca/radio/asithappens/as-it-happens-wednesday-edition-1.3336554/nunavut-family-outraged-after-fashion-label-copies-sacred-inuit-design-1.3336560, accessed 30 November 2015.

CHAPTER 7: THE EAST

1 Jill Tyrer, 'When Fortune Smiles (or not)', http://www.gulfshorelife.com/May-2010/When-Fortune-Smiles-or-not/, accessed 6 November 2015.

2 http://international.loc.gov/intldl/awkbhtml/kb-1/kb-1-2-1.html#track1, accessed 28 October 2015.

3 Quoted by Stuart Banner, *How the Indians Lost their Land* (Cambridge: Belknap/Harvard University Press, 2005), p. 78.

4 John A. Garraty, 'Tisquantum', American National Biography Online, February 2000 http://www.anb.org/articles/20/20-00975.html, accessed 6 November 2015.

5 Suggested by Gregory Evans Dowd; see Patrick Griffin, 'Empires, Subjects, and Pontiac: [review of] *War under Heaven: Pontiac, the Indian Nations, and the British Empire* by Gregory Evans Dowd', *Reviews in American History* 31(3) (2003), pp. 363–71, at p. 364.

6 Jon William Parmenter, 'Pontiac's War: Forging New Links in the Anglo-Iroquois Covenant Chain, 1758–1766', *Ethnohistory* 44(4) (1997), pp. 617–54, at p. 621.

7 Jack M. Sosin, 'The British Indian Department and Dunmore's War', *Virginia Magazine of History and Biography* 74(1) (1966), pp. 34–5, at p. 38.

8 Joseph-François Lafitau, *Customs of the American Indians Compared with the Customs of Primitive Times* (Toronto: Champlain Society, 1974), vol. 1, p. 94.

9 Ibid., vol. 1, p. 217.

10 Elisabeth Tooker, 'The United States Constitution and the Iroquois League', *Ethnohistory*, 35(4) (1988), pp. 305–36, at p. 309.

11 Barbara Graymont, 'Thayendanegea', in *Dictionary of Canadian Biography*, vol. 5, http://www.biographi.ca/en/bio/thayendanegea_5E.html, accessed 28 October 2015.

12 Quoted by Alan Taylor, 'The Divided Ground: Upper Canada, New York, and the Iroquois Six Nations, 1783–1815', *Journal of the Early Republic* 22(1), pp. 55–75, at p. 66.

13 Quoted by Samuel Gardner Drake, *The Book of the Indians of North America* (Boston: Joshua Drake, 1833), p. 79

14 Elisabeth Tooker, 'On the Development of the Handsome Lake Religion', *Proceedings of the American Philosophical Society* 133(1) (1989), pp. 35–50, at p. 48.

15 Ralph Linton and A. Irving Hallowell, 'Nativistic Movements', *American Anthropologist The* NS 45(2) (1943), pp. 230–40, at p. 230.

16 Friedrich Engels, *The Origin of the Family, Private Property, and the State* (1884), available at https://www.marxists.org/archive/marx/works/download/pdf/origin_family.pdf, accessed 28 October 2015, at p. 50.

17 See Lewis H. Morgan and Elisabeth Tooker, 'The Structure of the Iroquois League: Lewis H. Morgan's Research and Observations', *Ethnohistory* 30(3) (1983), pp. 141–54, and Elisabeth Tooker, 'Lewis H. Morgan and His Contemporaries', *American Anthropologist*, NS, 94(2) (1992), pp. 357–75.

18 Donald B. Smith, "Deskaheh," in *Dictionary of Canadian Biography*, vol. 15, http://www.biographi.ca/en/bio/deskaheh_15E.html, accessed 28 October 2015.

19 *Globe and Mail*, 5 September 2013, A7.

20 Patrick Howley, 'Documents: Anti-Redskins Indian Leader Not a Legitimate Member of His Tribe', *Daily Caller*, np, 14 October 2013, at http://dailycaller.com/2013/10/14/documents-anti-redskins-indian-leader-not-a-legitimate-member-of-his-tribe/, accessed 25 October 2011.

21 Josh Gerzetich, 'Oneida Enrollment', np, http://publications.newberry.org/indiansofthemidwest/identities/legal-identity/tribal-enrollment/video-transcript-josh-gerzetich-01/, accessed 26 October 2011.

22 Jessica S. Cattelino, quoted by Christopher Arris Oakley, 'The Native South in the Post-World War II Era', *Native South* 1 (2008), pp. 61–79. at p. 70.

23 Kathryn Fort, 'Disruption and Impossibility: The New Laches and the Unfortunate Resolution of the Modern Iroquois Land Claims', *Wyoming Law Review* 11(2) (2011), pp. 376–405, at p. 405.

24 Rebecca Bateman, 'Naming Patterns in Black Seminole Ethnogenesis', *Ethnohistory* 49(2) (2002), pp. 227–57, at p. 244.

25 John H. Dossett, 'Re: United States v. Al Bahlul, CMCR CASE NO. 09-001. To the Honorable Judges of the Court of Military Commission Review', np, National Congress of American Indians, 11 March 2011, available at https://www.law.msu.edu/indigenous/papers/2011-01.pdf, accessed 6 November 2015.

26 Ibid.

27 John DeGroot, 'James Billie: Born as Outcast, Leader Still Very Much a Man Alone', 1986, http://www.sun-sentinel.com/sfl-billie-sunshine-story.html, accessed 28 October 2015.

28 'Gaming, n.', OED Online, Oxford University Press, September 2015, http://www.oed.com/view/Entry/76505?rskey=gIuTCX&result=1#eid, accessed 28 October 2015.

29 Jessica S. Cattelino ' "One Hamburger at a Time": Revisiting the State–Society Divide with the Seminole Tribe of Florida and Hard Rock

International: With CA comments by Thabo Mokgatlha and Kgosi Leruo Molotlegi', *Current Anthropology* 52 (Supplement 3), 'Corporate Lives: New Perspectives on the Social Life of the Corporate Form: Edited by Damani J. Partridge, Marina Welker, and Rebecca Hardin' (2011), pp. S137–S149, at p. S145.

30 In the subtitle of Joseph B. Herring's, 'Kenekuk, the Kickapoo Prophet: Acculturation without Assimilation', *American Indian Quarterly* 9(3) (1985), pp. 295–307.

31 Brooks McNamara, 'The Indian Medicine Show', *Educational Theatre Journal* 23(4) (1971), pp. 431–45, at p. 431.

CHAPTER 8: THE WEST

1 See Victor Golla, *California Indian Languages* (Berkeley, Los Angeles and London: University of California Press, 2011).

2 Gifford and Kroeber, 1939, quoted by Sally McLendon and Robert L. Oswalt, 'Pomo: Introduction', in William C. Sturtevant (ed.), *Handbook of North American Indians*, vol. 8: *California*, ed. Robert F. Heizer (Washington, DC: Smithsonian Institution Press, 1978), pp. 274–88, at p. 276.

3 Quoted by Quincy Newell, ' "The Indians Generally Love Their Wives and Children": Native American Marriage and Sexual Practices in Missions San Francisco, Santa Clara, and San Jose', *Catholic Historical Review* 91(1) (2005), pp. 60–82, at p. 75.

4 Edward D. Castillo, 'An Indian Account of the Decline and Collapse of Mexico's Hegemony over the Missionized Indians of California', *American Indian Quarterly* 13(4) (1989), pp. 391–408.

5 Travis Hudson, 'The Chumash Revolt of 1824: Another Native Account from the Notes of John P. Harrington Journal', *Journal of California and Great Basin Anthropology* 2(1) (1980), pp. 123–6.

6 R. L. Bettinger and E. Wohlgemuth, 'California Plants', in William C. Sturtevant (ed.), *Handbook of North American Indians*, vol. 3: *Environment, Origins, and Population*, ed. D. H. Ubelaker (Washington, DC: Smithsonian Institution, 2006), pp. 274–83.

7 Quoted by Kimberly Johnston-Dodds, *Early California Laws and Policies Related to California Indians* (Sacramento: California Research Bureau, 2002), p. 15.

8 Ibid., p. 20

9 Ibid., p. 9.

10 Peter G. Christensen, 'Minority Interaction in John Rollin Ridge's *The Life and Adventures of Joaquin Murieta*', *MELUS* 17(2), (1991–2), pp. 61–72, at p. 69.

11 Helen Hunt Jackson, *Ramona*, 1884, np, available at http://www.gutenberg.org/cache/epub/2802/pg2802.txt, accessed 6 November 2015.

12 D. A. Hufford, *The Real Ramona of Helen Hunt Jackson's Famous Novel* (Los Angeles: D. A. Hufford & Co., *c.* 1900), p. 6.

13 Quoted by Margaret D. Jacobs, 'Making Savages of Us All: White Women, Pueblo Indians, and the Controversy over Indian Dances in the 1920s', *Frontiers: A Journal of Women Studies* 17(3) (1996), pp. 178–209, at p. 192.

14 http://www.webpages.uidaho.edu/~rfrey/PDF/329/IndianDances.pdf, accessed 1 March 2014.

15 Quoted by Martin B. Duberman, 'Documents in Hopi Indian Sexuality: Imperialism, Culture and Resistance', *Radical History Review* 20 (1979), pp. 99–130, at p. 113.

16 Quoted by Stephen J. Kunitz and John Collier, 'The Social Philosophy of John Collier', *Ethnohistory* 18(3) (1971), pp. 213–29, at p. 216.

17 Kenneth Philp, 'Albert B. Fall and the Protest from the Pueblos, 1921–23', *Arizona and the West* 12(3) (1970), pp. 237–54, at p. 239.

18 Tisa Wenger, 'Land, Culture, and Sovereignty in the Pueblo Dance Controversy', *Journal of the Southwest* 46(2) (2004), pp. 381–412.

19 Quoted by E. A. Schwarts, 'Red Atlantis Revisited: Community and Culture in the Writings of John Collier', *American Indian Quarterly* 18(4) (1994), pp. 507–31, at p. 513.

20 Quoted in Taos, 'Blue Lake', 2013, np, available at http://www.taospueblo-powwow.com/about-taos-pueblo/blue-lake, accessed 6 March 2013.

21 William A. Dobak, 'Killing the Canadian Buffalo, 1821–1881', *Western Historical Quarterly* 27(1) (1996), pp. 33–52, at p. 34.

22 For railroads and crony capitalism see R. White, *Railroaded* (New York: Norton, 2011), and A. Smith, review of *Railroaded: The Transcontinentals and the Making of Modern America* (review no. 1155), http://www.history.ac.uk/reviews/review/1155, accessed 9 January 2015.

23 http://collections.mnhs.org/MNHistoryMagazine/articles/38/v38i03p115-115.pdf, accessed 28 January 2014.

24 Quoted in Abraham Lincoln, 'Second Annual Message, December 1, 1862', in Gerhard Peters and John T. Woolley, *The American Presidency Project*, http://www.presidency.ucsb.edu/ws/?pid=29503, accessed 28 January 2014.

25 John LaBatte, 'Oral History – Interview, Narrator John LaBatte, Interviewer Deborah Locke, made in New Ulm, MN, Tuesday, May

31, 2011', available at http://usdakotawar.org/stories/contributors/john-labatte/1069, accessed 28 January 2014.

26 Linea Sundstrom, 'Mirror of Heaven: Cross-Cultural Transference of the Sacred Geography of the Black Hills', *World Archaeology* 28(2) (1996), pp. 177–89, at p. 183.

27 Bethany R. Berger, 'Elouise Cobell: Bringing the United States to Account', in Tim Alan Garrison (ed.), *'Our Cause Will Ultimately Triumph': The Men and Women Who Preserved and Revitalized American Indian Sovereignty* (Durham, NC: Carolina Academic Press, 2014), pp. 181–93.

CHAPTER 9: THE NORTH

1 *Historia natural y moral de las Indias* (Seville, 1590), discussed by David Henige, 'Impossible to Disprove Yet Impossible to Believe: The Unforgiving Epistemology of Deep-Time Oral Tradition', *History in Africa* 36 (2009), pp. 127–234, at p. 230.

2 Alessandro Achilli et al., 'Reconciling Migration Models to the Americas with the Variation of North American Native Mitogenome', *PNAS* 110(3) (2013), pp. 14308–13, at p. 14308.

3 Ibid.

4 Maanasa Raghavan et al., 'Genomic Evidence for the Pleistocene and Recent Population History of Native Americans', *Science* 349(6250) (21 August 2015), pp. 1–10, available at http://www.sciencemag.org/content/349/6250/aab3884.full.pdf, accessed 7 November 2015; Pontus Skoglund et al., 'Genetic Evidence for Two Founding Populations of the Americas', *Nature*, 525(7567) (3 September 2015), pp. 104–8, available at http://www.nature.com/nature/journal/v525/n7567/pdf/nature14895.pdf, accessed 7 November 2015.

5 Johann Nichols, 'Language Spread Rates and Prehistoric American Migration Rates', *Current Anthropology* 49(6) (2008), pp. 1109–17.

6 Ivan Lind Christensen and Søren Rud, 'Arctic Neurasthenia:The Case of Greenlandic Kayak Fear 1864-1940', *Social History of Medicine* 26(3) (2013), pp. 489–509.

7 Tom Lowenstein, *Ancient Land: Sacred Whale: The Inuit Hunt and Its Rituals* (New York: Farrar, Straus and Giroux, 1993), p. 101.

8 Hiroko Ikuta, 'Iñupiaq Pride', *Études/Inuit/Studies* 31(1–2) (2007), pp. 343–64, at pp. 351–2.

9 Carey Restino, 'Trip to Kivgiq Inspires Respect', 2013, np, available at http://www.alaskadispatch.com/article/trip-kivgiq-inspires-respect, accessed 11 November 2013.

10 www.aewc-alaska.com, accessed 12 November 2013.

11 Jessica S. Lefevre, 'A Pioneering Effort in the Design of Process and Law Supporting Integrated Arctic Ocean Management', *Environmental Law Reporter* 43(4), pp.10893–10908, at p. 10898.

12 'Statement Released by George Ahmaogak, Sr. on Wife's Federal Charges', *Alaska Dispatch*, 22 September 2011, http://www.alaskadispatch. com/article/statement-released-george-ahmaogak-sr-wifes-federal-charges, accessed 11 November 2013; http://www.fbi.gov/anchorage/press-releases/ 2012/, accessed 12 November 2013.

13 Colin Scott, 'Knowledge Construction among the Cree Hunters: Metaphors and Literal Understanding', *Journal de la Société des Américanistes* 75 (1989), pp. 193–208, at p. 205; Lynn Whidden, *Essential Song* (Waterloo, ON: Wilfrid Laurier University Press, 2007).

14 Quoted by Arthur Lazarus, Jnr, and W. Richard West, Jnr, in 'The Alaska Native Claims Settlement Act: A Flawed Victory', *Law and Contemporary Problems* 40(1) (1976), pp. 132–65, at pp. 133–4.

15 Ibid., p. 165.

16 Kirk Dombrowski, 'The Praxis of Indigenism and Alaska Native Timber Politics', *American Anthropologist* NS 104(4) (2002), pp. 1062–73.

17 Wyden-Murkowski Letter, 10 March 2013, available at http://tongasslowdown.org/TL/docs/Wyden-Murkowski%20Letter.pdf, accessed 3 November 2015.

18 Benjamin W. Thompson, 'The De Facto Termination of Alaska Native Sovereignty: An Anomaly in an Era of Self Determination', *American Indian Law Review* 24(2) (1999/2000), pp. 421–54.

19 Fredrica de Laguna, 'Eyak', in William C. Sturtevant (ed.), *Handbook of North American Indians*, vol. 7: *Northwest Coast*, ed. Wayne Suttles (Washington, DC: Smithsonian Institution Press, 1990), pp. 189–96, at p. 195.

20 http://www.sba.gov/content/control-eligibility, accessed 3 November 2015.

21 http://www.eyaktek.com/index.pl?id=3528;isa=Category;op=show, accessed 5 November 2013; Tom Schoenberg, 'Contract Fraud Entangling Eyak Corp. Subsidiary Was on Target to Reach $1 billion', 2013, available at http://www.adn.com/2013/07/12/2972964/contract-fraudentangling-alaska.html, accessed 5 November 2013.

22 Charles J. Marecic, 'Nunavut Territory: Aboriginal Governing in the Canadian Regime of Governance', *American Indian Law Review* 24(2) (1999/2000), pp. 275–95, at p. 283.

23 Chenega Corporation, available at http://www.chenega.com/exceptional-performance, accessed 12 December 2013.

24 Majority Staff Analysis Prepared for Chairman Claire McCaskill, United States Senate Committee on Homeland Security and Governmental

Affairs: *Subcommittee on Contracting Oversight New Information about Contracting Preferences for Alaska Native Coporations (Part II)*, Washington, DC, 2009.

25 Robert O'Harrow, Jnr, and Scott Higham, 'Alaska Native Corporations Cash in on Contracting Edge', http://www.washingtonpost.com/wp-dyn/articles/A11550-2004Nov25.html, accessed 7 November 2015.

26 Ken Battle and Sherri Torjman, *Poverty and Prosperity in Nunavut* (Ottawa: Caledon Institute, 2013).

27 Thomas R. Berger, 'The Nunavut Project', Ottawa, 2006, p. 24, available at http://www.aadnc-aandc.gc.ca/eng/1100100030982/1100100030985, accessed 6 November 2014.

28 P. Whitney Lackenbauer and Mathew Farish, 'The Cold War on Canadian Soil: Militarizing a Northern Environment', *Environmental History* 12(4) (2007), pp. 920–50, at p. 926. Philip Godsell, *Alaska Highway* (London: Samson Low, *c.* 1944), pp. 141 and 172.

29 http://www.makivik.org/corporate/makivik-mandate/, accessed 3 November 2015.

30 Nick Sibbeston, 'Land Claims as an Engine of Growth', *Hill Times*, 18 June 2012, http://www.hilltimes.com/policy-briefing/2012/06/18/land-claims-should-be-an-engine-of-growth/31113, accessed 6 November 2015.

31 Christopher Alcantara and Greg Wilson, 'Aboriginal Self-Government through Constitutional Design: A Survey of Fourteen Aboriginal Constitutions in Canada', *Journal of Canadian Studies/Revue d'études canadiennes* 44(2) (2010), pp. 122–45.

32 Jens Dahl, 'Greenland: Political Structure of Self-Government', *Arctic Anthropology* 23(1/2) (1986), pp. 315–24, at p. 319.

33 OMA, 'De Beers Canada Victor mine continues to add sparkle to Ontario's economy', 2012, available at http://www.oma.on.ca/en/News/index.aspx?newsId=d67198fd-61e3-498b-9341-9bc244238a9a, accessed 12 December 2013.

34 Comments after Gloria Galloway, 'Attawapiskat Audit Raises Questions about Millions in Spending', available at http://www.theglobeandmail.com/news/politics/attawapiskat-audit-raises-questions-about-millions-in-spending/article6995751/comments/, accessed 12 December 2013.

35 Raphael Fireman, in Jaqueline Hookimaw-Witt, 'We Stand on the Graves of Our Ancestors', MA thesis, 1997, Trent University, Peterborough, Ontario, p. 122, available at http://www.collectionscanada.gc.ca/obj/s4/f2/dsk2/tape15/PQDD_0016/MQ30219.pdf, accessed 6 November 2015.

36 Marie-Louise Hookimaw, in ibid., pp. 205–6.

CHAPTER 10: THE PACIFIC NORTHWEST COAST

1 Frederica de Laguna (ed.), *The Tlingit Indians by George Thornton Emmons* (Seattle: University of Washington Press, 1991), p. 83.

2 Jerome S. Cybulski, 'Skeletal Biology: Northwest Coast and Plateau', in William C. Sturtevant (ed.), *Handbook of North American Indians*, vol. 3: *Environment, Origins, and Population*, ed. D. H. Ubelaker (Washington, DC: Smithsonian Institution, 2006), pp. 532–57, at p. 533.

3 Quoted by Virginia L. Butler, 'Relic Hunting, Archaeology, and Loss of Native American Heritage at the Dalles', *Oregon Historical Quarterly* 108(4) (2007), pp. 624–43, at p. 634.

4 Anne C. Stone, 'Ancient DNA', in William C. Sturtevant (ed.), *Handbook of North American Indians*, vol. 3: *Environment, Origins, and Population*, ed. D. H. Ubelaker (Washington, DC: Smithsonian Institution, 2006), pp. 840-47, at p. 846.

5 Richard A. Lazenby and Peter McCormack, 'Salmon and Malnutrition on the Northwest Coast', *Current Anthropology* 26(3) (1985), pp. 379–84.

6 Edward D. *Castillo*, 'The *Impact of Euro-American* Exploration and Settlement', in William C. Sturtevant (ed.), *Handbook of North American Indians*, vol. 8: *California*, ed. Robert F. Heizer (Washington, DC: Smithsonian Institution Press, 1978), pp. 99–127, at p. 109.

7 Peter L. Macnair, 'Descriptive Notes on the Kwakiutl Manufacture of Eulachon Oil', *Syesis* 4(1–2) (1971), pp. 169–77.

8 Quoted in Donald Mitchell and Leland Donald, 'Sharing Resources on the North Pacific Coast of North America: The Case of the Eulachon Fishery', *Anthropologica* 43(1) (2001), pp. 19–35, at p. 22.

9 Gregory G. Monks, Alan D. McMillan and Denis E. St Claire, 'Nuu-Chah-Nulth Whaling: Archaeological Insights into Antiquity, Species Preferences, and Cultural Importance', *Arctic Anthropology* 38(1) (2001), pp. 60–81.

10 Eugene Arima, *The West Coast People* (Victoria: Provincial Museum of British Columbia, 1983), p. 41

11 Comment by Martin Shaughnessy on Gottlieb, 'U.S. Halts Makah Whaling Study after Seven Years over "New Scientific Information", np, http://www.peninsuladailynews.com/article/20120523/NEWS/305239 987/us-study-of-makah-whaling-out, accessed 21 December 2013.

12 See Robert Galois, 'Clah, Arthur Wellington', in *Dictionary of Canadian Biography*, vol. 14, http://www.biographi.ca/en/bio/clah_ arthur_wellington_14E.html, accessed 6 November 2015.

13 See Robin K. Wright, 'Edenshaw, Charles', in *Dictionary of Canadian Biography*, vol. 14, http://www.biographi.ca/en/bio/edenshaw_charles_14E.html, accessed 4 November 2015. For Bill Reid, see Karen Duffek and Charlotte Townsend-Gault (eds.), *Bill Reid and Beyond: Expanding on Modern Native Art* (Seattle: University of Washington Press, 2004).

14 http://avalon.law.yale.edu/18th_century/proc1763.asp, accessed 6 November 2015.

15 http://www.bctreaty.net/files_3/pdf_documents/delgamuukw.pdf, accessed 6 November 2015.

16 Christopher F. Roth, 'Without Treaty, Without Conquest: Indigenous Sovereignty in Post-Delgamuukw British Columbia', *Wicazo Sa Review* 17(2) (2002), pp. 143–65, at p. 159.

17 John J. Cove, 'The Gitksan Traditional Concept of Land Ownership', *Anthropologica* 24(1) (1982), pp. 3–17.

18 http://www.aiatsis.gov.au/ntru/documents/NeilSterritt.pdf, accessed 6 August 2013.

19 Geoff Dembicki, 'Foreign Giants Line up to Develop Chunks of BC's Coast. Libs' LNG Plans Invite Installations by Petro Firms with Combined $2 Trillion in Revenues', 23 April 2013, available at TheTyee.ca, accessed 26 April 2013.

20 http://www.answers.com/topic/sealaska-corporation#ixzz2Ufn7H3an, accessed 26 April 2013.

21 http://tongasslowdown.org/TL/docs/Wyden-Murkowski%20Letter.pdf, accessed 26 April 2013.

22 http://www.fs.fed.us/spf/coop/library/private_forest_report.pdf, accessed 26 April 2013.

23 http://www.sealaskaheritage.org/about, accessed 8 November 2015.

24 http://www.braidedriver.org/authors?view=employee&id=2, accessed 4 November 2015.

25 http://www.duwamishtribe.org/oralhistory.html, accessed 4 November 2015.

26 See the discussion at: http://www.culturalsurvival.org/publications/cultural-survival-quarterly/united-states/legacy-restored-another-perspective-boldt-dec, accessed 6 November 2015.

27 https://www.hoopa-nsn.gov/?s=language, accessed 21 December 2013.

28 Kristan Korns, 'Rural Areas "Under Siege" by Marijuana', *Two Rivers Tribune*, 8 November 2012.

29 Quoted by Arnold R. Pilling, 'Yurok Aristocracy and "Great Houses"', *American Indian Quarterly* 13(4), pp. 421–43, at p. 422.

List of illustrations and Maps

Illustrations

p. 3 The Revd Samson Occum (British Museum images, © The Trustees of the British Museum); **p. 4** Colonel Ely S. Parker (US National Archives, Wikimedia Commons); **p. 4** Charles Eastman (Smithsonian, Department of Anthropology, Smithsonian Institution); **p. 5** Jim Thorpe (US National Archives , Wikimedia Commons); **p. 5** Tom Longboat; **p. 6** Charles Curtis; **p. 6** Buffalo Child Long Lance; **p. 7** Open Coffin of Jackson Barnett; **p. 7** Ojibwe Anishinaabe protest; **p. 8** Myra Yvonne Choteau; **p. 9** Canadian Cree activist; **p. 10** Sacheen Littlefeather; **p. 10** Chief Dan George; **p. 11** Mercier Bridge, Quebec; **p. 11** Quirino Romero; **p. 12** Karen Jim; **p. 13** Foxwoods Resort Casino (Alamy, © Alamy); **p. 13** The Battle of Hayes Pond, 1957 (AP, AP/PA Images); **p. 14** Suzan Shown Harjo (Wikipedia, © Lucy Fowler); **p. 14** Whiteford's Indian Burial Pit

p. 53 Henry Roe Cloud; **p. 54** Representatives of tribes (NCAI, JK, NCAI NARA); **p. 54** Russell Means; **p. 55** Louis Tewanima and Jesse Owens; **p. 56** Truman receiving a Seminole shirt; **p. 56** John Echohawk (NCAI/ Flickr 2010); **p. 57** Morongo Casino (LOC ©The Jon B. Lovelace Collection of California Photographs in Carol M. Highsmith's America Project, Library of Congress, Prints and Photographs Division); **p. 57** Helen Petersen; **p. 58** Ben Nighthorse Campbell; **p. 58** William Wayne Keeler; **p. 59** Billy Mills; **p. 60** Wilma Mankiller; **p. 60** Edison Chiloquin; **p. 61** LaDonna Harris; **p. 61** Indian Pavilion at Expo 1967; **p. 62** Elijah Harper (CPI Images © THE CANADIAN PRESS/Tom Hanson); **p. 63** Vine Deloria Jnr; **p. 63** Julian Pierce; **p. 63** President Barack Obama meets Elouise Cobell (Creative Commons Attribution 3.0 License)

p. 103 Segesser Hide Paintings, (NM, Palace of the Governors, Santa Fe, Segesser II, Courtesy of the Palace of the Governors Photo Archives (NMHM/DCA), Negative Number 149804); **p. 104** Nicholson map 1723

Mungo Martin (Royal BC Museum); **p. 507** Jenny Thlunaut (Sheldon Museum and Cultural Centre Archive); **p. 507** Elizabeth Peratrovich; **p. 508** Petition, 1951; **p. 508** Bill Reid (Dr Martine Reid, CC licenses prior to Version 4.0); **p. 509** Makah whaling (Library of Congress); **p. 509** Salmon bake (Property of Museum of History & Industry Seattle); **p. 510** Poster by Kik-Ke-In (© Kik-Ke-In); **p. 510** Makah programme (the Makah Nation); **p. 511** Shawn Atleo (Flickr, Photo by Ian Gill. Read more on Ecotrust Canada's blog, www.ecotrust.ca/first-nations/atleo-afn Creative Commons); **p. 512** Bryan Mallott (Flickr, James Brooks photo Creative Commons Attribution 2.0 Generic); **p. 512** Jody Wilson Raybould (by ERICH SAIDE (ERICH SAIDE) [CC BY-SA 3.0 (http://creativecommons.org/licenses/by-sa/3.0)], via Wikimedia Commons)

Maps

Index

Page references in *italic* indicate maps and illustrations or their captions.